A+ Certification For Dummies®

The IDG Books Worldwide logo is a registered trademark under exclusive license to IDG Books Worldwide, Inc., from International Data Group, Inc. The ...For Dummies logo is a trademark, and - - - - For Dummies and ...For Dummies are registered trademarks of IDG Books Worldwide, Inc. All other trademarks are the property of their respective owners.

Intel processors

CPU	Package	Data Bus (bits)	Co-processor?
8086	DIP	16	No
80286	PGA	16	No
386DX	PGA	32	No
386SX	PGA	16	No
486DX	PGA	32	Yes
486SX	PGA	32	No
486DX2	PGA	32	Yes
486DX4	PGA	32	Yes
Pentium	PGA	64	Yes
Pentium MMX	PGA	64	Yes
Pentium Pro	PGA	64	Yes
Pentium II	SEC	64	Yes

RAID disk drive types

RAID 0: Striped disk array without fault tolerance.

RAID 3: Parallel transfer with parity.

RAID 5: Data striping with parity.

Preparing a hard disk

SCANDISK	Check for media problems
FDISK	Partition the disk
FORMAT	Prepare the disk and load system files

Default IRQ assignments

IRQ	Typical Assignment
1	Keyboard
2	Video card
3	COM2, COM4
4	COM1, COM3
5	Sound card
6	Floppy disk controller
7	Parallel port (LPT1)
9	Cascaded IRQ 2
12	PS/2 mouse
14	Hard disk controller

Electrical measurments

Amps	Measures a current's strength or rate of flow.
Ohms	Measures a conductor's resistance to electricity.
Volts	Measures the electrical pressure in a circuit.
Watts	Measures the electrical power in a circuit.
Continuity	Indicates the existence of a complete circuit.

PCMCIA card types

Type I	Up to 3.3 mm thick and used primarily for adding RAM to a portable computer
Type II	Up to 5.5 mm thick and commonly used for modem cards
Type III	Up to 10.5 mm thick and used to install portable disk drives

Bus architectures

Architecture	Data Bus Width
Industry Standard Architecture (ISA)	16-bit
Micro-Channel Architecture (MCA)	The first 32-bit bus
Extended ISA (EISA)	32-bit
Intelligent Drive Electronics (IDE)	
VESA Local Bus (VLB or VL-bus)	32-bit
Peripheral Component Interconnect (PCI) bus	32- or 64-bit

IDG BOOKS WORLDWIDE

...For Dummies®: Bestselling Book Series for Beginners

A+ Certification For Dummies®

Cheat Sheet

BESTSELLING BOOK SERIES

Laser printing phases

Cleaning, conditioning, writing, developing, transferring, fusing

Phrase to remember laser printing phases:

California Cows Won't Dance The Fandango

Layers of the OSI model

Physical, data link, network, transport, session, presentation, and application

Phrases to remember the OSI layers

Forward: Please Do Not Tell Secret Passwords Anytime

Backward: All People Seem To Need Data Processing

Windows 95 core components

Kernel	memory, file, and I/O management, and application support
User	mouse, keyboard, I/O ports, and desktop layout
GDI	graphical user interface and printing

On test day . . .

At the testing workstation, but before the test begins, write down:

- ✔ IRQs
- ✔ I/O adddresses
- ✔ Laser phases
- ✔ OSI layers

DOS/Windows 3.x memory management

Conventional memory	The first 640K of system memory
Upper memory area (expanded memory)	The upper 384K of the first megabyte of memory, above conventional memory
High memory area	The first 64K (less 16 bytes) of the second megabyte of memory
Extended memory	Any memory above the high memory area

DOS/Windows file systems

Operating Systems	File System
DOS	File Allocation Table (FAT)
Windows 3.x	Virtual File Allocation Table (VFAT)
Windows 95	VFAT and FAT32
Windows NT Workstation	Windows NT File System (NTFS)

Acronyms

CMOS: Complementary metal oxide semiconductor

ESD: Electrostatic discharge

GPF: General protection fault

HTTP: Hypertext transfer protocol

PCMCIA: Personal Computer Memory Card Interface Adapter

RAID: Redundant array of inexpensive (or independent) disks

SCSI: Small computer system interface

UART: Universal asynchronous receiver-transmitter

ZIF: Zero insertion force

...For Dummies®: Bestselling Book Series for Beginners

TM

...For Dummies

BESTSELLING BOOK SERIES

References for the Rest of Us!®

Are you intimidated and confused by computers? Do you find that traditional manuals are overloaded with technical details you'll never use? Do your friends and family always call you to fix simple problems on their PCs? Then the *...For Dummies*® computer book series from IDG Books Worldwide is for you.

...For Dummies books are written for those frustrated computer users who know they aren't really dumb but find that PC hardware, software, and indeed the unique vocabulary of computing make them feel helpless. *...For Dummies* books use a lighthearted approach, a down-to-earth style, and even cartoons and humorous icons to dispel computer novices' fears and build their confidence. Lighthearted but not lightweight, these books are a perfect survival guide for anyone forced to use a computer.

> "I like my copy so much I told friends; now they bought copies."
>
> — Irene C., Orwell, Ohio

> "Quick, concise, nontechnical, and humorous."
>
> — Jay A., Elburn, Illinois

> "Thanks, I needed this book. Now I can sleep at night."
>
> — Robin F., British Columbia, Canada

Already, millions of satisfied readers agree. They have made *...For Dummies* books the #1 introductory level computer book series and have written asking for more. So, if you're looking for the most fun and easy way to learn about computers, look to *...For Dummies* books to give you a helping hand.

IDG BOOKS WORLDWIDE

A+ CERTIFICATION FOR DUMMIES®

by Ron Gilster

IDG BOOKS WORLDWIDE

IDG Books Worldwide, Inc.
An International Data Group Company

Foster City, CA ♦ Chicago, IL ♦ Indianapolis, IN ♦ New York, NY

A+ Certification For Dummies®

Published by
IDG Books Worldwide, Inc.
An International Data Group Company
919 E. Hillsdale Blvd.
Suite 400
Foster City, CA 94404
www.idgbooks.com (IDG Books Worldwide Web site)
www.dummies.com (Dummies Press Web site)

Library of Congress Catalog Card No.: 98-89040

ISBN: 0-7645-0479-7

Printed in the United States of America

10 9 8 7 6 5 4 3 2

1O/QZ/QT/ZZ/IN

Distributed in the United States by IDG Books Worldwide, Inc.

Distributed by CDG Books Canada Inc. for Canada; by Transworld Publishers Limited in the United Kingdom; by IDG Norge Books for Norway; by IDG Sweden Books for Sweden; by Woodslane Pty. Ltd. for Australia; by Woodslane (NZ) Ltd. for New Zealand; by TransQuest Publishers Pte Ltd. for Singapore, Malaysia, Thailand, Indonesia, and Hong Kong; by ICG Muse, Inc. for Japan; by Norma Comunicaciones S.A. for Colombia; by Intersoft for South Africa; by Le Monde en Tique for France; by International Thomson Publishing for Germany, Austria and Switzerland; by Distribuidora Cuspide for Argentina; by Livraria Cultura for Brazil; by Ediciones ZETA S.C.R. Ltda. for Peru; by WS Computer Publishing Corporation, Inc., for the Philippines; by Contemporanea de Ediciones for Venezuela; by Express Computer Distributors for the Caribbean and West Indies; by Micronesia Media Distributor, Inc. for Micronesia; by Grupo Editorial Norma S.A. for Guatemala; by Chips Computadoras S.A. de C.V. for Mexico; by Editorial Norma de Panama S.A. for Panama; by American Bookshops for Finland. Authorized Sales Agent: Anthony Rudkin Associates for the Middle East and North Africa.

For general information on IDG Books Worldwide's books in the U.S., please call our Consumer Customer Service department at 800-762-2974. For reseller information, including discounts and premium sales, please call our Reseller Customer Service department at 800-434-3422.

For information on where to purchase IDG Books Worldwide's books outside the U.S., please contact our International Sales department at 317-596-5530 or fax 317-596-5692.

For consumer information on foreign language translations, please contact our Customer Service department at 1-800-434-3422, fax 317-596-5692, or e-mail rights@idgbooks.com.

For information on licensing foreign or domestic rights, please phone +1-650-655-3109.

For sales inquiries and special prices for bulk quantities, please contact our Sales department at 650-655-3200 or write to the address above.

For information on using IDG Books Worldwide's books in the classroom or for ordering examination copies, please contact our Educational Sales department at 800-434-2086 or fax 317-596-5499.

For press review copies, author interviews, or other publicity information, please contact our Public Relations department at 650-655-3000 or fax 650-655-3299.

For authorization to photocopy items for corporate, personal, or educational use, please contact Copyright Clearance Center, 222 Rosewood Drive, Danvers, MA 01923, or fax 978-750-4470.

About the Author

Ron Gilster (A+ Certified Service Technician, MBA, and AAGG) has been operating, programming, and repairing computers for more than 30 years. Ron has extensive experience training, teaching, and consulting in computer-related areas, including work on mainframes, minicomputers, and virtually every type of personal computer and operating system that exists. In addition to a wide range of positions that have included Customer Service Manager, Data Processing Manager, Management Information Systems Director, and Vice President of Operations in major corporations, Ron was a management consultant with an international auditing firm and operated his own computer systems consulting firm. He has also authored several books on computer and information literacy, and Visual Basic applications programming. Ron is presently semi-retired as an instructor at Walla Walla Community College, in Walla Walla, Washington, where he oversees and teaches the A+ certification, MOUS (Microsoft Office User Specialist), and CCNA (Cisco Certified Networking Associate) programs in the Computer Technology division.

ABOUT IDG BOOKS WORLDWIDE

Welcome to the world of IDG Books Worldwide.

IDG Books Worldwide, Inc., is a subsidiary of International Data Group, the world's largest publisher of computer-related information and the leading global provider of information services on information technology. IDG was founded more than 30 years ago by Patrick J. McGovern and now employs more than 9,000 people worldwide. IDG publishes more than 290 computer publications in over 75 countries. More than 90 million people read one or more IDG publications each month.

Launched in 1990, IDG Books Worldwide is today the #1 publisher of best-selling computer books in the United States. We are proud to have received eight awards from the Computer Press Association in recognition of editorial excellence and three from Computer Currents' First Annual Readers' Choice Awards. Our best-selling ...For Dummies® series has more than 50 million copies in print with translations in 31 languages. IDG Books Worldwide, through a joint venture with IDG's Hi-Tech Beijing, became the first U.S. publisher to publish a computer book in the People's Republic of China. In record time, IDG Books Worldwide has become the first choice for millions of readers around the world who want to learn how to better manage their businesses.

Our mission is simple: Every one of our books is designed to bring extra value and skill-building instructions to the reader. Our books are written by experts who understand and care about our readers. The knowledge base of our editorial staff comes from years of experience in publishing, education, and journalism — experience we use to produce books to carry us into the new millennium. In short, we care about books, so we attract the best people. We devote special attention to details such as audience, interior design, use of icons, and illustrations. And because we use an efficient process of authoring, editing, and desktop publishing our books electronically, we can spend more time ensuring superior content and less time on the technicalities of making books.

You can count on our commitment to deliver high-quality books at competitive prices on topics you want to read about. At IDG Books Worldwide, we continue in the IDG tradition of delivering quality for more than 30 years. You'll find no better book on a subject than one from IDG Books Worldwide.

John Kilcullen
John Kilcullen
Chairman and CEO
IDG Books Worldwide, Inc.

Steven Berkowitz
Steven Berkowitz
President and Publisher
IDG Books Worldwide, Inc.

WINNER

*Eighth Annual
Computer Press
Awards ➤ 1992*

WINNER

*Ninth Annual
Computer Press
Awards ➤ 1993*

WINNER

*Tenth Annual
Computer Press
Awards ➤ 1994*

WINNER

*Eleventh Annual
Computer Press
Awards ➤ 1995*

IDG is the world's leading IT media, research and exposition company. Founded in 1964, IDG had 1997 revenues of $2.05 billion and has more than 9,000 employees worldwide. IDG offers the widest range of media options that reach IT buyers in 75 countries representing 95% of worldwide IT spending. IDG's diverse product and services portfolio spans six key areas including print publishing, online publishing, expositions and conferences, market research, education and training, and global marketing services. More than 90 million people read one or more of IDG's 290 magazines and newspapers, including IDG's leading global brands — Computerworld, PC World, Network World, Macworld and the Channel World family of publications. IDG Books Worldwide is one of the fastest-growing computer book publishers in the world, with more than 700 titles in 36 languages. The "...For Dummies®" series alone has more than 50 million copies in print. IDG offers online users the largest network of technology-specific Web sites around the world through IDG.net (http://www.idg.net), which comprises more than 225 targeted Web sites in 55 countries worldwide. International Data Corporation (IDC) is the world's largest provider of information technology data, analysis and consulting, with research centers in over 41 countries and more than 400 research analysts worldwide. IDG World Expo is a leading producer of more than 168 globally branded conferences and expositions in 35 countries including E3 (Electronic Entertainment Expo), Macworld Expo, ComNet, Windows World Expo, ICE (Internet Commerce Expo), Agenda, DEMO, and Spotlight. IDG's training subsidiary, ExecuTrain, is the world's largest computer training company, with more than 230 locations worldwide and 785 training courses. IDG Marketing Services helps industry-leading IT companies build international brand recognition by developing global integrated marketing programs via IDG's print, online and exposition products worldwide. Further information about the company can be found at www.idg.com. 1/24/99

Dedication

To my loving, patient, and understanding wife, Diane, who I owe big time.

Author's Acknowledgments

I would like to thank the virtual "cast of thousands" at IDG Books who helped to get this book published, especially Jill Pisoni, Sherri Morningstar, Nancy DelFavero, Paula Lowell, Gwenette Gaddis, Chad Hughes, Colleen Esterline, Linda Stark, Jennifer Ehrlich, Christine Beck, Carmen Krikorian, and a special thanks to Mary Corder and Nate Holdread, who saved my sanity.

Publisher's Acknowledgments

We're proud of this book; please register your comments through our IDG Books Worldwide Online Registration Form located at http://my2cents.dummies.com.

Some of the people who helped bring this book to market include the following:

Acquisitions, Editorial, and Media Development

Project Editor: Nate Holdread

Acquisitions Editors: Sherri Morningstar, Jill Pisoni

Copy Editor: Paula Lowell

Editors: Christine Meloy Beck, Jennifer Ehrlich, Gwenette Gaddis, Kyle Looper, Linda S. Stark

Technical Editor: Chad Hughes

Media Development Editor: Marita Ellixson

Associate Permissions Editor: Carmen Krikorian

Editorial Manager: Mary C. Corder

Media Development Manager: Heather Heath Dismore

Editorial Assistant: Alison Walthall

Production

Associate Project Coordinator: Tom Missler

Layout and Graphics: Lou Boudreau, Angela F. Hunckler, Anna Rohrer, Brent Savage, Janet Seib

Proofreaders: Kelli Botta, Melissa D. Buddendeck, Nancy Price, Rebecca Senninger, Janet Withers

Indexer: Sherry Massey

Special Help

Nancy DelFavero, Colleen Esterline

General and Administrative

IDG Books Worldwide, Inc.: John Kilcullen, CEO; Steven Berkowitz, President and Publisher

IDG Books Technology Publishing: Brenda McLaughlin, Senior Vice President and Group Publisher

Dummies Technology Press and Dummies Editorial: Diane Graves Steele, Vice President and Associate Publisher; Mary Bednarek, Director of Acquisitions and Product Development; Kristin A. Cocks, Editorial Director

Dummies Trade Press: Kathleen A. Welton, Vice President and Publisher; Kevin Thornton, Acquisitions Manager

IDG Books Production for Dummies Press: Michael R. Britton, Vice President of Production and Creative Services; Cindy L. Phipps, Manager of Project Coordination, Production Proofreading, and Indexing; Kathie S. Schutte, Supervisor of Page Layout; Shelley Lea, Supervisor of Graphics and Design; Debbie J. Gates, Production Systems Specialist; Robert Springer, Supervisor of Proofreading; Debbie Stailey, Special Projects Coordinator; Tony Augsburger, Supervisor of Reprints and Bluelines

Dummies Packaging and Book Design: Patty Page, Manager, Promotions Marketing

♦

The publisher would like to give special thanks to Patrick J. McGovern, without whom this book would not have been possible.

♦

Contents at a Glance

Cartoons at a Glance

By Rich Tennant

page 427

page 273

page 383

page 53

page 439

page 9

page 175

Fax: 978-546-7747 • E-mail: the5wave@tiac.net

Table of Contents

Introduction

*I*f you have purchased or are considering purchasing this book, you probably fit one of the following categories:

- ✔ You know how valuable A+ certification is to a personal computer technician's career and advancement.
- ✔ You're wondering just what A+ Certification is all about.
- ✔ You think that reading this book may be a fun, entertaining way to learn about computer hardware maintenance and repair.
- ✔ You love all ...*For Dummies* books and wait impatiently for each new one to come out.
- ✔ You're a big fan of mine and can't wait to read my new book.

Well, if you fit any of the first four scenarios, this is the book for you! However, I'm not certified in the appropriate medical areas to help you if you chose the last category!

If you're already aware of the A+ Certified Computer Technician program and are just looking for excellent study aids, you can skip the next few sections of this introduction because your search is over. However, if you don't have the foggiest idea what A+ Certification is or how to prepare for it, read on!

Why Use This Book?

With nearly 20 years and layer on layer of microcomputer hardware and software technology to study, even the most knowledgeable technician needs help getting ready for the exam. This book should shorten your preparation time for the A+ exams.

As with all other ...*For Dummies* books, this book is a no-nonsense reference and study guide. It focuses on the areas likely to be on the exam plus provides a little background information here and there to help you understand some of the more complex concepts and technologies. This book presents the facts, concepts, processes, and applications included on the exams in step-by-step lists, tables, and figures without long explanations. The focus is on preparing you for the A+ exams, not on my obviously extensive and impressive knowledge of computer technology (nor on my modesty, I might add).

In developing this book, I made two assumptions:

- ✔ You have knowledge of electronics, computers, software, networking, troubleshooting procedures, and customer relations and are interested in finding a review and study guide for the exams.

- ✔ You have limited knowledge of electronics, computer hardware, and the processes used to repair, maintain, and upgrade PCs and could use a little refresher on the basics along with a review and study guide for the exams.

If my assumptions in either case suit your needs, then this book is for you.

Using This Book

This book is organized so that you can study a specific area without wading through stuff you may already know. I recommend that you skim the whole book at least once, noting the points raised at the icons. For your last-minute cram before the exam, each part and chapter of the book is independent, and you can study them in any order without confusing yourself.

Each chapter also includes a pre-test (Quick Assessment quiz) and post-test (Prep Test questions) to help you determine where your knowledge is weak and where you need to continue studying. The following sections tell you what I include between the covers of this book.

Part I: First, Some Fundamentals

Part I begins with an overview of what to study for the A+ exam and other general information about taking the exam. I also include some foundation and background information on the concepts of electricity, electronics, and numbering systems, including what you need to know about electronics and the numbering systems used on PCs. And finally, I cover the tools used in computer maintenance with emphasis on electrostatic discharge protection and prevention.

Part II: Inside the Case

Part II takes you down into the wonderful, incredible world of the motherboard and other electronic FRUs (field replaceable units) found inside the case so that you can explore what you need to know for the A+ exams about these really technical parts of the PC. This section is chock-full of information about all the components, systems, and field replaceable units found on or used with the main motherboard; various PC memory systems, including memory types, categories, installation, and optimization; data storage technologies and components commonly used in PCs, including installing and removing, troubleshooting, optimizing, and upgrading; an explanation and comparison of various bus architectures used on the PC; and a review of the purpose, voltages, connectors, upgrading and replacing, and diagnosis and solutions for common power supply problems.

Part III: Outside the Case

After you know everything you need to know about A+ basics and what's going on "under the hood," you need to know about interfacing to the system unit with input, output, printers, and serial and parallel connections, plus networking and data communications for the A+ exam. Part III covers input devices, such as the keyboard, mouse and other pointing devices, scanners, and input device drivers; output devices, including the monitor, sound card, connectors, device drivers, care of these components, and common failures found with these components; installing and troubleshooting serial and parallel port connections; printers, focusing on laser, inkjet, and dot matrix printer operations; communications and networking basics; and last but not least, an explanation of networking principles, terminology, and concepts as these principles impact how a PC operates on a network.

Part IV: Keeping the Computer (And the User) Happy

Part IV has everything you need to know about the tools and best practices to use for repairing, maintaining, and configuring PC hardware, as well as advice and common-sense information about effectively interacting and maintaining successful relationships with customers. Read about disassembling the PC, with a step-by-step guide to taking the computer apart, discussions on protecting the components, and conducting a thorough visual inspection of the assembly, cables, and connections. Then go on to reassembling the PC, with a step-by-step guide to reassembling the major components of the PC, including checks and tests for proper fit and function of FRUs, cables, and connectors. Next, read about installing new hardware: removing and installing individual FRUs and installing expansion cards, connectors, cabling, and software device drivers.

Discover everything you ever wanted to know about upgrading the motherboard, with a focus on upgrading processor, memory, and functionality of the motherboard. Portable systems follow, with information about setting up and configuring notebooks and other portable computer systems, including PCMCIA cards and communications. Then I move on to discuss the people who are most important to your business: your customers. Read about the best ways to interface successfully with your customers, concentrating on the value of customer relations and interpersonal skills in providing customer service on the phone, in person, or by e-mail. Finally, I dig into preventive maintenance. You can solve the mysteries of how to perform regular maintenance to ensure proper system function, including cleaning, vacuuming, washing keyboards, and so on.

Part V: The DOS/Windows World

This part of the book focuses specifically on the A+ DOS/Windows Service Technician exam. Although there is information throughout the book on how the various areas of the PC work in the DOS and Windows worlds, this part of the book is aimed at those areas unique to these environments. I cover PC configuration and upgrade as performed in DOS, Windows 3.*x,* and Windows 95 operating systems and then move on to the troubleshooting and repair procedures unique to the DOS and Windows environments.

Part VI: The Part of Tens

This section provides additional motivation and study guides to help get you ready for the test, with advice about how to be sure that you're ready to take the test on Test Day. This part also includes a list of ten great Web sites where you can find study aids.

Part VII: Appendixes

This section gives you even more practice test questions, with sample test questions on each domain. This section also provides information about what's on the CD in the back of this book and how to use the CD.

Studying Chapters

A+ Certification For Dummies is a self-paced method of preparing for the exam. You don't have to guess what to study; every chapter that covers exam objectives guides you with

- Preview questions
- Detailed coverage
- Review questions

This step-by-step structure identifies what you need to study, gives you all the facts, and rechecks what you know. Here's how it works.

First page

Each chapter starts with a preview of what's to come, including

- Exam objectives
- Study subjects

Not sure that you know all about the objectives and the subjects in a chapter? Keep going.

Quick Assessment questions

At the beginning of each chapter, you find a brief self-assessment test that helps you gauge your current knowledge of the topics that chapter covers. Take this test to determine which areas you already understand as well as to determine the areas that you need to focus on most.

- If you're in a hurry, just study the sections for the questions you answered incorrectly.
- If you answered every question correctly, jump to the end of the chapter and try the practice exam questions to double-check your knowledge.

Study subjects

When you study a chapter, carefully read through it just like any book. Each subject is introduced — very briefly — and then you discover what you need to know for the exam.

As you study, special features show you how to apply everything in the chapter to the exam.

Labs

Labs are included throughout the book to step you through some of the processes you need to know for the exam, such as installation or configuration of a particular component. Here's an example of what a lab looks like:

Lab 7-1	Accessing IRQs in Windows 95

1. **Click the My Computer icon on the Desktop with the right-button of the mouse to display a shortcut menu.**

2. **Choose Properties from the menu to display the System Properties box.**

3. **Choose the Device Manager tab, click the "Computer" level icon, and choose Properties.**

4. **From the System Resources display, choose the View Resources tab and click the interrupt requests (IRQ) option to display the IRQ settings.**

Tables

Sometimes you need just the facts. In such cases, tables are a simple way to present everything at a glance, like the following:

Table 4-1	DRAM versus SRAM
DRAM	**SRAM**
Slow and must be constantly refreshed	Fast and doesn't require refreshing
Simple	Complex
Inexpensive	Expensive
Physically small	Physically large

Prep Tests

The Prep Tests at the end of each chapter gauge your understanding of the entire chapter's content. These Prep Test questions are structured in the same manner as those you may see on your exam, so be sure to try your hand at these sample questions. If you have difficulties with any questions on the Prep Test, review the corresponding section within the chapter.

Icons Used in This Book

 Time Shaver icons point out tips that can help you manage and save time while studying or taking the exam.

 Warning icons flag problems and limitations of the technology that may appear on the exam and things to avoid when working with certain technologies.

 Instant Answer icons highlight tips to help you recognize correct and incorrect exam answers by context and point out information that is likely to be on the test.

 Shocking Information icons point out electrostatic discharge (ESD) and other electrical dangers that you should be aware of for the test and on the job.

 Remember icons point out important background information and advantages of the technology that may appear on the exam or help you understand test questions.

 Tip icons flag information that can come in extra-handy during the testing process. You may want to take notes on these tidbits!

Feedback

I'd like to hear from you. If an area of the test isn't covered as well as it should be, or if I provide more coverage than you think is warranted about a particular topic, please let me know. Your feedback is solicited and welcome. You can send e-mail to me at `rgilster@bmi.net`.

Part I
First, Some Fundamentals

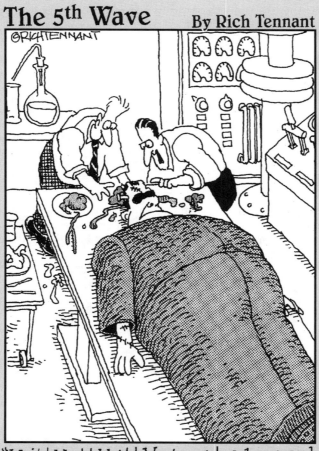

The 5th Wave   By Rich Tennant

@RICHTENNANT

"Wait! Wait! Wait! You've got a lung and two eyeballs in there! I thought you said you were A+ Certified?"

In this part . . .

Not everything about the world of PC service technicians is on the A+ exams. There are some things you are just expected to know; for example, basic electronics, electricity, number systems, and the use of hardware, software, and electronic tools. CompTIA, the A+ test company, has assumed that you know this stuff or you wouldn't be either working (or wishing to be working) as a PC service technician or getting ready to take the A+ exams.

Before you begin preparing for the test, use this part of the book to learn about the tests and review some of the basic and underlying knowledge you need for the exams.

Chapter 1
The A+ Certification Exam

In This Chapter

▶ Knowing what to study

▶ Taking the A+ exam

A+ certification, officially known as *CompTIA Certified Computer Technician,* assures employers and computer owners that an individual has the requisite knowledge to build, upgrade, troubleshoot, and repair microcomputer systems. The A+ examinations measure this ability and knowledge at the level a technician should have after six months of on-the-job training. Certified computer technicians are always in great demand, so passing the A+ certification exams is well worth any time that you have to spend preparing for the exams. A+ certification is a lifetime certification that, so far, doesn't require retesting and renewing on a regular basis.

Who Is CompTIA?

Computing Technology Industry Association (CompTIA) is a membership trade organization formed in 1982 to promote standards of excellence in computer technology. Its goals are to develop ethical, professional, and business standards and provide educational opportunities to the industry. Its members include more than 7,500 computer resellers, VARs (value-added resellers), distributors, manufacturers, and training companies in the United States and Canada, ranging from large multinational corporations to smaller local computer repair shops and individual entrepreneurs.

Why Get A+ Certification?

That's a fair question — why would you want to cram for a test and sweat bullets over taking it, just to get a piece of paper that says, "You know computer repair stuff?" Well, I can think of a number of good reasons, first of which are the more than 65,000 A+ Certified Technicians worldwide. Here are a few more:

✔ **Proof of professional achievement:** The A+ credential validates to your employer and your customers that you have reached a level of competence established by the computer industry, using criteria that is accepted and valued by the industry.

✔ **Increases your marketability:** A+ certification makes you a more desirable employee who can often attract a higher starting wage because the cost to train you is lower than that for a noncertified employee. Many employers now make A+ certification a minimum requirement for employment.

✔ **Provides opportunity for advancement:** A + certified employees are generally more efficient workers, which means they are more productive. In most companies, the most productive people get ahead.

✔ **Fulfill training requirements:** A+ certification meets the prerequisite classes and training requirements for other certification or advanced training courses.

✔ **Raises customer confidence:** As more and more technicians are putting the A+ certification logo on their business cards, the public is starting to accept it as a sign of repair excellence, believing that an A+ certified technician is more qualified to work on computers than an uncertified technician.

✔ **The envy of all your friends and the respect of your peers:** Having the gratification that verifies that you truly do know your stuff is a good thing. Earning the A+ certification is a matter of personal pride. You have new self-worth; you get that big job; and it may even get you a date!

What Do the A+ Exams Cover?

The exams are the result of an industrywide analysis of what service technicians with six months of on-the-job experience need to know to be considered competent in their jobs. The results of this analysis were validated in a worldwide survey of more than 5,000 A+ certified professionals.

The two A+ certification exams are the Core exam, with 69 questions on microcomputers, displays, storage media, printers, basic operating systems, modems, buses, and CD-ROMs, (and a 70th question, but it just asks permission to release your name, and so forth) and the Microsoft DOS/Windows exam, with 70 questions. Each test is geared to measure your knowledge in a number of technical domains.

Each test domain focuses on a specific area of technical service procedures, tools, skills, and customer relations. Some domains are emphasized more than others, so the number of questions on the test from any one domain varies.

Tables 1-1 and 1-2 list the domains and the percentage of coverage that each domain has on the total test, as well as the approximate number of test questions that you can expect for each domain.

Table 1-1	A+ Core Test Module Domains		
Domain	*Percentage of Test*	*Number of Questions*	*Content*
Installation, Configuration, and Upgrading	30%	20	Identify, install, configure and upgrade components, and peripherals
Diagnosing and Troubleshooting	20%	13	Diagnosing and trouble-shooting common problems and malfunctions
Safety and Preventive Maintenance	10%	7	Requires knowledge of safety and preventive maintenance, including the potential hazards of lasers, high-voltage equipment, ESD, and working with items that require special disposal procedures; knowledge of preventive maintenance products, procedures, environmental hazards, and precautions
Motherboard/ Processors/ Memory	10%	9	Specific terminology, facts, and means of dealing with motherboards, processors, and memory systems
Printers	10%	7	Basic types and concepts of printers and components, including all aspects of their operations, care, service techniques, and common problems
Portable Systems	5%	3	Portable computers and their unique components and problems
Basic Networking	5%	4	Basic networking concepts and terminology, network interface cards, and repairs on a networked computer

(continued)

Table 1-1 *(continued)*

Domain	Percentage of Test	Number of Questions	Content
Customer Satisfaction	10%	6	The factors, actions, and interpersonal skills that contribute to a quality technician-customer interaction

The Customer Satisfaction domain of the Core Module Exam is scored, but it doesn't impact your final score. However, it's noted on your score report for your information and use. For example, some employers want to know your score in the Customer Satisfaction domain as a part of their hiring criteria.

Table 1-2	A+ DOS/Windows Test Module Domains		
Domain	**Percentage of Test**	**Number of Questions**	**Content**
Function, Structure, Operation, and File Management	30%	23	The functions, structure, file management, navigation, and program execution in DOS, Windows 3.*x*, and Windows 95
Memory Management	10%	7	The types of memory used by DOS and Windows and the potential for memory address conflicts
Installation, Configuration, and Upgrading	25%	15	Installing, configuring, and upgrading DOS, Windows 3.*x*, and Windows 95, including system boot sequences
Diagnosing and Troubleshooting	25%	13	Diagnostic and troubleshooting procedures relating to DOS, Windows 3.*x*, and Windows 95
Networks	10%	6	Network capabilities and connections in DOS and Windows, and Internet concepts and system setup

Who Can Get Certified?

A+ certification is completely open to anyone who pays the test registration fees and passes the exams. You don't have to be a repair technician, work for a particular company, or have any prerequisite training from a specific company.

How to Get Certified

To become A+ certified, you must get a 65% on the Core exam and a 66% on the DOS/Windows exam. When you take the test, you have 1 hour to complete the Core module, and 1 hour and 15 minutes to complete the DOS/Windows module. You don't have to take them at the same time, although both Sylvan Prometrics and I recommend it. I believe that one period of test anxiety is enough. If you want to study for the tests separately, then schedule them apart. If you do take and pass only one of the tests, you must pass the other exam within 90 days.

After you pass both exams — which is a lead-pipe cinch with the help of this book — you get a bundle of goodies. In addition to the gratification and pride you get from having passed the test, you receive your official A+ certificate — suitable for framing — a lapel pin with the A+ Certified logo, and a wallet-size credential card proving that you are, in fact, A+ certified.

Where to Go

The A+ exams are given by Sylvan Prometric testing centers at over 700 locations worldwide. To schedule an appointment to take one or both exams, contact them at 800-776-4276. Don't wait until the day you're ready to take the test; give Sylvan at least one day's notice. Sylvan helps you find a convenient location and time and sets up payment of the test fee.

How Much Does It Cost?

The cost of one exam alone is $120 U.S. ($85 if you or your company is a member of CompTIA). Both exams cost $215 U.S. ($140 to CompTIA members).

Where to Begin

If I've convinced you that A+ certification is a good thing, you can begin by reading this book. Use the Quick Assessment quizzes at the beginning of each chapter to identify the areas you need to study the most. In addition to this book, many excellent resources to help you prepare for the exams are available. I list some World Wide Web resources at the end of this chapter and in The Part of Tens.

World Wide Web Sites to Help You

Here are some URLs that have either free information or products, or both, to help you prepare for the test:

- AFSMI: www.afsmi.org/aplus/
- Certify, Inc.: www.apluscertification.com/
- CompTIA: www.comptia.org
- Dali Design: www.dalidesign.com/prepap/aplus_cert.html
- ForeFront: www.ffg.com
- Heathkit Educational Systems: www.heathkit.com/
- Marcraft International: www.mic-inc.com/Aplus/
- MindWorks: www.mindwork.com
- Wave Technologies: www.wavetech.com/

Mommy, Make the Mean Man Stop!

If you're really committed to earning your A+ PC technician certification by taking and passing the two CompTIA exams, you have chosen wisely, grasshopper. My advice is to use the study tool that best suits your study habits and the time available. Don't be too cocky or overconfident about this test. Even if you have worked as a PC techician for 20 years, you probably have not been able to work on every FRU (field replaceable unit) in every PC configuration. If you have, so much the better, but some review can't hurt. Along with questions about commonly used terminology, practices, and FRUs, these exams have questions that ask about little-known information on obscure devices or tasks — an obvious attempt to separate the worthy from the pretenders.

When you request a test date from the nice helpers at Sylvan Prometrics, give yourself time to study, if only for a couple days. At over $200 a pop, you can probably afford the time more than the cost of retaking the test. Best of luck!

You really need to know DOS memory management, laser printers, ESD, and system resource assignments. Spend the most time focusing on areas that you don't get much experience with on the job. By all means, review everything you can and take as many sample tests as possible.

Chapter 2

Basic Electronics and Number Systems

· ·

Exam Objectives

▶ Identifying the concepts, terminology, and properties of electronics and electricity in the PC

▶ Identifying ESD (electrostatic discharge) and ESD protection devices

▶ Reading and converting binary, decimal, and hexadecimal number systems

· ·

*E*mbedded in the fundamentals of computer troubleshooting, repair, and maintenance is a knowledge and understanding of electricity, electronics, and number systems. You need to have a basic knowledge of electricity and electronic principles to even begin preparing yourself for the A+ Certification exams. Although no specific electronics or electricity questions are on the test, many questions assume a basic understanding of electricity concepts and terminology and the function of a few electronic components. Even if you know enough about electricity to repair a PC without destroying either the equipment or yourself, you may need a refresher on the names, definitions, concepts, and applications of electricity and electronics. Therefore, in this chapter I provide you with some groundwork that includes a very brief review of electricity and basic electronics.

Binary and hexadecimal number systems are used in the PC for addressing and data display. You may be asked to convert a binary number or two on the exam, and you can count on seeing binary and hexadecimal references in several questions. That's why this chapter takes a quick look at the binary and hexadecimal number systems. I also include a couple of labs to help you review the process of converting hexadecimal and binary numbers to and from decimal values.

Quick Assessment

Identifying the concepts, terminology, and properties of electronics and electricity in the PC

1 _____ measures the electrical pressure in a circuit.

2 _____ measures an electrical current's strength.

3 A semiconductor that can store one of two toggled values is a _____.

4 Households use _____ current electricity.

5 PCs use _____ current electricity.

6 A _____ is a device that can measure more than one property of electricity.

Identifying ESD and ESD protection devices

7 ESD stands for _____.

8 Antistatic bags are treated to become _____.

9 The _____ number system uses only the numbers 1 and 0.

Reading and converting binary, decimal, and hexadecimal number systems

10 The _____ number system uses the numbers 0–9 and the letters A–F.

Answers

1 *Voltage.* Review "Counting electrons."

2 *Amps.* See "Counting electrons."

3 *transistor.* Check out "Resistors, capacitors, transistors, and diodes."

4 *alternating.* Review "Switching from AC to DC."

5 *direct.* Direct yourself to "Switching from AC to DC."

6 *multimeter.* Check out "Measuring the current."

7 *electrostatic discharge.* Read "Don't Give Me Any Static."

8 *conductive.* Peruse the sidebar, "Using antistatic bags."

9 *binary.* Review "Reading binary numbers."

10 *hexadecimal.* See "Working with hexadecimal numbers."

Understanding Electricity

Everything inside or attached to the PC system unit runs on electricity. Electricity is both the lifeblood and the mysterious evil of the personal computer. It's a flowing entity, measured in amps, ohms, and volts that should be approached with respect, if not outright fear.

Nothing helps you understand a complex technical topic better than a real-life analogy that you can relate to. I tried hard to come up with a new and original analogy to help you understand electrical properties and measurements and to dazzle you with my cleverness, but, unfortunately, I have failed. One analogy that I thought had a lot of potential involved Twinkies and beer, but it fell flat. So I am forced to use the same old water-in-the-hose analogy that you have probably seen and heard at least a thousand times. If you have heard it before, skip the next few paragraphs, but if it's new to you, read on.

Electricity flowing through a circuit is very much like water running through a hose. When you open a water faucet, the pressure in the water line forces the water to flow at some gallons-per-minute rate into the hose. Friction reduces the force and rate of the water before it exits the hose. When electricity flows into a wire from a source such as a battery, some of its pressure is lost to resistance in the wire.

The "electricity is like water in a hose" analogy points out the forces of electricity that can be measured. These forces are measured in volts, amps, and ohms. At the risk of running the analogy into the ground, Table 2-1 lists the water hose analogous element against its electrical equivalent.

Table 2-1	May the Force Be with You
Water Forces	*Electrical Forces*
How much pressure?	What's the voltage?
How much water is flowing?	What's the volume of the electrical current in amps?
Is there any friction in the hose?	What's the wire's resistance in ohms?

Table 2-2 may put this analogy into a little better perspective. The electrical measures are listed with a description and an example of how they're applied on the PC.

Counting electrons

The forces of electricity inside the computer can be measured, and each type of measurement tells you something different about the computer. I include the electrical measurements in Table 2-2 to provide you with an introduction to these units of measurement. Chapter 8 provides more information on the power used in the PC and how it is measured.

Table 2-2	Common Electrical Measurements	
Measurement	*Description*	*Application*
Amps	Measures a current's strength or rate of flow	The amount of current needed to operate a device; for example, a hard disk drive needs 2.0 amps to start up, but only 0.35 amps for typical operation.
Ohms	Measures a conductor's resistance to electricity	Resistance of less than 20 ohms means that current can flow through a computer system.
Volts	Measures the electrical pressure in a circuit	A PC power supply generates 4 levels of voltage: +5 volts (V), –5V, +12V, and –12V.
Watts	Measures the electrical power in a circuit	A PC power supply is rated in a range of 200 to 600 watts.
Continuity	Indicates the existence of a complete circuit	A pin in a DIN connector registers 5V on a digital voltage meter (DVM or multimeter) when grounded to another pin.

Measuring the current

The primary measurements of electricity are volts and amps. Volts measure pressure, and amps measure current. Current isn't needed to have voltage. When a water faucet is off, water pressure still exists. There is just no current. Likewise, when an electrical circuit is open, voltage (pressure) is still in the line although no current is flowing. If you touch the wire and close the circuit, the current begins to flow, and you can feel all of its pressure as a *shock*.

You can use a variety of devices to read the power and fury of an electrical current. Ammeters, ohmmeters, and voltmeters measure specific properties, but using a multimeter or DVM is more efficient for you to use because it combines these instruments into one tool.

Switching from AC to DC

Current is the flow of electrons in a wire. Electricity has two current types: AC (alternating current) and DC (direct current). AC is what you get from the outlets in your house or office, and DC is the type used inside the computer.

In alternating current, the current changes directions about 60 times per second, moving first one way, and then the other. The voltage changing rapidly from a positive charge to a negative charge causes the current to also switch the direction of its flow in the wire. AC power exists because it has advantages for the power company and for your household electrical appliances, but these advantages have little value on a low-voltage system like a PC.

When the flow of the electricity is in one direction only, it is direct current. What happens in direct current is that negatively charged particles seek out and flow toward positively charged particles, creating a direct electrical current flow. DC power maintains a constant level and flows in only one direction — always, predictably, and measureably, from a negative charge to a positive charge.

For example, wire a light bulb to a battery, and the current flows from the negative terminal to the positive terminal through the light bulb. Because the current of electricity causes heat and light in the right materials, the lighter materials in the light bulb glow.

The PC uses DC power. The PC's power supply converts power from the AC wall outlet into DC power for the computer. Peripheral devices, such as printers, external modems, and storage drives, including CD-ROM and Zip drives, use an AC power converter to convert AC power into DC power.

Okay, so the computer runs on direct current electricity. What does this fact have to do with the A+ exam?

When answering a question about the power supply, you must know what −5V, +5V, −12V, and +12V represent (minus 5 volts, plus 5 volts, minus 12 volts, and plus 12 volts, which are the four DC power levels produced by the power supply).

Focus on the following electrical terms or concepts:

- ✔ Voltage and volts
- ✔ Amperes or amps
- ✔ Electrical resistance
- ✔ Ohms
- ✔ Watts
- ✔ Alternating current
- ✔ Direct current
- ✔ 5 or 12 volts DC current

Reviewing Elementary Electronics

Now that you know a little about electricity, you should review basic electronics principles. What follows is a series of definitions and concepts that both prepare you for any direct questions on electronics (not very many) and provide you with background information for questions in other areas. This stuff is pretty basic, so if you're an electronics whiz, you may want to skip over it.

Digital circuits

A digital circuit is an electronic circuit that accepts and processes binary data using the rules of Boolean algebra — the logic of AND, OR, NOT, and so on. Digital circuits are made up of one or more electronic components placed in series to work cooperatively to achieve the logical objective of the circuit.

Conductors, insulators, semiconductors

A *conductor,* such as copper, carries an electrical current. An *insulator,* such as rubber, doesn't carry an electrical current, which is why a copper wire conductor is usually wrapped with a rubber insulator.

In the conducting electricity scheme of things, halfway between a conductor and an insulator is a *semiconductor.* Although its name technically means "half-conductor," it's really neither a conductor nor an insulator. When a semiconductor is zapped with electricity or light, it toggles to either a conductor or an insulator, depending on what it was at the time it was zapped.

Confused? Don't be. It's actually very simple: A semiconductor is simply an extremely simple on/off switch. Zap it once, it's on; zap it again, it's off. Zap it, on; zap it, off — and so on.

Resistors, capacitors, transistors, and diodes

These four electronic components are the building blocks on which virtually every electronic circuit in the computer is built. Each plays a distinctly different and valuable role in a circuit, as I explain in the following:

- A *resistor* acts much like a funnel to slow down the flow of current in a circuit.

- A *capacitor* is like a storage bin to hold a charge. The PC has a few large capacitors that can literally kill you if you make contact with them, such as the capacitors in the monitor and in the power supply.

- A *diode* is a one-way valve that allows the current to flow in only one direction.

- A *transistor* is a semiconductor that stores one binary value.

- Transistors, resistors, capacitors, and diodes produce logic gates. *Logic gates* create circuits, and *circuits* make up electronic systems.

Don't Give Me Any Static

The term *static* has a variety of meanings in computer technology. To the computer technician, it's *static electricity* (electrostatic charge) and its evil twin — *electrostatic discharge* (ESD), also called electrical static discharge, that have the most importance by far. If you were a superhero named PC Repairperson, you would battle the evil nemesis ElectroStat Dis, a negatively charged evil-doer of the first order. ESD, as it is infamously called, is the evil demon that lies in wait for the unsuspecting service technician who fails to don the sacred wrist strap before kneeling at the PC altar.

Throughout this book, you see repeated warnings, cautions, and preventive actions for ESD, something that can't be emphasized too much. Focus your attention on the prevention of ESD damage.

You should always wear a grounded wrist strap that's connected to either a grounding mat or the PC chassis when you work on any part of the computer except the monitor. If you're curious about why you don't wear your strap when working on a monitor, see Chapter 10.

Static electricity is what makes your hair stand on end when you rub a balloon against your head. Of course, this assumes that you have hair — and that you'd have occasion to rub a balloon against your head. Static electricity also occurs when you walk across a carpet. Static electricity is not by itself a problem; it's a fact of nature. It's in the potential danger of its discharge that evil old ESD lurks. You know, when you reach for the door knob and zap! A blue spark as big as a tow rope jumps from your finger to the metal. Although this may seem harmless (other than the pain), the potential for a lot of damage to a PC exists in that seemingly harmless spark. Remember that lightning is ESD in its most dreaded form.

This is on the test. Just because you can't feel an electrostatic discharge doesn't mean that it can't do harm to an electronic component. A human feels ESD at around 3,000 volts, but only around 30 volts are needed to damage electronic components. ESD is a far greater threat to the PC than anything else the PC service technician might accidentally do.

Looking at the dark side of ESD

Most PCs are designed to have some ESD protection as long as their cases are intact and closed properly. Cases are chemically treated or have copper fittings designed to channel electrostatic discharge away from the sensitive components inside.

The danger from ESD damage begins when the case is opened and the fragile components on the motherboard are exposed. When a human with a static electrical charge touches anything inside the case, the charge can travel along the wires interconnecting the various electronic components. One of the wires may lead inside a component, and when the charge nears a metal part with an opposing charge, the effect is that the internal wires and elements of components can explode or weld together.

So, ElectroStat Dis is real, and it's YOU!

Take a look at some ESD facts:

- ✔ Most of the computer's electronic components use from 3 to 5 volts of electricity.
- ✔ An ESD shock of 30 volts can destroy a computer circuit.

✔ An ESD shock you can *feel,* such as on a doorknob, has around 3,000 volts. You only feel a charge that has more than 2,500 volts.

✔ An ESD shock you can *see* carries about 20,000 volts.

The real problem with ESD damage is that not all of it is obvious. If an entire component is destroyed, you know it, and you replace the piece. When a component has been damaged but continues to work, though, days, weeks, or even months may pass before the component fails completely. More frustrating is intermittent partial failures that can't be isolated.

Eliminating static electricity

You can avoid static electricity. Good environmental preventive measures that help to eliminate, or at least reduce, static electricity follow:

✔ You can treat carpeting inexpensively with antistatic chemicals to reduce static buildup. Aerosol cans of these chemicals are available in most computer or carpet stores. If your employer doesn't carry some, tell your customers to ask for antistatic carpet treatment.

✔ Store all electrical components in antistatic bags when not in use.

✔ Install a grounded pad under the PC. Before you touch the computer, touch the pad, and discharge any built-up static electricity.

✔ If all else fails, install humidifiers to replace moisture in the air. Keep the humidity above 50 percent. Dry air can cause static electricity. The primary thing you can do to avoid the threat of ESD damage to the PC is to always wear a ESD grounding strap on your wrist or ankle that is connected to either the chassis of the PC or to a grounding mat when working inside the PC.

However, when working on the monitor, do not, I repeat, do not wear a grounding strap. There is a very large capacitor in the monitor and a grounding strap only invites all of its stored charge to run through your body — not always a pleasant experience.

For all my ranting and raving on the threat of electrostatic discharge, ESD does have some good uses. For example, it's used to apply toner to paper in copy machines and laser printers and is used to clean the air of unwanted pollen, dust, and other debris.

WARNING!

Using antistatic bags

Replacement components are generally shipped in plastic or foam bags and wrapping that are treated to be antistatic. This means that they are treated to be conductive. An antistatic bag absorbs static electricity from the components it protects. Many people don't understand this fact and believe that antistatic bags are nonconductors — when just the opposite is true.

Never place a circuit board on antistatic material and then turn on the power. Using the conductive antistatic material, every pin and part on the back of the circuit board shorts to every other pin or part. Any 5-volt component connected to a 12-volt component is certain to be destroyed.

Polishing Up on Number Systems

On the A+ exams, you encounter questions that reference hexadecimal addresses for items such as IRQs and COM ports. The ability to read and understand binary and hexadecimal values helps you understand some questions.

For example, one test question you may get asks you for the address where BIOS is commonly located in memory. The answer choices listed are hexadecimal values such as A0000 to AFFFF, B0000 to BFFFF, C0000 to CFFFF, and F0000 to FFFFF. Your ability to rationalize which of the numbers represents the range closest to the 1MB boundary for the upper memory area is your key to the answer.

Your ability to work with binary and hexadecimal numbers can also help you in dealing with questions related to troubleshooting and debugging situations, as well as on the job.

Reading binary numbers

The binary number system is the foundation upon which all logic and data processing in the PC is built. For no other reason than that, you should know something about it. In its simplest form, the *binary number system* consists of only two digital values: 1 and 0. Because a transistor is a semiconductor that can only store one of two toggled values, the binary number scheme and the electronics of the PC are made for each other.

Binary values are the result of the number 2 being raised to various powers. This is true for all number systems. The decimal number system is based on values of the number 10 raised to increasing powers. For example, 2^3 is 8, and 2^{10} is 1,024. An 8-bit byte can store the value 255, which is a number that should sound familiar to you, because it is virtually the limit on everything in the PC.

You may see a question on the test asking you to convert a binary number like 00000101 to a *decimal value* — you know, ordinary numbers. The key is to remember that each position represents a power of 2, starting with 0 on the right end up through 7 at the left end. For example, the binary number 00001010 contains

0×2^0 = 0 (any number to the zero power is worth 1)

1×2^1 = 2 (any number to the one power is the number)

0×2^2 = 0 (two times two)

1×2^3 = 8 (two times two times two)

Totaling 10 (the remaining positions are all zero)

So, 00000101 in binary is the same as 10 in decimal. Just count the positions, starting from the right with zero, and then calculate the powers of two for each position with a one.

Follow the steps in Lab 2-1 to convert the numbers in your street address to a binary number. (If your house number is greater than 65,536, use a lower number.)

Lab 2-1   Converting Decimal to Binary

1. **Figure out the largest power of two value that can be subtracted from the number.**

   For a house number of 63,529, the largest binary value that can be subtracted is 32,768, or 2^{15}. Probably, a very scientific way exists to determine this number, but I use trial and error to find the largest power of 2 that can be subtracted from the starting number. For example, 2^{16} is 65,536 and that was too big, so I had to use the next lower power of 2. Because this value is 2^{15}, a 1 can be placed in position 16 of the binary number (remember the first power of two is a zero — so values of 2^{15} go in the 16th position. Got it?). I have 1000000000000000 for the binary number so far. This represents the following:

2^{15}	2^{14}	2^{13}	...	2^2	2^1	2^0
1	0	0	...	0	0	0

2. Subtract 32,768 from your original number.

The difference in this example is 30,761. Repeating the process used in Step 1, the highest value that can be subtracted from this number is 16,384, or 2^{14}. The binary number is now 1100000000000000.

Continuing the process through each remaining value of the original decimal number and for each digit in the binary number, the final binary number for this example is 1111100000101001.

How did your house number come out?

Of course, if you have one handy, you could use a scientific calculator to convert these numbers, but you won't always have one with you, so being able to convert decimal numbers to binary is a good skill for a PC repair technician to have. Luckily, you don't have to demonstrate this skill on the A+ test. They don't let you use a calculator on the test anyway.

Addressing in binary

Because all data is stored as a binary value in the computer, the size of the computer's bus (8-, 16-, 32-, or 64-bits) controls both the highest address that can be stored (and accessed) and the largest value that can be stored at any address. A 16-bit address bus can store an address or value of 2^{15}, or 32,768 — my lucky number! A 32-bit word length handles 2^{31}, or 2,147,483,648, and 64 bits stores a really big number with lots of commas.

The largest number that can be stored in a certain number of bits is calculated by raising two to a power represented by the number of bits minus one.

Working with hexadecimal numbers

The word *hexadecimal* means *six and ten,* and that's just what this number system is about. Whereas binary includes only zero and one, hex, as it's known to its friends, includes the decimal numerals 0 to 9 (the ten) and replaces the decimal values of 10 to 15 with the symbols A, B, C, D, E, and F (the six).

You can expect to be asked for the hexadecimal number addresses of one or more IRQs, LPT, or COM ports on the test. For example, 2F8 is the default address of IRQ3 and COM2. The decimal equivalent of this number is absolutely unimportant, but the ability to convert hexadecimal numbers is a good basic skill for PC repair technicians, because you often need to convert a range of addresses to decimal to determine the size of a memory, storage, or address range. For example, the DOS DEBUG program gives memory locations in hexadecimal with a hexadecimal offset to indicate its size. You need to be able to convert this number to know how big an area it is.

Concentrate on the hexadecimal addresses of the IRQs, COM, and LPT ports and not the decimal equivalents of these hexadecimal values.

Converting hexadecimal numbers

As I show in Lab 2-1 earlier in this chapter, converting any nondecimal number system to decimal is a matter of knowing two things: the *radix* (base value) of the number system and the numeric value of each position. In binary numbers, each position represents a different power of two; the same holds true in any number system, including hexadecimal. The difference with hexadecimal is that each position represents a different power of 16.

The radix of a number is the value that 10 represents in that number's number system. The radix of decimal is 10, the radix of binary is 2, and the radix of hexadecimal is 16.

What is the decimal equivalent of the hexadecimal number A012F? Use the process in Lab 2-2 to convert it.

Lab 2-2	Converting Hexadecimal to Decimal

1. **Because each position represents a power of 16, the A in A012F represents the positional value of 16^4. The A has the decimal equivalent of 10. So, this position is worth 10×16^4, or 655,360.**

2. **The next position of value is a 1 in the position of 16^2, which is worth 256.**

3. **The next position has a value of 2×16^1, or 32.**

4. **The last position has the value of F (15) $\times 16^0$, or 15. Any number to the zero power is worth 1, so this is the same as 15×1.**

5. **Add up the values: $655360 + 256 + 32 + 15$. The sum is 655,663 — the decimal equivalent of A012F hexadecimal.**

Hexadecimal numbers are usually written with a small *h* following them. For example, the number used in the preceding lab is written as A012Fh.

Hexadecimal numbers are by far easier to convert with a calculator, but knowing how to convert them can come in handy, especially when working with debugging and troubleshooting tools or when taking an A+ exam.

Prep Test

1 The decimal equivalent of 00000110 is

A ○ 8

B ○ 5

C ○ 110

D ○ 6

2 When servicing a PC, where do you attach the ground strap to prevent ESD?

A ○ To the inside of the case

B ○ To the static shielding bag that came with the computer

C ○ To the ground mat

D ○ To a wall outlet

3 Electrical current is measured in

A ○ Amps

B ○ Ohms

C ○ Volts

D ○ Watts

4 What is the most common threat to PC hardware when being serviced by a technichian?

A ○ ESD

B ○ Accidental breakage of a component

C ○ Improper tools damaging a component

D ○ Placing components on the wrong type of surface to work

5 Electrical resistance is measured in

A ○ Amps

B ○ Ohms

C ○ Volts

D ○ Watts

6 You should ground yourself with an ESD wrist strap when working on which of the following? (Choose all that apply.)

A ❑ Memory board

B ❑ Motherboard

C ❑ Hard drive

D ❑ System board

7 The microcomputer operates on _____ current electricity.

A ○ Alternating
B ○ Direct
C ○ Switchable
D ○ Directional

8 The decimal equivalent of A00h is

A ○ 44
B ○ 32,768
C ○ 2,560
D ○ 65,536

9 Computer components can be damaged by an ESD charge of

A ○ 2,000V
B ○ 30V
C ○ 30,000V
D ○ 3 to 5V

10 What does ESD refer to?

A ○ Electronically safe device
B ○ Electrical static discharge
C ○ Electric surge protector
D ○ None of the above

Answers

1 *D.* The binary number 00000110 is the same as adding 2^2 (4) and 2^1 (2) to get 6. *Take a look at "Reading binary numbers."*

2 *C.* You should attach the wrist ground strap to the ground mat if possible. *Check out "Don't Give Me Any Static."*

3 *A.* The strength of an electrical current is measured with an ammeter in amps. *Review "Counting electrons."*

4 *A.* ESD damage is far more common than any other damage inflicted by the repair person or user. *Look at "Don't Give Me Any Static."*

5 *B.* Electrical resistance, or the amount of resistance in a conductor to the flow of electricity, is measured with an ohmmeter in ohms. *See "Counting electrons."*

6 *A,B,C,D.* Wear an ESD grounding strap when working all of these FRUs. The only part of the computer you don't want to be grounded to is the Cathode Ray Tube (CRT) — see Chapter 10 for more information. *Check out "Resistors, capacitors, transistors, and diodes" and "Don't Give Me Any Static."*

7 *B.* Household appliances operate on alternating current, but the computer operates on direct current. The power supply converts AC to DC. *Take a look at "Switching from AC to DC."*

8 *C.* A00h is the same as 10×256 (16^2), or 2,560. *Review "Converting hexadecimal numbers."*

9 *B.* It doesn't take very much of an ESD charge to zap the internal components of a computer. *Check out "Looking at the dark side of ESD."*

10 *B.* ESD is the abbreviation for either electrical static discharge or electrostatic discharge; both terms are used interchangeably. *Zap over to "Don't Give Me Any Static."*

Chapter 3
Using the Right Tools

Exam Objectives

▶ Using common hand tools appropriately

▶ Applying diagnostic tools to troubleshoot and isolate problems

▶ Using a multimeter to measure voltage

*M*uch of the A+ exam relates to troubleshooting and diagnosing PC problems and installing, configuring, and upgrading FRUs. In order to do this, the PC service technician must have and know how to apply the appropriate tools effectively. The application of specific tools is a minor consideration of the A+ exam, but I believe that you must have knowledge of the repair process itself and the tools used in it to be completely successful on the test, as well as on the job.

The PC repair technician uses tools in two different situations: locating the source of a PC problem and affecting the fix. This doesn't require two separate tool kits. In fact, a single tool can often used in both situations effectively. For example, a DVM (digital volt meter) can be used to determine if an AC line carries the proper voltage and it can also be used to test that a new FRU is installed properly. Often the real difference between one use of a tool and another is only the mental processes applied by the repair technician in a given situation.

You can do most customer-site diagnostics and repairs with about a dozen or so tools and a few pieces of software, so you don't need to carry around a suitcase full of stuff. On the other hand, a good tool kit is specialized enough that you can't get away with just an all-in-one tool kit.

You can divide the service tool kit into three groups: hardware tools, software tools, and measurement tools.

As I indicate earlier, the A+ exam has very few questions on the specific use of a tool. You won't be asked the purpose of a screwdriver, wire cutter, tweaker, or the like. However, you might see a question about when a tool is used, or which tools are used in a diagnostics situation. For example, on a question about checking the power available from the power supply, you may be asked what tool you would use to make this measurement (DVM). Preparing you for this type of questioning is my primary mission in this chapter.

Quick Assessment

Using common hand tools appropriately

1 The _____ is an absolute necessity in any tool kit.

2 _____ is a supply item that's used for cleaning fans, grill work, inside the case, keyboards, and other parts of the PC.

Applying diagnostic tools to troubleshoot and isolate problems

3 _____ are used to diagnose a parallel or serial port on a PC.

4 The _____ is one of the most effective diagnostics tools available and runs every time you boot the system.

5 _____ software performs troubleshooting, system tune-ups, hardware checks, and system status.

Using a multimeter to measure voltage

6 A(n) _____ is a voltmeter, ammeter, and sometimes ohmmeter rolled into one.

7 The range of values used when measuring VDC is _____ to _____.

8 Placing one probe on a pin at an end of a serial cable and the other probe on a pin at the other end of the cable checks for _____.

Answers

1 *ESD wrist strap*. Review "ESD wrist strap."

2 *Compressed air*. Check out "Supplies."

3 *Loop-back plugs*. Look at "Loop-back plugs."

4 *BIOS POST*. See "The domestic tools."

5 *Diagnostic*. Visit "The foreign tools."

6 *Multimeter*. Review "Measurement Tools: The Multimeter."

7 *3V to 12V*. Look at "Measurement Tools: The Multimeter."

8 *Continuity*. Check out "Measurement Tools: The Multimeter."

Hardware Tools

That you can appropriately use tools in troubleshooting, diagnosing, and repairing a PC is basically assumed in the newest version of the A+ exams. You should at least skim through the first few sections of this chapter to familiarize yourself with the tools included. Focus your attention on software tools and using a multimeter. It's hard not to know these tools. They're the *hard tools;* that is, they are hard to the touch. You use hard tools to diagnose, repair, remove, and install hardware. (This is where I break into a chorus of "Hard Day's Night" and drive the point straight into the ground.) I think you get the idea — hardware tools are hard and you generally use them on hardware.

In the general category of hardware tools, you have literally hundreds of different types. Some tools are specific to particular tasks and others are more generic. Luckily for PC-repair technicians, most of the necessary tools are fairly generic, which saves money when buying tools. The more specific a tool is to a task, the more it costs.

You can buy an adequate tool kit that has most of the basic tools you need at your local computer or electronics store or online for less than $20. (They often come in nifty little zippered cases.) When buying a tool kit, be sure that it has an ESD (electrostatic discharge) grounding wrist strap.

The PC-repair technician's tool kit consists of two groups of hardware tools. The never-go-to-the-customer-site-without-these-tools and the tools-that-are-kept-at-the-shop-for-major-surgery. Like a doctor's bag, only the instruments and generic medicines that are needed for general care are carried in the bag and the really strange and specific tools are left back in the operating room.

The following sections discuss the general categories of hardware tools, separating each category into those tools that go into the doctor's bag and those that should be left in the operating room.

Tools you shouldn't leave home without

Many tools come in handy often enough that you should carry them with you to all customer sites. They're the staples of your tool kit. Don't leave home without 'em.

Screwdrivers

Screwdrivers are mostly used in assembly and disassembly tasks, which are common activities in repairing and even diagnosing PC problems. For this purpose, you don't need a huge assortment of screwdrivers. The screws used in the PC come in basically four flavors: Phillips (cross-head recess or star), slotted (standard), hex head, or Torx. If you have one or two good screwdrivers for each type of screw, you'll be in good shape.

Know the different screw heads by sight, especially the Phillips and Torx.

Magnetic screwdrivers, while very convenient for you, can be dangerous to the sensitive electronic components inside the computer. I suggest you adopt a better-safe-than-sorry attitude and, to be safe, use nonmagnetic tools.

Needle-nose pliers

While not completely necessary, you can use needle-nose pliers to hold screws and connectors when your fingers are just too big. They can also come in handy for working with wire, and most needle-nose pliers have a wire-cutter near the hinge. Whether this tool is in your tool kit is a matter of personal preference, but I suggest carrying a set with you, just in case.

One caution about pliers handles: The handles on some pliers are plastic or rubber to improve the grip and may also vary in color by size. The plastic or rubber is not for electrical shock protection. Pliers that are insulated against shock are marked as such, but are very rare.

Parts retriever

This tool has a small set of retractable claws that extend when a button on the spring-loaded handle is pressed. Once they are extended, you can place the claws around an item to be retrieved, such as the screw that fell down onto the motherboard, and release the spring to grasp the item. For me, this tool is a real necessity.

Diagonal cutters (dikes)

Manufacturers are developing the habit of bundling all the cables, including the one you need, with cable ties. A small pair of diagonal cutters, also known as dikes, are useful for cutting cable ties and any other thicker wire or plastic that you need to cut. Of course, cutting a cable tie should remind you to put some extra cable tie in your tool kit. This is a tool you won't need until you need it — take it along.

Loop-back plugs

You rarely need to diagnose or repair a parallel or serial port on a PC. However, if necessary, *loop-back plugs,* which create the illusion to the port that it is connected to another device, used in conjunction with a diagnostics software package (such as Norton Diagnostics), can help determine whether the cause of a communications error problem is in the port by performing a full operations test on a port.

ESD wrist strap

This tool is an absolute necessity in every tool kit for travel and in the shop. Using the doctor analogy, an *ESD wrist strap* is akin to the mask worn by the surgeon over his or her mouth and face. They are both worn for the safety of the patient. An ESD wrist strap is an elastic or Velcro wristband that usually has a coiled wire attached to it that also has a clip or snap or both at the other end. The clip or snap is used to attach to a computer chassis or to a grounding mat, or both, to ground you and eliminate the potential for ESD damage from you or your tools.

You can connect the ESD wrist strap to the case of the PC, or preferably attach it to a static ground mat placed under the PC. But, because most repair technicians don't carry a ground mat to customer sites (it isn't always easy to place the mat under the customer's PC), the next best grounding method is attaching a wrist strap to the PC chassis.

Flashlight

A flashlight is another must-have. Many gloomy shadows lurk inside the computer where screws and other small parts can fall. Also, you need to read some very small print, such as the pin markings on a connector, that can be hard to read in the shadows. A small flashlight can really come in handy.

Operating tools

I carry a small set of dental and medical tools that includes angled mirrors (see Figure 3-1), hemostats, and probes. They have no specific repair purpose, but these tools come in handy when I need to see a connector or wire deep inside the computer. You can find these tools at most tool shops. The better commercial tool kits now include these items.

Sharp edge

At times you may need to cut through something and having a utility knife or blade of some type can be helpful. If you carry one with you, be sure that it has a retracting edge or snug-fitting cover.

Figure 3-1:
Angled
mirrors, like
the kind
dentists
use, can
really come
in handy.

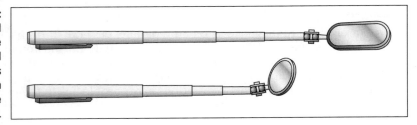

Tools you can safely leave at the shop

The following tools may show up in questions concerning their use. There are no surprise tools here, but review it, just in case. These tools aren't used often enough to warrant lugging them around to every site, but that doesn't mean that they don't come in handy back in the shop. The following sections discuss tools that have fairly specific purposes, and that aren't called to duty quite as often.

- ✔ **Wire cutters/strippers:** You rarely need to cut a wire in a computer or to strip the insulator on a wire or cable. But when you do, you need a wire cutter or wire stripper. Usually the tool shown in Figure 3-2 does both of these jobs. Should the repair require this level of activity, take it to the shop — where you can have this tool waiting.

- ✔ **Chip tools:** You can use chip tools in two ways: inserting DIP chips and extracting DIP chips. Just about every commercial tool kit comes with a DIP chip inserter/extractor tool. As the name implies, you use this tool when removing DIP chips and when inserting new chips. Because you rarely do this, the DIP chip inserter/extractor falls into the category of nice-but-unnecessary. If you don't have one of these gadgets, try using a slotted screwdriver to unseat a DIP chip. It often works better and damages fewer chip pins.

- ✔ **Soldering iron:** Many technicians say that a soldering iron is a useless tool and should be omitted from commercial tool kits. I agree that at a customer site, this tool should never see the light of day, but in the shop, it can come in handy for repairing cables and for other light soldering tasks. As long as it's kept away from circuit boards, it can't do much damage. Leave the soldering iron at home.

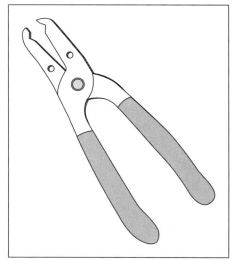

Figure 3-2:
Wire cutter
and
stripper.

Supplies

Not all hardware tools are actually *tools,* in the common sense of the word. Some actually fall more into the category of supplies. Consider keeping the following supplies close at hand. They're cheap, easy to find, and may save your bacon sometime:

- ✔ **Electrical tape:** The black plastic kind, for wrapping wire ends and insulating other components.
- ✔ **Compressed air:** For cleaning fans, grill work, inside the case, keyboards, and so on.
- ✔ **Soft, lint-free cloth:** For cleaning the glass and plastic components of the computer and peripherals.
- ✔ **Spare parts:** Having an assortment of screws, expansion card inserts, faceplaces, cables, and so on can be handy when working at a customer site. For example, if you need to remove a card and can't immediately replace it, you can cover its hole with an expansion card insert. You know the customer didn't save the one that came out of the PC, if one ever existed.

Software Tools

Of the tools that you use to troubleshoot and diagnose the problem on a customer's PC, the software tools described in this section are the tools that the A+ exam cares about. You will definitely encounter questions that ask about when, why, and what to expect from the software tools in this section.

A PC's problem is not always apparent. Only once in a blue moon do you arrive to find the power supply on fire and are fairly certain that the problem is the power supply. If you've worked with PCs long enough, you know that no problem is ever 100 percent what it seems. The problem often lies deep inside the computer, and you must employ something other than hardware tools.

This situation is where diagnostic and troubleshooting software comes in. These software tools are as much an essential part of your tool kit as the Phillips screwdriver. Whether they're a part of your travel tool kit is a policy matter for you or your employer. Installing and uninstalling the tools after each use or getting your customer to purchase a license may be involved.

Luckily, some of these tools often come as a part of the operating system, as is the case with those discussed in "The domestic tools." Some must be licensed (purchased) for use on one or more computer. This group of software tools is discussed in "The foreign tools."

The domestic tools

Consider this group of diagnostic software tools as a part of your travel tool kit:

- ✔ **BIOS POST**: One of the most-effective diagnostic tools available to you is built right into the PC and runs automatically every time the PC is powered on. If a serious hardware problem exists, most likely the POST finds it and reports it to you.

- ✔ **POST card:** A piece of hardware that you may want to consider to make the POST an even better tool. Not the kind Aunt Milly sends from Iowa, but a dedicated circuit that interprets the POST error codes written to address 80h. A POST card saves you the trouble of counting beeps and decoding them.

- ✔ **MSD.EXE:** (also known as Microsoft Diagnostics): This DOS utility creates and reports a brief inventory of your PC. This inventory is useful for seeing a system's configuration, including the BIOS, disks, memory, and system resource assignments, such as IRQs (interrupt requests) and I/O (input/output) addresses to LPT and serial ports.

    MSD.EXE will run under Windows 95. Although it is on the Windows 95 release CD and can be copied to the system, it isn't included in a normal Windows 95 installation. Run MSD.EXE in DOS mode and not in a DOS window under Windows 95.

- ✔ **SCANDISK.EXE:** This program, installed as a part of Windows 95, checks and reports hard disk problems, including file system corruption and hard disk read errors.

- ✔ **MEM.EXE:** Another DOS and Windows 95 utility that provides details about the memory configuration and usage on a PC.

- ✔ **DEFRAG.EXE:** A DOS and Windows 95 utility that arranges the data clusters on the disk to improve disk efficiency.

- ✔ **SYSEDIT.EXE:** A Windows 95 tool that's used to view or edit .INI, AUTOEXEC.BAT, CONFIG.SYS, and other system files.

- ✔ **Windows 95 Device Manager:** This tool can be useful on Windows 95 systems, if you suspect a problem is caused by a resource conflict, IRQ, DMA channel, or I/O address. The Properties feature shows the device driver, resource settings, and much more for a specific hardware device. More information is available on this feature in Chapter 24.

The foreign tools

You can use three types of software tools to help troubleshoot, diagnose, or repair PC problems. These tools are

- ✔ **Antivirus:** Due to the increase in e-mail, Web, and other Internet access, PCs need some immunity against computer viruses. A variety of antivirus software packages are on the market. Having an antivirus program available on a floppy disk can help you solve a customer problem before it spreads.

- ✔ **Diagnostic and troubleshooting:** A number of diagnostics packages are available, such as Nuts & Bolts, First Aid 98, or QAPlus, that perform troubleshooting, system tune-ups, hardware diagnostics, and system status reporting. Often these packages include other features such as file encryption and file compression.

- ✔ **Uninstaller:** If you haven't already noticed, the Windows environment uses the first-in-stays-here mode of file management. Windows programs leave behind more junk than NASA, which is why uninstall software, such as Remove-It 98, can be an essential tool. That you are ever called upon to clean up a customer's files is doubtful, but you may need to remove conflicting or out-of-date DLLs or the like.

Measurement Tools: The Multimeter

The A+ exam expects you to know how to use, when to use, and what to measure with the digital multimeter. You can expect questions on which multimeter settings to use when measuring volts, amps, and ohms on the PC. If you don't have much experience with a multimeter, you should get one and work with the booklet it comes with or get a more-experienced service technician to work with you so that you are comfortable making the standard electrical measurements on the PC.

Most PC technicians carry a multimeter in their travel tool kit. A multimeter is a voltmeter, an ammeter, and sometimes a ohmmeter all rolled into one. A multimeter measures electrical resistance, voltage, and current. Most multimeters used by field technicians are battery powered, but some of the higher-end models use AC power from a wall plug.

When you set up a multimeter for use, you must set three things:

- ✔ **The type of current you're measuring:** AC or DC (also known as VDC — voltage direct current).

- ✔ **What you're measuring:** You set the appropriate indicator or dial to either voltage (volts), current (amps), or resistance or continuity (ohms).

✔ **The range of values expected:** If you're measuring voltage from the power supply, the voltage range is 3V to 12V, and for the AC wall plug's output, the range is around 105V to 125V. You can find Autorange multimeters that sense the incoming power and set the range automatically.

A multimeter has two probes: a red (positive) probe and a black (negative) probe. When you test a device, place the red probe on the *hot point,* or high point, of the current and place the black probe on the *ground,* or low point. The voltage of the circuit is calculated as the difference in the readings of these two points.

Lab 3-1 gives you some general experience using the multimeter. Lab 3-2 shows you how to check the continuity on a cable. If you have a digital voltmeter (DVM) that doesn't measure continuity, skip Lab 3-2. The purpose of these labs is to enable you to focus on the process of using the multimeter and not the actual results.

Lab 3-1   Using the Multimeter

1. **Turn on the multimeter and set it to measure DC current voltage in the range of 5V to 12V.**

2. **Open the computer case and remove the top cover.**

3. **With the power on, carefully locate a power cord connector to either a floppy disk, hard disk, or internal CD-ROM drive. The device power connector has either a Molex or Berg plug.**

   Remember to put on your wrist strap and connect to either a static ground mat or the PC case.

4. **Place the red (positive) probe on the leftmost wire and place the black (negative) probe on the wire next to it.**

   You should get a reading of between +11.5V and +12.6V. If you get around 5V, you have the connector reversed.

5. **Place the red probe on the right lead and the black probe next to it.**

   You should now have a voltage reading between +4.8V to +5.2V.

Lab 3-2   Checking Continuity on a Cable

1. **Set the multimeter to measure resistance (continuity, which is measured in ohms).**

   See your multimeter's manual for how to set this.

2. **Get a null modem cable, the cable from an external modem, or another serial device.**

   Be sure to disconnect the cable from any devices.

3. **Place either probe on Pin 2 of at one end of the cable and the other probe on Pin 2 at the other end of the cable.**

If you're unable to make a good contact at the female end of the cable, use a short bit of wire, or a straightened paper clip, to extend it.

The multimeter should give a reading, buzz, or beep to indicate continuity in the cable. If you do not get buzzed or beeped, either no continuity exists in the cable, or you have not made a good connection. Try a few more times, and if you still get no reading — chances are there is not continuity.

A paper clip is an excellent tool in the right cases. In addition to extended cable pins for continuity readings, you can use it to open a stuck CD-ROM drive.

Prep Test

1 When servicing a PC, on which of the following do you attach the grounding wrist strap to prevent ESD?

A ○ To the chassis inside the case

B ○ To the static shielding bag that came with the computer

C ○ To a static ground mat

D ○ To the chassis, but only if a ground mat is not available

2 What procedure is used to measure continuity between two points with a multimeter?

A ○ Set the meter to ohms and test the circuit with power to it.

B ○ Set the meter to ohms and test the circuit without power to it.

C ○ Set the meter to amps and test the circuit with power to it.

D ○ Set the meter to amps and test the circuit without power to it.

3 In which of the following situations do you not use a multimeter?

A ○ When measuring DC volts

B ○ When measuring RAM

C ○ When measuring resistance

D ○ When measuring AC volts

4 The Windows 95 software tool used to view and edit .INI files, AUTOEXEC.BAT, and CONFIG.SYS is

A ○ File Manager

B ○ Sysview

C ○ Regedit

D ○ Sysedit

5 An IC is best removed using a(n)

A ○ Needle-nose plier

B ○ Phillips screwdriver

C ○ IC chip tool

D ○ Expansion card slot filler

6 The screwdriver that is made especially for screws with an internal, faceted, star-like hole is a

A ○ Phillips screwdriver

B ○ Torx screwdriver

C ○ Nut driver

D ○ Tweaker

7 The software tool that's used to find and repair hard-disk problems is

A ○ MSD.EXE

B ○ MEM.EXE

C ○ DEFRAG.EXE

D ○ SCANDISK.EXE

8 The type of software that's used to remove orphaned or unwanted files is

A ○ Uninstaller

B ○ Diagnostics

C ○ Troubleshooting

D ○ Antivirus

9 The abbreviation *DVM* stands for

A ○ Direct voltage monitor

B ○ Digital volt meter

C ○ Direct voltage meter

D ○ Direct variable meter

10 If you use a screwdriver set with interchangeable tips, be sure that the tips are

A ○ Magnetic

B ○ Carbon steel

C ○ Nonmagnetic

D ○ Insulated

Answers

1 *D. To the chassis, but only if a ground mat is not available.* The best possible place to attach an ESD wrist strap and grounding cord is to a static ground mat. If a mat isn't available, attach the wrist strap to the chassis frame with the computer plugged into a wall outlet. *See "ESD wrist strap."*

2 *B. Set the meter to ohms and test the circuit without power to it.* Continuity is measured in ohms. With power running through a cable, you're testing current or power. Without the power, you're testing continuity. *Review "Measurement Tools: The Multimeter."*

3 *B. When measuring RAM.* RAM is measured in bytes or bits. A multimeter is used to test for voltage, power, resistance, and continuity. *Look at "Measurement Tools: The Multimeter."*

4 *D. Sysedit.* SYSEDIT.EXE is used to view or manually edit Windows 95 configuration and system files. *See "The domestic tools."*

5 *C. IC chip tool.* Although a slotted screwdriver also works well, IC chip tools are specifically made for this task. *See "Tools you can safely leave at the shop."*

6 *B. Torx screwdriver.* The Torx screwdriver is considered to be tamper-proof and less likely to be damaged. It's used in Apple and Compaq cases. *Review "Screwdrivers."*

7 *D. SCANDISK.EXE.* SCANDISK is a Windows 95 tool that finds and repairs problems with the hard disk and the folders and files stored on it. *Look up "The domestic tools."*

8 *A. Uninstaller.* An uninstaller program identifies system files left behind by removed applications, temporary files, and unwanted Internet files for possible removal. *Check out "The foreign tools."*

9 *B. Digital voltmeter.* Some multimeters don't measure continuity and so they're called digital volt meters. *See "Measurement Tools: The Multimeter."*

10 *C. Nonmagnetic.* Magnetic tips can cause damage when in contact with sensitive components on the motherboard and disk drives. *Look at "Screwdrivers."*

Part II
Inside the Case

The 5th Wave   By Rich Tennant

JAWS OF LIFE

"Here's a little tip on disassembly that you won't find on the A+ Certification test."

In this part . . .

Most of the PC service technician's world exists inside the PC case in the form of the motherboard, memory, the power supply, disk drives, and the bus structure. In a way, this is the techie part of a techie job. Almost half of the Core exam and one third of the DOS/ Windows exam concern the computer components found inside the case. So, this part of the book should be a first stop in your preparation for the test.

Chapter 4
The Motherboard

Exam Objectives

▶ Identifying popular motherboards, their components, and architecture

▶ Distinguishing CPU chips by their basic characteristics

▶ Identifying the concepts and procedures of the BIOS

▶ Identifying CMOS's purpose and how to change its parameters

*T*he A+ exam tests your knowledge of the central role played by the motherboard in the system. The motherboard is by far the most important electronic circuit in the computer. It acts as the gatekeeper to the CPU — all outside devices wishing to have an audience with the CPU must pass through the motherboard. It is all-powerful. It is all-knowing. Ignore that man behind the curtain!

At least 10 percent of the Core exam contains questions on the motherboard and bus structures, CMOS, BIOS, chipsets, and compatibility. One-third of the remaining questions (around 20 or so) relate to CPUs, memory, installation, and troubleshooting the motherboard and its components. You can expect to see questions like

> What is the size of the 386SX data bus?

> What are some common types of motherboard form factors?

> What was the first 32-bit architecture?

> What are the CMOS settings for a hard disk drive?

You need to know about data and address buses, processor capabilities and compatibilities, the contents of the CMOS and how they are updated, and the role of the system ROM and BIOS in booting the system.

I can hear you saying, "Is that all!" It is only natural that an exam with "Core" in its name tests you on the core components and issues of the PC. In the PC, nothing is more "core" than the motherboard, processor, and memory. Because so much of the A+ Core exam deals with these areas, I chose to spread out the review on motherboards, processors, and memory systems over a few chapters. This should help prevent a brain overload while you review.

Quick Assessment

Identifying popular motherboards, their components, and architecture

1 The three standard motherboard types are _____, _____, and _____.

2 The four primary types of bus structures found on most motherboards are _____, _____, _____, and _____.

Distinguishing CPU chips by their basic characteristics

3 The _____ processor was the first to feature a built-in math coprocessor.

4 The Pentium processor generates about _____ degrees Fahrenheit.

5 MMX is short for _____.

Identifying the concepts and procedures of the BIOS

6 BIOS is an acronym for _____.

7 The BIOS process that verifies the integrity of the hardware is the _____.

8 Using software to control the upgrading of the BIOS ROM is called _____.

Identifying CMOS's purpose and how to change its parameters

9 You can use a _____ to reset the CMOS settings, including the startup password.

10 CMOS settings are changed by running the BIOS _____ program.

Answers

1   *AT, Baby AT, and ATX.* Take a look at "Motherboard form factors."

2   *Address, control, data, and power.* Review "Riding the Bus."

3   *486DX.* Review the table in "Intel processors."

4   *185.* Peruse "Keeping the processor cool (and applying some grease)."

5   *Multimedia extensions.* Read "Putting it in overdrive."

6   *Basic Input/Output System.* See "Understanding the BIOS."

7   *POST.* See "Looking at the Boot Sequence" and "The POST."

8   *Flashing.* See "Understanding the BIOS."

9   *Jumper.* Review "The startup password."

10 *Setup.* Take a look at "Accessing the BIOS setup program."

Understanding the Motherboard

This section focuses on preparing you to meet the exam objective of identifying popular motherboards and their components and architecture. I can't overly emphasize the importance of knowing this material for the exam. Not only does it have its own domain on the test, but it seems to have seeped into all parts of the test.

Most experts, and some writers, have theories on the importance of the motherboard. You have probably seen many references to the motherboard that characterize it in human anatomy terms. It has been called the heart, backbone, spine, soul, and brain of the computer. However, it is much more than one single organ.

Every essential component directly or indirectly involved with making the PC function as it should is either on, attached, or connected to the motherboard. For all intents and purposes, the motherboard is the computer. A computer without a printer, a CD-ROM, or a monitor is still a computer. However, a computer without a motherboard is just an empty metal box that just sits there giving very bad response time.

You will commonly hear the motherboard referred to as the systemboard. In most usage, a systemboard goes beyond a motherboard by integrating video, audio, graphics, and other device support into the board's architecture. IBM has called its motherboard a systemboard from the beginning. Apple Computer calls theirs a logic board, and still others call it a planar board. These terms are still around today, but mostly they are now interchangeable because most motherboards are now systemboards and vice versa. I tend to favor the term motherboard, but from time to time I will slip in a systemboard for variety.

A motherboard is usually designed to be one of the following two types:

✔ **Nonintegrated:** The traditional style of motherboard that requires the circuitry for major subsystems, such as video, disk controllers, audio, and others, to be added through expansion cards; the upside is that if a card goes bad, only it needs to be replaced.

✔ **Integrated:** This motherboard style incorporates most of the circuitry that would normally be added through expansion cards: video, disk controllers, and others; the downside of this simplicity is that if one of the circuits goes bad, the whole board must be replaced.

As illustrated in Figure 4-1, a motherboard integrates the most significant components of the computer on a single circuit board. It is common for the motherboard to include the CPU and its associated support chips, memory, device controllers, and expansion slots that give peripheral devices access to the computer's internal bus.

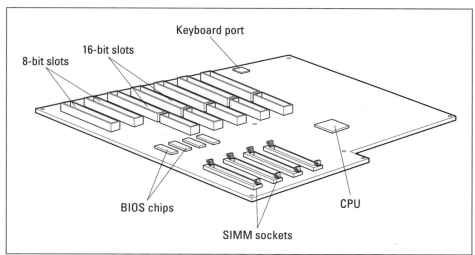

Figure 4-1:
A Pentium
motherboard.

Keyboard port

16-bit slots

8-bit slots

BIOS chips

CPU

SIMM sockets

Motherboard form factors

The shape, packaging, and to a certain extent, the function of a motherboard is called its form factor. For the A+ Core exam, you should know the three most common PC form factors in use.

Three standard forms of motherboards exist:

- ✔ **AT:** A motherboard patterned after the original IBM AT motherboard
- ✔ **Baby AT:** A smaller motherboard used in clone machines
- ✔ **ATX:** Smaller like the Baby AT board, but installed with a 90-degree rotation

The ATX motherboard allows for easier installation of full-length expansion cards and cables and is easier to cool.

The motherboard components

The motherboard consists of layers of components added to the basic circuit board very similar to those of a pizza. For the A+ exam, you need to know not only what makes up the crust but each of the ingredients as well. In this chapter, I cover some of the major ingredients (the processor and CMOS), but each of the other major components are covered in following chapters.

In addition to the motherboard, processor, and CMOS, you need to know each of the following ingredients, I mean, components, listed in Table 4-1. These components are typically found inside the system unit and considered to be, after they are installed, a part of the motherboard's sphere of control.

Table 4-1	Motherboard Components You Must Know for the A+ Exam
Component	*Where You Can Find It in This Book*
Memory	Chapter 5 — "Memory Systems"
Disk Drives	Chapter 6 — "Storage Systems"
Motherboard and expansion bus	Chapter 7 — "Bus Structures"
Power supply	Chapter 8 — "Power"
I/O ports	Chapter 11 — "Serial and Parallel Ports"

Looking at Microprocessors

A microprocessor is an integrated circuit that contains millions of transistors interconnected with very small aluminum wires. Its processing capabilities are used to control and direct the activities of the PC by interacting with the other electronic components on the motherboard. The exact functions performed by a microprocessor are dictated by software.

One of the objectives of the exam is to measure how well you can identify a central processing unit (CPU) by its basic characteristics. If you are given a key characteristic of a microprocessor, you should be able to tell which one it is. For example, when asked (and you will be) which CPU was the first to have a math coprocessor built into it, you confidently choose the answer "486DX."

You need to know microprocessors in detail for the exam. I mean, little nit-picky stuff like clock speeds, bus widths, features included or supported, mountings, packaging, manufacturer, and evolution. This seems to be a favorite area of the test writers to get very specific. In most areas of the test, a sound, solid, experienced, and general knowledge of a subject can be enough to get you by, but not here. You need to know this stuff.

Since 1981, microprocessors have been packaged in a form factor (package style) called the Pin Grid Array (PGA), which arranges its transistors into a square shape (see Figure 4-2). The PGA microprocessor installs on the motherboard in a special socket called a ZIF (Zero Insertion Force). You can probably gather how easy it is to install a chip in one of these sockets by its name.

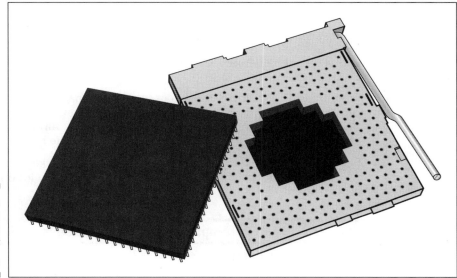

Figure 4-2:
The Pin Grid
Array (PGA)
and ZIF
socket.

Newer ZIF sockets, such as ZIF Socket 7, also come with a lever (ZIF handle) to lock and release the chip, making it even easier to install or replace the processor.

Intel processors

Most of the microprocessors you come into contact with as a PC repair technician are manufactured by the Intel Corporation. Intel began manufacturing CPUs before PCs existed and has been the dominant microprocessor manufacturer in the PC market since IBM decided not to build its own chips. What began with the 8088 CPU in the first IBM PC has carried through to the Pentium II and beyond.

For the exam, about the only thing you need to remember specific to Intel is the numbering and naming schemes it has used for its CPUs, and how that contrasts to the processors of other manufacturers. You won't be asked to identify the manufacturer of a CPU, but knowing Intel's evolution may help you to identify bad choices in a question.

According to the published objectives of the A+ Core exam, know the type of mounting, voltages, clock speed, and bus width for each of the popular (meaning Intel) microprocessors. Table 4-2 includes information for the CPUs that you should know for the test.

In Table 4-2, the packaging abbreviations used mean:

- ✔ DIP — Dual Inline Packaging. This is the most common package for all types of integrated circuits. It is usually a black plastic or ceramic body with a row of metal pins along each side.

- ✔ PGA — Pin Grid Array. There are various sizes of PGA packages and mountings. For example, the 486 uses a 169-pin package; the Pentium processor mounts in either a 273- or 296-pin socket; and the Pentium Pro uses a 387-pin mounting. This also changes the physical size of the chip, but don't worry about the physical sizes for the test.

- ✔ SEC — Single Edge Contact. This nifty new type of package mounts the processor as a single module into a specially designed slot on the motherboard.

Table 4-2			Microprocessor Characteristics				
CPU	Package	Voltage	Speed (MHz)	Data Bus (bits)	Memory (MB)	Co-processor?	Cache (K)
8086	DIP	5	8	16	1	No	0
80286	PGA	5	20	16	16	No	0
386DX	PGA	5	40	32	4096	No	0
386SX	PGA	5	25	16	16	No	0
486DX	PGA	5	25, 33, 50	32	4096	Yes	8
486SX	PGA	5	20, 25, 33	32	4096	No	8
486DX2	PGA	5	40, 50, 66	32	4096	Yes	8
486DX4	PGA	5	75, 100	32	4096	Yes	16
Pentium	PGA	5	100, 133, 150, 166	64	4096	Yes	16
Pentium MMX	PGA	5	150, 166, 200	64	4096	Yes	32
Pentium Pro	PGA	1.5	166, 200	64	4096	Yes	16
Pentium II	SEC	1.5	166, 180, 200, 266, 300+	64	4096	Yes	64

The 486DX was the first CPU with an integrated math coprocessor; the Pentium Pro offers a 64-bit data bus; and the Pentium and Pentium II processors offer MMX.

The Pentium processor is basically a combination of two 486DX chips that create a parallel processing environment that Intel calls superscalar.

Competing processors

You may see references to other (that is, other than Intel) processors in the choices (wrong answers) of questions on motherboard and chipset compatibility. Be able to spot the processors mentioned in this section as real processors by their identities, but don't worry about anything else.

Intel is the big kahuna in microprocessors, but other companies do manufacture CPUs. The two prominent competitors are Advanced Micro Devices, Inc. (AMD) and Cyrix.

AMD's K5 and K6 and Cyrix's 6x86 and M2 processors compete with Intel's Pentium and advanced Pentium processors. The AMD microprocessors, which are found in many popular PC brands, offer a wide variety of clock and bus speeds and are generally compatible with most motherboard support component chipsets.

Putting it in overdrive

You may or may not run into overdrive chips on the exam. Just in case you do, here's some information on them.

Intel's 386 Overdrive and 486 Overdrive processors provide 386 and 486 processor owners with Pentium-level performance without the need to pay for a new Pentium computer. The Overdrive processor increases the speed of the processor about 2.5 times the motherboard's bus speed. For example, with an Overdrive processor installed, a 33 MHz motherboard runs at approximately 80 MHz.

Intel has recently announced a Pentium II Overdrive upgrade chip for Pentium Pro users who want to add speed to their systems without buying a new computer. The only warning is that this chip may also require a BIOS upgrade as well.

Extending out to multimedia

MMX (short for multimedia extensions) technology has added three features to the Pentium processor:

- ✔ Fifty-seven new instructions to improve video, audio, and graphics capabilities
- ✔ SIMD (Single Instruction Multiple Data) technology, in which one instruction can control several data items
- ✔ Cache doubled to 32K

Speeding up the works with a coprocessor

You may see one or two questions on the test relating to math coprocessors. As I indicate by its repetition in earlier sections, most likely the question will be which processor first incorporated the coprocessor. You should also know that earlier processors could have one added to the motherboard.

Until the 486DX came along, it was often advisable to add a coprocessor to the motherboard to help speed up the system. The coprocessor, also called a math coprocessor or a numeric processor, allowed the CPU to offload much of its number-crunching tasks, which really helped applications like CAD, spreadsheets, and graphics.

The coprocessor is installed in a socket located adjacent to the CPU on 808x, 286, 386DX and SX, and 486SX motherboards. Coprocessors were numbered relative to the system each was designed to support. For example, the coprocessor for the 80286 was the 80287; the 80387DX worked with the 386DX; and the 80487SX was installed on the 486SX board.

Understanding chipsets

A chipset is a set of microchips that work as a unit to set or control the amount of memory and the type of RAM chips that can be used, and provide support for certain peripherals. The term *chipset* is commonly used to mean the basic functions of a motherboard, as in "What's its chipset?"

The chipset on a motherboard has an impact on any upgrades you may apply to it. They determine which processors, memory, and peripherals with which the motherboard is compatible. Be sure you check out the chipset on a motherboard before making any upgrade recommendations.

Keeping the processor cool (and applying some grease)

With the Pentium processors came heat and cooling problems for the PC. The Pentium chip runs much hotter than earlier CPUs and requires special heat dissipation and cooling. You need to know a few things about the heat problems and cooling requirements of the Pentium chips.

The Pentium processor operates at 185 degrees Fahrenheit. The cooling system is designed to keep the processor in this range. Therefore, you want to keep the PC's case closed to ensure that its cooling system is operating efficiently. In fact, the cooling system on a Pentium PC sucks air into the case, whereas earlier systems blew air out of the case.

In addition to the air flow system of the PC, the Pentium processor also uses special motherboard configurations to help cool it. This may include a fan or a heat sink, or both, mounted directly on top of the processor. The fan sucks the heat away from the chip and up into the PC's air flow to be blown away. A heat sink is a device that looks something like a bed of nails that wicks the heat into its tines where the air flow cools it. If a processor has both, the fan sits on top of the heat sink. These devices are attached to the processor with clips and special chemical materials called thermal grease.

Thermal grease (also known as heat sink jelly, heat sink compound, thermal gunk, thermal compound, or thermal goo) improves the heat conductivity between the processor and its heat sink. It eliminates any gaps between the two, working along the lines of denture adhesive, allowing the CPU's heat to transfer to the heat sink more efficiently.

Because most thermal grease is mercury based, avoid getting it on your skin, and definitely don't use it for denture cream.

Riding the Bus

A part of understanding the operation of the motherboard is understanding its bus structure. Most of the motherboard exam questions are about bus architectures. This section provides you with a brief overview of this area, but take a look at Chapter 7 for a much deeper review of this important part of the test.

The CPU moves data values and signals around the computer on a network of very small wires that interconnect it to all the other components on the motherboard. This network is called the *bus*.

The lines used to move data around inside the computer is the internal bus. The lines used to communicate with peripherals and other devices attached to the motherboard is the external bus. You can think of the internal bus as being the hallways within a large building, such as a very large hospital or the Pentagon. In this example, the external bus would be the hallways that lead directly to outside doors.

You can find four primary types of bus structures on most motherboards:

- ✓ **Address:** The components on the motherboard pass memory addresses to one another over the address bus.
- ✓ **Control:** Used by the CPU to send out signals to coordinate and manage the activities of the motherboard components.
- ✓ **Data:** Because the primary job of the computer is to process data, logically the data must be transferred between peripherals, memory, and the CPU. Obviously, the data bus can be a very busy hallway.
- ✓ **Power:** The power bus is the river of life for the motherboard's components, providing each with the electrical power it needs to operate.

The number of wires in a bus controls the number of bits that can be transferred over the bus. For example, a 32-bit bus must have 32 wires.

Don't Forget the Memory Chips

While I'm on the subject of the motherboard, I want to cover all the chips that would be plugged into it, including memory chips and ROM BIOS, and the physical chips, their type, size, number, and selection. (See Chapter 5 for more information on how memory systems work and how they're configured.)

Memory chips come in three handy package sizes, with one right for every system:

- ✓ **Dual inline package (DIP):** Small byte-size pieces installed individually, shown in Figure 4-3
- ✓ **Single inline memory module (SIMM):** Large economy-size pieces that combine multiple DIPS on a single module, shown in Figure 4-3
- ✓ **Dual inline memory module (DIMM):** High capacity modules that have memory on each side of the module board that connects through a single connector

Along with the 386 and its 32-bit bus, the 30-pin SIMM was introduced. As illustrated in Figure 4-3, a SIMM is a series of RAM chips that have been soldered together on a small circuit board. Each SIMM essentially replaces one bank of DIP memory chips. A DIMM is a double-sided memory board that combines two SIMMs.

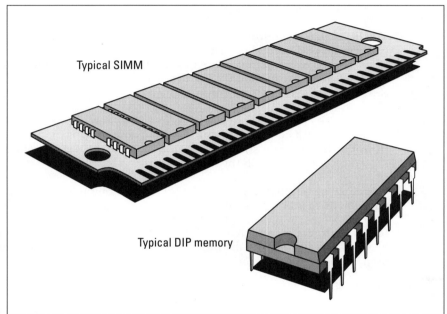

Typical SIMM

Typical DIP memory

Up through the 80286, computers use the DIP type of memory chips. Prior to the 286, systems used either 64-kilobit or 256-kilobit chips. Because the 286 can address more memory, a 1-megabit chip can be used on that system. For those systems that use can them, DIP chips are installed in banks of up to 16 chips each. The 1-megabit chip is two pins longer than the other chips, but some motherboards can take both sizes.

It is very unlikely that you will be asked any questions regarding the installation of memory on an 80286 board, or that you will ever actually do it. It's much better simply to upgrade the motherboard or buy a whole new computer.

Understanding the BIOS

One of the central functions of the motherboard is the BIOS. Several exam questions relate to the BIOS system and its major components and features, including the POST process and the system boot procedures. This is very important material, if for no other reason than to prove you can't have too many acronyms in one chapter.

The BIOS (basic input/output system) contains the programming used to control the keyboard, disk drives, monitor display, and data communications, as well as a few miscellaneous hardware-related actions. It serves as an interface between the PC's hardware and the operating system, monitors the hardware settings, and controls the boot sequence of the PC.

Several types of BIOSes are in a PC. Many peripheral units, such as video cards, hard disk controllers, and SCSI host adapters, have their own BIOS. However, the one you should worry about is the main system BIOS, which is stored on a ROM chip on the motherboard.

You must keep reminding yourself that all the computer (that is, the processor) can do is follow instructions. No matter how sophisticated the hardware becomes, to date, it can't perform even the simplest task without being told what to do. When you first turn on your computer, the first set of instructions available to the processor comes from the BIOS ROM chip mounted on the motherboard.

The BIOS code is installed on the motherboard in a ROM chip.

All microprocessors look in the same physical location for their first instruction. Not by coincidence, this location is the same location used for the first instruction of the BIOS. When the BIOS program begins running, it invokes the system's boot sequence, which in turn invokes other programs, including the operating system. However, the process starts with that one instruction, called the *jump instruction*.

The jump instruction of the BIOS program is located at address FFFF0h of conventional memory.

Because RAM is faster than ROM, some manufacturers design their systems to perform *shadowing,* a procedure that copies the BIOS code from ROM into RAM when the computer boot sequence begins.

The BIOS is made up of several parts and features, with more features added to every new version. One of the challenges of the PC repair technician is keeping current with the error detection, features, and functions of the various BIOS types and versions.

On newer systems, the BIOS system is installed on the motherboard on an electrically erasable, programmable, read-only memory (EEPROM) chip that can be updated under software control. On older systems, the BIOS could be updated only by replacing the BIOS ROM chip, which is one of the reasons PC repair tool kits actually have a chip-puller tool, which you use to pry off a keyboard's keycaps.

The BIOS ROM is installed in a motherboard socket and is easily found because of its shiny foil label that identifies its version, date of manufacture, and the name of the manufacturer.

The version number printed on a BIOS ROM chip's label may not be the version actually installed because most newer BIOS ROM can be updated through a software procedure called flashing. A BIOS ROM chip that is not on a flash memory chip must be physically replaced.

Flashing is updating the contents of a ROM chip under software control. Many of the newest ROM BIOS chips are EEPROM (electrically erasable programmable read-only memory), which allows them to be erased and re-written by software.

A BIOS that's always implemented on a flash memory chip is Plug-and-Play BIOS. This type of BIOS supports Plug-and-Play (PnP) devices and will detect them during POST processing. Its ability to be updated with flashing ensures that it can stay current to the latest devices.

Some motherboard or computer manufacturers buy BIOS code from a BIOS company and then modify it to work with their hardware. In these cases, the BIOS ROM label may identify the PC or motherboard manufacturer.

It is rare that you would need to fuss with the BIOS at all. In general, if the BIOS ROM becomes corrupted and the PC will not boot, you may need to replace the BIOS ROM.

Looking at the Boot Sequence

One of the first objectives of the A+ Core exam is for you to identify the basic terms, concepts, and functions of a PC's boot processes. This includes the actions and the sequence of the actions involved in starting the computer from a power-off status (cold boot) or restarting a PC that is already running (warm boot). The cold boot starts when the PC's power is switched on and the warm boot is performed whenever the PC is restarted or reset with the power still on. One of the most common ways to start the warm boot is by using the service technician's secret club official keystrokes (Ctrl+Alt+Delete), but then you already knew that.

A cold boot is the whole BIOS enchilada. It causes the BIOS to guide the computer's boot sequence through a series of steps that verify the computer's integrity. The exact steps vary slightly, depending on just about everything about or in your computer (manufacturer, BIOS, and hardware configuration), but the steps listed in Table 4-3 are what generally happens when you cold boot a PC.

Expect one or two questions on the cold boot process and the sequence of its actions in the "Motherboard, memory, and processors" Core exam domain. You may also see two or three boot sequence or POST questions in the "Installation, configuring, and upgrading" and "Diagnosing and trouble-shooting" domains as well.

Table 4-3	Cold Boot Processing
Step	*Activity*
Power initialization	The motherboard chipset holds the CPU at bay until the power supply initializes.
BIOS startup	The processor reads the jump address and starts the BIOS program.
POST (Power-On Self Test)	The BIOS checks the hardware system — any errors are signaled with error beep codes.
Video and peripheral BIOS	The video card and any other device BIOSes execute.
System check	After displaying its startup screen, BIOS checks memory, storage drives, ports, and other devices — any errors are signaled with error messages on the screen.
Plug-and-Play (PnP) check	If BIOS supports this standard, it detects and configures any Plug-and-Play devices.
Summary screen	The BIOS displays a summary of the PC's configuration. On some systems, it displays long enough to read, but on many others it usually flashes by very quickly and is unreadable.
Boot device	The BIOS determines which drive is the boot drive (either A: or C:) and looks for the volume boot sector (A:) or the master boot record (C:).
Op Sys running	Control passes to the boot sector code and the operating system.

A warm boot bypasses the majority of the POST process and begins its boot sequence at about the same point as the cold boot's system check.

The POST

Any questions on the boot sequence you encounter will most likely be about the POST process. The POST is a hardware diagnostic routine built into the BIOS that checks the PC's hardware to make sure that everything that's supposed to be there is, and that everything is working properly. The POST process ensures that the system is ready to begin the boot sequence.

Should the POST process detect errors, it generates a signal to indicate where in the process the error occurred and which device had the error. Not all POST errors are fatal; the POST process generally continues past non-fatal problems. If a fatal error is detected, such as no memory is found, the POST process signals its error code and halts the boot process immediately. If the POST detects an error very early in the process, before the device drivers for the monitor are loaded, it must signal an error the only way it can: using sounds, actually beeps, issued through the PC's system speaker.

The meaning of a beep code depends on the manufacturer of the BIOS. Each BIOS maker has its own set of beep codes, which can also vary from one version to the next. Something like having a different Morse code scheme for every ham radio. Well, maybe not really *that* bad!

Just about all BIOS programs will sound a single beep right before displaying the BIOS startup screen. As long as the boot sequence continues, the beep doesn't indicate a problem. BIOS beep codes can be used to troubleshoot hardware failures occurring in the POST procedure.

Decoding POST messages

After the POST and boot sequence have advanced to the point that they have use of the video to display messages, they can display a numerical error message to indicate a failure that occurred during the POST or boot sequence. For instance, a POST message code in the 300 series indicates a keyboard error was detected during the POST.

For the exam, know the major groups of numerical error codes, such as those listed in Table 4-4, which lists the major groups of the POST hardware diagnostics messages commonly used on PC systems. Each of the different BIOS systems uses many of the codes listed, but no single BIOS uses all of these codes. I include only those codes that you are likely to encounter on the test. There are many more, especially in the IBM system world. One of the problems of these error codes is that the list continues to grow without much ever being deleted.

Table 4-4   POST Hardware Diagnostic Message Groups

Code	Description
1xx	Systemboard errors
2xx	Main memory errors
3xx	Keyboard errors
5xx	Color monitor errors
6xx	Floppy disk controller errors
14xx	Printer errors
17xx	Hard disk disk controller errors
86xx	Mouse error

Did you beep?

Don't worry about beep codes for the test, but here is some information you may find interesting. If you are cramming for the test, ignore this stuff.

The BIOS system on a PC most likely came from one of three companies: American Megatrends International (AMI), Award, or Phoenix. Each of these BIOS system providers has its own unique set of POST error beep codes.

The Phoenix BIOS uses as many as 100 different beep codes in very complicated patterns. With this many codes, a Phoenix BIOS is sure to give you the most beeping details about exactly where and when a problem occurred. However, it may also complicate the task of accurately decoding the signal and identifying the error. The Phoenix BIOS issues beep codes in groups. For example, one beep, a pause, two beeps, another pause, and finally four more beeps means that the motherboard is bad and should be replaced.

The AMI BIOS uses 1 to 11 beeps to identify a POST problem. For example, a two-beep error is the approximate equivalent of the Phoenix BIOS 1-2-4 beep code (motherboard error). The very latest AMI BIOS versions have additional two-part codes (such as one long beep, pause, eight short beeps!) to indicate memory and video problems.

Unfortunately, Award BIOS is sold to motherboard or system manufacturers who then customize the BIOS code. This can really complicate error message decoding during the POST process. In general, the Award BIOS POST only beeps if the video system can't start. Award BIOS prefers to display its messages on the screen. You need to look in the systemboard manuals or visit the manufacturer's technical support Web site for a list of the error codes for any particular PC using an Award BIOS system.

The BIOS startup screen

After the POST completes, assuming you have not been beeped to death, a screen is displayed that, except for the memory numbers running up, you have probably been ignoring. After first displaying information about the video adapter (which also signals the point at which the BIOS can now display its messages), the BIOS startup screen displays.

The BIOS startup screen is where you can find its information. On the exam, you may be asked where the identity and version of the BIOS can be found or what key is used to start the BIOS setup utility. Although this information is often different from PC to PC, it displays as a part of the BIOS startup screen. A common BIOS startup screen includes the following:

- **Identity:** The name of the BIOS manufacturer and the BIOS version number.
- **Setup key:** The key (or keys) to press to enter the BIOS's setup program — commonly Del or F2.
- **Energy Star Logo:** Usually in the upper-right corner, this logo displays if the BIOS supports the Energy Star ecology standard.
- **BIOS Serial Number:** If displayed (normally at the bottom of the screen), the serial number may help you identify a specific motherboard and customized BIOS version.

Configuration summary display

At the end of the POST process, the BIOS displays information about the PC's configuration. On some systems, the display is in the form of an ASCII graphics box drawn with asterisks around the confirmed contents of the CMOS, and on others, it's a series of text lines. Regardless, it provides important information to the repair technician who is just starting to troubleshoot a PC — the customer may not remember his PC's configuration, but the BIOS almost never forgets.

The information in this display is important because it verifies the hardware configuration of the PC. However, on many PCs this information is not displayed long enough for you to be able to read it carefully. It is always better to view the system configuration with the BIOS setup utility, discussed in the next section.

Storing the PC's Configuration

During the boot sequence, the BIOS and the operating system need to know the hardware configuration of the PC. This setup data is stored a couple different ways, depending on the age of the system. You need to be familiar with both methods, but really pay attention to storing the system configuration using the BIOS setup utility.

Setting the configuration through DIP switches

Older computers (like those ancient PCs before 286s) store their setup data through a series of DIP switches located on the motherboard, as illustrated in Figure 4-4. The combination of on and off switches is used to indicate the presence and type of memory, expansion cards, and device types installed on the PC. DIP switches are either the rocker type or the slide type.

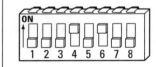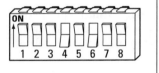

Figure 4-4:
A DIP
switch.

 Use a probe, ballpoint pen, or another sturdy tool to change the settings of a DIP switch. Never use a pencil! The pencil's graphite point could break off, leaving conductive material in the switch, possibly damaging it.

The early IBM computers used only 8 to 12 individual DIP switch positions to designate a variety of configuration settings, including the number of floppy drives, whether a system had a coprocessor, the type of monitor, and the amount of memory installed.

For example, to set the amount of memory installed to 256K or higher required that positions 3 and 4 of switch block 1 both be set to off. To set the number of floppy drives to 2 required positions 1 and 7 to be off, and position 8 to be on.

CMOS memory

Since the introduction of the 286 processor, PCs have stored their system configuration information on CMOS (complementary metal oxide semiconductor) memory chips. CMOS is one of the technologies used to manufacture integrated circuits (ICs). This material was chosen in the early days because of its special properties, which include low power requirements and long data retention. Today, although many ICs are made using the CMOS technology, including many processors, the name CMOS is synonymous with the storage of the PC's BIOS configuration data.

The CMOS used to hold the BIOS setup is a special memory type that's powered by a low-voltage battery. As long as the battery holds out, the CMOS retains its contents, which is usually years.

The battery used to power CMOS memory is usually a lithium battery that's about the shape of a medium-sized button. The battery is usually installed on the motherboard. Other types of batteries used are a 3.6-volt cylindrical lithium battery, an alkaline 4.5-volt battery, or a pair of common size AA batteries installed in a holder attached with Velcro to the side of the case.

Using the BIOS setup utility

Although the A+ exam lists CMOS and BIOS under separate objectives, these two areas come together under the BIOS setup utility. This utility, which is a part of the BIOS software, is used to access, view, and, if needed, modify the system configuration settings stored in CMOS. Because this is the part of the BIOS system that most people actually interact with, this routine is often called "the BIOS" or "the CMOS."

I recommend that you access the CMOS configuration settings on your computer as the fastest way to orient yourself to using the BIOS setup utility and the contents of CMOS. Although your particular PC may have a different display format, its CMOS contents and BIOS setup utility functions virtually the same in all cases.

Accessing the BIOS setup program

The BIOS setup program is opened only during the boot process by pressing the key designated for that purpose. The BIOS system displays the key used on the screen along with the system status information. The F1 or F2 function keys are commonly used, as is the Del (Delete) key. However, some older BIOS versions may use a variety of key combinations, including Esc, Ctrl+Esc, Alt+Esc, Ctrl+Alt+Esc, or others.

After the setup program starts, it may display a menu of options that can be used to view or edit the different types of settings saved in CMOS. Unless you have actually changed the hardware configuration of the PC, don't mess with the BIOS settings.

No two setup programs are exactly alike. Even two Pentium motherboards, manufactured by the same company and both with the same BIOS type and version, may not have the same BIOS settings.

BIOS CMOS settings

The settings managed by the BIOS setup utility are essentially those displayed during the boot sequence. However, newer PCs are storing additional settings and advanced and more complex settings as well. The settings in computers with CMOS setups (286 and later) have included, among others, the values shown in Table 4-5.

Table 4-5	CMOS Entries and Possible Settings
Entry	*Settings*
Parallel port	Unidirectional, bidirectional, ECP, EPP, enabled/disabled
Serial port	COM port assignment, I/O address, IRQ, enabled/disabled
Floppy drive	Boot sequence level, size, speed, density
Hard drive	Size and standard AT type number (used to indicate volume, cylinders, heads, capacity, and so on)
Processor	CPU type and speed
Memory	Size and type
Standard system	Date, time, passwords values

The startup password

Many PCs protect their CMOS settings behind a startup password, also called a power-on password. This password is required to boot the system and without it, the boot process halts. It also serves the purpose of protecting the BIOS CMOS settings from tampering.

You may find a question on how the startup password can be reset on the exam, but first you need to understand what it is. The startup password is stored in the CMOS and is managed by the BIOS setup program. This is all well and good until you forget the password, or some joker enters the CMOS setup and puts a password in without telling you. Luckily, the engineers who designed this feature were either brilliant or forgetful.

A three-pin jumper located near the CMOS battery on virtually all motherboards can be used to reset CMOS settings to their default values, including the password — and this is good. Another and quicker way to reset the CMOS is to remove the CMOS battery, if possible. You must bear in mind that any changes that have been made to the CMOS are also reset — and this is bad.

Using jumpers in setup

Beyond the configuration data held in the CMOS, additional information can be set using jumpers on the motherboard. A *jumper* is a set of two or three pins that are covered with a block to indicate different values. Jumpers are used to indicate the presence or absence of certain types of hardware or conditions.

Jumpers, like the one used to reset the CMOS, are used to set a variety of conditions and values on motherboards in addition to turning on or off toggle indicators like the CMOS jumper. In the past, jumpers have been used much like the BIOS CMOS is today. For example, the IBM AT motherboard included a jumper to set the video to color or monochrome.

Prep Test

1 Startup passwords can be disabled by

A ○ Formatting the hard drive

B ○ Running the Fdisk utility

C ○ Editing the autoexec.bat file

D ○ Jumping the CMOS jumper pins

2 POST refers to

A ○ Power-On Startup Test

B ○ Power-On Self Test

C ○ Pre-Operating System Test

D ○ Protected Online Startup Test

3 MMX stands for

A ○ Multimegahertz

B ○ Multimedia extensions

C ○ Maximum megahertz

D ○ Multisession extension

4 The primary functions of the ROM BIOS are

A ○ Gathering configuration information and initializing the computer when powered on

B ○ Storing configuration data for use by the CMOS

C ○ Providing software to communicate directly with hardware components when the OS is functioning

D ○ A and C

5 You open the case on a PC that has been making a strange sound and find that the cooling fan has fallen off the CPU. What is one possible reason this has happened?

A ○ The onboard connector for the cooling fan's cable was loose.

B ○ The thermal grease was never applied to the top of the processor.

C ○ The ZIF handle broke off of the CPU.

D ○ The CPU overheated and expanded.

6 Which computer component contains the circuitry necessary for all components or devices to communicate with each other?

A ○ Systemboard

B ○ Adapter board

C ○ Hard drive

D ○ Expansion bus

7 The main chip found on the motherboard that executes instructions is the
A ○ Math coprocessor
B ○ CMOS memory
C ○ Microprocessor

D ○ ROM chip

8 How can you remove an unwanted password or erase CMOS settings?
A ○ By using a DOS boot disk and typing **clear password** at the DOS prompt
B ○ By going into setup and choosing default settings
C ○ With the CMOS jumper on the systemboard

D ○ By removing any .PWL files found on the hard drive

9 Which of the following is used to keep a Pentium processor cool?
A ○ Liquid nitrogen
B ○ A fan
C ○ A heat sink
D ○ No special equipment is needed
E ○ B and C

F ○ A and B

10 CMOS refers to
A ○ Ceramic Metal Oxide Semiconductor
B ○ Complementary Metal Oxide Semiconductor
C ○ Continuous Metal Oxide Signal

D ○ Capacitive Memory for Operating Systems

11 What makes a systemboard different from a motherboard?
A ○ More RAM.
B ○ Built-in video and drive controllers.
C ○ Built-in sound and graphics systems.

D ○ No difference exists.

12 A POST diagnostics message code in the 300 range indicates an error in the
A ○ Hard disk controller
B ○ Mouse
C ○ Keyboard
D ○ Main memory

Answers

1 *D*. Moving the CMOS battery jumper block to its opposite position resets the CMOS values to their default settings. *See "The startup password."*

2 *B*. The Power-On Self Test validates that the hardware is ready and operating. *Review "Looking at the Boot Sequence."*

3 *B*. Fifty-seven new instructions are added to Pentium MMX processors to handle multimedia activities. *Look up "Putting it in overdrive."*

4 *D*. In addition to handling startup functions for the processor, BIOS is the basic input/output system. *See "Understanding the BIOS."*

5 *B*. Thermal grease acts somewhat like an adhesive as well as a heat transfer material. *Review "Keeping the processor cool (and applying some grease)."*

6 *A*. The bus structures are located on the motherboard/systemboard. Check out *"Riding the Bus."*

7 *C*. If you answered anything else, go back and read *"Looking at microprocessors."*

8 *C*. Yes, I did ask you this already, but I wanted to give you another version of what may appear on the exam. *See "The startup password."*

9 *E*. Sometimes both a fan and a heat sink are used. *See "Keeping the processor cool (and applying some grease)."*

10 *B*. Review *"CMOS memory."*

11 *B*. Most newer boards should technically be called systemboards for this reason. *Visit "Understanding the Motherboard."*

12 *C*. This error includes stuck or bad keys, as well as a bad connection. *Review "Decoding POST messages."*

Chapter 5
Memory Systems

Exam Objectives

▶ Identifying the terminology, location, and physical characteristics of memory

▶ Differentiating between types of logical memory

*A*bout 10 percent of the A+ core exam deals with questions on memory and memory management. The actual percentage may be closer to 3 percent, because the exam domain that includes memory also covers motherboards and processors.

It's difficult to say how much of the remaining 90 percent of the test touches on memory, IC packages, and subjects like parity, error checking, and other topics I include in this chapter along with memory systems.

The DOS/Windows Specialty Exam is a little more explicit in that 10 percent of that exam is directly on memory management in the DOS and Windows environments. Most of this chapter applies to this area indirectly, but I present the more specific material in Chapter 21.

After the CPU, memory may be the next most important component on the PC. Every PC repair professional should have a good understanding of memory systems, how they work, how they are configured, how to avoid some problems, and how to track down those problems that spring up.

You should at least review this chapter to make sure that you're familiar with the concepts and terminology of a rapidly changing technology — especially if you're one of the old duffers who, like me, are still clinging to their XT waiting for the overdrive chip to come out.

Quick Assessment

1 On older PCs, the _____ package form was installed in sockets directly on the motherboard.

2 The most common type of DRAM used is the _____ technology.

3 _____, much faster and more expensive than DRAM, is used for memory caching.

4 Nonvolatile memory used to permanently store instructions is _____.

5 Individual DRAM chips soldered to a small circuit board are called a _____.

6 _____ involves the use of an additional bit for each 8 bits of data.

7 _____ can detect and correct 1-bit errors in data.

8 _____ is the combination of physical memory and hard disk space, which gives the appearance of more memory than is actually available.

9 The first 640K of system memory is called _____.

10 The upper 384K of the first megabyte of memory is _____.

11 All memory above 1MB is called _____.

Answers

1 *DIP*. See "DRAM packages."

2 *EDO*. Review "DRAM technologies."

3 *SRAM*. See "Static RAM (SRAM)."

4 *ROM*. Look at "Read-Only Memory (ROM)."

5 *SIMM*. Review "Using Modern Memories."

6 *Parity*. Review "Understanding parity."

7 *ECC or Error Correction Code*. See "Looking at Error Correction Code (ECC)."

8 *Virtual memory*. Review "Real Versus Virtual Memory."

9 *conventional memory*. See "Logical memory layout."

10 *expanded or upper memory area*. Look at "Upper memory area."

11 *extended memory*. Review "Extended memory."

Refreshing Your Memory: Memory Basics

You can look at memory in two ways:

- ✔ As the physical chips that plug into the motherboard
- ✔ As the scratch pad space that holds the data and instructions in use

For purposes of the A+ exams, you need to know something about both, including the names and purposes of memory components, some of the memory configuration issues, and just a little on troubleshooting processes.

As a subject, memory systems are complex and offer a depth of material — the kind of stuff engineers get misty-eyed over. For such a physically small thing, memory is a large subject. But not here! I give no lengthy diatribes on why parity memory is better or the like. I give you just the facts along with a small amount of background information to help you understand the exam's questions — a trick in itself sometimes.

Two basic types of memory are in the PC:

- ✔ **RAM (random access memory):** Holds the instructions and data in use by the operating system and software applications before and after they pass to the CPU. RAM is volatile; to hold its contents, it must have a steady power source. Should the power stream be broken, anything stored in RAM is erased. No power — no data; pretty straightforward.
- ✔ **ROM (read-only memory):** Is nonvolatile and retains its contents through even the darkest power outage.

RAM is by far the faster of the two types of memory. In fact, RAM is often used to shadow the BIOS ROM to improve its performance during the boot process.

You will be asked what copying the contents of the BIOS ROM into RAM for faster access to the instructions by the CPU is called. The answer is *shadowing*.

Random Access Memory (RAM)

RAM is the primary memory of the PC and is generally installed directly on the motherboard in a variety of package types, which I deal with later. Many types of RAM exist, but the most common are DRAM (dynamic RAM) and SRAM (static RAM).

You need a solid understanding of RAM, its packaging forms, and its technologies for the exam. Many questions assume you know what the types of RAM are, where they are installed, and their characteristics. For example, you may be asked which is the fastest of the RAM types (SRAM), or how SIMM memories are installed (in vertical sockets on the motherboard).

Dynamic RAM (DRAM)

DRAM is the RAM everyone talks about. It's the most commonly used type of memory. It's not a complex circuit compared to some and, as a result, is not expensive. However, its design also requires that it be refreshed regularly or it loses its contents. This need for constant refreshing gives DRAM its dynamic tag.

DRAM must be refreshed every two milliseconds. A special refresh logic circuit reads and then rewrites the contents of each DRAM address, whether it's in use or not.

DRAM is also the slowest of the memories, clocking in with access speeds around 50 nanoseconds (ns) or higher (remember that higher here means slower). Older DRAM had an access speed of around 120 ns.

DRAM packages

DRAM chips come in three package forms: DIP (Dual In-line Package), SOJ (Small Outline J-lead), and TSOP (Thin, Small Outline Package). It is likely that you will only see the DIP package form mentioned on the A+ exams, along with other newer packaging forms (see "Using Modern Memories"). Here is a definition for each type of DRAM packaging:

- ✔ DIP DRAM is used to install memory directly on a motherboard. The DIP form is a through-hole electronic component, which means it installs through the holes of a socket directly into a circuit board's surface.
- ✔ SOJ and TSOP DRAM gained popularity with the development of the SIMM (single inline memory module). These components mount directly on a circuit board's surface. These packaging forms make it possible to build memory modules, SIMMs and DIMMs (dual inline memory modules), that contain many separate DRAM chips.

DRAM technologies

DRAM comes in three popular technologies: Fast page mode (FPM), extended data out (EDO), and burst EDO. Recent addtions are synchronous DRAM (SDRAM) and video RAM (VRAM). Which technology can be used on a particular system is controlled by its processor and motherboard (see Chapter 4). The following lists the characteristics of each of the DRAM technologies:

- ✔ Extended Data Out (EDO) is the most common type DRAM, although it is only slightly faster than FPM memory. It's common in most Pentium and later PCs, except those with memory buses over 75MHz.

- ✔ Fast Page Mode (FPM) DRAM is occasionally called non-EDO RAM. It's generally compatible with all systemboards except those with memory buses with speeds over 66MHz.

- ✔ Burst Extended Data Out (BEDO) DRAM is EDO memory with pipelining technology added for faster access times. BEDO allows much higher bus speeds than EDO. But, this standard has little chipset support.

- ✔ Synchronous DRAM (SDRAM), like its SRAM cousins (see the next section), is tied to the system clock and reads or writes memory in burst mode. SDRAM could very well be the next PC memory standard because it works at higher bus speeds and asynchronous DRAM (EDO, FPM, and so on) doesn't.

- ✔ Video RAM (VRAM) is a specialized DRAM physically separated from main memory. VRAM applies dual porting, which allows the processor and the video card's refresh circuitry to access the memory at the same time. Another video RAM is Windows RAM (WRAM), also called Windows Accelerator RAM, which has essentially the same properties as VRAM.

You will definitely see the DRAM technologies on the A+ exams. Familiarize yourself with the general descriptions provided here, which should be enough for FPM, EDO, burst EDO, and SDRAM. Video RAM is covered in more detail in Chapter 10.

Some but not all systems allow you to install EDO memory in one bank and FPM memory in another. Even those that do will downgrade memory speeds to the slower FPM memory. Always check the motherboard's manual before upgrading its memory.

Static RAM (SRAM)

SRAM is static, which means it holds its charge and doesn't need to be refreshed. As long as it has a power stream, it holds its charge. SRAM also has very fast access times, in the range of 15 to 20 ns (comparing to the 50 ns to 120 ns of DRAM). Its only problems are that it's physically two pins longer in size than DRAM and because it's a more complex technology, it costs a lot more.

SRAM is packaged as either a single DIP chip or as a COAST (Cache On A Stick) module in a variety of increments. The type of SRAM and the amount a motherboard will support, like everything else, depends on the motherboard.

SRAM is available as either synchronous or asynchronous. Synchronous SRAM uses the system clock to coordinate its signals with the CPU, and asynchronous doesn't. Because of its high cost and bigger size, SRAM is used primarily for memory cache.

Memory caching: DRAM and SRAM working together

Memory caching allows the CPU to work more efficiently. Cache memory is used to store data and instructions that the motherboard fetches in anticipation of what the CPU will want next. When it is correct, which is about 90 percent of the time, the CPU is able to get what it needs from the much faster SRAM. The following steps describe how memory caching works in detail:

1. A cache controller anticipates the data or program module that the CPU is likely to request next.

2. The data or program code is copied from DRAM and stored in SRAM.

3. If the cache controller guesses right, which is about 90 percent of the time, the CPU's next request is satisfied from SRAM at a much faster rate than possible from DRAM.

Prior to the 486, cache controllers were on a discrete chip. On the 486 and later, cache controllers are a part of the CPU along with a small amount of SRAM.

The SRAM that is included along with the cache controller is internal, or level 1 (L1), cache. Many newer systems now include additional SRAM, which is called external, or level 2 (L2), cache. It is common for a system to have 256K of internal cache and another 256K of level 2 cache. Cache is also discussed in Chapter 4.

DRAM versus SRAM

Okay, in case you're trying to keep score.

Table 5-1 summarizes what you need to know about the characteristics of DRAM and SRAM for the A+ Core exam.

Table 5-1	DRAM versus SRAM
DRAM	*SRAM*
Slow and must be constantly refreshed	Fast and doesn't require refreshing
Simple	Complex
Inexpensive	Expensive
Physically small	Physically large

Is there a winner? No, I think we have a tie.

In spite of its constant thirst, DRAM works better for PC main memory because it's cheaper and needs less space. SRAM costs too much and takes way too much space to use it for main memory. However, SRAM is perfect for cache memory because of its speed and physical size.

PCMCIA memory

Notebook and palmtop computers can have flash memory added through a PCMCIA (Personal Computer Memory Card Interface Adapter) slot. A PCMCIA card, which is also called a PC Card, looks a little like a credit card, as shown in Figure 5-1, and slips into a slot usually located on the side of the notebook's base. One feature of PCMCIA cards is *hot swapping,* which allows you to remove and replace the card while the system is running. Chapter 18 covers portable systems and PC Cards in more detail.

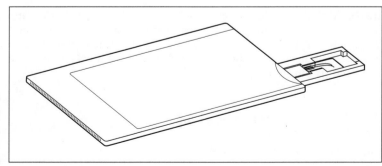

Figure 5-1:
PCMCIA
card.

You need to know the three types of PCMCIA (PC Cards) in use for portable PCs. Refer to Chapter 18 for further information, but briefly the three standard types of PCMCIA cards are

- ✔ **Type I:** Up to 3.3 mm thick and used primarily for adding RAM to a portable computer
- ✔ **Type II:** Up to 5.5 mm thick and commonly used for modem cards
- ✔ **Type III:** Up to 10.5 mm thick and used to install portable disk drives

Read-Only Memory (ROM)

The problem with ROM on the A+ test is that it can pop up in many places on the tests. However, for purposes of the A+ exam, ROM is ROM. What I mean is that while many different applications exist for ROM, most people equate ROM to BIOS ROM. You should expect to see at least one or two questions directly about ROM and its characteristics on the Core exam.

Officially, ROM is the nonvolatile memory used to permanently store instructions and data that can't be altered in normal operations.

While virtually all ROM chips are packaged in a DIP (dual inline packaging) form, there are three types of ROM in use. You should know the ROM types and the process used to update each type, if it can be updated. The following describes each type of ROM chip (remember that as the ROM type gets newer and gains capability, it also gains more letters in its name):

- ✔ **PROM** (Programmable Read-Only Memory): Stores data or instructions as firmware and can't be reprogrammed.

- ✔ **EPROM** (Erasable Programmable Read-Only Memory): Can be erased by exposure to ultraviolet light through a little window on the chip's top and can be reprogrammed with a chip burner; the BIOS ROM on most older computers is likely an EPROM.

- ✔ **EEPROM** (Electrically Erasable Programmable Read-Only Memory): Can be flash programmed with software and is now commonly used for BIOS ROM; also called flash ROM.

To upgrade the BIOS on any computer with an EPROM BIOS, you must remove the BIOS EPROM and replace it with the upgraded EPROM. I seem to remember a test question on chip creep. Nearly all DIP chips, including ROM chips, suffer from a condition called *chip creep*. DIP chips inserted into through-hole sockets can and will squirm out of the socket in time. This movement can cause reliability, boot, and parity problems. You should occasionally check older motherboards that have DIP-style memory and ROM chips for creep.

The first code that the CPU has access to is on the ROM.

Using Modern Memories

In the next few sections, I cover the memory packages on most new computers. The only questions from this area that you will encounter on the exam deal mostly with definitions and generic memory configurations and problems. If most of your experience is with older systems, you may really want to review this section, if for no other reason than the terminology.

I think the A+ exam recognizes that you are not an electrical engineer and focuses more on what the acroynms mean and the number of connector pins than any other features. However, I suggest you also look over Chapter 4.

SIMMs

In most newer PCs, about the only place you find a DIP memory is soldered on a memory module. A Single Inline Memory Module (SIMM) is made up of surface-mounted SOJ and TSOP DRAM memory soldered on a small circuit board that has either a 30-pin or 72-pin connector. SIMM's capacities range from 1 to 16MB in either a one-sided or two-sided style, with chips soldered to one or two sides of the board. SIMMs are currently the most common memory type in use.

As illustrated in Figure 5-2, SIMMs are installed on the motherboard in special sockets designed with clips and clamps to eliminate chip creep (discussed in the previous section), as well as to maximize the amount of memory installed in a minimal space.

SIMMs must be installed in pairs. Each bank of memory for a SIMM has two sockets. You must fill the bank before moving on to another bank.

DIMMs

The Dual Inline Memory Module (DIMM) is emerging as the new standard for larger PCs. A DIMM has 168 discrete contact pins as opposed to the 30 and 72 pins of the SIMM.

DIMMs come in different voltages: 3.3V and 5.0V, and as buffered or unbuffered, which yields four possible combinations. The current de facto standard is the 3.3V unbuffered DIMM that is used by most computers. A smaller version of the DIMM is Small Outline DIMM (SODIMM). The SODIMM is a smaller package module used primarily in laptop computers.

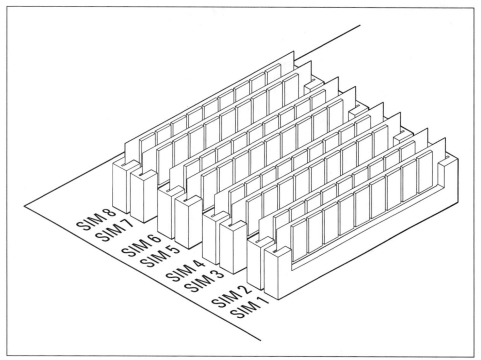

Figure 5-2:
SIMM
installed in
SIMM
sockets.

Putting gold in a tin cup

Two different metals are used for both the pins on SIMMs and DIMMs and the sockets on the motherboards: gold and tin. Older motherboards have gold SIMM sockets, and newer boards have tin sockets. Gold is, of course, gold; and tin is a silvery color (not gold anyway). "So what?" you ask. Read on.

It's important that *only* memory modules with gold contacts are installed in gold sockets, and *only* modules with tin contacts are placed in tin sockets. Mixing the two

metals, gold and tin, creates a chemical reaction over time (months, even years), and tin oxide can build up on the gold and create an unreliable electrical connection. Here is the most commonly found mineral content for each memory module:

- ✔ **30-pin SIMM:** Gold
- ✔ **72-pin SIMM:** Tin
- ✔ **168-pin DIMM:** Gold

Ensuring Memory Integrity

In addtion to all that you should know about memory for the A+ exams, one very important aspect of memory that is included in several domains is memory data integrity. It's one thing to store data in memory and quite another to be sure that what's there is still valid, especially if it hasn't been accessed in eons, or one or two hundred milliseconds, whichever comes first. As leaky as DRAM is, a mechanism has to exist to verify the integrity of the data.

Lucky for us, a mechanism does exist. In fact, two methods are used to ensure the integrity of data stored in memory: parity and Error Correction Code (ECC).

First, however, you need to know a little about the memory controller. The memory controller oversees the movement of data into and out of memory and, in doing so, determines the type of data integrity checking used. In both parity and ECC, the memory controller is key to the process. The memory controller generates the signals used to control the reading and writing of data from and to memory.

Understanding parity

Parity has been around for a very long time, or as long as the PC anyway. DRAM memory that implements parity checking has an additional bit for every 8 bits of data. This extra bit allows the system to verify the data format using two parity protocols — odd parity and even parity — that work very much the same. In a nutshell, if the system is using even parity, the extra bit is used as necessary to make the total number of positive (ones) bits an even number. In an odd parity world, the extra bit is used to create odd number totals. "Parity" is achieved when the total number of one bits in a byte add up to either an even or odd number, depending on the parity techique in use.

When a character fails to have the appropriate number of bits, it causes a parity error. A parity error can be the first signal of a host of problems, ranging from one-time anomalies to faulty memory. Faulty memory can be the cause of repeated memory parity errors.

The limitation with the parity method for data integrity is that it can only detect an error. It has no mechanism to do anything about it. It doesn't know which of the bits are wrong and which are correct. When it detects a parity error, it only knows the count is wrong.

Some chips on the market use *fake parity*. Fake parity simply makes every bit count even or odd, depending on the method being used. In effect, this method is the same as no parity checking at all.

Nonparity memory

Because parity and ECC memory are more expensive than nonparity memory, nonparity memory is much more common. Nonparity systems don't perform data integrity checks. Fortunately, parity and ECC memory are dropping in price and becoming more common on systems. You can't use nonparity memory in a parity system. Doing so generates a parity error as soon as the system boots up. You can turn off parity checking on some systems in the BIOS setup. Parity memory works fine in a nonparity system — the extra bit is ignored.

Parity memory chips contain an extra bit used to check the integrity of the data stored in each byte and nonparity memory does not.

Looking at Error Correction Code

You could see this type of data integrity checking on the Core exam, so be familiar with its meaning and function. Error Correction Code (ECC) is a data integrity method that is used in high-end PCs and file servers. The difference between ECC and the parity method is that ECC can both detect *and* correct errors. The good news is that ECC can detect up to a 4-bit memory error. The not-so-bad news is that it can only correct 1-bit errors. This problem isn't that big of a deal because a 4-bit error (that's not the same as a 50-cent error) is very rare, and 1-bit errors are much more common. Like the parity method does with all errors, when ECC sees a multiple-bit error, it reports it as a parity error. Believe me, if your memory has a 4-bit error, you want to know about it.

Timing memory access

Memory access time is the time it takes for memory to make data available. This time is measured in nanoseconds (ns). Most of the memory around today has access times that range from 5 to 70 nanoseconds, with the higher number being the slower. This memory access speed is used as a rating of sorts for DRAM.

Of course, everyone prefers to have the fastest memory available, but that is not always possible. The speed of the existing memory may limit the ability for a PC to add faster memory. You should avoid mixing memory speeds in the same computer, but if you must, follow these precautions:

  ✔ **Use identical memory in a bank:** You should only use the same type, speed, and technology of memory within a memory bank (a pair or group of memory module sockets). For example, never mix EDO and FPM memory within a bank of memory.

✔ **Put the slowest memory in the first bank:** Some systems use autodetection to determine the speed of the memory installed on the system. If 60 ns memory is installed in bank 0 and 70 ns in bank 1, the system sets the former as the timing rate, causing problems for the 70 ns memory. Install the 70 ns memory in the first bank.

Real versus Virtual Memory

Physical memory, also called real memory, refers to the actual memory chips installed in the computer and used to store the programs and data actually in use by the computer. Larger programs or multitasking support can create a demand for memory that exceeds the amount of real memory available. On these occasions, it would be nice if the processor could borrow some additional memory for a while. To allow this borrowing, you can create some virtual memory. Virtual memory works much like a memory credit card in that it uses memory that doesn't really exist. It goes like this:

1. In a computer with 64MB of physical memory, the memory demand exists for 100MB of RAM.

2. The operating system creates a virtual memory space on the hard disk and assigns a virtual memory manager, which immediately opens a 36MB swap space (100 – 64) to handle the current excess demand.

3. The operating system smugly proceeds as if it now has 100MB of RAM, leaving the virtual memory manager to handle the swapping of inactive blocks in and out of RAM and the virtual memory swap space.

Virtual memory is the combination of installed physical memory and hard drive space that gives the appearance of more memory than is actually installed on the system.

Virtual memory is the basis for multitasking in Windows 95. Without virtual memory, you would not be able to run most of the software in use today. Windows 3.*x* and Windows 95 both implement virtual memory in files called swap files. Chapter 21 has additional information on this feature.

Real mode versus protected mode

Before I dive into PC logical memory layout, I should review real-mode and protected-mode memory addressing. These two terms come up frequently in discussions of the memory space located above the conventional memory area (see "Logical Memory Layout"). In addition, and probably of more importance, these terms are on the A+ exams.

Installing a RAM drive

Although it seems somewhat contradictory, creating a RAM drive assigns a part of memory to serve and act like a hard disk drive. The advantage gained from a RAM drive is the speed of loading whatever is stored in it. RAM drives are used to store programs that are loaded to memory frequently and to reduce the load time of copying programs to RAM. However, with the increased file sizes of today's software, RAM drives are rarely practical.

To create a RAM drive, the RAMDRIVE.SYS device driver is loaded to memory as a terminate-and-stay-resident (TSR) program and allocates a certain amount of RAM. Assign the drive a device designator (perhaps D: or E:) and use it just like a hard disk. The following code statement added to the CONFIG.SYS file creates a RAM drive of 1MB:

```
DEVICE=C:\DOS\RAMDRIVE.SYS 1024
```

This statement causes the operating system to create a 1024K drive and assign it the next available device designator.

Among other more esoteric things, *real-mode* memory addressing means that software, such as DOS or DOS applications, can address only 1MB of RAM.

The counterpart to real-mode is *protected-mode* memory addressing. In this mode, a program is limited to its own memory space allocations, but it can access memory above 1MB. It gets its name from the fact that programs in this mode are protected from other programs desiring its memory.

Just about every operating system other than DOS runs in protected mode, which can lead to some trouble. For example, if you boot your Windows system in MS-DOS mode, DOS can't access your protected-mode drivers. You need real-mode drivers for any of the peripherals you take for granted under Windows: CD-ROM, sound card, and so on. Loading these drivers to real mode may also run you out of memory quickly.

Logical Memory Layout

How memory is divided into its logical types may be the most important thing you should know about memory, beyond the terms DRAM and ROM. The logical memory divisions of RAM are the subjects of direct and specific questions as well as referenced in questions in other domains. Spend the time to memorize the information included in this section.

Memory on the PC is broken into four basic divisions, as illustrated in Figure 5-3 and discussed in Table 5-2:

Table 5-2	Memory Layout
Memory	*Description*
Conventional memory	The first 640K of system memory. Used by standard DOS programs, device drivers, TSRs, and anything that runs on standard DOS.
Upper memory area	The upper 384K of the first megabyte of memory, located right above conventional memory. Reserved for system devices and special uses such as BIOS ROM shadowing. Also called expanded memory or reserved memory.
High memory area	The first 64K (less 16 bytes) of the second megabyte of memory. Although it's the first 64K of extended memory, it can be accessed in real mode. Used by DOS to preserve conventional memory.
Extended memory	Technically, this is all memory above 1MB, but in actuality it is any memory above the high memory area. Used for programs and data in protected mode, such as under Windows.

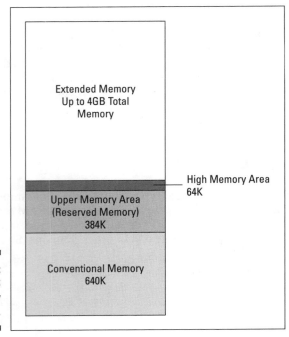

Figure 5-3:
MS-DOS
memory
layout.

Conventional memory

Conventional memory is the first 640K of system memory (refer to Figure 5-3). This fixed size is the result of two early developments:

✔ Early processors could not address more than 1MB of total RAM.

✔ IBM's decision to allocate the upper 384K of memory to BIOS and utilities, leaving 640K for the user and operating system.

✔ Conventional memory is used to run the operating system files, application programs, memory-resident routines, and device drivers.

Upper memory area

This is the upper 384K of the first megabyte of system memory. This area is typically allocated to special purposes such as the BIOS ROM, adapter ROMs, and video RAM.

It wasn't long before those developers who had grown tired of the 640K limitation began lusting after this space. So, it was redesignated as expanded memory, and special drivers were created to allow its use. The primary device driver used for this purpose is EMM386.EXE. This program frees up conventional memory by allowing unused portions of the reserved memory area to be used for DOS drivers and memory-resident programs.

The best way to implement EMM386 is by adding the following lines to the CONFIG.SYS file in the DOS root directory:

```
DEVICE=C:\DOS\EMM386.EXE
DOS=UMB
```

where UMB stands for upper memory blocks.

If you don't want to run EMS emulation, but you do want the ability to load drivers and TSRs to upper memory, the NOEMS option is added:

```
DEVICE=C:\DOS\EMM386.EXE NOEMS
DOS=UMB
```

Be sure you know and understand both of the previous examples of EMM386.SYS implementations for the tests.

High memory area

The high memory area (HMA) is the first 64K of the extended memory area. It's also the only part of extended memory that a program in real mode can access. This space is normally used by DOS after the following specification is included in the CONFIG.SYS file (know this and what it does):

```
DOS=HIGH
```

This statement tells DOS to load most of its code to HMA instead of in conventional memory, freeing about 45K of conventional memory space for other programs.

Don't confuse high memory area with upper memory area. You will definitely see questions on the test that refer to both.

Extended memory

This one is pretty simple to understand: Extended memory is all the memory above the first megabyte. Every computer has an upper limit for extended memory that ranges from 16MB on the 286 to 4GB on a Pentium. It also can't be accessed, beyond its first 64K, in real mode.

Some people confuse extended memory with expanded memory. Expanded memory expands base memory to its full 1MB. Extended memory extends memory on up to the clouds.

Accessing higher memory areas

Many good things were included in the 80286 processor. One in particular was the capability for programs to address more than 1MB of RAM. In fact, they could address as much as 16MB of RAM, which caused great joy at the time. That is, until it was remembered that DOS could still not address more than 1MB.

To get around this problem, software was developed to extend DOS so that it could run in protected mode and work above the 1MB bar. Naturally, these programs are called DOS extenders, and the most commonly used one is HIMEM.SYS. With HIMEM.SYS running, DOS is magically extended to see extended memory.

To add expanded memory emulation, move some of the drivers and TSRs to upper memory, move DOS into the high memory area, open up the extended memory frontier, and include the following code in the CONFIG.SYS file:

```
DEVICE=HIMEM.SYS
DEVICE=EMM386.EXE
DOS=HIGH,UMB
```

You should definitely know and understand the statements used to activate HIMEM.SYS and EMM386.EXE.

All versions of Windows 3.*x* need HIMEM.SYS running to access extended memory. You could see a question about what must be running for Windows 3.*x* to load. The answer is HIMEM.SYS.

Optimizing memory

You can optimize memory with either hardware or software. This section looks at some of the more common methods used to optimize memory with software. For the A+ exams, you should know the effect of including each of the commands included in this section.

The DOS configuration files CONFIG.SYS and AUTOEXEC.BAT have value even in the Windows environments, and a quick look at some of the other entries you can include for optimizing memory may help you on the exams.

The `LOADHIGH` and `DEVICEHIGH` commands also put upper memory blocks (UMB) to use. The `LOADHIGH` and `LH` commands are used on the DOS command line or in the AUTOEXEC.BAT file to start a program and direct the operating system to place it into the upper memory area. For example:

```
C:\> LOADHIGH C:\PxP\PxP.EXE
```

loads the driver PxP into the upper memory area. This statement works only if HIMEM.SYS and EMM386.EXE device commands have been included in the CONFIG.SYS file.

`DEVICEHIGH` is used in the CONFIG.SYS file to assign a device driver to UMB, commonly done with the mouse driver, as shown in this example:

```
DEVICE=HIMEM.SYS
DEVICE=EMM386.EXE
DOS=HIGH,UMB
DEVICEHIGH=C:\MOUSE\MOUSE.SYS
```

The above CONFIG.SYS command statements are an accumulation of the commands discussed in this section. Be sure you review the reason for and the syntax of each command for both A+ exams.

Checking memory space with MEM

You can't just assign all drivers to UMB (upper memory blocks) because you may not have enough space. The DOS command MEM reports the status and usage of all memory, including how UMB has been assigned.

Typically, you run MEM with its /C option. This option produces a classified (which is what the "C" stands for) report that lets you know how memory is being utilized. Use the MEM report before assigning too many programs to upper memory.

Use the DOS command MEM /C /P to display the conventional memory allocation at a given instance. You may see the "/C" switch listed as "/CLASSIFY" on the A+ exams.

Using MemMaker

MemMaker, available in MS-DOS 6.0 or later, manages UMB and extended memory. It scans the CONFIG.SYS and AUTOEXEC.BAT files and automatically edits or inserts the commands discussed previously as needed. It also decides whether device drivers should be placed high or left in conventional memory and makes the necessary adjustments.

MemMaker is a memory management utility available in DOS 6.0 and later that is used to automatically optimize memory usage.

Managing memory in Windows 3.x

The memory management techniques used in the Windows environment are not much different between Windows 3.x and Windows 95, but you should know a few things.

In its 386 enhanced mode, Windows 3.x needs HIMEM.SYS to execute from the CONFIG.SYS file before it can load. Enhanced mode also creates a virtual memory environment using swap files. Windows 3.x uses either a temporary (WIN386.SWP) or a permanent swap space file (386SPART.PAR). It's usually better to use the permanent swap space option, because temporary files can become fragmented over time.

You can change the size and nature of the virtual memory swap file, which affects the performance of your system. If you have 8MB of RAM or less, you should use a fairly large swap space. On systems with larger RAM sizes, you should decrease the swap space proportionally to their RAM size to encourage Windows to use the RAM and not the swap space.

Windows 3.*x* uses three core files to manage memory and other system resources:

- **KRNL386.EXE:** The kernel file handles memory management as well as loading and executing Windows applications. Depending on the system, KRNL286.EXE could be used instead.
- **GDI.EXE:** The Graphics Device Interface (GDI) handles graphic display and printing tasks.
- **USER.EXE:** The user interface handles user input, communication ports, and the display and interaction of icons, windows, and dialog boxes.

Windows 3.*x* arranges portions of its memory in heaps that are allocated to GDI.EXE and USER.EXE to use for recording and tracking every icon, mouse click, window resizing, and other user interface actions. The total of the heaps allocated to these two functions, along with those allocated to the system and text functions, creates the Windows systems resources.

Commonly, an "out of memory" error can occur when the heaps for the system and GDI.EXE fill up. Even a system with 128MB of RAM can have "insufficient memory" errors. In Windows 3.*x*, you can view the amount of system resources available in the Windows Help➪About Program Manager option.

Managing memory in Windows 95

You can expect to see quite a few questions from both exams on Windows 95 memory mangement. Windows 95 manages memory much differently than DOS and Windows 3.*x*. The primary differences are in how Windows 95 implements memory heaps, virtual memory, and device drivers. Chapter 21 includes coverage on Windows 95 memory management. Be sure you review it carefully.

Windows 95 has effectively eliminated the need for DEVICE entries in the CONFIG.SYS file with the advent of a group of 32-bit protected-mode device drivers. Windows 95 automatically loads these drivers into extended memory when it loads. These new 32-bit drivers are called virtual device drivers (VxD drivers) and have .VXD or .386 file extensions.

Managing memory in Windows NT

Just for your information. If you compare memory management under the various operating systems, DOS is a trailer park driveway with speed bumps; Windows 3.1 is a two-lane state highway with stop signs; Windows 95 is a four-lane expressway with tollbooths; and Windows NT is the autobahn, free of all obstructions. Under Windows NT, memory is one large wholly address-able resource that allows programs and drivers to address any part of its memory.

Windows NT memory management allocates memory from all available sources to satisfy an application's demand for memory. The allocated space may come from RAM, virtual memory, or both. The application can't stipu-late which memory it wants, only that it wants memory. Applications interface with the Virtual Memory Manager, which controls the real and virtual memory resources.

Prep Test

1 Protected mode memory addressing was introduced with which processor?

A ○ 8086
B ○ 80286
C ○ 80386
D ○ 80486

2 Frequent general protection faults could be caused by

A ○ Poor quality memory chips
B ○ An incorrectly connected hard drive cable
C ○ Not enough RAM
D ○ All the above

3 You have installed four 4MB SIMMs on your PC, but when you boot the system, only 12MB are counted up. How can you determine what may have happened to the other 4MB?

A ○ Run BIOS Setup and check the CMOS memory settings
B ○ Use MEM to view the contents of the memory banks
C ○ Replace the SIMMs in pairs to determine which is failing
D ○ B and C

4 Parity memory validates the integrity of the data stored in RAM by

A ○ Checking the header of each packet of data received
B ○ Checking every eighth bit for errors
C ○ Checking the RAM table in BIOS
D ○ Counting the number of even or odd bits set to 1 in the data

5 BIOS programs are most often loaded to which area of memory?

A ○ Conventional memory
B ○ Upper memory
C ○ Extended memory
D ○ Virtual memory

6 Windows organizes memory into

A ○ Conventional, Upper, Extended
B ○ Used and Free
C ○ Heaps
D ○ Blocks

7 Which Windows environments are not bound by the memory limitations of MS-DOS?

A ○ Windows 3.*x*

B ○ Windows 95

C ○ Windows NT

D ○ B and C

8 All memory above 1MB is called

A ○ Extended memory

B ○ Expanded memory

C ○ Upper memory

D ○ Base memory

9 What is the first 640K of memory called?

A ○ Upper memory

B ○ Extended memory

C ○ Conventional memory

D ○ Expanded memory

10 Windows 3.*x* and Windows 95 store virtual memory in a

A ○ Swap file

B ○ EMM386.EXE file

C ○ CONFIG.SYS file

D ○ HIMEM.SYS file

Answers

1 *B.* The 80286 processor is able to address up to 16MB of RAM. *See "Accessing higher memory areas."*

2 *A.* Faulty memory can cause repeated memory parity errors. *Review "Understanding parity."*

3 *C.* SIMM assemblies must be installed in pairs, so the troubleshooting procedure is to remove a pair of SIMMs and replace them together or to swap banks and individual SIMM assemblies to eventually isolate the bad assembly. *See "SIMMs."*

4 *D.* Parity checking involves using an additional bit with each 8 bits to set the total number of ones bits to either an even or odd number depending on the protocol in use. *See "Understanding parity."*

5 *B.* The upper memory area is used to hold BIOS programs and memory-resident drivers. *See "Upper memory area."*

6 *C.* Windows organizes memory into heaps that are allocated to support system, user, graphics, and text activities. *See "Managing memory in Windows 3.x."*

7 *C.* Windows NT addresses all memory as one resource without the logical divisions used in DOS and Windows 3.*x* and 95. *Review "Managing memory in Windows NT."*

8 *A.* Memory above 1MB is called extended memory. *See "Extended memory."*

9 *C.* The first 640K of memory is conventional memory. *See "Conventional memory."*

10 *A.* Windows stores its virtual memory disk areas in a file called a swap file. *See "Real Versus Virtual Memory."*

Chapter 6

Storage Systems

● ●

Exam Objectives

▶ Identifying basic terms, concepts, and functions of storage systems

▶ Adding and removing storage devices

▶ Optimizing disk drive performance and space

▶ Managing data storage

● ●

Several different ways exist to store data with a PC. Some are familiar to everyone and some are not so well known. One of the problems with an industrywide certification exam is that it expects you to know about all the various devices you may find in a customer's computer. I've attempted to cram as much as possible into this chapter for you, focusing on the storage devices you should encounter on the A+ exam.

Remember that the exams will not necessarily test you on the newest, latest, or greatest technologies on the market at the time you take the test. I don't envy the task of writing a test on current computer technology. So, don't spend your time reading the latest PC magazines to bone up on storage devices. Your time will be spent wisely if you expand your knowledge of the storage devices and related topics included in this chapter. You should review

✔ **Floppy disks:** Once the data center of the computer, and like all past champions that just won't retire, they no longer receive the respect they're due.

✔ **Hard disks:** Including each of the drive, storage, and interface technologies in use along with their installation and configuration.

✔ **Hard disk and storage management techniques:** Including partitioning, backups, compression, and other related processes.

✔ **CD-ROMs and other storage devices**

My assumptions are that you understand how bits are organized into bytes and that bytes are used to store both text and numeric data. You also know that data stored in memory are temporary, and if you want to store data permanently, you use a form of permanent storage media, such as tape or disk. These are the assumptions of the A+ exams, too. If you know this much, you're off to a good start.

Quick Assessment

Identifying basic terms, concepts, and functions of storage systems

1 Tape storage is a _____ access media.

2 A hard disk cluster is a collection of _____.

3 _____ and _____ are the two primary data encoding schemes used to translate data into flux transitions on disk media.

Adding and removing storage devices

4 A(n) _____ should never be low-level formatted.

5 You can connect _____ hard drives to a single ATA IDE cable.

6 You must install _____ at the beginning and end of the SCSI chain.

7 RAID level _____ provides for disk striping without parity.

Optimizing disk drive performance and space

8 The two primary utilities used for maintaining and optimizing hard drives in DOS and Win95 are _____ and _____.

9 Under DOS and Windows 3.*x*, _____ is the size of the largest hard disk partition that can be created.

10 You can use a _____ utility to reduce the space used by files on the disk.

Managing data storage

11 A(n) _____ backup copies all the data modified since the last previous backup.

Answers

1 *Serial or sequential.* Review "Storing data on tape."

2 *Sectors.* Look at "Organizing data on disk."

3 *FM, RLL.* See "Reading and writing to a disk."

4 *IDE disk drive.* Check out "Installing and configuring IDE/EIDE hard drives."

5 *Two.* See "IDE technology."

6 *Terminating resistor pack,* or *terminators.* Look at "SCSI Technology."

7 *0 (zero).* Review "Raid!?!."

8 *SCANDISK and DEFRAG.* See "Protecting Your Investment."

9 *2GB.* Check out "Partitioning the hard disk."

10 *Disk compression.* Look at "Compressing the disk."

11 *Incremental.* See "Creating a data backup."

Understanding the Basic Terms

You may not always think of the floppy disk as a removable storage system, but it is — along with CD-ROMs, optical disks, and tape cartridges. Removable storage, also known as removable media, allows for expansion of the hard disk storage space whenever it's needed and the ability to store data outside and away from the PC.

Hard disk technologies

Four types of hard disk technologies have been used in PCs over the years: the ST506, ESDI, IDE, and SCSI. Time has passed the first two by, along with the AT computer in which they were used. Most of the PCs in use today use either an IDE or a SCSI hard disk drive.

The A+ exam includes questions on IDE and SCSI (including RAID) drive technologies. Focus your review on disk storage in these technology types.

ST506/ESDI technologies

These systems are significant in that they were the first hard disk technologies. Besides being big and slow, they are complex to install and replace. Their cabling had to be installed in a certain sequence and with the twist at a certain connector, and then a set of jumpers was used to indicate their drive select setting.

As I contrast in the next section, these devices had to be low-level formatted (the process of creating the disk's cylinders and checking for bad surface media), then high-level formatted (preparing the device for files), and finally the operating system was installed. It is not important that you remember what low-level formatting is for the A+ test beyond the fact that it is not done on all drive technologies after the ST506 and ESDI drives. It is also not important that you know what ESDI stands for.

IDE technology

IDE (Integrated Drive Electronics) technology was originally developed as an alternative to the expensive SCSI technology (see "SCSI technology" later in this chapter) by Compaq and Western Digital. In a nutshell, this technology integrates the controller board into the disk drive. IDE is still one of the most popular disk drive interfaces in use.

IDE, also known as AT Attachment (ATA) interface, is a simple interface technology compared to its predecessors. With the interface controller built into the disk drive itself, only a passthrough board is needed to connect the device to the motherboard. The interface card that's plugged into the motherboard for an IDE disk drive is often a multifunction card supporting the floppy drives, game ports, serial ports, and more. Some newer designs incorporate an IDE controller right into the motherboard.

IDE supports up to two 528MB drives. A newer version of IDE, EIDE (Enhanced IDE) enlarges the capacity into four multigigabyte drives. Beyond that capacity, you must use SCSI or some other technology.

IDE drives are low-level formatted at the factory. A low-level format is one that scans the disk storage media for defects and sets aside sectors with defects so that they are not used for data, preventing later problems. IDE drives should never be low-level formatted by a user or a technician. Only a high-level format (such as that performed by the DOS/Windows command FORMAT) is necessary to prepare that disk partitions for the operating system and data. (See "Formatting the disk" later in this chapter.)

Here's a brain teaser for you that could show up on the A+ Core exam: Beginning from zero (no pins connected), what is the highest digital value that can be represented on a three-pin jumper? What's your answer? A three-pin jumper can be used to indicate a total of eight values, ranging from 0 to 7; more on this later in "Installing and configuring a SCSI hard disk."

Tape drives

You can attach a tape drive to the PC as an internal or external device. Whether you eat up a slot in your case for one depends on how much data you back up and how often. Tape cartridges come with either 4mm or 8mm tape. The latest tape type is DAT (Digital Audio Tape), an 8mm high-capacity technology.

Tape drives are used primarily for backing up large databases and hard disks. Because of its streaming capabilities, it is perfect for recording data in a serial format. This is discussed later in this chapter in "Creating a data backup."

Floppy disks and drives

Unless you have been repairing computers in Elbonia for about ten years, I'm very confident that you know what a floppy disk is and how it's used. You may even know that the current most popular size of floppy disk is 3 1/2 inches.

A floppy disk is perfect for transporting files of around 1MB in size between computers (a technique known as *sneaker net*). Multiple floppy disks can also be used to record large files or backups. However, there are some dangers involved in using a floppy disk in many computers, not the least of which are computer viruses, which are discussed in Chapter 22. I discuss the organization used on a floppy disk later in "Organizing data on disk."

CD-ROM technologies

The CD-ROM is one of the optical storage technologies that uses a laser to read its data from its media. For purposes of the A+ test, it's a read-only media (memory), which is where it gets its name. The compact disc (CD) media used on the computer is exactly the same as that used for recorded music. In fact, most Windows PCs have software to play your favorite music CDs.

A CD-ROM has the capability of storing up to 650MB of data. Its data is recorded exactly backward to the old vinyl phonograph records — you remember those, they sell them at yard sales a lot. Data on a CD-ROM is recorded in one long continuous strand beginning on the inside edge and winding to the outside edge.

CD-ROM drives are available in a wide range of transfer speeds. In fact, the transfer speed of a CD-ROM drive sets its type. CD-ROM types are stated as "X" factors. Each increment of the X is worth 150K in transfer speed. For example, a 1X CD-ROM has a transfer speed of 150K, an 8X CD-ROM has a transfer rate of 1200K, and a 24X CD-ROM has a transfer rate of 3600K.

In the storage scheme of things, the CD-ROM is the slowest of the devices found on the average PC. Of course, RAM is the fastest, followed by the hard disk, and poking along in last is the CD-ROM. This is not usually a problem because users don't use the CD-ROM for its speed. The CD-ROM is valuable to its users for the content of its discs.

Most external CD-ROM drives use a SCSI interface and come with their own host adapter cards. Not all SCSI CD-ROMs come with an adapter, so you may need to verify whether the customer's machine already has one or whether an adapter card is needed.

 To operate a PC's CD-ROM drive in a DOS environment, its device driver must load from the CONFIG.SYS file during the boot process. If the CD-ROM drive is to be installed internally, you have the choice of either an IDE or SCSI. The IDE is less expensive, but the SCSI offers greater future expandability. Anyway, give the customer the choice.

 When installing an IDE CD-ROM drive to a system that has an IDE hard disk installed, you must configure the CD-ROM as a slave. See the drive manual for the correct setting. If no IDE hard disk exists, the CD-ROM can be set to be the master, but some CD-ROMs only run as slaves.

Optical disks

Like the CD-ROM, the optical disk uses lasers to read and write data. However, optical disks have one major exception: They can be written to and read from more than once.

Optical disks also provide a large volume alternative to the floppy disk. They can store up to 6GB of data, and in addition to the CD-ROM, are available in the following technologies:

- ✔ **WORM (Write-Once, Read-Many):** An optical disk that can be written to, but only once. After that, the WORM disk is just like a CD-ROM. The WORM drive records data by making permanent physical marks on the media's surface with a low-power laser.

- ✔ **EO (Erasable Optical):** Disks that are erasable, can be overwritten with new data, and can be used much like magnetic disks. The laser erases any existing marks on the media by relaxing the mark, allowing the media to be reused.

The three major optical technologies (CD-ROM, WORM, and EO) each require a different type of disk drive and media and are not compatible with each other.

SCSI technology

The Small Computer Systems Interface (SCSI — pronounced "scuzzy," rhymes with fuzzy) is a collection of interface standards that covers a wide range of peripheral devices, including hard disks, tape drives, optical drives, CD-ROMs, and disk arrays (RAID). Up to eight SCSI devices can connect to a single SCSI controller by sharing the common interface, called a SCSI bus or SCSI chain.

SCSI devices are like IDE/EIDE devices in that the device controllers are built into the device itself. Each device on the SCSI bus is assigned a unique device number. These numbers are configured to the device with jumpers or DIP switches located on the device. When the SCSI controller (which counts as one of the eight devices) wishes to communicate with one of the devices on the bus, it sends a message encoded with the unit's device number. Any reply to the SCSI controller includes the sender's number. To ensure that messages stay on the bus, the bus is terminated at each end with a terminating resistor pack.

Because SCSI devices are the intelligence supplied by their onboard controllers, they are able to control their own data access or capture activities and interpret requests from the PC system that are passed along by the SCSI controller for specific information.

Meeting the SCSI clan

Much like World War I was not given a number until World War II began, the original SCSI interface is now SCSI-1. This implementation of the SCSI standard has a 5MB transfer rate, uses either a Centronics 50-pin or a DB-25 connector, and has an 8-bit bus.

The major improvements to the SCSI-1 interface are

- ✔ SCSI-2: Also called SCSI Fast-Wide, includes 16-bit bus (Wide SCSI), and twice-as-fast transfer rate (Fast SCSI).

- ✔ SCSI-3 and beyond: Includes Ultra SCSI, Wide Ultra SCSI, SCSI Parallel Interface (SPI), and Ultra2 SCSI, which all feature 16-bit bus and from 40 to 80MBps transfer rates.

Watching your As and Bs and Ps and Qs

Skim through the following information on SCSI cabling. I've not seen a question from this area, but that doesn't mean one doesn't exist.

SCSI systems connect to the host adapter in a daisy-chain fashion. This means that the devices are connected in series one to the other in a kind of high-tech conga line. SCSI devices installed as internal devices use a 50-pin ribbon cable very much like the floppy disk cable without the twist. External SCSI devices may require one or more of a series of 50-pin and 68-pin cables, depending on the standard in use. For example, a SCSI-2 device requires an A-cable (50-pin) and a B-cable (68-pin). The B-cable should not be confused with the SCSI-3 P-cable (68-pin) that must be used with a Q-cable (68-pin), and so it goes. When installing a SCSI device, read the manual carefully before you start connecting stuff.

All SCSI devices should be powered on before the PC to allow the SCSI host adapter (usually inside the system) to detect and interrogate each of the devices on the SCSI bus.

RAID!?!

A Redundant Array of Independent Disks (RAID) is a category of disk drives that employs two or more drives in combination for fault tolerance (error recovery) and performance. RAID disk drives are used frequently on servers but aren't generally necessary for personal computers.

One of the fundamental concepts of RAID drives is data striping. In this process, data files are subdivided and written to several disks. This technique allows the processor to read or write data faster than a single disk can supply or accept it. While the first data segment transfers from the first disk, the second disk is locating the next segment, and so on.

Another common feature of RAID systems is data mirroring. This feature involves writing duplicate data segments or files to more than one disk to guard against losing the data because of a device failure.

Ten different RAID levels exist — 0 through 7, 10, and 53, each more complicated than its predecessor. The three you should know for the A+ Core exam are 0, 3, and 5, which are also the most common:

- **RAID 0:** Striped disk array without fault tolerance. This level provides for data striping but doesn't include mirroring or redundancy or any protection against device failure (fault tolerance).

- **RAID 3:** Parallel transfer with parity. This level is very much like Level 0, except that it sets aside a dedicated disk for storing parity and error correction code (ECC) data.

- **RAID 5:** Data striping with parity. This level provides data striping at the character level and also implements stripe error correction. The ECC data is recorded on a separate disk for each level of data stripe.

Working with Disk Storage

You'll find questions on disk storage scattered throughout the domain areas of the A+ exams. It is hard to predict just how many questions you can expect, but my guess is between five and ten on the Core exam and about the same on the DOS/Windows exam.

Organizing data on disk

Much like you need an organization scheme to file documents in a file cabinet so you can find them later, the disk also needs one. If you aren't interested in finding the data later for some reason, then you really don't need to worry about organization. This is called the FISH file-organization technique — First In Stays Here. But you do care, so some organization scheme must be used.

Even before you can get your data organized, the PC and disk drive must have an organization technique that helps them to place and find data stored on the media. Following are the building blocks of disk media organization (which you can also see in Figure 6-1):

- **Tracks:** Concentric circular areas of the disk. A length of a track is one circumference of the disk. On a hard disk, there may be 1,000 or more tracks. When data is written to the disk, it begins with the outermost track first.

- **Sectors:** Cross-sectioning divisions of the disk that intersect all the tracks. In addition to dividing each track into manageable pieces, sectors provide addressing references. For example, a floppy disk has nine sectors on each side of the disk.

- **Cylinders:** Unique to hard disk drives, cylinders are a logical grouping of the same track on each disk surface in a disk unit. For example, if a hard disk drive has four platters, it has eight surfaces and eight track

52s. All eight of the track 52s make up cylinder 52. This feature allows data to be written to each platter on the same track, eliminating the need to move the read/write heads.

✔ **Clusters:** Groups of sectors used by operating systems to track data on the disk. There are normally around 64 sectors to a cluster, but the size of the disk drive determines the actual number of sectors in a cluster.

You should be very familiar with the above terms for the A+ exams.

Reading and writing to a disk

Before data can be read from a disk, it must be written to the disk through a process called *flux transition,* which means that the storage media is altered with an electromagnet to either a positive or a negative charge. Primarily, two different encoding schemes have been used to convert data into flux transitions:

✔ **FM (frequency modulation) and MFM (modified frequency modulation):** Some of the first widely used encoding methods. These schemes simply recorded a 1 or a 0 as different polarities on the recording media.

✔ **RLL (run length limited):** Allows for higher track and data density by spacing one-bits farther apart and specially encoding each byte. RLL introduced data compression techniques, and most current disk drives (IDE, SCSI, and so on) use a form of RLL encoding.

Interleaving data on a disk

You may see a question on the A+ exam about interleaving, but understand that most of the newer disk drives no longer need it due to increased efficiencies. Also be careful not to confuse interleave with interlace. *Interleave* relates to PC hard disks and *interlace* relates to PC monitors. Be sure of the question before answering.

Interleaving is a technique that allows the read/write head to use the rotation of the disk to its advantage. If a disk drive has an interleave ratio of 3:1 (or 3 minus 1), it writes one sector and then skips two before writing the next. Likewise, an interleave of 2:1 means that it writes to every other sector (2 minus 1 equals 1). An interleave of 1:1 is the same has having no interleaving at all.

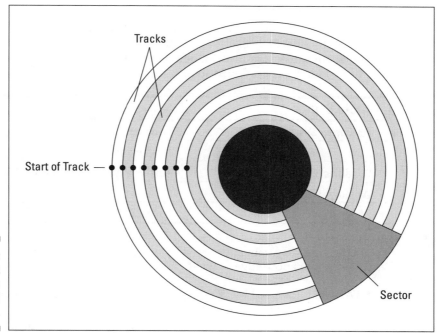

Figure 6-1:
A disk platter with tracks and sectors.

Formatting the disk

A disk drive has two levels of formatting done to prepare it for use in the PC. The low-level format is one that most PC repair technicians should no longer be concerned with because it's done at the factory during manufacturing. Low-level formatting accomplishes two major things:

- ✓ Builds the File Allocation Table (FAT) file and records the location of all tracks and sectors on the device
- ✓ Physically scans the disk media for defects and records the location of any unusable areas found

The FAT is always located at Track 0 because different disks have different sizes, number of tracks, and so on. Track 0 is predictably always in the same place.

During the procedure to install an operating system on a disk, a high-level format usually is done. This format varies slightly between operating systems. For example, in the DOS or Windows installation, the high-level format creates a separate FAT table that's used by the operating system to track disk clusters.

Creating a file system

Different operating systems use different file systems to manage disk storage. A high-level format creates the operating system's file system and management tables and files. Table 6-1 lists the file systems used by DOS and the Windows operating systems.

Table 6-1	File Systems
Operating Systems	*File System*
DOS	File Allocation Table (FAT)
Windows 3.*x*	Virtual File Allocation Table (VFAT)
Windows 95	VFAT and FAT32
Windows NT Workstation	Windows NT File System (NTFS)

Focus on the file system supported by each operating system. But, just so you have some knowledge of what each is about, review the following items:

- **FAT** is a table used by DOS to place and locate files on a disk. It also tracks the pieces of fragmented files.

- **VFAT** is the file system used in Windows 3.*x* and older releases of Windows 95. VFAT serves as an interface between applications and the physical FAT. I think its most outstanding feature is that it allows long filenames.

- **FAT32** is the file system used in Windows 95 service release 2 and Windows 98. It supports larger disk capacities (up to two terabytes) and because it uses a smaller cluster size, it produces more efficient storage utilization.

- **NTFS** is one of the two file systems used by the Windows NT operating system (the other is the FAT file system). NTFS features transaction logs to help recover from disk failures, the ability to set permissions at the directory or individual file level, and allows files to span across several physical disks. Any Windows NT questions you encounter will likely be about storage systems.

Partitioning the hard disk

You should know the reason for partitioning the hard disk, something about the partitions themselves, and that FDISK is the command used in both Windows and DOS. The FDISK utility is used to partition the hard drive into logical subdivisions, which are seen by the operating system as separate logical (as opposed to physical) hard disks.

You would partition the hard disk to do the following:

- ✔ Divide the disk into logical subdrives that are addressed as separate drives; for example, C:, D:, and E:

- ✔ Create separate areas of the disk to hold multiple operating systems, such as Windows and Linux in their own partitions

- ✔ Separate programs from data into separate partitions to ease the backup process

Hard disks are divided into primary and extended partitions. Typically, the primary partition is the one used to boot the system. Any other partitions on the drive are extended partitions and can be used for another operating system or subdivided further (up to 23 more times). A hard disk can be divided into a maximum of four primary partitions, but some systems, such as DOS, require that only one primary partition be active or visible at a time.

Partitioning disks can improve disk efficiency. Under DOS and Windows, cluster sizes are automatically assigned in proportion to the disk size. The bigger the disk, the bigger the clusters, and large clusters can result in slack space (wasted disk space). Reducing the size of the disk through partitioning has the effect of reducing the cluster size as well. A wide range of software tools is available to help partition a hard disk effectively.

In DOS, Windows 3.x, and early releases of Windows 95, a hard disk over 2GB in size must be divided into partitions each smaller than 2GB if you want to use the entire disk. Windows 95 OSR2 and Windows 98, which implement FAT32, can create a primary partition of 8GB.

After a hard disk is partitioned, the first sector on cylinder 0 (the outermost track) is reserved for the master boot record that contains the partition table. All partitions have a partition table that's used to track its contents. However, the master boot record partition table contains the mapping for all partitions on all drives. The master boot record uses the partition table to locate and use the active primary partition to boot the system.

Compressing the disk

Disk compression uses data compression techniques to reduce the amount of disk space a file needs. The effect is that more files fit into the same space. For example, after compression, the available space on a disk may be 50 to 100 percent higher than before compression.

After a disk is compressed, a disk compression utility must reside in memory and work between the operating system and the disk controller. Any file actions to the compressed disk are intercepted by this utility. For example, when the operating system saves a file to disk, the compression utility intercepts the file and compresses it before it's written to disk. The same holds true when the operating system opens a file — the compression utility intercepts the file, decompresses it, and then passes it to the operating system. This utility does add some overhead to the process and slows down all file access from the compressed disk.

One caution about booting a system with a compressed disk from a floppy disk: If the floppy disk does not contain the disk compression utility used to access the compressed drive, the contents of the compressed disk will not be available for access. This is especially a problem if you are trying to reformat or re-set up Windows or its configuration.

A number of third-party disk compression utilities are available for DOS and Windows, all of which work essentially the same. DOS and Windows 3.*x* use a routine called DBLSpace. Windows 95 includes a disk compression utility called DriveSpace, which goes DBLSpace one better because it can compress and uncompress data on floppy disks, removable media, or hard disk drives, whereas DBLSpace works only with floppy and hard disks.

DriveSpace works by creating a new uncompressed logical drive, called the host drive, where it stores the CVF (Compressed Volume File), a form of VFAT for the compressed drive. The uncompressed drive also contains files that should not or cannot be compressed, such as system files. Any unused space is available to the user.

The Windows 95 version of DriveSpace creates compressed drives of up to 512MB. Large disk drives usually can't be compressed as a single volume. The version available in Microsoft Plus! and Windows 98 can compress drives up to 2GB.

Creating a data backup

Tape is a good medium to use for creating a backup of hard disk data. Making a backup of files is a safety precaution taken to ensure that data outlives the device on which it's stored. A cardinal rule of computing is to back up files regularly, and then back up the backups.

Most operating systems include utilities for creating a backup. Usually backup software is included with a tape or other backup media drive. You can also purchase backup software separately. Backup software offers some advantages over just copying a file to a removable medium. Most offer compression that reduces the number of disks or tapes needed to hold data. Many also offer cataloging routines and single directory or file restore capabilities.

You can create four different types of backups (expect to see these on the test):

- An *archival* backup (or full backup) is one that contains every file, program, table, and so on from the hard disk.

- An *incremental* backup contains only the files that have been modified since the last previous backup.

- A *differential* backup copies all the data added or modified since the last full backup.

- A *copy* backup is created by using a copy command to write a duplicate of a file, directory, or disk to another media.

It's usually wise to rotate a series of tapes or other media relative to the number of increments to be regularly captured. For example, if daily backups are made, you should use seven sets of backup media. It's also good practice to make an archival backup once per cycle with incrementals filling out the rest of the cycle. Perhaps doing an archival backup once a week with incrementals the rest of the week would work. Whatever cycle you use, the backup should be a comfortable safety net for the system.

Storing data on tape

There was a time, back in the dark ages of personal computing, back even before floppy or hard disks, when the only permanent storage media available was cassette tapes — the same ones used for music. Before then, except for some very early use of punched paper tape, you just didn't store data between runs of the PC. Each time you wanted to run your BASIC program, you had to re-enter it and the data. Regardless of how you feel about tape today, at one time, it was a godsend.

Tape is a somewhat unique medium in comparison to the other writeable permanent data storage media available to PC users today. Whereas most of the other media are direct access, tape is a serial, or physically sequential, access media. If you want to hear the third song on a music cassette, you must first fast forward over the first two songs. The same is true for accessing the third record of a tape file.

Tape is primarily a backup media today, and many larger systems, especially network servers, have either an internal or external tape drive. This is a good use of the media, its serial nature, and its relative compact size. Some problems exist with using tape, but they are avoidable with proper care and diligence. You should rotate tapes regularly, store them in a cool dry place, and replace them at least once a year.

In the situation where a rotated group of tapes is used for daily backups of a server, and intermittent problems start occurring on different days and at different points in the backup process, the problem could be in the age of the tapes.

Installing and Configuring Storage Devices

The process of installing and configuring a floppy, hard, or CD-ROM disk drive is basically the same. Only a few subtle and specific tasks differentiate these tasks. The task on which the A+ exam focuses in every case is aligning and attaching the device cabling. As you review the procedures used for each device in the following sections, pay particular attention to how its cabling is aligned and installed.

Installing and configuring floppy disk drives

In the A+ world, the 5 1/4-inch floppy disk still exists, even as it's becoming rare in actual use. This situation is because a vast number of older computers are still in use with owners who wish to have them repaired on occasion. The three things you must consider when installing a floppy disk drive in a PC are

- **Media:** Which diskette sizes has the user been using to back up data or install software? Don't do the customer a favor and upgrade the system to a 3 1/2-inch floppy drive when all of his files are on 5 1/4-inch floppies.

- **Physical size:** Three package sizes (also called form factors) for floppy disk drives exist: full-height, half-height, and combination half-height. A full-height drive, which is big, bulky, and takes about two expansion slots, is common in older PCs. The half-height drive is one-half as tall as a full-height drive and is the size of one expansion slot on a PC case. This drive is the *de facto* standard in use today. The third form combines both a 3 1/2-inch and a 5 1/4-inch drive into a single half-height drive.

- **Capacity:** Floppy disks range in their storage capacity. Depending on how many sides and the media density of the disk, 5 1/4-inch floppy disks hold in the range of 360K to 1.2MB. Depending on the same variables, 3 1/2-inch disks hold from 720K to 1.4MB.

Installing a floppy disk drive

To install a floppy disk drive in a computer, you must install the floppy disk drive controller card in the motherboard. Three types of floppy disk controller interfaces are used in PCs:

- **Standalone cards:** Usually not a single purpose card, floppy controller cards install into an expansion slot on the motherboard. For example, many floppy controller cards also include a game port, a serial port or two, a parallel port, and, of course, the disk interface.

- **Disk controller cards:** It has been common for a single card to provide the interface for the hard disk and the floppy disk since the days of the 286. This practice reduces the number of expansion slots needed to install what are considered system necessities.

- **Built-in controllers:** Some motherboards (called all-in-ones, or less sarcastically — integrated systemboards) include the interface circuitry for the floppy disk. While this is handy, it can be an expensive nightmare should a circuit fault cause the floppy disk drive to stop working, which means that the entire motherboard must be replaced.

Cabling the floppy disk drive

The common floppy disk cable is a 34-wire ribbon cable that is usually light blue in color with one edge painted either red or blue. Usually three connectors are on the cable. The three connectors connect to the controller card and up to two floppy disk drives.

To be sure you have the floppy cable installed correctly, you can use two tricks: 1) remember "Big Red is Number One," and 2) in most cases, the red edge should point toward the AC power cord. I apologize for the sports metaphor, but it works for me.

A floppy cable is installed in a specific way. In addition to worrying about the alignment of the cable and getting Pin 1 installed on the controller card (Pin 1 is either marked with a "1" or a white dot on the controller card connector), you must also make sure that you use the correct connector with the proper disk drive. Some computer manufacturers go one step further to make this even easier. For example, Compaq uses a keyed cable connector for its floppy and IDE drives that can be connected in only one way.

As shown in Figure 6-2, two two-connector sets for floppy disk drives are on the cable. The first set of connectors, the ones in the middle of the cable, are for the B: floppy disk drive. After the twist in the cable, that is, at the end of the cable, are the A: floppy disk connectors.

Configuring the floppy disk drive

Fortunately, the drive cable takes care of any configuration problems you may have, unless you are installing a used drive. The drive select jumpers that assign an identity to the drive are usually set to DS2, or drive select 2, at the factory. The twist in the cable near the A: connector tricks the system into thinking that the drive connected after the twist is DS1, or drive select 1.

Terminating the relationship

The last floppy drive (usually A:) must be terminated at one end. This is especially true of older full-height and some half-height drives. These 5 ¹/₄-inch drives have a terminating resistor plugged into the end of the cable to absorb all signals and prevent signal echoes bouncing back down the line and crashing into new incoming data.

Once again, technology is taking care of you, because all 3 ¹/₂-inch drives have a preinstalled, nonconfigurable terminating resistor. With 3 ¹/₂-inch drives, each drive shares the role of termination. If you have only one drive on the chain, it terminates itself. If you mix 5 ¹/₄-inch and 3 ¹/₂-inch drives on the same chain, the terminator on the 5 ¹/₄-inch drive should be removed unless it's the end. Terminating resistors look like 16-pin memory DIP chips.

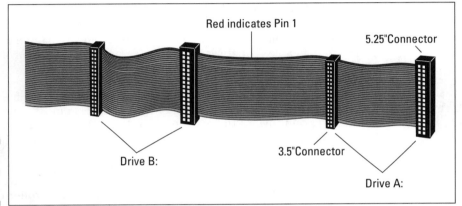

Figure 6-2:
The floppy
disk cable.

Installing and configuring IDE/EIDE hard drives

You do not low-level format an IDE/EIDE or SCSI drive. If you did low-level one of these drives, you may render it totally useless by wiping out its sector translation information.

You can expect one or two questions on the number of drives supported by IDE (2) and EIDE (4) and how its cable is aligned. Chapter 15 also has information on installing these drive types.

IDE and EIDE drives are installed with a 40-pin ribbon cable that must also be aligned to pin 1. The alignment is performed exactly the same as for the floppy ribbon cable. Only two IDE drives can be installed in a system, with one the master and the other the slave. Up to four EIDE drives can be installed with two drives each on two cables, but only one master.

IDE/EIDE drives must be designated either as a master or a slave. The master is the primary disk drive from which the system is normally booted. The slaves are not. Regardless of whether you install two IDE or four EIDE drives, one drive on each cable should be designated as the master. You must set any other drives as slaves. This is done with jumpers on each drive controller. This step is very important because two masters will fight each other to the death, and two slaves will stand around lost, waiting for instructions. The result in either case is no disk access. Read the manuals for the drives carefully to locate and set the jumpers appropriately. Remember to also set the CMOS AT drive type for each drive according to the setting prescribed by its manual.

Installing and configuring a SCSI hard disk

Each SCSI device must be assigned an ID number. As I indicate earlier in this chapter, the number is assigned through a jumper or a DIP switch block. Because the SCSI bus supports eight devices, including the host adapter, the numbers range from zero to seven. Device ID 7 is reserved for the SCSI host adapter. You can assign the other devices any of the other numbers, but slower devices such as CD-ROMs should be assigned a higher SCSI ID. This gives them lots of time to process data on the SCSI bus. A SCSI hard disk used to boot the system is assigned SCSI ID 0.

If you have both an IDE disk drive and a SCSI disk drive on a system, the IDE drive should be the boot drive.

A three-pin jumper can be used to indicate a total of eight values, the highest of which is 7. Just in case you need to see how this is done, review Table 6-2.

Table 6-2		Three-Pin Jumper Values		
Value	**Pin #1**	**Pin #2**	**Pin #3**	**Binary**
0	off	off	off	000
1	off	off	on	001
2	off	on	off	010
3	off	on	on	011
4	on	off	off	100
5	on	off	on	101
6	on	on	off	110
7	on	on	on	111

The SCSI host adapter is set to 7; the boot hard disk drive is set to 0.

Protecting Your Investment

While it has become an excellent value on a per-byte basis, the hard disk still represents a substantial investment for most customers. The value of a hard disk comes not only from the cost of a new one, but in the value of the data stored on it. The obvious and easiest way to protect the value of data is to back it up regularly. In addition, you can use some preventive maintenance steps to ensure the disk drive is working properly. Here are some tools, all three of which you can expect to find on the exam, you can use to help protect data:

- **DOS CHKDSK:** Looks for disk clusters that aren't associated with existing data files. Running this program with an / f switch harvests these clusters, gives them names like FILE0000.CHK, and places them in the root file directory. You really can't recover any data found in these clusters, but you can look at them and try to figure out what you may have lost before you delete them and free up the space.

- **SCANDISK:** A DOS utility that's also available in Windows 95. It's a more sophisticated program that detects disk media errors and file errors, and attempts to repair them.

- **DEFRAG:** Another DOS/Windows 95 tool used to remedy slow access by defragmenting the hard disk. Fragmentation occurs when files are updated frequently, and, due to changing file sizes, end up fragmented in different clusters than other parts of the same file. DEFRAG attempts to pull files back into the same clusters, improving file access speeds.

Prep Test

1 Which RAID level provides for disk striping with parity?

- A ○ 0
- B ○ 1
- C ○ 4
- D ○ 5

2 When should high-level formatting be done on an IDE hard drive?

- A ○ By the manufacturer at the factory
- B ○ Before it's partitioned with FDISK
- C ○ After it has been partitioned with FDISK
- D ○ IDE drives should never be high-level formatted

3 The term *interleave* applies to a hard disk as

- A ○ The rotation speed of a hard drive
- B ○ The space placed between records on the hard drive
- C ○ A technique used to speed up data access
- D ○ Does not apply to the hard disk

4 One of the features of the Windows 95 VFAT is

- A ○ 32-bit access
- B ○ Long filenames
- C ○ 8.3 filenames
- D ○ A 32-bit FAT

5 The compression program that ships with Windows 95 is called

- A ○ Stacker
- B ○ DoubleSpace
- C ○ DriveSpace
- D ○ PKZIP

6 To operate a PC's CD-ROM drive in a DOS environment,

A ○ Its device driver must load from CONFIG.SYS
B ○ The Windows CD-ROM driver must be loaded to RAM
C ○ LASTDRIVE must be set to "Z"
D ○ No special requirements are needed

7 A fragmented file is not stored in

A ○ Consecutive sectors
B ○ Consecutive clusters
C ○ Consecutive bytes
D ○ Consecutive tracks

8 A hard disk cluster is made up of

A ○ Cylinders
B ○ Tracks
C ○ Sectors
D ○ Hard disk drives

9 When installing IDE/EIDE disk drives, you must assign one of the drives as the

A ○ Slave
B ○ Host
C ○ Controller
D ○ Master

10 How many devices can be attached to a SCSI chain?

A ○ Two
B ○ Four
C ○ Six
D ○ Eight

Answers

1 *D*. RAID 5 provides data striping at the character level and implements stripe error correction. *See " RAID!?!."*

2 *C*. IDE disk drives never need low-level formatting, but they should be high-level formatted after being partitioned to load the operating system to the drive. *Review " IDE technology."*

3 *C*. Interleave is a technique that allows the read/write head to use the rotation of the disk to its advantage. If a disk has an interleave ration of 3:1, it writes to one sector and then skips over two before writing again. See *"Interleaving data on a disk."*

4 *B*. VFAT is the file system used in Windows 3.*x* and older releases of Windows 95. One of its features is the support of long filenames. Look at *"Creating a file system."*

5 *C*. Windows 95 includes a disk compression utility named DriveSpace. *Review "Compressing the disk."*

6 *A*. To operate a PC's CD-ROM drive in a DOS environment, its device driver must load from the CONFIG.SYS file during the boot process. *See "CD-ROM technologies."*

7 *B*. Fragmentation occurs when files are updated frequently and, due to changing file sizes, end up fragmented in different clusters than other parts of the same file. Review "Protecting Your Investment."

8 *C*. Clusters are groups of sectors. Normally around 64 sectors are in a cluster, but the size of the disk drive determines the actual number of sectors in a cluster. *Look at " Organizing data on disk."*

9 *D*. When installing IDE/EIDE drives, you must designate one of the drives as the master. Designate any other drives as slaves. *See "Installing and config-uring IDE/EIDE hard drives."*

10 *D*. Up to eight SCSI devices can connect to a single controller-sharing SCSI bus. *Review "SCSI technology."*

Chapter 7

Bus Structures

• •

Exam Objectives

▶ Identifying PC motherboard expansion buses

▶ Explaining the function of Plug-and-Play

▶ Defining the PCMCIA (PC Card) interface

▶ Configuring IRQs, DMAs, I/O addresses, and logical devices

• •

*I*nterfacing with the system is one area of the A+ exams that's very detail oriented and precise. In many of the exam domains, a general knowledge of basic concepts is usually sufficient, but that's not the case with the topics in this chapter, and rightly so.

As a PC repair technician, much of your job is adding new or replacing old hardware, which involves installing new adapter cards and cabling in customer PCs. To do it right, you must thoroughly understand the bus structures, IRQs, DMA functions, and input/output addressing associated with each particular motherboard. A solid understanding of how these technologies function is what gives you the confidence to plug a new high-priced video card into the appropriate expansion slot and set it up correctly with the operating system. Without a doubt, installing, configuring, and cabling new peripherals and adapter cards is the most techie part of being a PC technician.

Although its specific domain will have only around ten questions, as much as 40 percent of both A+ tests may have questions relating to this chapter's topics. So, this is one chapter you may want to look at a little more carefully, especially if you don't do this kind of work very much. I really condense a lot of facts and concepts into this chapter to help you prepare for the questions that I bet trip up most of the people who fail the exams.

Quick Assessment

Identifying PC motherboard expansion buses

1 The two general types of bus structures on every motherboard are _____ and _____.

2 The system bus provides four different system necessities: _____, _____, _____, and _____.

3 The ISA architecture provides a _____-bit bus.

4 _____ was the first 32-bit architecture.

Explaining the function of Plug-and-Play

5 _____ is a configuration standard that allows the BIOS and operating system to automatically configure expansion boards and device adapters.

Defining the PCMCIA (PC Card) interface

6 The Type II PC Card is primarily used to add _____ or _____ to portable computers.

7 _____ are the resources used to interface, communicate, and control individual device adapters and controllers.

Configuring IRQs, DMAs, I/O addresses, and logical devices

8 A(n) _____ channel allows a device to bypass the processor to access memory directly.

9 A(n) _____ is a signal from a device to the processor that a service or special action is needed.

10 The default IRQ for COM1 is _____.

11 The default I/O address for LPT1 is _____.

Answers

1 *Internal, external*. See "Bus structures."

2 *Power, control signals, addresses,* and *data*. Review "Understanding the internal bus."

3 *16*. Study "Plugging into the expansion bus."

4 *MCA (Micro-Channel Architecture)*. Review "Plugging into the expansion bus."

5 *Plug-and-Play*. Review "Fun with Plug-and-Play."

6 *Modems or NICs (network interface cards)*. Take a look at "Upgrading notebooks and portables."

7 *System resources*. See "Working with System Resources."

8 DMA (direct memory access). Review "Accessing memory directly with DMA."

9 *Interrupt*. Study "Requesting an interrupt, or how to get IRQed."

10 *IRQ 4*. Take a look at "Using input/output (I/O) addresses."

11 *3F8h*. See "Using input/output (I/O) addresses."

Bus Structure Basics

Although you may see a question on the exam that involves the definition of a bus, most of this first section is background for the real techie stuff that follows. If you look at the bottom of any PC motherboard, you can see an interconnecting maze of pathways that are used to transport data, addresses, and instructions around the system. Each of these pathways is a *bus,* which is a group of tiny, very thin wires that carry signals from one part of the motherboard to another.

Two general types of bus structures are on every motherboard:

 ✔ **Internal bus:** Interconnects main memory, the CPU, and all other components on the motherboard

 ✔ **External (expansion) bus:** Connects the outside world of peripherals to the motherboard

When I compare a bus to a multilane highway, I'm referring to the size, or width, of a bus. The width of a bus determines the amount of data, and how large an address it can transmit. The width of a bus is stated in bits. A 16-bit bus can transmit 16 bits of data and a 32-bit bus can transmit 32 bits of data. Obviously, the wider a bus is in bits, the more data it can carry.

The speed that data moves on a bus is controlled by its clock speed, which is measured in megahertz (MHz). The higher the bus speed, the more data that can be moved on the bus. Think of it this way: If a bus (a passenger bus) needs to carry 300 people from point A to point B, but has capacity for only 66 at a time, it obviously must make several trips. The faster the bus goes in making its out and back trips, the sooner all the people get to beautiful downtown point B. Likewise, a faster bus (the computer kind now) allows more data to be transferred faster, which in turn makes the operating system and applications run faster.

What's a megahertz?

So what is or are megahertz? The term *megahertz,* which is plural (like data) and is abbreviated as MHz, is a measurement for the processing speed of a microcomputer.

Within the CPU is a quartz crystal that vibrates as electricity passes through it. This vibration creates a signal with a steady pulse to which the CPU and every other component of the computer synchronize. Each wave of this pulsating signal represents one system cycle, or one hertz. The speed at which these cycles occur, millions per second, is the clock speed of the computer. These mega (millions) of hertz (cycles), or megahertz, are used to indicate the processing speed of the computer.

In the mid-1980s, a typical PC operated at 4.77 MHz. Today, a common microcomputer operates at 200 to 300 MHz or more.

Understanding the internal bus

You should have a good understanding of general bus architectures for the exam. You may not be asked any specific questions from this area, but it will sure help you understand some of the questions you will be asked.

A big difference exists between the specific system bus structures of a 386 processor and those of the latest Pentium technology, but don't worry about it for the exam. Concentrate on the various bus architectures used in device I/O, which is where you as a repair technician most likely come into contact with the bus, anyway.

The internal bus, also known as the system bus, is that maze of wires you see on the bottom of the motherboard. It provides the internal components of the computer with four different necessities:

- **Power:** Power comes to the motherboard straight from the power supply. The motherboard uses the system bus to distribute power to its ICs and other components.

- **Control signals:** The control unit within the CPU sends out control signals to coordinate the activities of the system. These signals are carried on a part of the internal bus called the control bus.

- **Addresses:** PC components pass data and instructions between one another using memory location addresses to reference the location of the data or instructions in memory. These addresses are transmitted on a part of the internal bus called the address bus.

- **Data:** The actual data or instructions being transferred between components are transmitted around the system on the part of the internal bus called the data bus.

On Pentium motherboards, the system chipset is the communications controller between all the components that interact with the system bus. The system chipset coordinates with each component or device to ensure that each device properly interacts with every other one.

For the exam, you must understand the compatibilities, capabilities, and limitations of the various bus architectures detailed in this chapter.

In the context of the PC, when most people refer to "the bus," they are referring to the data bus and, without knowing it, the address bus. The external bus must connect and coordinate with these two internal bus workhorses.

PC buses carry data, instructions, or the addresses of data or instructions. In the same way that a passenger bus stops at different places to pick up or drop off people, a PC bus deposits or collects addresses or data at the different components (CPU, memory, and so on) to which it is connected. The address carried on the address bus references the source or destination location of the data or instruction carried on the data bus.

In a way, the contents of the address and data buses are like a letter going through the postal service mail. The envelope (the letter's address bus) has the address of the letter's destination, and the message inside of the envelope (the letter's data bus) is its data.

Defining the external (expansion) bus

For the exam, you really need to know what each of the expansion bus features are and for what each is used. Focus on gaining a general understanding of how and why they are applied. Not only will this understanding help you on the test, but later in this chapter as well.

Earlier in this chapter, I list the external bus as one of the general bus structures of the PC. This bus, also called the *expansion bus,* allows peripheral devices to communicate with the motherboard and its components, almost as if they were a part of the motherboard itself. To add a new device to the PC, the device's adapter card is plugged into the expansion bus via a compatible expansion slot on the motherboard. After it's plugged in, the device is able to communicate with the CPU and other system components.

The expansion slot for any of the supported expansion bus architectures comprises a certain number of small copper spring connectors that line each side of the connector slot. For an expansion board designed for a particular slot style, the slot connectors match up with the copper tabs on the edge connector of the expansion card. Like pins in a serial or parallel cable, each connection between the slot and card form a channel that services a particular need of the expansion card. Some channels carry power, some connect to the address and data buses, and others are used for *clock signal, IRQ,* and *DMA* interfaces. Here is a brief description of each of these features:

- ✓ **Clock signal:** This connection provides the card with the signal of the bus clock so that it can synchronize its communications with the buses of the motherboard.

- ✓ **Interrupt request (IRQ):** A request telling the CPU to interrupt what it's doing and take care of the special needs of the device sending the IRQ. So that the CPU knows which device is the rude one, devices are assigned IRQ numbers. When you install a new device, it is assigned an

IRQ number, which enables the CPU to know who to blame, I mean, which device to service. On occasion, devices may share an IRQ, provided both devices do not attempt to interact with the CPU at the same time.

✔ **Direct memory access (DMA):** DMA channels allow certain devices to bypass the processor and access main memory directly. Some architectures allow more DMA channels than others, but a DMA channel can't be shared by two devices.

✔ **Input/Output (I/O) address:** Assigned to each device via the device's expansion slot. The I/O address, also called an *I/O* or *hardware port,* allows the CPU to send commands directly to the device. The I/O address is a one-way-only line that works like a reverse IRQ. The CPU uses the I/O address to send a command to the device. If the device responds, it uses the data bus or DMA channel to do so. Only one device can be assigned to an I/O address.

✔ **Bus mastering:** Another feature attached to expansion slots and expansion cards that allows one device to interact directly with another. Usually, the expansion card plugged into a slot has a bus master processor on the card that directs this activity.

Fun with Plug-and-Play

Plug-and-Play (PnP) is a configuration standard that allows the system BIOS and the operating system to automatically configure expansion boards and other devices without the user worrying about setting DIP switches, jumpers, and system resources (IRQ, DMA, and so on). In effect, you just plug in the device or adapter card and play with it.

In order to use Plug-and-Play on a system, four requirements must be met:

✔ The system BIOS must support PnP.

✔ The motherboard and its chipset must support PnP.

✔ The operating system running on the PC must support PnP.

✔ The bus of the expansion slot that the device occupies must be compatible with PnP.

Windows 95 fully supports Plug-and-Play, although Windows NT only partially supports it. Plug-and-Play is compatible with ISA, EISA, MCA, PC Card (PCMCIA), and PCI devices and adapters. All PCI devices are Plug-and-Play, but not all Plug-and-Play devices are PCI devices.

Plugging into the expansion bus

For the exam, you need to know what differentiates one expansion bus architecture from another and which are the most commonly used types.

One bit of terminology adjustment is in order here: An expansion bus architecture is the same as an expansion slot type.

A variety of expansion architectures have been used in PCs over the years, including 8-bit, ISA, EISA, MCA, VLB, and PCI. When you open the PC's case and look at the motherboard's expansion slots, the expansion slots you likely see are ISA, VLB, and PCI. A motherboard can often support several types of expansion slots.

I show only a couple of the expansion card connectors and slots, because the visual of the cards is not important to the A+ exam. Which expansion bus is used with what type of card and device is much more important.

Here is a brief description of each of the expansion slot architectures that have been used in PCs:

✔ **8-bit bus:** Not many of these left around, so don't worry about it for the exam. However, it's characterized by a single slot that supports eight interrupts and four DMA channels, with all of them preassigned. Almost all the architectures that followed are backward compatible with 8-bit cards.

✔ **Industry Standard Architecture (ISA):** Pronounced "ice-ah," it was introduced with the IBM AT and also called the AT bus; it provided a 16-bit data bus. As shown in Figure 7-1, the ISA bus is characterized by adding an additional short slot to a slot on the 8-bit bus to create the 16-bit connector. ISA added eight additional IRQs and doubled the number of DMA channels. ISA expansion cards were designated to the appropriate IRQ or DMA numbers through jumpers and DIP switches. The ISA architecture also separated the bus clock from the CPU clock to allow the slower data bus to operate at its own speeds. ISA slots are found on 286, 386, 486, and some Pentium PCs.

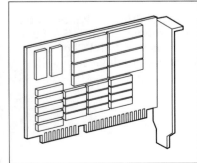

Figure 7-1:
An ISA card fits into an ISA expansion slot.

✔ **Micro-Channel Architecture (MCA):** Introduced with the IBM PS/2, MCA was the first 32-bit option, and featured bus mastering and a 10 MHz bus clock for expansion cards. The MCA expansion slot is about the same size as the ISA slot, but has about twice as many channels. MCA cards are also configured to their IRQ and DMA assignments by software, an improvement over the jumpers and DIPs of the ISA architecture.

✔ **Extended ISA (EISA):** Pronounced "ee-sah," this architecture was developed by a group of companies to overcome the limitations of ISA and to compete with MCA. In effect, EISA takes the best parts of MCA and builds on them. It has a 32-bit data bus, uses software setup, has more I/O addresses available, and ignores IRQs and DMA channels. EISA uses only an 8 MHz bus clock to be backward compatible to ISA boards.

✔ **Intelligent Drive Electronics (IDE):** This architecture is used almost exclusively for disk drives. An IDE adapter card connects up to two different devices on each expansion slot, providing a low-cost way to add additional drives without needing another expansion card. The *Extended IDE (EIDE)* architecture allows up to four drives to be connected into a single slot.

✔ **VESA Local Bus (VLB or VL-bus):** VLB was used first on 486 systems and grew out of the need for the data bus to run at the same clock speed as the CPU. VLB was developed by the Video Electronics Standards Association (VESA) to place a port more or less directly on the system bus with what was called a bus slot or a processor direct slot. This 32-bit architecture is called *Big ISA* because beyond the local bus slot, it's basically an ISA architecture — jumpers, DIP switches, and all. VLB slots are mostly proprietary and support expansion cards only from the PC's manufacturer.

✔ **Peripheral Component Interconnect (PCI) bus:** Introduced with the Pentium PC, PCI is a local bus architecture that supports either a 32- or 64-bit bus, which allows it to be used with both 486 and Pentium computers. The PCI bus is also processor independent because of a special bridging circuit contained on PCI boards. Its bus speed is 33 MHz, giving it much higher throughput than earlier cards. The PCI architecture and expansion slot, shown in Figure 7-2, also supports ISA and EISA cards. PCI cards are also Plug-and-Play, which means they automatically configure themselves to the appropriate IRQ, DMA, and I/O port addresses.

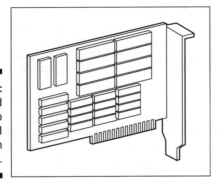

Figure 7-2:
A PCI card
plugs into
a PCI
expansion
slot.

✓ **Universal Serial Bus (USB):** A newly developed architecture that allows for the connection of up to 127 external serial devices. The USB technology is supported only on Pentium motherboards, where it's a built-in feature on most. It can also be added to motherboards that don't include it through a PCI slot. USB provides support for both low-volume serial I/O devices, such as a mouse or keyboard, and some higher volume devices, such as a modem, CD-ROM, or scanner. All USB devices are Plug-and-Play, and you can *hot-plug* or *hot-swap* them; that is, remove or insert them with the system power on.

For the exam, remember the bus width in bits for each bus structure, especially the ones that are 32 or more bits. Table 7-1 summarizes the basic characteristics of the bus structures discussed earlier.

Table 7-1	Bus Architecture Characteristics		
Bus	*Bus Width (bits)*	*Bus Speed (MHz)*	*How Configured*
8-bit	8	8	Jumpers and DIP switches
ISA	16	8	Jumpers and DIP switches
MCA	32	10	Software
EISA	32	8	Software
VL-Bus	32	Processor speed	Jumpers and DIP switches
PCI	32/64	Processor speed	Plug-and-Play

Upgrading notebooks and portables

The *PC Card,* or its original name *PCMCIA (Personal Computer Memory Card International Association) bus,* is used to add external devices to a notebook or hand-held computer. PC cards, which are about the size of a credit card, are used to add memory, modems, network interface cards, and even hard disk drives to portable computers. These cards slide into slots that are usually on the side of a notebook computer. Three standards exist for PC Cards:

- ✔ **Type I:** Cards that are 3.3mm thick, are used for memory additions, and have a single row of connectors.

- ✔ **Type II:** Cards that are 5mm thick and used primarily to add modems or network interface cards (NICs). Type II cards have two rows of connectors.

- ✔ **Type III:** Cards up to 10.5mm thick, which are often used to add an external hard disk to a notebook computer. Type III cards have four rows of connectors.

Plan on seeing a question on the type of devices supported by the PCMCIA (PC Card) types.

You can hot-swap PCMCIA, or PC Cards, which means you can remove or insert them with the system's power on.

Using SCSI

The *Small Computers System Interface* (*SCSI,* pronounced "skuzzy") is an interface, and not an architecture. It is used to connect a wide variety of both internal and external devices, such as CD-ROM drives, printers, and scanners. You can connect up to eight different SCSI devices in a daisy-chain fashion to the host adapter card installed in a SCSI slot. SCSI is not actually a bus architecture itself, but is actually a technology used for interfacing multiple devices through a single connection on the motherboard. SCSI adapter cards can themselves be PCI, VL-Bus, EISA, or ISA. Chapter 6 includes a more in-depth discussion on the SCSI interface and its various technologies.

Bus interfacing

Here is some additional background information to help you understand how bus architectures communicate with one another. Most 486 and Pentium systems support multiple bus interfaces. On these systems, some provision must be made to connect the different bus architectures and allow their devices to communicate with one another. This objective is accomplished through the use of a *bridge,* which connects two dissimilar systems. This term means the same thing in networking, as well. The most common bridge is the PCI-ISA bridge found in virtually all Pentium systems. As shown in Figure 7-3, the Windows 95 Device Manager displays a list of any bridges on a system, along with any other supported system devices, on its System Devices tab.

Local versus standard bus

A *local bus* provides a high-speed input/output bus structure alternative that puts production-critical devices "local" to main memory, the chipset, and the processor, or connected directly to the internal bus. This structure allows the devices to run at or near the processor's clock speed, which is usually much faster than the system's expansion bus clock speed. Local bus architecture is generally used for video cards, disk storage devices, and high-speed network interfaces. VESA Local Bus (VLB) and the Peripheral Component Interconnect Bus (PCI) are the most common local bus architectures.

The *standard bus* is used to connect slower devices, such as the mouse, a modem, a standard (8- or 16-bit) sound card, and low-speed network interfaces. It's also useful for compatibility issues with older 8-bit devices. On most PCs, the standard bus is the Industry Standard Architecture (ISA) bus.

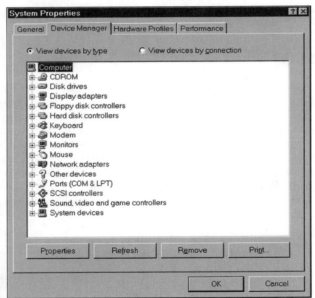

Figure 7-3:
The
Windows 95
Device
Manager.

Working with System Resources

In the realm of PC configuration, the word *system resources* refers to the mechanisms used to interface, communicate, and control individual device adapters and controllers, along with the serial, parallel, and mouse ports. All the PC's devices, including the motherboard, expansion cards, and peripherals, must share system resources.

For the exam, unfortunately, a bit of memorization is required in this area. You need to know which IRQs are used with which devices (see "Requesting an interrupt, or how to get IRQed"), and which devices are assigned to which I/O addresses (see "Using input/output (I/O) addresses"). You must also be familiar with the common uses of DMA channels (see "Accessing memory directly with DMA"). In other words, you must know the relationships of the system resources and the physical and logical devices (see "Naming the logical devices") to which they are assigned.

Requesting an interrupt, or how to get IRQed

An interrupt is a signal from one part of the computer (the requesting device) to the processor indicating that a service or special action be taken that only the CPU can perform. If you've ever dined at one of the large coffee shop chains, you've seen a form of interrupt processing in use. Usually, above the kitchen service window is a sign with a bank of numbers that can be individually lighted. When the very busy server has an order ready, the cook lights up the server's number on the sign. When the server is able to interrupt what he or she is doing, he or she serves the food or coffee to the customer.

The server number that alerts the server that an order is ready is much like the interrupt request used in PC interrupt processing. When a device needs the CPU to perform a task, transfer data from memory, issue an I/O, and so on, it signals the CPU using its IRQ line. Each device is assigned a specific IRQ number (much like our food server) so that the processor knows the device to which it needs to respond.

Interrupt requests are sent to a special system component, called an *interrupt controller,* which either is a separate chip on the motherboard or is incorporated into the chipset. The interrupt controller receives and verifies requests and passes them on to the processor.

Two interrupt controllers have been on PCs since the 286, each managing eight IRQ lines with each IRQ tied directly to a particular device. The two interrupt controllers are linked, or *cascaded,* through IRQ 2, which is set aside for this purpose. PC/XT systems that used IRQ 2 (they used only one set of eight IRQs) now use IRQ 9 instead.

Conflicting interrupts

For the exam, understand the ramification of IRQ conflicts and how to avoid them.

An IRQ is assigned to one specific device, and it just doesn't work to have more than one device assigned to an IRQ at one time. If two devices were assigned the same interrupt, the processor could become confused and send its response to the wrong device at possibly the wrong time, causing untold horrors to happen. Assigning two devices to the same IRQ creates an *IRQ conflict,* a serious system no-no.

An IRQ conflict can cause both devices to perform sporadically — in the best case — or not to work at all — in the worst case. Similar devices can share IRQs, but they can't be used at the same time. IRQs are assigned by the system BIOS during POST and the boot process. Reassigning an IRQ or changing the assigned IRQ of a device is done differently depending on the adapter card and perhaps the operating system. On most DOS (which includes Windows 3.*x*) machines, the IRQ of a device is set by either a jumper on its adapter card or through the use of proprietary installation software. On a Windows 95 PC, the IRQ can be changed through the Device Manager. Lab 7-1 lists the steps you use to access IRQ settings in Windows 95.

Lab 7-1	Accessing IRQs in Windows 95

1. **Right-click on the My Computer icon on the Desktop to display a shortcut menu.**

2. **Choose Properties from the menu to display the System Properties box.**

3. **Choose the Device Manager tab, click the "Computer" level icon, and then choose Properties.**

4. **From the System Resources display, choose the View Resources tab and click the Interrupt request (IRQ) option to display the IRQ settings, shown in Figure 7-4.**

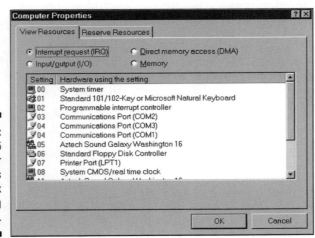

Figure 7-4:
Windows 95
Computer
Properties
dialog box
showing
IRQs.

In Windows 95, IRQ settings are changed or assigned in the properties of the individual device.

Assigning IRQs

For the exam, study Table 7-2 carefully. You should know the IRQ assignments for devices standard to all PCs.

Table 7-2		IRQ Assignments
IRQ#	**Default Use**	**Description**
0	System timer	Reserved interrupt for the internal system timer.
1	Keyboard controller	Reserved interrupt for the keyboard controller.
2	Bridge to IRQs 8–15	In cascaded interrupt systems, IRQ 2 is used as a link to IRQs 8 to 15, which means it's not available for general use; if needed by an older (IBM PC/XT) system, it's replaced by IRQ 9 (see "Requesting an interrupt, or how to get IRQed" for information on cascaded interrupts).
3	COM2 and COM4	Many modems are preconfigured for COM2 on IRQ 3. It's also used as the default interrupt for COM4.
4	COM1	Normally used by the serial mouse. It's also the default interrupt for COM3.
5	Sound card	Often the default IRQ for network interface cards. Also used by PC/XT systems for the hard disk drive and is the default interrupt for LPT2. Most sound cards are preset to IRQ 5.
6	Floppy disk controller	Reserved for the floppy disk controller.
7	LPT1	Although not reserved for it, this interrupt is normally used for the first parallel port and printer.
8	Real-time clock	Reserved for the real-time clock timer, which is used by software to track events to "real world" time. (IRQs 8–15 are not available in 8-bit systems.)
9	None	A popular choice for network interface cards, but it's generally available for any use. It does replace IRQ 2 in cascading interrupt systems, so it should not be used if IRQ 2 is in use.

(continued)

Table 7-2 *(continued)*

IRQ#	Default Use	Description
10	None	Generally available and unencumbered because no other devices are vying for it.
11	None	Often used by the SCSI host adapter if present, but normally this line is open and available. Some PCI video cards and IDE sound cards try to use IRQ 11.
12	Motherboard mouse (PS/2) connector	On motherboards supporting a PS/2 mouse (mini-DIN connection on the motherboard), this IRQ is reserved for the PS/2 mouse. A PS/2 mouse on this interrupt frees up IRQ 4 (and COM1) for other uses. Otherwise, this IRQ is available.
13	Math coprocessor or floating point unit	Reserved for the integrated floating point unit (386DX and later) or a math coprocessor (386SX and earlier).
14	Primary IDE adapter	Reserved for the primary IDE controller, which controls the first two IDE (ATA) disk drives. On PCs with no IDE devices, it can be reassigned in the BIOS setup for other uses.
15	Secondary IDE adapter	Reserved for a secondary IDE controller, if present. Can be reassigned in BIOS.

Using input/output (I/O) addresses

For the exam, remember the starting I/O address for devices common to all PCs. Every device must have a unique address, without exception, so you won't find trick questions in this area.

Every device in the PC uses *input/output addresses* (called I/O addresses or port addresses). The address in the I/O address points to the location in memory that's assigned to a specific device to use for exchanging information between itself and the rest of the PC. The I/O address is a device's internal post office box number.

All devices have an I/O address assigned to them along with a segment of memory to hold messages and data. The size of the memory segment varies with the amount of data a device needs to pass on to other devices, but in general, the memory segment assigned to a device ranges from 1 to 32 bytes, with 4, 8, or 16 bytes being common. These areas of memory allow a device to do its work without worrying about what other devices or the processor may be doing.

For example, when a modem receives data, it wants to pass the data along to the PC for processing, but where can the data be put? The modem writes the data to the I/O address of the COM port to which the modem is attached, and when the CPU is ready to process this data, it knows right where to look. This process of using I/O addresses to complete input/output operations is called *memory-mapped I/O*.

I/O addresses are expressed in hexadecimal and written as 3F8h. The lowercase "h" indicates it's a hexadecimal address. When working with I/O addresses, it's not important that you can determine the size of the memory segment assigned or even if you can decipher the hex address itself. Just remember these addresses are in hexadecimal and ignore the *h*.

For the exam, memorize only the starting addresses of devices that are common to all PCs, such as the keyboard, LPT1, and COM1.

Table 7-3 lists many, but not all, of the common I/O address assignments used in PC systems.

Table 7-3	Common I/O Address Assignments
I/O Address Range	*Device or Port Commonly Assigned*
000-00Fh	DMA channels 0–3 controller
020-021h	IRQ 0–7 interrupt controller
060h, 061h	Keyboard
0F0-0FFh	Math coprocessor
130-14Fh	SCSI host adapter
170-177h	Secondary hard disk controller
1F0-1F7h	Primary hard disk controller
200-207h	Game port
220-22Fh	Sound cards
278-27Fh	LPT2 or LPT3
2E8-2EFh	COM4
2F8-2FFh	COM2

(continued)

Table 7-3 *(continued)*

I/O Address Range	Device or Port Commonly Assigned
300-30Fh	Network cards
3B0-3BBh	VGA video adapter
3C0-3DFh	VGA video adapter
378-37Fh	LPT1 or LPT2
3E8-3EFh	COM3
3F0-3F7h	Primary disk adapter
3F8-3FFh	COM1

You can view I/O address assignments on a PC in Windows 95 using the Device Manager's Computer Properties dialog box, shown in Figure 7-5.

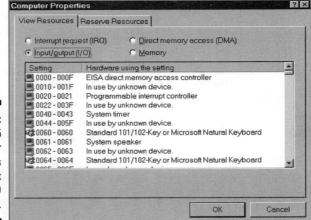

Figure 7-5: Windows 95 Computer Properties dialog box showing I/O addresses.

Accessing memory directly with DMA

A *direct memory access* (DMA) channel allows a device to bypass the processor to directly access memory. Those devices with a DMA channel assignment gain the advantage of faster data transfers that do not have to pass through the CPU. DMA use is common in some disk drives, tape backup drives, and sound cards. One drawback to using DMA is that while the DMA device is working faster, the CPU may be put on hold, slowing everything else, until the DMA data transfer is complete.

Table 7-4 lists common DMA channel usage.

Table 7-4	DMA Channel Assignments
DMA Channel	*Assignment*
0	DRAM refresh
1	Available
2	Floppy disk controller
3	Available
4	Link to second DMA controller
5	Available
6	Available
7	Available

Channels 0 through 3 are generally available in all PCs, but channels 4 through 7 are available only in 286 and later systems. Each group of four channels has its own DMA controller chip that services its requests. DMA channel assignments are made through the BIOS setup utility, with the dedicated configuration software of a device, or with DIP switches or jumpers on the device adapter card.

You can view DMA channel assignments in Windows 95 using the Device Manager's Computer Properties dialog box, shown in Figure 7-6.

Figure 7-6:
Windows 95
Computer
Properties
dialog box
showing
DMA.

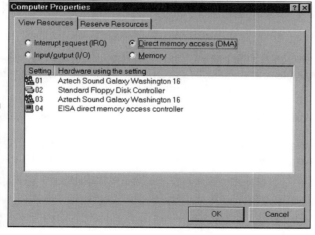

To view DMA channel assignments, follow these steps:

1. **Select My Computer from the Desktop.**
2. **Use the right mouse button to display the shortcut menu and choose Properties.**
3. **Choose the Device Manager tab.**
4. **Highlight Computer at the top of the device hierarchy shown, and click Properties.**
5. **Choose Direct Memory Access (DMA) to display the channel assignments on your system.**

You can also use these steps to view the status of the other system resources: interrupt request (IRQ), I/O address, and memory assignments.

Naming the logical devices

Many devices are assigned both a physical address and a logical name. Logical device names are assigned to serial ports (which are given the logical names COM1 to COM4) and parallel ports (LPT1 and LPT2). Logical names eliminate the need for software to use what could be the moving target of I/O addresses.

Logical device names are assigned during the POST process by the system BIOS. The BIOS searches the I/O addresses for devices in a preset order and assigns them a logical name in numerical order each time the system boots.

Table 7-5 lists the default assignments for COM and LPT ports.

Of the tables shown in this chapter, the following table may be the best one to review right before the exam. It's brief and holds most of the information about logical devices you should memorize for the test.

Unfortunately, to see logical device assignments in Windows 95, you must view each device separately. From the Device Manager dialog box, select the logical device from the device hierarchy and choose the Resources tab to see the device's system resource assignments, as shown in Figure 7-7.

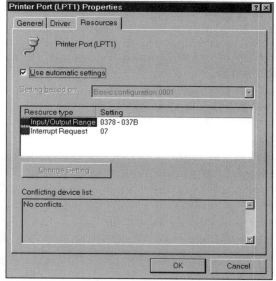

Figure 7-7:
Windows 95
Device
Manager
dialog box
showing
device
resources.

Table 7-5	Logical Device Name Assignments	
Port	*I/O Address*	*Default IRQ*
COM1	3F8-3FFh	4
COM2	2F8-2FFh	3
COM3	3E8-3EFh	4
COM4	2E8-2EFh	3
LPT1	378-37Fh	7
LPT2	278-27Fh	5

One way to remember at least one IRQ assignment is to add the 1 from
COM1 to the 3 from COM3 to get the 4 from IRQ4. Yes, this memory aid is
fairly complicated, and perhaps convoluted, but it worked for me.

Prep Test

1 The default I/O address for COM1 is

A ○ 2F8-2FFh

B ○ 3F8-3FFh

C ○ 378-37Fh

D ○ 3F0-3F7H

2 The first 32-bit bus was

A ○ PCI

B ○ EISA

C ○ MCA

D ○ VESA

3 A PC has a sound card that locks up whenever the parallel tape backup unit is used on the system. What is most likely the problem?

A ○ A DMA channel conflict

B ○ An IRQ conflict

C ○ The sound card is installed in an incompatible bus slot

D ○ There is no system problem other than a defective sound card

4 To automatically configure a PnP device, a system must have all the following except

A ○ A PnP BIOS

B ○ PnP hardware devices

C ○ A PnP OS

D ○ A PCI system bus

5 COM1 normally uses which IRQ?

A ○ IRQ 2

B ○ IRQ 3

C ○ IRQ 4

D ○ IRQ 5

6 The CPU uses an IRQ to

A ○ Control devices attached to the system
B ○ Generate a log file containing interrupt requests
C ○ Identify a peripheral and find the software that controls it
D ○ Protect the system from hardware device failures

7 What IRQ is often used for LPT1?

A ○ IRQ 2
B ○ IRQ 10
C ○ IRQ 7
D ○ IRQ 5

8 What should you do about an IRQ conflict?

A ○ Reassign the device IRQ settings using the best appropriate method.
B ○ Nothing, as long as the I/O addresses of the devices aren't in conflict.
C ○ Nothing, as long as the devices are never used at the same time.
D ○ Always refer to the devices by their logical device names.

9 Bus clock speed refers to

A ○ The external speed of the CPU
B ○ The internal speed of the CPU
C ○ The speed of the hard drive
D ○ The speed at which data on the bus moves

10 A PCMCIA hard drive fits in which type of slot?

A ○ Type I
B ○ Type II
C ○ Type III
D ○ Type IV

Answers

1 B. See "Using input/output (I/O) addresses"

2 C. Micro-Channel Architecture was the first 32-bit expansion bus architecture. *Review "Plugging into the expansion bus."*

3 B. When two devices are directly affecting how each other works, it most likely is a system resource conflict, and very likely an IRQ conflict. *Check out "Conflicting interrupts."*

4 D. Plug-and-Play devices are available in just about every bus architecture. All PCI devices are Plug-and Play, but not all Plug-and-Play devices are PCI. *See "Fun with Plug-and-Play."*

5 C. IRQ 4 is the default IRQ assignment for COM1. *Review "Assigning IRQs."*

6 A. Interrupts and IRQs (interrupt requests) are used by the processor to communicate and control the activities of peripheral devices. *Look at "Requesting an interrupt, or how to get IRQed."*

7 C. LPT1 (the first parallel port) is virtually always assigned IRQ 7. *See "Assigning IRQs."*

8 A. IRQ assignments can be made, depending on the device and operating system through a jumper on the card, installation software for the device, or through the operating system (Windows 95). *Check out "Conflicting interrupts."*

9 D. The bus clock controls the transfer rate of data on the data bus. *Review "Bus structures."*

10 C. Type I PCMCIA (PC Card) cards are used to install RAM, Type II cards are used to install a modem or network card, and Type III cards are used to install disk drives. *Take a look at "Upgrading notebooks and portables."*

Chapter 8

Power

Exam Objectives

▶ Recognizing PC power supply terms, concepts, and functions

▶ Explaining PC power supply safety procedures

▶ Detecting common PC power supply problems

*O*ne of my favorite you-never-can-tell stories is the "Case of the Fibbing Sibling." Anyone who has had the pleasure of being a brother or a sister has experienced the "Not me's." This happens when your loving sibling has done something worthy of parental consternation and when asked about it says, "Not me!" This translates to mean that *you,* the innocent bystander, must have done it.

This story reminds me of a power supply that was also the fibbing sibling. A brand-new computer gave a POST disk drive error right out of the box. A new disk drive was sent for and installed. When the system was rebooted, it had the same error. The hard disk cables were replaced, but to no avail. The motherboard was replaced, and the system finally booted. However, a few days later the problem returned. Eventually, with no other parts to swap, the power supply was replaced. End of problem.

The power supply has one of the highest failure rates of any PC component. In spite of this, it's often the last component suspected for a problem. A faulty power supply or weak battery can cause untold damage to the computer and, as the preceding story relates, can send the repair technician on a wild goose chase.

Quick Assessment

Recognizing power supply concepts & functions

1 The PC power supply converts _____ power into _____ power.

2 The power supply also contains the main cooling _____ of the PC.

3 The PC power supply generates five voltages: _____, _____, _____, _____, and _____.

4 The PC power supply's output is measured in _____.

Describing power supply safety procedures

5 A(n) _____ happens when disturbances create a temporary high-voltage burst that travels down the power line.

6 _____ are small variations in the voltage of the power line.

7 A _____ reduces power problems by absorbing spikes and smoothing line noise.

8 UPS stands for _____.

9 A Green Star device reduces its power consumption by _____ in sleep mode.

Detecting common power supply problems

10 During the POST processing, an error code of 021 indicates a _____ error.

Answers

1 *AC, DC.* See "Power to the 'Puter' and "Internal power."

2 *Fan.* Study "Cooling it."

3 *+5V, −5V, +12V, −12V, +3.3V.* See "Converting power."

4 *Watts.* Review "The impact of moving up on the power supply."

5 *Power surge.* Look at "The paradox of external power."

6 *Line noise.* Review "The paradox of external power."

7 *Surge suppressor.* Check out "Suppressing the surge."

8 *Uninterruptable power supply.* Take a gander at "Hedging your bet."

9 *99 percent.* See "Saving the planet."

10 *Power supply, or Power Good signal.* Review "Diagnosing POST problems."

Power to the 'Puter

In spite of the power supply's importance, you won't find many questions on the A+ exam specifically about it. When you boil it down, all it does is supply power and cool the case. However, expect questions on system voltages, the cooling system, surge suppressors, UPCs, and why they are needed. Two basic facts of computer power are that the computer runs on 5 to 12 volts of direct current (DC) power internally, and the electrical outlet on the wall supplies alternating current (AC) at about 110 to 115 volts. The PC's power supply bridges these obviously incompatible worlds by converting raging AC power from the wall into the docile DC power used by the computer.

Obviously, the computer can't run without a power supply, which supplies power to all the components in the computer. It also regulates incoming power voltage to eliminate the spikes and electrical noise common to most electrical systems. It is also the main part of the cooling system.

To the PC power supply, two types of power exist: external and internal.

The paradox of external power

External power, which comes from your home or office wall outlet, is the power everyone tends to take for granted — as long as it's there, it's fine. You may be surprised at the number of problems external power can have: line noise, spikes, surges, brownouts, and blackouts. Most of these problems go unnoticed, because they are usually small enough that the computer's power supply can deal with them (all except a blackout, of course). But, these power problems can lead to reliability problems in your computer.

When you plug your computer directly into the wall socket, you are subjecting your computer to several problems. Some of these problems your computer can handle, but over time, even unnoticed problems can take their toll and result in major damage. You should know the kinds of problems that the PC can experience from external power for the test. These problems are

> ✔ **Line noise:** Consists of small variations in the voltage of the power line. A small amount of line noise is normal in just about every system, and all but the very cheapest power supplies can handle it. If you have the PC plugged into its own circuit (unshared line), you should have little trouble from line noise. However, if your computer shares an extension cord with the pop machine or its circuit with a megaton air conditioner, line noise is a certainty, and it will soon cause some major problems. Usually, the power-regulating circuits in your power supply burn out, and any line noise passes through to the motherboard or disk drives.

✔ **Power surges:** A power spike or overvoltage happens when disturbances, such as distant lightning strikes or other anomalies in the electrical supply grid, create a voltage spike that travels down the line and to your wall plugs. The surge lasts only a few thousandths of a second, but that's plenty of time for the voltage to increase to 1,000 volts or higher. High voltage spikes degrade the power supply. Multiple surges over time can destroy it.

✔ **Brownouts:** Also known as undervoltage, a brownout is the opposite of a power surge and happens when a sudden dip occurs in the power line voltage. A brownout usually doesn't last too long, but it can. Usually, the power level drops below normal levels for a time and then returns to normal. Brownouts are extremely common during periods of heavy load on the electrical system, such as hot afternoons or cold mornings. The reduced voltage level causes many devices to run slower than normal or malfunction in other ways.

✔ **Blackouts:** Occur when the power fails completely. The problems caused by a blackout are usually more frustrating than damaging, but the fluctuation of power surrounding a blackout can harm your system. If you're in the middle of a long document (that you hadn't yet saved), or were defragmenting or fixing other hard disk problems (and the allocation tables weren't completely rebuilt) when the power goes out — you very likely have problems. More often, though, the damage occurs when the power returns suddenly, usually in the form of a huge spike.

✔ **Lightning strikes:** This biggest spike delivers a million volts or more. I don't need to tell you what would happen if one were to hit your home or office directly. However, a strike even in your vicinity can result in a very high voltage spike. I have witnessed what a lightning strike can do to a building. Everything plugged in was completed destroyed or melted down: computers, copiers, fax machines, telephones, and more.

Internal power

The PC runs on DC. The computer's power supply converts AC power into the various DC voltages and signals used by the PC's components and circuits. The computer power supply, like that shown in Figure 8-1, is a switching power supply. It reduces the 110V incoming voltage to the 3.3V, 5V, and 12V charges used by the PC by switching the power charge off and on. In a very simplified explanation, you get 20 watts from a 100-watt signal by leaving it on 20 percent of the time and off 80 percent of the time. In this way, only the amount of power needed is generated.

The PC power supply only functions when it has demand. It has to know how much power to produce from the switching process used to generate its DC voltages. A power supply without some demand will not function properly and may even damage itself. Never "test" a power supply without connecting it to at least one 12V line — for example, a disk drive.

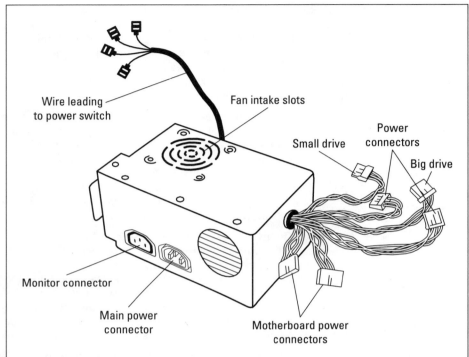

Figure 8-1:
A computer
power
supply.

Protecting Against Power Evils

There are certainly ways you can fight back against the evils of external power. In fact, several levels of protection exist, ranging from none to too much, that you can use to protect your computer system from power problems. It's all in how much you want to spend, with costs ranging up to several hundred dollars or more.

For the A+ exam, be very familiar with the benefits and limitations of the various types of power protection devices described in this section. The exam has few trick questions, but one that you might look for is, "Which of these devices provide surge suppression?" The answer is that almost every one of these devices provides surge suppression.

Two types of damage can be done to the PC by electrical forces: catastrophic and degradation. Catastrophic damage is when the device is destroyed all at once in a single event. Degradation is when a device is damaged over a period of instances and begins to fail or has intermittent problems.

In the following section, I discuss some of the ways you can practice safe power.

Never, never, never, cut the grounding pin off an PC power plug cord. This is like looking the power monster in the face and smugly daring it to bite you.

Suppressing the surge

Most users plug their computers into a power strip or surge suppressor. These devices, which provide protective levels ranging from psychological to pretty good, are generally available. At the psychological level is the less-than-ten-dollars power strip, which is not much more than a fancy extension cord. At the pretty-good level are full surge suppressors that include line conditioning. You will see the following line so often in the discussion on power protection that you will think it is my mantra, but — typically, the more you pay, the better the protection.

The primary component of a surge suppressor is a Metal Oxide Varistor (MOV). The MOV protects the computer by taking the hit from voltage spikes. The problem with MOV is that one big spike or an accumulation of small surges over time can knock it out. Some surge suppressors have a light to indicate that the MOV is still all right.

A surge suppressor reduces power problems by absorbing spikes and surges and by smoothing out line noise (this is called line conditioning). Surge suppressors at the high end of the cost range offer more protection, but some protection is always better than none. Unfortunately, how much protection you have really depends on how much you pay.

Consider two main features when choosing a surge suppressor: *clamping voltage* and *clamping speed.* Clamping voltage is the voltage at which the suppressor begins to protect the computer. Clamping speed is the time lapse before the protection begins, or how much time elapses between detection and protection. Know this for the test.

Not all surge suppressors include line conditioning. Check the box and any literature carefully when buying one.

Here are some other things to look for (familiarize yourself with the units of measures — Joules, decibels, and watts — used in the following descriptions):

✔ **Energy Absorption:** Surge suppressors are rated in Joules, which measures their capability to absorb energy. The higher the rating, the better the protection: 200 Joules is basic protection, 400 is good protection, and 600 is superior protection. You need to be familar with Joules for the test.

- ✔ **Line Conditioning:** The line conditioning capability of a surge suppressor is measured in decibels. The more decibels of noise reduction, the better the line conditioning.

- ✔ **Protection Indicators:** If you have a surge suppressor, then you are familiar with the LED that indicates you are protected. Unfortunately, how reliable the indicator is depends on how much you paid. Less-expensive units will absorb enough power over time to degrade them. However, one thing is for sure — if the LED is out, get a new suppressor. You have no way of knowing whether you're protected if a suppressor has no indicator.

- ✔ **Levels of Protection:** Surge suppressors have three levels of protection that indicate the maximum number of watts the suppressor allows to pass through to anything plugged into it. The standard ratings are 330 (best), 400 (better), and 500 (good).

Underwriters Laboratories (UL) has established a standard (UL 1449) for surge suppressors. A suppressor with UL approval has met this standard and should protect your system.

Conditioning the line

Line conditioners filter the power stream to eliminate line noise. Because they are usually expensive, few PC users use a true line conditioner, preferring to purchase this capability in other devices, such as a surge suppressor.

Protecting the back door

A connection to the computer that most people forget when securing the power is the telephone cord connected to the internal modem. In the event of an electrical storm or lightning strike, power can surge up the telephone lines just as mean, fast, and nasty as on the power lines. When installing a surge protector, be sure it has phone-line protection. Another way to get this protection is to install a separate phone/modem isolator, an inexpensive device you can buy at any electronics or computer store. This may not be on the test, but you should know it anyway.

Hedging your bet

An uninterruptable power supply (UPS) tries to live up to its name by providing a constant (uninterrupted) power stream to the computer. Under normal conditions, it's a surge protector that can also handle brownout conditions. When the power drops below a certain level or is disrupted completely, the UPS kicks in and provides power for a certain number of minutes, or even hours in some cases. Expect a question or two on UPSs.

Two types of UPS units are available: standby and in-line. All UPS units have two sets of circuits. One side is the AC circuit that, in effect, is an expensive surge suppressor. The other side is the battery and DC to AC conversion. Yes, that's right — DC to AC conversion. The batteries store a DC charge that must be converted to AC because that's what the PC expects.

The standby and in-line differ in the following ways:

- ✔ The standby UPS operates normally from its AC side. When the power drops, it switches over to its battery backup side.
- ✔ The in-line UPS operates normally from its DC or battery backup side. The AC side is only used in the event of a problem with the battery-powered circuits.

UPS units are often confused with a standby power supply (SPS), or battery backup, which only supplies power when none is available and has no power-conditioning abilities.

Never plug a laser printer into a conventional PC UPS. Laser printers draw a tremendous amount of power at startup and few UPS units have enough power to handle the demand.

Saving the planet

The A+ exam tests you on environmental issues surrounding the PC and its peripherals, including the hazards and safeguards.

To reduce the amount of electricity consumed by computers, the U.S. Environmental Protection Agency (EPA) established guidelines for energy efficiency under a program called U.S. Green Star, also known as Energy Star. On Green Star systems, the power supply works with the computer's components and some peripherals to reduce the power they use when idle.

Green Star devices have a standby program that puts them into sleep mode after the device has been idle for a certain period of time. In sleep mode, the device reduces 99 percent of its power consumption and uses no more than 30 watts of power.

The Power Supply

This section concentrates on the first exam objective listed at the beginning of the chapter: recognizing PC power supply terms, concepts, and functions. There are a few questions you should expect on the test, which are covered in this section.

The power supply is a black or silver box with a fan inside and cables coming out of it. It's located either at the back of a desktop case or at the top of a tower or mini-tower case. The power supply is distinctive because of its big yellow warning label with scary-looking symbols and warnings. The purpose of this label is to warn you not to try to fix a power supply.

A caution sticker (you'll know it — it says "Caution") on an electric or electronic device in a PC alerts you to possible equipment damage. A warning label (says "Warning" and has lightning bolts, a skull and crossbones, or the like) alerts you to possible bodily injury.

Just to quench your curiosity, inside the power supply, one part in particular should keep you out: a 1000 microfarad capacitor. Capacitors store electricity, even when the power is off. This particular capacitor performs line conditioning by absorbing too much power and replacing missing power. If you were to touch it, it would shock you — potentially with bodily harm or worse. Because you can buy a new power supply in the range of $25 to $80, I'm not sure it's worth the risk to open up the power supply to try to fix it. A good quality power supply should last for years, providing the computer with stable electrical current, assuming that it has been protected adequately. On the other hand, a low quality, faulty, or overloaded power supply can cause all kinds of problems in a system. A bad power supply can cause hard disks to develop bad sectors and affect memory to cause what seem like software bugs — problems that are hard to pin on the power supply.

Anatomy of the power supply

Be familiar with the parts of the power supply for the exam, especially the passthrough connector.

The features you have access to on the outside of the power supply are incredibly standard even between form factors. The primary power supply components are

- **Power cord:** I think you know what this is and for what it is used.
- **Passthrough connectors:** Located on the back of the power supply. In the past, these connectors were used primarily to plug a monitor into the power supply, which enables you to turn the monitor on and off with the computer's power switch.
- **Power switch:** On older PCs, this switch extended through the case wall from the power supply on a back corner of the PC. More recently, the power switch is now on the front of the case. In the newer ATX power supply, the power switch works differently altogether. Instead of a physical on/off switch connected directly to the power supply, the switch is now electronic. You don't so much turn on or off the computer as you request the motherboard to do it.

> ✔ **110V/220V Selector switch:** Allows you to select between the two voltages. If a power supply has one, be sure that it's set correctly. This switch comes in handy when you jaunt over to Europe with your PC.

When the monitor is plugged into the power supply's passthrough connector, it's not powered by the PC's internal power supply. You have only gained the convenience of turning the monitor on and off with the PC.

Cooling it

The power supply also contains the main cooling fan that controls air flow through the PC case. The power supply fan is the most important part of a PC's cooling system. Air is forced to flow through the computer case and over the motherboard and electronic components, which generate heat as they work. Any interruption to the air flow can cause sensitive components to degrade or fail. The power supply fan should be kept clean and clear.

Only with the case closed and intact will the PC cooling system function at its optimum.

If a power supply's wattage rating is sufficient to supply the computer's electrical requirements, the fan should be adequate to handle the computer's cooling needs, although Pentium series processors still require additional cooling and heat sinks of their own.

As I expand on later in this chapter, two popular form factors for power supplies exist: the Baby AT and the ATX. I bring up form factors here only because these two types of power supplies cool the system differently.

> ✔ The Baby AT, which has been the standard up until the past year or two, cools the system by pulling air out of the case and blowing it out through the fan. You can feel the air blowing out of the fan on this type of power supply. If you've ever opened up an old PC AT computer that has been in use for a while without the case being opened, you know firsthand one of the primary problems with this type of cooling. Room dust, smoke, chalk in school settings, and all else is sucked into the computer to accumulate on grills, wires, components, and so on. This buildup can impact the cooling system's capability to cool the motherboard and drives by restricting the air flow.

> ✔ The ATX form of power supply sucks air into the case. This method helps to keep the case clean by pressurizing the inside of the case. The power supply is situated on the board so that air blows straight onto the processor. This is meant to eliminate the need for a CPU fan, but it is a good idea to always use a CPU fan.

In either case, all expansion slot filler slides should be in place and the case should be in place and intact to allow the cooling system to do its job.

The impact of moving up on the power supply

A PC's power supply directly controls its expandability. Every power supply has a maximum power demand, expressed in watts, that it can support. When you upgrade a PC by adding an additional drive, replacing the motherboard, or installing a new processor, the responsibility falls on the power supply to produce the power the PC now requires. I mention earlier in this chapter the problems that come with an overloaded power supply.

Power supplies are rated in watts capacity, which should not be confused with watts used. A 250-watt power supply has the capacity to convert up to 250 watts of power, but if its system only demands 100 watts, then it only converts 100 watts. You can't burn up a system with a high wattage power supply; it doesn't work that way. However, it will run up your electric bill.

Converting power

What the power supply does is basically simple: It converts AC to DC. Any number of devices exist to help convert currents one way or another, for example, the power converter I plug into my van's dashboard so my kids can watch videotapes as we motor along. Another type allows my portable CD player to plug into the wall when the batteries are dead. If only it were that simple for the computer power supply. The PC power supply must provide a variety of voltages at different strengths and manage some power-related signals for the motherboard.

Know this stuff for the test. The power supply provides the following voltages to the motherboard and drives:

- ✔ **+5V:** The standard voltage of motherboards for all 8086, 286, 386, 486 processors below 100 MHz, and peripheral boards.

- ✔ **+12V:** Used primarily for disk drive motors and similar devices. Modern motherboards pass this voltage to ISA bus expansion slots.

- ✔ **–5V and –12V:** Included in most power supplies for compatibility with older systems. Most modern motherboards don't use either of these voltages. Power supplies that produce these values do so at very low (less than 1) amperage. Check the label on your power supply.

- ✔ **+3.3V:** A 486 100 MHz or above, and all Pentium, Pentium Pro, and equivalent chips run at 3.3V (some use even lower voltages internally). Upgraded motherboards must convert the 5V signal from the power supply into 3.3V for the processor, requiring a voltage regulator on the motherboard. Newer power supplies provide the 3.3V power for the CPU directly.

Concentrate on which voltages are used with which type of devices. For example, disk drives use the +12V lines, the Pentium processor uses 3.3V, and the other lines (+/–5V and –12V lines) are primarily used for backward compatibility.

Fitting it in the box

Form factor refers to the shape and dimensions of a device. PC cases are designed to hold a particular power supply form factor. The power supply must match the designed form factor of the case as well as match its power to the motherboard. The form factor of a power supply is not often an issue except for upgrades and build-your-owns, because the power supply is usually purchased already installed in the case. The form factor of the case is usually more of an issue.

In general, the form factors of the motherboard are the same for the case and the power supply. The most common form factors used today are the Baby AT, the oldest standard that has been used for PCs until recently, and the ATX, the newest form factor.

The Baby AT is what most people think of as the standard desktop case and power supply. It will be around for quite some time, given the number of PCs in use with this form factor. The ATX form factor has essentially replaced the Baby AT for new systems.

The ATX power supply differs from the Baby AT power supply in three primary ways:

- ATX has additional voltage and power lines that are used to signal and control the power supply.

- The fan blows into the case instead of out like the Baby AT, which helps keep the case clean.

- The ATX power supply turns on and off with electronic signaling and not a physical power switch. It can also be switched on and off by software, such as a Windows shutdown.

Connecting the Power

Power questions relating to the motherboard, disk drives, and other devices are on the test. Some of these questions may appear to be about the device but will, in fact, be power and power connection questions. Review this section carefully.

The bundles of wire hanging out of the power supply are what the power supply is all about. They are the lines that carry juice to the various parts of the computer. Depending on the form factor, four or five bundles of wire are coming from the power supply.

Always be positive that the power supply is unplugged by removing its power cord from its back before you attach its connectors inside the PC.

Motherboard connectors

Don't expect to see any questions on the A+ exam on the specific pinouts of power supply connectors. In fact, any questions on the test dealing specifically with the power supply and the motherboard together refer to the older AT or Baby AT form factors.

You can definitely tell which form factor you have by the motherboard power connectors. The Baby AT power supply has two 6-wire connectors, and the ATX has a single 20-wire keyed connector.

✔ **Baby AT:** The two connectors of the Baby AT power supply attach to the motherboard right next to each other. Sometimes, the connector blocks are labeled P8 and P9, the plug positions of their mates on the motherboard. But you're still left with the dilemma of which side is 8 and which is 9, and they look almost identical.

The P8 and P9 connectors are oriented correctly if all four of the black wires, or grounds, (two on each plug) are together in the middle. Any other orientation will likely damage the motherboard.

✔ **ATX:** The ATX power supply must be used with an ATX motherboard. Together, they eliminate any confusion with the power connection with a single 20-wire keyed connector. A keyed connector usually has a prong, lip, or finger that prevents it from being connected incorrectly. The ATX power supply also has power connectors for the front panel.

The ATX power supply is always on. Power is supplied to the motherboard even when the system power is off. Always disconnect the power cord from the back of the case before working on one.

Drive power connectors

Most power supplies have either three or four four-wire power connectors for internal drives. Two types and sizes of connectors exist and are easy to tell apart, as shown in Figure 8-2. The larger plug, called a Molex connector, is used to connect almost all hard drives, CD-ROM drives, and 5$\frac{1}{4}$-inch floppy drives. The smaller plug, a Berg connector, is used by 3$\frac{1}{2}$-inch floppy drives and a few others. These connectors are keyed, so they can't be installed backward, try as I might.

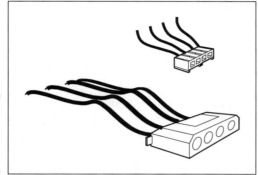

Figure 8-2:
Power
supply drive
connectors.

Troubleshooting the Power Supply

Although I don't recall any questions about troubleshooting the power supply on the tests, that doesn't mean there won't be any. At least review this section to remind yourself of the situations mentioned.

The power supply is obviously a very important component of the PC, but did you know that it's also the one most likely to fail? Day in and day out it suffers the slings and arrows of mean and nasty electrical power, sacrificing itself for the good of your computer. A recent study shows that, on average, the common workstation or desktop PC suffers over 120 power "events" every month. Not surprisingly, it can develop problems.

Three conditions exist in which you need to check out a power supply:

✔ After switching on the PC's power, nothing happens.

Solution: The first problem is the easiest to diagnose. After determining that the power cord is plugged into the power supply, the power cord is plugged into the surge suppressor, the surge suppressor switch is on and working properly, and power is available at the wall plug, you know that either the power switch is bad or the power supply itself has completely failed. In either case, you should replace the power supply.

Never stick anything into the fan to try to get it to rotate. This approach does not work, and it's way beyond dangerous.

✔ You've tried everything else to track down an intermittent problem to no avail. Like the fibbing sibling, the power supply can be the real culprit in a power-related failure. However, determining the power-related part may prove difficult.

Solution: How can you tell whether the power supply is going bad? You can look for a number of symptoms: overheating, occasional boot failures or errors, frequent parity errors, noisy operation, or mild electrical shocks when you touch the case.

If you ever receive a shock, other than ESD, when touching the case, you have power supply problems of the first magnitude — replace the power supply immediately!

✔ You're planning a big upgrade (new motherboard, new hard drive, DVD, and more), and you're worried that your power supply may be too weak to handle the new load.

   Solution: When upgrading, remember that power supplies are rated by the wattage they produce. You can currently get from 100 to 600 watt units today. Unless you're building a super server with quad Pentium IIs and four or five internal SCSI drives, a power supply rated between 230 to 300 watts should work well for most average systems.

A quick and easy way to troubleshoot a computer power supply is to put your hand in front of the cooling fan. If it is not blowing out air, chances are the power supply is bad, unless it is an ATX form factor case, in which case the system board may have a bad power switch.

To unplug or not to unplug

The exam may include a question on whether you should unplug the computer before working on it. My advice follows:

✔ If no particular form factor is mentioned, assume it to be the AT or Baby AT form factors and answer that the PC should be plugged in when working on it (which provides a positive ground). This is most likely the question you will be asked on the current test.

✔ If the ATX form factor is mentioned specifically, then the PC should be unplugged when you're working on it. ATX motherboards are hot — they have power going to them even when the power supply is powered off. This is likely the answer on the next version of the test.

Diagnosing POST problems

You may run into situational questions on the Core exam that require you to know which FRU is involved from certain types of symptoms. Here are a few symptoms that indicate a power supply problem:

✔ The power light on the front panel is off.

✔ The power supply fan isn't operating.

✔ The computer sounds either a continuous beep or doesn't beep at all.

✔ The computer sounds a repeating short beep.

✔ The computer displays either a POST error in the 020–029 series (Power Good signal error) or a parity error.

Taking preventive measures

A number of actions can lengthen the life of a power supply. Many are
environmental, some require equipment, and some are just plain common
sense. They are

- Run the computer in a cool, moderately humid environment. The cooler
  the air entering the fan, the better. The power supply produces heat
  like all other transformers. Use an air-conditioned room if possible.

- Either reduce the amount of dust and smoke in the air around the
  computer, or plan to clean it often. Blow the dust bunnies off of the fan
  and power supply grills frequently by using compressed air. It can't
  hurt to do the same for the inside of the case once in a while either.

- Use a surge protector, or better yet, a true line conditioner.

Prep Test

1 A device that can supply backup power to a PC when the electricity fails and provides for line conditioning as well is called a(n)

- A ○ SPS
- B ○ UPS
- C ○ Surge suppressor
- D ○ Line conditioner

2 A device that protects a PC against overvoltage is called a

- A ○ UPS
- B ○ Power conditioner
- C ○ Surge suppressor
- D ○ All the above

3 While you repair a PC, it should be

- A ○ Plugged in
- B ○ Unplugged
- C ○ Turned on
- D ○ None of the above

4 A PC conforming to the Green Star standard reduces what percentage of its power consumption in Sleep mode?

- A ○ 99
- B ○ 90
- C ○ 92
- D ○ 96

5 What electronic component in the PC power supply absorbs most power spikes?

- A ○ Resistors
- B ○ Varistors
- C ○ Coils
- D ○ Capacitors

6 What are two important factors to consider when selecting a surge suppressor?

- A ○ Switching rate and Joules dispersed
- B ○ Switching speed and clamping speed
- C ○ Clamping speed and clamping voltage
- D ○ Joules dispersed and wattage

7 Which of the following devices should not be connected to a UPS?

    A ◯ A laser printer.

    B ◯ A monitor.

    C ◯ A PC power supply.

    D ◯ You can connect any device to a UPS.

8 When the electrical power system fails completely, it's called a

    A ◯ Brownout

    B ◯ Blackout

    C ◯ Overvoltage

    D ◯ Undervoltage

9 A power supply failure detected during the POST may be indicated with

    A ◯ A constant beeping sound

    B ◯ No beep codes at all

    C ◯ An error code in the 020–029 range

    D ◯ All the above

10 What are the two types of uninterruptable power supplies?

    A ◯ Standby and interactive

    B ◯ In-line and out-line

    C ◯ Standby and in-line

    D ◯ In-line and interactive

Answers

1 *B.* A battery backup only supplies backup electricity. A surge suppressor provides line conditioning protection as does a true line conditioner. The uninterruptable power supply (UPS) does both. *See "Hedging your bet."*

2 *C.* Overvoltage is the same as a power surge or a spike. A surge suppressor absorbs the spike and prevents it from damaging your computer. *Review "Suppressing the surge."*

3 *A.* Keep in mind the two ways to answer this question and why. AT and Baby AT form factor power supplies should be plugged in to provide a ground. ATX form factor power supplies should be unplugged because of hot connectors that it supports. *See "To unplug or not to unplug."*

4 *A.* A device that conforms to the U.S. Green Star standard reduces its power consumption to less than 30 watts and reduces its overall consumption by 99 percent. *See "Saving the planet."*

5 *D.* A capacitor is used to absorb a power spike and can be used to provide power to bring up an undervoltage condition. *Charge over to "The Power Supply."*

6 *C.* The clamping voltage is the voltage level at which the surge suppressor engages; the clamping speed is how soon after detection suppression begins. *See "Suppressing the surge."*

7 *A.* Laser printers draw a tremendous amount of power at startup, and few UPS units have enough power to handle the demand. *See "Hedging your bet."*

8 *B.* A blackout is the complete loss of power from the general electrical power supply system. *See "The paradox of external power."*

9 *D.* All of these are indications that there may be a power supply failure. *Review "Diagnosing POST problems."*

10 *C.* The standby UPS is like a big surge suppressor with a battery backup; the in-line UPS is a big self-charging battery that runs your computer with an emergency AC line, just in case. *Review "Hedging your bet."*

Part III
Outside the Case

In this part . . .

*J*ust as important as the previous part, with its coverage of the inside of the PC case, is the coverage in this part on peripheral devices. Without peripherals, there would be no interface for the PC with its user. In the latest version of the test, two areas included in this part of the book have been expanded. These two areas are laser printers and network communications, especially interacting with the Internet.

Chapter 9
Input Devices

Exam Objectives

▶ Identifying basic terms, concepts, and functions of input devices
▶ Identifying common peripheral ports and their connectors
▶ Identifying preventive maintenance procedures
▶ Troubleshooting common input device symptoms and problems

Input devices are included on the A+ Core exam in a couple of areas, but primarily under installing, configuring, and upgrading FRUs (field replaceable units). You can also expect to see input devices included under the preventive maintenance and troubleshooting areas as well. Don't expect to find many questions directly about input devices on the exam, such as "How many keys are on the keyboard?" or "How does a mouse work?" This, I think, is because the major input devices, the keyboard and mouse, are essentially throw-away technology. It's often cheaper, in both materials and labor, to buy a new unit than to waste any time trying to fix the old one.

I can't prove it with statistics, and I looked for them, but I bet that right after power problems ("It worked fine this morning before the power failure") and printer problems ("What does on-line mean?"), that the next most common service problem involves keyboards or mouse units. By now, I'm sure you've heard the joke about the user and his foot pedal. If I'm right, and I can't be too wrong on this, then as a working PC repair technician, you should understand how input devices work, connect, and fail.

Quick Assessment

Identifying basic terms, concepts, and functions of input devices

1 The _____ keyboard uses a capacitive membrane module.

2 The most commonly used PC keyboard format is the _____ keyboard.

3 Two popular types of mouse units are _____ and _____.

Identifying common peripheral ports and their connectors

4 A _____ mouse connects to a serial computer port.

5 A _____ mouse connects to a mini-DIN-6 connector.

6 The bus mouse attaches to its own _____.

7 The standard IRQ assigned to the mouse is _____.

Identifying preventive maintenance procedures

8 To remove paper bits and food crumbs from a keyboard, you turn it upside down and _____ it.

Trouble-shooting common input device symptoms and problems

9 _____ and _____ are best for cleaning the ball of a mouse.

10 A 300-range error code displayed during the boot sequence indicates a _____ error.

Answers

1 *Capacitive.* Review "Capacitive keyboards."

2 *Enhanced.* Check out "Keyboards."

3 *Mechanical, optical.* Click on "The Mouse."

4 *Serial.* See "Connecting the mouse."

5 *PS/2.* Peruse "Connecting the mouse."

6 *Adapter or expansion card.* Review "Connecting the mouse."

7 *IRQ 12.* Check out "Driving Miss Mousey."

8 *Shake.* Review "Practicing keyboard preventive maintenance" for the common keyboard preventive maintenance actions.

9 *A swab, mild soap.* Take a look at "Taking good care of your mouse."

10 *Keyboard.* See "Solving boot sequence problems" for information on common keyboard errors during POST.

Keyboards

The A+ exam focuses on three areas of keyboards: connectors, preventive maintenance, and troubleshooting. If you're confident that you know how a keyboard works, skip to "Connecting the keyboard." Otherwise, review the following sections for background and terminology.

The obvious place to begin your review of input devices is with the most common input device of all — the keyboard (see Figure 9-1). The keyboard's role on a PC system should be fairly obvious. However, for those of you who have not given it much thought, the keyboard allows the user to communicate with the computer with keystrokes, which provide the computer with character data and commands that it will interpret and perform actions on accordingly.

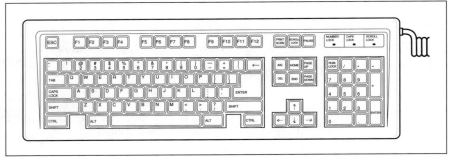

Figure 9-1:
An
enhanced
PC
keyboard.

The keyboard formats found on any DOS or Windows PC can be grouped into one of four categories:

- ✔ **XT:** 83 keys, 10 function keys, numeric keypad and cursor control keys combined, keyboard processor in keyboard.

- ✔ **AT:** 84 keys, with the addition of the SysRq key, a larger Return key, and the keyboard processor on system board.

- ✔ **Enhanced:** 101 keys, which includes 12 function keys, cursor and screen control keys, and numeric keypad (refer to Figure 9-1). Enhanced is the most common keyboard type.

- ✔ **Ergonomic:** Enhanced keyboard with built-in wristrest, and arched or bowed keyboard shape; may also separate into segments (see Figure 9-2).

XT keyboards and AT keyboards are incompatible because they each assume the keyboard microprocessor is located someplace different. You can't install an AT keyboard on an XT system; likewise, an XT keyboard will not work on an AT system. The XT wants the microprocessor to be inside of the keyboard, and the AT wants it to be on the motherboard.

Some of the generic clone keyboards get around this problem by having an AT/XT switch on the back of the keyboard. Enhanced keyboards (most ergonomic keyboards are just modified enhanced keyboards) work with either AT or XT.

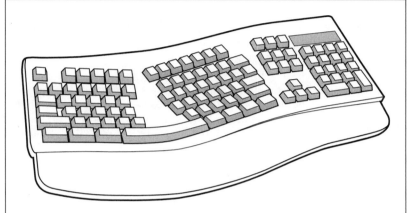

Figure 9-2:
An ergonomic or "natural" keyboard.

The enhanced keyboard, also called the 101-keyboard, is the most popular type in use. Most newer keyboards, including the ergonomic keyboards, are enhanced keyboards underneath their fancy cases.

The keyboard is very simple to operate, and touch-typing aside, most people can operate a keyboard well enough. The keyboard is usually the primary input device for a PC, which is why people can become emotional when it breaks.

The common keyboard is a matrix of mechanical keys. Each key generates an electrical signal that's translated into a specific character or command value in the following way:

1. When you press a key, an electrical circuit closes and a "make code" signal is created.

2. When you release the key, the circuit reopens and a "break code" signal generates.

3. Using these codes, plus the location of the key on the keyboard grid, the keyboard microprocessor generates the "scan code."

4. The keyboard driver, usually a part of the system BIOS, converts the scan code into the character assigned to that code, depending on the language configured to the keyboard.

Typecasting keyboards

Two types of key mechanisms are used in PC keyboards: *mechanical* and *capacitive*. Usually, you know one from the other just by lifting it. As the name suggests, the mechanical is cheaper, bigger, heavier, and bulkier. The capacitive keyboard is sleeker, lighter, more reliable, and more expensive. Understand that the cost comparisons here are not like the difference between a Yugo and a Mercedes, but more like the relative difference between a plain hamburger and a deluxe cheeseburger.

Mechanical keyswitch keyboards

A mechanical keyboard is usually heavier than other keyboards and provides a more positive tactile click to the key action. Although, as with most things, age can play a part in how well the key's action holds up. Each key is a separate electromechanical device called a keyswitch. Inside of each keyswitch is a spring to return the key after it is pressed. This spring can lose its bounce with age and cause operating problems. Keyswitch keyboards operate as follows (see Figure 9-3):

1. The user presses down the keycap.

2. The plunger is pushed down.

3. The two metal or foil contacts are pushed together.

4. A circuit closes and a signal is created.

5. The signal is detected by the keyboard controller.

6. Using the key's location and signal, the controller sends the character value to the computer.

7. The user releases the key and the return spring raises the plunger and keycap to their original positions.

Capacitive keyboards

A capacitive keyboard, also called a membrane keyboard, is common on many brand-name systems. It's more reliable and expensive than a mechanical keyboard, although it's very similar in appearance, construction, and operation. It's much lighter than the mechanical keyboard as well. The one major exception is that in place of metallic contacts, it uses a capacitive membrane module to generate its signals.

The capacitive keyboard is more reliable, slightly more expensive, and found in name-brand keyboards like IBM, Compaq, DEC, KeyTronic, and so on.

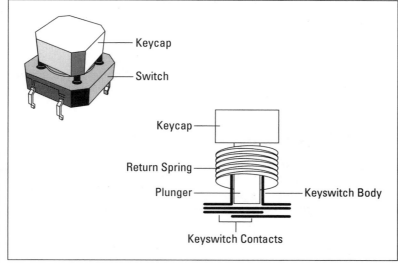

Figure 9-3:
A
mechanical
keyswitch
and its
components.

Table 9-1 summarizes the characteristics of the two keyboard types.

Table 9-1	Differences between Mechanical and Capacitive Keyboards	
Mechanical	*Capacitive*	
Uses electromechanical keyswitches		
A plunger presses two contacts together, creating a signal	A paddle contacts the capacitive membrane, creating a signal	
Less expensive to manufacture	Expensive to manufacture	
Used in clones and generic brand keyboards	Used in brand-name and high-quality OEM keyboards	
Heavier than capacitive keyboards	Lighter and more compact than mechanical keyboards	
More reliable		

Connecting the keyboard

Unless a keyboard is one of the new wireless breeds, it must be physically connected to the computer. This connection is made with one of two connector types: a DIN-type 5-pin connector or a mini-DIN 6-pin, also known as a PS/2 connector. These connectors are also called DIN-5 and mini-DIN-6 connectors, respectively. The mini-DIN connector gets its name due to its smaller overall size. Some proprietary keyboards connect with the RJ-11 style plug, but they are disappearing.

DIN connectors have a notch or key slot that prevents an incorrect connection.

Understanding device drivers

Keyboards, like all peripheral devices, require several types and layers of software to help them work. One of these software layers is the device driver, without which a peripheral device can't function. The more sophisticated the device, the more layers of software are required to make it work. Keyboards and other input devices are relatively unsophisticated as a rule and don't require much beyond the two fundamental layers: firmware and device driver.

Just for the record, a peripheral device is any piece of hardware used for input, output, storage, or communications purposes.

✔ **Firmware:** Stored on a ROM (read-only memory) chip either inside the device or on the interface card installed on the motherboard. The firmware contains hardware and BIOS (basic input/output system) interface information, such as IRQ (interrupt request), COM (serial) port assignments, and boot sequence support data.

✔ **Device driver:** The software that communicates directly with the device itself and interacts with the operating system during normal operations. Device drivers are started during the system boot sequence from either the CONFIG.SYS in DOS and Windows 3.*x* or by the Windows 95 device management utilities.

The keyboard is typically assigned IRQ 1 and I/O address 060h. Anytime you see an IRQ, I/O address, or DMA channel assignment, remember it for the test.

Practicing keyboard preventive maintenance

Keyboards, especially mechanical ones, should be cleaned periodically. You can clean a keyboard with the computer turned off using the following steps:

1. **Turn the keyboard upside down and shake out any paper, potato chips, cookie crumbs, paper clips, or the like.**

2. **Use an aerosol can of compressed air to dislodge any stubborn bits.**

3. **Use an all-purpose cleaner and soft cloth to clean the key tops.**

4. **Use a lint-free swab and the cleaner to clean between the keys.**

If soda pop or some other sticky stuff spills on your keyboard, you can rinse the soiled subject with water, soak it in a sink or tub, or even put it through a dishwasher rinse cycle without soap. That is, unless you live out in the boondocks and have really gunky well water, in which case, use distilled water or Perrier or such to rinse the keyboard. In any case, be extremely sure the keyboard is dry before reconnecting it to the computer and turning the power back on. Otherwise, any water left on the keyboard can at best cause phantom key connections or at worst, short out the keyboard membrane or switches. I don't know that I'd actually wash the keyboard; if it's really that bad, perhaps a new keyboard is a better idea.

Troubleshooting the keyboard

Keyboards are considered throw-away technology. Mechanical keyboards can be repaired, but most aren't. It's far less expensive to replace a keyboard than to spend time troubleshooting and repairing it. Individual keyswitches may be replaced on a mechanical keyboard, but that should be the prudent limit.

To determine whether a keyboard electrical failure is in the keyboard or on the system board, use the following steps:

1. **Power off the computer.**

2. **Unplug the keyboard connector from the motherboard.**

3. **Power on the computer.**

4. **Use a digital multimeter to check the voltages of the connector pins.**

If any of the voltages are out of range, in the vicinity of +2 volts to +5.5 volts, depending on the pin, the problem is likely in the keyboard circuits of the motherboard. See the keyboard's documentation for the specific voltage and pinouts. Otherwise, the problem is probably in the keyboard.

Expect several exam questions about your interface with the customer on a repair call. When servicing a keyboard problem, or any problem for that matter, listen carefully to the user's explanation and avoid jumping to a conclusion. Don't assume that you know the problem or its solution ahead of time. Don't waste the customer's time or your energy troubleshooting a keyboard problem that would be solved less expensively with a new keyboard. More information is available on dealing with the customer in Chapter 19.

Solving boot sequence problems

Keyboard-related problems may also occur during the POST process. Should the problem occur early in the POST process, you hear the beep codes for the particular BIOS on that computer.

If the failure occurs later in the POST (power-on self test) or boot sequence, an error code in the 300 to 399 number range displays, indicating a keyboard error. The most common reason for this error is a keystroke detected during the POST processing. This could be a stuck key, an accidentally pressed key, someone leaning on the keyboard, or the owner's manual laying on the keyboard. The remedy is to clear the problem and reboot the computer.

Don't try to memorize all POST error codes that relate to keyboards. As far as keyboard problems go, it's enough to know that the 300 series error codes relate to keyboard problems. For the entire list of numeric codes used during POST, see Chapters 3 and 6.

Avoiding operator injury

You may see a question or two on the text regarding the safe and ergonomic use of the keyboard. Ergonomics address the physical interface between the computer and the user.

People who use keyboards frequently sometimes develop repetitive stress injuries (RSI) in their hands and wrists. The most common injury is carpal tunnel syndrome (CTS). Ergonomic keyboards attempt to help remedy the stress on hands, arms and wrists, but some simple keyboard hand, wrist, and arm mechanics can help prevent problems.

You can prevent CTS by keeping your elbows at the same level as the keyboard and keeping your wrists straight and higher than your fingers.

The Mouse

Like the keyboard, a mouse keeps company with nearly every PC in use. Some diehard users still refuse to move to a Windows environment and may not have a mouse on their systems. There was a time when you could get by fairly well in the Windows environment without a mouse, but those days are long gone. Systems without a mouse or other type of pointing device will eventually go the way of the dinosaur.

You may encounter exam questions that cover any of these areas:

- Connecting the mouse to the computer
- The internal parts and operation of the mouse
- Device drivers (see Chapters 16 and 21)
- Common preventive maintenance procedures

Most mouse units in use today are the mechanical type. A few optical units are still around. The mechanical mouse uses a rubber ball, which is moved by the user's hand. The ball rotates a set of rollers, which in turn drive sensors that drive the screen pointer. As the user moves his hand, the distance traveled and the speed of the ball is detected by the rollers and sensors and displayed on the monitor.

The optical mouse uses optical sensors and LEDs and a special grid mouse pad to detect motion. Sometimes also called an opto-mechanical mouse, this mouse detects movement over the grid from the reflection of the LED being detected by sensors. As with the ball-type mouse, the distance and speed of the mouse is detected and translated into motion of the screen pointer on monitor display.

Table 9-2 lists other pointing devices that you can attach to the PC.

Table 9-2	PC Pointing Devices
Device	*Usage*
Joystick	Popular with flight and navigation games, and as a backup mouse
Trackball	In effect, an upside-down mouse where the ball is rotated to move the screen pointer
Touchpad	A reliable alternative to the mouse that can be integrated into the keyboard
Digitizing tablets	Used with drawing or CAD (computer-aided drafting) software to create line or vector graphics

Connecting the mouse

In case you've been on a remote desert island or in a deep dark cave for about ten years: A mouse is a pointing device commonly used on the PC. It's safe to say that every PC sold today comes with a mouse as standard equipment, although this standard is only about five years old.

Four species of mouse units are available for the PC. These units differ in how they connect to the computer. The four mouse types and their connectors are

- ✔ **Serial:** Connects via a 9- or 25-pin serial port usually with a DB-9 or DB-25 connector
- ✔ **PS/2:** Connects with a mini-DIN 6-pin plug to a port usually mounted on the motherboard
- ✔ **Combination:** Connects with either a mini-DIN (PS/2) 6-pin connector to a port on the motherboard or with a DB-9 or DB-25 connector through an adapter card to either a DB-9 or DB-25 serial port
- ✔ **Bus:** Connects to its own adapter card. Bus mouse units usually connect with a mini-DIN-6 plug to an adapter added to the PC specifically to support the mouse.

The most commonly used mouse units are the serial and PS/2 types.

Driving Miss Mousey

In addition to physically connecting the mouse to the PC, the mouse needs to have a device driver installed. In the DOS and Windows 3.*x* worlds, the device driver that is supplied with the mouse on a floppy disk is installed on the hard drive, and a command, like the following, is added to the CONFIG.SYS file.

```
DEVICE=C:\MOUSE\MOUSE.SYS
```

Windows 95 has built-in device drivers for virtually every type of mouse unit and can detect and support the mouse automatically.

The mouse is typically assigned IRQ 12 and an I/O address of 238h. Actually, IRQ 12 is assigned to the motherboard's in-port, but because that is where the mouse is typically plugged, it defaults to the mouse. The mouse, like most input devices, is not assigned a DMA channel.

Taking good care of your mouse

Periodically, you need to clean the mouse's moving parts — the ball and rollers inside the ball housing. Cleaning should be a part of a normal periodically performed maintenance routine because a dirty mouse can cause the screen pointer to move erratically across the screen, or it may not move up and down, or it may not move side to side. In any case, use the following steps to clean the mouse:

1. Open the ball access cover.

You can usually do this by either rotating or sliding the locking collar that holds the mouse ball in place. You can usually tell how to remove the cover by the large arrows embossed into it, showing the direction you need to push or twist.

2. Use a swab and a mild soap clean the ball.

You may have heard that rubbing the mouse with a pencil eraser is a good way to clean it. Not! And neither is using anything that could react with the rubber to cause flat spots or make the mouse ball out-of-round, such as contact cleaner or alcohol, two commonly recommended cleaning solutions for the mouse housing.

3. Blow out the ball housing.

I recommend using aerosol compressed air rather than your breath. It for sure has less germs, and likely less moisture as well. Replace the ball and reinstall the retaining ring, and you're back in business. Be sure to test the mouse immediately, and correct any problems that show up.

Sight and Sound Inputs

You're not likely to be asked anything directly about sound or video capture devices. Just to be on the safe side, I cover them very briefly for you. Most of the service issues with these systems involve system compatibility, which I detail in Chapter 6.

Multimedia and desktop publishing are less hardware issues than they are applications. Nevertheless, both are becoming standard functions of the PC. This standardization is evidenced by MMX instructions being added to processors and most PCs now coming with speakers, extended RAM, and graphics enhancement as a standard part of the package.

Capturing visual images

You can use two types of devices to capture images directly into the computer — scanners and digital cameras:

✔ **Scanners:** Available as either a flatbed scanner or as a hand-held scanner and used to convert printed text and images into digital form for editing and manipulation. Flatbed scanners act pretty much like a copy machine. You place the picture on the glass, click to scan, and the light/sensor unit beneath the glass starts moving and reading. Hand-held scanners are manually operated, which means that you move them with your hand, and have a limited scanning width.

✔ **Digital cameras:** Two types are available — full-motion capture and still-image capture.

- **Full-motion:** Installed on your PC to capture your good-looking self for transmission as part of a live video-teleconferencing session. Full-motion digital cameras require support from software, such as Microsoft NetMeeting and White Pine CUSeeMe.

- **Still-image:** Hand-held independent devices. They are used just like a regular analog camera; that is, your regular 35mm camera that requires film and developing. A digital still-image camera stores its images on a diskette. Digital still-image cameras are still new to most computer users. It looks like a camera, and acts like a camera, but still isn't a camera quality-wise.

Video capture cards are assigned to an available IRQ and I/O address. Many also use and are assigned DMA channels, but no default settings exist for these devices. Don't worry, no trick questions about this are on the exam.

Installing sound

You probably think of sound playback when you consider sound and the PC, but devices exist that you can use to capture sound as well. Sound capabilities, both input and output, are installed in a PC through a sound card, a special type of expansion card. Usually, a sound card has connection ports for microphones and speakers to enable it to capture sound and play it back.

Sound cards act like a modem of sorts, in that they are involved in the conversion of analog sound to digital data, and vice versa. Grossly simplified, sound capture involves grabbing a piece of the sound every so often to build a digitally reproducible facsimile of the original sound, also known as *sampling*. The sampled sound file is stored as a digital file on the computer, usually as a .WAV or similar file type.

The sound card is generally assigned to IRQ 5 and I/O address 220h. A sound card can use up to three DMA channels. Channels 0, 1, and 3 for an 8-bit card, and channels 5, 6, and 7 for a 16-bit card.

Prep Test

1 The keyboard and mouse are considered to be

- A ○ Throw-away technology
- B ○ Shop-repairable items
- C ○ Factory-only repairable items
- D ○ Not repairable

2 You can prevent carpal tunnel syndrome by

- A ○ Keeping your wrists straight and lower than your fingers
- B ○ Keeping your back straight
- C ○ Keeping your elbows at the same level as the keyboard and your wrists straight and higher than your fingers
- D ○ Resting your wrists and hands on a wrist pad while you type

3 Which mouse type is the most commonly used?

- A ○ Trackball
- B ○ Mechanical mouse
- C ○ Touch pad
- D ○ Optical mouse

4 What are the two types of keyboards in use today?

- A ○ Standard and nonstandard
- B ○ Mechanical and optical
- C ○ Resistive and capacitive
- D ○ Mechanical keyswitch and capacitive

5 The larger of the common keyboard connectors is a

- A ○ BNC
- B ○ mini-DIN-6
- C ○ DIN-5
- D ○ maxi-DIN-9

6 What is the most commonly used PC keyboard format?

- A ○ Ergonomic
- B ○ Natural
- C ○ XT
- D ○ Enhanced

7 What type of mouse connects to either a serial port or a port mounted on the motherboard?

A ○ Serial

B ○ PS/2

C ○ Bus

D ○ Combination

8 A keyboard error code displayed during the boot sequence would be in what number series?

A ○ 1700–1799.

B ○ 300–399.

C ○ 100–199.

D ○ It may be a number from any series.

9 Device drivers provide

A ○ Boot sequence support for peripheral devices

B ○ Operating support for peripheral devices

C ○ ROM-based interface instructions

D ○ User help information

10 The joystick is

A ○ A special tool used for RAM

B ○ The lever on a ZIF socket

C ○ A type of pointing device

D ○ A type of output device

Answers

1 *A.* The cost of repairing a keyboard or mouse for anything but the simplest problems can be more expensive than just replacing it with a new one. *See "Troubleshooting the keyboard."*

2 *C. Review "Avoiding operator injury."*

3 *B.* Others may come and go, but the little mechanical mouse keeps on going, and going . . . . *Review "The Mouse."*

4 *D. See "Typecasting Keyboards."*

5 *C.* The two types of connectors are the larger DIN-5 and the smaller mini-DIN-6. *Review "Connecting the keyboard."*

6 *D.* Even the newer natural, ergonomic, and separating keyboards are essentially enhanced keyboards in new packages. *Take a look at "Keyboards."*

7 *D.* The combination mouse can be adapted to fit either type of connector, which allows it to work with just about any system. *See "Connecting the mouse."*

8 *B.* Any POST error code in the 300 to 399 range is a keyboard fault. Check with the BIOS manual for the specific error. *Look at "Solving boot sequence problems."*

9 *B.* Boot sequence support is provided by firmware. See *"Understanding device drivers."*

10 *C.* The joystick is very popular with flight-simulation games. *Review "The Mouse."*

Chapter 10

Output Devices

Exam Objectives

▶ Identifying common output devices and their normal operation

▶ Identifying output device connectors

▶ Using preventive maintenance products

▶ Disposing of environmentally hazardous equipment

▶ Following safety procedures for high-voltage equipment

*U*nlike their input device cousins, which are adapted to gather data at their myriad sources, output devices are limited by the human senses of sight and hearing. As a result, the PC is designed to provide its users with things they can read, watch, or hear. Output devices have only one purpose: to display (print or sound) the results of instructions and data entered by the user and processed by the PC.

On the common, everyday PC, one you are likely to repair, typically only two or three types of output devices exist: monitors, printers, and sound systems. A direct result of this fact is that the A+ exam includes questions focused primarily on monitors and printers, because virtually every PC has them. Sound is still somewhat new to the A+ world, but you may see a question on these devices as well.

On the A+ exam, monitors and displays are included in three separate parts, but are primarily in the domain of "Installation, Configuration, and Upgrading." I interpret the configuration part to include picking the right device for the customer's needs as much as it means setting the jumpers or DIP switches, or configuring software.

This chapter also includes a quick overview on PC sound devices. Printers are left for Chapter 12 because they now have their own domain on the A+ exam.

Quick Assessment

Identifying common output devices and their normal operation

1 The _____ is the primary component of the PC monitor.

2 A CRT paints its image using _____, which are tiny clusters of color dots.

Identifying output device connectors

3 The VGA/SVGA standard connector has _____ pins.

4 A sound card usually supports both the _____ and the _____ standards.

5 A sound card typically uses IRQ _____.

Using preventive maintenance products

6 The monitor's glass builds up _____ and holds dust on its surface.

Disposing of environmentally hazardous equipment

7 The CRT is considered an environmental hazard because it contains _____.

Following safety procedures for high-voltage equipment

8 A Green monitor is one that reduces its power by _____ in sleep mode.

9 A CRT has a large _____ inside that holds an electrical charge.

10 You should not wear a(n) _____ when working inside a monitor.

11 A process called _____ eliminates most of the magnetization inside the CRT.

Answers

1 *CRT*. See "Looking Inside the Monitor."

2 *Pixels*. Check out "Looking Inside the Monitor."

3 *15*. Look up "Making the connection."

4 *SoundBlaster and General MIDI*. Review "Hearing all about the standards of sound."

5 *5*. Take a look at "Connecting to sound."

6 *Static electricity*. Charge to "Cleaning the monitor."

7 *Lead*. See the sidebar "CRTs and the environment."

8 *99 percent*. Boldly go to "Saving the planet."

9 *Capacitor*. Mosey over to "Keeping the lid on."

10 *ESD grounding strap*. Zap to "Keeping the lid on."

11 *Degaussing*. Review "Exorcising the magnetic evils."

Looking Inside the Monitor

The PC monitor is not an item that PC service technicians are often called on to fix, and rightly so. The A+ people recognize this fact and have included very few questions on the internal workings of the monitor. Study this section as background material for the terminology and concepts concerning monitors in general.

You don't need to know how the internal combustion engine works to put gas in a car. Likewise, you really don't need to know the inner workings of a CRT to install and configure a monitor. However, you need to have a general idea. After the system unit, the monitor represents the customer's next largest investment and is the only part of the system that actually holds its value. Your focus on the job and for the A+ exams should be the technologies that allow the monitor to work at its best.

The primary component in the PC monitor is the cathode ray tube (CRT). Although its name makes it sound a little like a demonic weapon from a science fiction movie, it is the technology used in virtually all computer monitors (and televisions) to produce the displayed image.

The way a monitor works is that an electron beam moves back and forth, working top to bottom and left to right one row at a time, lighting up phosphor dots on the inside of the glass CRT tube. This action illuminates the dot that's located on the back of the display screen, and together all the illuminated dots create images in a fraction of a second. However, the illuminated dot also fades just as fast, requiring the entire display to be refreshed by repeating the process many times per second.

On a color monitor, each dot carries one of three colors: red, green, and blue. Three dots, one of each color, are arranged together to create a *pixel* (short for *picture element*). Three electron beams illuminate a pixel's dots in varying degrees. This variation produces different color shadings. When all the pixels on the screen are lit up, a picture forms in living color.

Here are a couple of monitor terms you may find in monitor-related questions on the exam:

 ✔ **Refresh rate:** This rate represents the time it takes the CRT's electron beam to paint the screen from top to bottom. Refresh rates are expressed as hertz (Hz), which is one complete screen refresh cycle. Different monitors have different refresh rates. For example, the VESA organization has set the minimum refresh rate as 70 Hz for the SVGA monitor.

- **Interlacing:** Interlaced monitors draw the screen in two passes, drawing only the even count lines on the first pass and just the odd count lines on the second pass. An interlaced monitor usually has more screen flicker than a noninterlaced monitor, which draws the entire screen in each pass. (Don't confuse interlacing with interleaving, which is used to improve hard disk performance.)

Inside the monitor is a controller board that performs the communication with the adapter card, directs the drawing of the CRT's display, and responds to the adjustment controls located on the monitor to adjust the display. The monitor's internal controller also determines the technology used in creating the display.

The names of the technologies used to control the illumination of the CRT's phosphor sound like bad old movie titles: the *shadow mask* and the *aperture grill*. Here is how they work:

- **Shadow mask:** A metal screen with thousands of very small holes. The mask is placed so that the holes are directly in line with the dots of each pixel. The shadow mask absorbs unwanted electrons and prevents the phosphor material between the pixels from being illuminated, which leaves a black border around each pixel.

- **Aperture grill:** Very thin vertical wires instead of the shadow mask's little openings. These wires let more electrons through, creating a deeper color display. Horizontal wires hold the vertical wires in place to keep the verticals from vibrating.

The definitions of resolution and dot pitch are very likely on the test, so review the following paragraphs closely.

The number of and distance between pixels determines the quality of the images produced — regardless of the technology used to light the pixels. The number of displayable pixels on a screen is the *resolution*. The more pixels available for display, the higher the resolution, which results in a much better display. Resolution is stated as the number of pixels available horizontally on the screen by the number of rows of pixels available vertically on the screen. For example, 640 x 480 represents 640 pixels in each horizontal row and 480 vertical pixel rows on the screen.

The distance between pixels is the *dot pitch*. Technically, the dot pitch is the distance in millimeters between dots of the same color in two adjacent pixels, but in effect, it is the distance between the pixels. Common dot pitch sizes are .39mm, .35mm, .28mm, and .25mm. The smaller the dot pitch, the better the picture quality. (You will usually see the dot pitch expressed without the "mm" unit of measure.) It also stands to reason that a smaller dot pitch makes room for more pixels, which improves the monitor's resolution.

One more thing about resolution. The higher the resolution, the smaller each pixel appears on the screen. If a user complains that his Windows icons are too small on his new monitor, lower the resolution.

The Video Adapter Card

The video card, also called the graphics adapter, converts a graphic image from a software application into a series of instructions that tell the monitor's internal controller how to draw the image on the screen and what colors to use. When monitors displayed only monochrome, the video card was very simple in design. However, graphics adapters now have their own onboard processors and memory, supporting better and faster graphic images. A few of the different video adapter cards follow:

- ✔ **Monochrome Display Adapter (MDA):** Does just what its name says — displays mostly text on a monochrome monitor. This digital adapter is still used for servers, process control, and monitoring systems where the display contains only text and a color display is not needed. Resolution is not an issue on MDA monitors.

- ✔ **Color Graphics Adapter (CGA):** This digital adapter was the first color adapter. It's capable of displaying four colors. CGA monitors support 320 x 200 (four colors) or 640 x 200 (two colors).

- ✔ **Enhanced Graphics Adapter (EGA):** This digital adapter supports 16 colors at a resolution of 640 x 350.

- ✔ **Video Graphics Array (VGA):** Introduced by IBM and soon copied by the *Super VGA (SVGA)* and *Ultra VGA (UVGA)* adapters. SVGA and UVGA monitors and cards did not define new graphics standards, but merely added a few features to the IBM VGA standard. The VGA card supports up to 640 x 480 (16 colors) or lower resolutions in 256 colors. The SVGA and UVGA adapters are available with resolution as high as 1,280 x 1,024 and up to 16 million colors.

The video card and monitor must use the same graphics standard to work properly.

Accelerating the video

Virtually all modern video cards are accelerators, getting their smarts from their *video chipset*. An accelerated video card, sometimes called a *Windows accelerator,* has a video coprocessor that enables it to calculate many of the display calculations previously handled by the CPU. Accelerator cards allow the processor to issue commands rather than instructions. For example, when the processor wants a circle drawn on the screen, it sends a command instructing the video adapter to draw a circle along with the screen coordinates of where it wants the circle placed on the screen. Without an accelerated video card, the processor must compute which pixels and which colors are to be used in creating the circle.

Accelerated video cards include a video coprocessor that offloads video image production from the CPU.

Buffering the video image

Monochrome monitors display about 2K of data, and processors can afford to set aside a portion of system memory to hold it. However, the amount of data needed to designate the display on a color monitor can be quite large. As the size of the data grew, putting some memory on the video card itself began to make sense. The memory on a video card is called *video memory,* or the *frame buffer*.

The first video memory was standard DRAM, which proved to be impractical because of its need to be continually refreshed, the fact that it can't be accessed during the refresh process, and the very fast clock speeds in video systems. This impracticality led to the development of specialized video memory technologies:

✓ **Video RAM (VRAM):** Dual-ported DRAM that requires far less refreshing than ordinary DRAM and can be written to and read from at the same time

✓ **Windows RAM (WRAM):** Also dual-ported, but is accessible in blocks, which results in slightly faster transfers over VRAM

✓ **Synchronous Graphics RAM (SGRAM):** Represents improvements in the technology of single-ported DRAM that enables the chips to run as much as four times faster than conventional DRAM memories

For the exam, you want to be familiar with video memory types. You can expect to see a question like the following:

Which of the following is not a type of video RAM?

    A. WRAM

    B. SGRAM

    C. FRAM

    D. VRAM

Of course, the answer is FRAM — it is not a type of video RAM, but a maker of oil filters!

Remember that graphics support is also integrated into some systemboards, using a unified memory architecture, so named because it uses system RAM for video memory. This name is pretty spiffy for a technology that almost always produces poorer graphics.

Sizing video memory

You will very likely see a question or two on each of the A+ Core module and DOS/Windows exams on how to determine the amount of video memory needed by a system.

The memory on a video card must be sufficiently large that it can hold an entire screen of data. Video memory must be large enough to store the entire digital bitmap produced by the processor. Video memory is usually sized as 256K, 512K, 1MB, 2MB, and so on. Above 1MB, always jump to the next whole megabyte of video memory. Lab 10-1 demonstrates how to calculate the amount of video memory needed.

Lab 10-1	Calculating the Frame Buffer Size

1. **On the Windows 95 Control Panel, select Display.**

2. **Click the Settings tab to see the settings for your display.**

3. **You're interested in two numbers here: the number of colors and the display resolution.**

4. **Multiply the resolution: 800 times 600 = 480,000.**

5. **Multiply the product of Step 4 by the color bits: 480,000 times 8 = 3,840,000.**

6. **Divide the product of Step 5 by 8 bits: 3,840,000 divided by 8 = 480,000.**

   Yes, when using an 8-bit color scheme, you really don't need Steps 5 and 6 and can convert the results in Step 4 straight to bytes. However, if you were calculating the frame buffer for 16-bit color, in Step 5 you would multiply by 16 to get 7,680,000, then in Step 6 you divide by 8 bits (the number of bits in a byte) to convert to bytes (960,000).

Dealing with driver software

The device driver software used with a video card directly impacts its performance and the features it can offer. The driver software decides the most efficient way to use the features of the graphics processor and translates what an application wants to display into instructions that the video card can understand.

Exploring the Great RAMDAC

You won't see RAMDAC on the test, but I think it's one of the greatest names in computing and very good background material.

Sounding like one of the bad guy monsters that fought the old (and good) Godzilla, *RAMDAC* is short for Random Access Memory Digital-Analog Converter. RAMDAC converts the digital signals of the processor and video

RAM into analog signals for the monitor. Several times per second, RAMDAC converts the contents of video memory into analog signals and sends them to the monitor. RAMDAC also controls the video card's refresh rate and the number of colors supported at a certain resolution.

Usually, a video card has a separate software driver for each resolution or color depth used, which is why you must reboot the PC after you change the display settings of your monitor in Windows — to load a new device driver. Chapter 21 covers the installation of the device driver in more detail.

Making the connection

You can expect a question about the sizes of the different plugs used to connect the monitor to the system. The monitor connects to the system through a connector on the back of the adapter card or through a connector on the systemboard. Different plugs are used, each with a different number of pins. The number of pins on the connector is somewhat indicative of the adapter card's capabilities. Here are the different connectors for monitors:

- ✔ **15-pin:** This is the standard monitor and video card cable and connector size in use today. It's also called the VGA, after the standard that first used it. Virtually all VGA and SVGA cards and nearly all standard monitors use the 15-pin connector.

- ✔ **9-pin:** Most older monitors, usually digital displays (CGA, EGA, and early VGA) use a 9-pin connector. The 9 pins represent the 8 data pins and the control pin.

- ✔ **BNC connector:** Some very high-end monitors use a special cable that connects with a standard 15-pin connector at the adapter card and a group of five BNC connectors at the monitor.

Monitor Power and Safety

Two areas of particular concern to the CompTIA that are strongly reflected in the A+ exams are safety and environmental issues concerning monitors. You can count on seeing one or more questions from this section in the Core module exam.

Cleaning the monitor

Dust collects on the glass of the monitor, held there by static electricity that also builds up over time. Never clean the monitor's glass with any liquid solution while it's powered on. A danger of personal and equipment damage exists. The static electricity built up on the screen can be conducted straight to you by the liquid cleaner when you wipe it off. If you want to use a spray cleaner, turn off the monitor, spray a cloth, and then wipe the monitor. You can also find antistatic wipes that are made just for this purpose.

Saving the planet

In active mode, the monitor uses more power than the whole rest of the PC system. However, reducing its power consumption in its idle states is a focus of the United States Environmental Protection Agency (EPA) program called *Energy Star,* or *Green Star.* The purpose of this program is to certify PCs and monitors that use less than 30 watts in all power modes and reduce their power consumption by 99 percent in sleep or suspend mode. PCs that meet this standard can display the Energy Star logo.

Monitors meeting the Green standard must reduce their power consumption by 99 percent in suspend mode.

VESA's *Display Power Management System (DPMS)* protocol shuts down the parts of the monitor or motherboard that have been inactive for a certain period of time. PCs with both a motherboard and a monitor supporting the DPMS protocol significantly reduce the system's power consumption.

Protecting against electromagnetic evils

Because of how they work, CRTs produce strong electrical and electromagnetic emissions. These emissions are formidable and can wreak havoc on other electrical or magnetic systems. Debates are ongoing within the computing and health worlds regarding the possible threat of these emissions to humans. Some people believe that extended exposure can increase a person's risk of cancer, and others believe no risk at all exists. Everyone agrees that limiting your exposure to electromagnetic emissions can't hurt.

CRTs and the environment

Because as much as 70 percent of some of the CRT's components contain lead, the CRT comes under the Land Disposal Ban Program of the Resource Conservation and Recovery Act (RCRA). This law states that you can't just throw your old CRT display into the trash or haul it to the landfill. According to the regulations of the Environmental Protection Agency (EPA), to dispose a CRT properly, it must be dismantled, crushed, and encapsulated in cement. Salvage companies exist that can properly dispose of your CRT for a small fee, after first salvaging any usable components from it. I guess this means that I shouldn't just casually dump my old TVs into the landfill anymore.

The Swedish government, which is the leader for lower-emissions standards for monitors, has issued two standards, MPR I and II, and many monitor manufacturers have adopted these standards. It's also always a good idea to separate one form of electromagnetic device from another. In other words, placing your stereo's speakers or storing your diskette library on top of your monitor is not a great idea.

Keeping the lid on

For the exam, memorize this section word for word. You can expect to see this coverage on the test, and the information may just save your life.

You have no reason to open up a monitor to work on it. Chances are that you

- ✔ Don't have the foggiest idea what you're doing in there.
- ✔ Don't have the right tools or equipment to affect a fix.
- ✔ Will most likely kill yourself — the monitor holds 20,000 volts or more and is still present even when the power is off.

If you must open the case to work on a monitor, *do not* wear an ESD grounding strap. Also, unplug the AC cord from the power source, and use the buddy system (never work alone on a monitor).

To be safe, send the monitor to the manufacturer to be fixed or to a salvage company to be disposed of properly.

Monitors use very high voltages and hold other hazards that can cause serious injury or even death, even when the power is off and disconnected. Never use a regular multimeter or other test equipment to measure the voltages on a monitor. Much like the PC's main power supply, some large *capacitors* inside the monitor hold some big nasty charges, and you don't want any part of them.

Exorcising the magnetic evils

Because preventive maintenance is an important part of the repair technician's job, the A+ exam requires you to know about monitor cleaning and preventive maintenance techniques. Chapter 20 covers this area in more detail. The next couple of sections deal with two specific preventive techniques you need to know.

The powerful electromagnetic forces in the monitor or any placed nearby can cause the internal components of the monitor to become magnetized. When this happens, the image resolution and color quality produced by the monitor can be distorted or faded, especially in the display's corners.

A process called *degaussing* eliminates most of the magnetization inside the CRT. Most color monitors have a built-in degaussing protocol that can usually be accessed from the monitor's front panel. A monitor should be degaussed fairly regularly, but be careful not to overdo it. Degaussing a circuit too much can damage it.

Adding Sound to the PC

You may see an exam question directly related to sound reproduction and capture technology on the A+ exam, outside of the IRQ that's usually occupied by the sound card (IRQ5), or where the CD-ROM's audio cable connects (to the sound card).

Sound, beyond the little system speaker on the front of the system unit, is added through an adapter card in an expansion slot. Sound cards are often included with a CD-ROM drive in a multimedia upgrade kit, but most of the newer computers now have a sound card (a CD-ROM and a set of speakers) as standard equipment.

Hearing all about the standards of sound

Essentially, three sound card standards have existed: the 8-bit AdLib, the higher-end SoundBlaster, and the General MIDI (musical instrument digital interface). Most of the sound cards in use today support both the SoundBlaster and General MIDI standards for recording and playback. The AdLib card has all but disappeared. Most sound cards are CD-quality, which means that they capture and reproduce digital audio at the same resolution (CD-A) used for audio CDs. For the test, remember that the two standards in use are the SoundBlaster and the MIDI standards.

CD-ROM drives produce sound through a phone jack on its face, or its sound can be piped through the sound card for broadcast to the PC's speakers. You can find an audio cable on the CD-ROM that connects to the sound card for this purpose.

The audio cable of the CD-ROM is attached to the sound card.

Connecting to sound

For the exam, know which IRQ (interrupt request), DMA (direct memory access) channel, and I/O address are typically assigned to the sound card. You can learn more about IRQs, DMAs, and I/O addresses in Chapter 7.

SoundBlaster-compatible sound cards, the current standard, are normally configured to support

- ✔ DMA Channel 1
- ✔ IRQ5
- ✔ I/O address 220

The connectors found on virtually all sound cards are

- ✔ A 15-pin MIDI connector that can also be used for a joystick controller
- ✔ One or two speaker-out jacks
- ✔ A line-out jack for providing sound input to external devices
- ✔ A microphone-in jack

Prep Test

1 The sound card normally uses which IRQ?

A ○ IRQ 2

B ○ IRQ 5

C ○ IRQ 11

D ○ IRQ 9

2 To support a monitor with a resolution of 1024 x 768 pixels and 65,000 (16-bit) colors, a video card with at least how many MB of video RAM is needed?

A ○ 2

B ○ 4

C ○ 8

D ○ 1

3 A customer calls you claiming that his floppy disk drive is going bad because files are often missing or corrupted after they're saved to the floppy disk. When you arrive at the customer's site ready to troubleshoot the floppy disk drive, you discover a stack of floppy disks sitting on top of the monitor. What do you now think may be the problem?

A ○ The customer is not actually saving the data to the disks.

B ○ The cause may be a bad box of disks, which the customer should throw out and replace with new disks.

C ○ The floppy drive is bad and you need to replace it.

D ○ Magnetic emissions from the CRT are possibly erasing the disks.

4 A monitor that uses two passes to draw the entire screen, drawing every other line on each pass, is what type of monitor?

A ○ Noninterlaced

B ○ Interlaced

C ○ Interleaved

D ○ Multiscan

5 Which of the following is not a type of video RAM?

A ○ WRAM

B ○ VRAM

C ○ SGRAM

D ○ ZRAM

6 The audio wire that connects to the sound card is attached to

A ○ The ground lead of the motherboard's power connection.

B ○ The audio jumper on the motherboard.

C ○ The CD-ROM drive.

D ○ Nowhere, it is a never-used extra wire.

7 A monitor conforming to the Energy Star standard reduces its power by what percentage in sleep or suspend mode?

A ○ 99

B ○ 80

C ○ 100

D ○ 96

8 An ESD grounding strap should always be worn when working on the PC, except when working on a

A ○ Memory board

B ○ CRT

C ○ Hard drive

D ○ Motherboard

9 The distance between pixels on the CRT screen is measured as

A ○ Resolution

B ○ Interlacing

C ○ Dot pitch

D ○ Dot triad

10 Which of the following is not a type of video adapter card?

A ○ CGA

B ○ VGA

C ○ LPGA

D ○ SVGA

Answers

1 *B.* A sound card that is SoundBlaster-compatible, the current standard, supports DMA channel 1, IRQ 5, and I/O address 220. *See "Connecting to sound."*

2 *A.* This is calculated as 1,024 times 768 times 16 divided by 8. *Check out "Sizing video memory."*

3 *D.* The CRT produces electrical and magnetic emissions strong enough to corrupt the diskettes. *Look at "Protecting against electromagnetic evils."*

4 *B.* An interlaced monitor uses two complete screen cycles to completely build the display or refresh the display. *Review "Looking Inside the Monitor."*

5 *D.* WRAM, VRAM, and SGRAM are all types of memories used on a video card. *See "Buffering the video image."*

6 *C.* The audio wire is actually a part of the CD-ROM assembly and is connected to the sound card to provide sound audio support. *Look up "Hearing all about the standards of sound."*

7 *A.* The EPA Energy Star standard certifies equipment that reduces their power consumption by 99 percent in sleep or suspend mode. *Check out "Saving the planet."*

8 *B.* Never work on the internal system of a monitor without proper equipment, but if you decide to do so, please don't wear an ESD wrist strap. *Zap over to "Keeping the lid on."*

9 *C.* Dot pitch is the distance between two dots of the same color in adjacent pixels. *Slide up to "Looking Inside the Monitor."*

10 *C.* LPGA may mean anything, but it definitely is not a video adapter card type. *Review "The Video Adapter Card."*

Chapter 11

Serial and Parallel Ports

● ●

Exam Objectives

▶ Identifying common peripheral ports, their cabling, and connectors

▶ Troubleshooting procedures for serial and parallel ports

● ●

*I*f you've ever spent hours trying to get a parallel port to accept a serial printer connected to a serial-to-parallel converter to salvage a customer's old system printer, then you and I have a deeper appreciation for the differences of serial and parallel ports and communications. To many PC technicians and users, a parallel port is used for printers, and the serial port is where the modem plugs in. While this is not an altogether bad summarization of their differences, you will need to know their other subtleties for the A+ exams.

Parallel ports carry many times more data than serial ports in the same amount of time, which is why they are used for all the connections where speed is an issue, such as for monitors and printers, among others.

So why don't all communications between the computer, peripherals, modems, and the wide world of the user use a parallel port? Good question — and one I attempt to answer for you in this chapter. Afterward, if you understand the reasons serial ports are used for some things and parallel for others, you'll know what you need to for the A+ exams on these two port types. Don't expect too many questions on this material, perhaps three or four.

Don't try to memorize everything about serial and parallel ports. Review the serial port material to gain some background and understanding of its function, familiarize yourself with the terminology, and remember the COM port, IRQ, and I/O address linkages. Chapter 13 looks at serial ports in regard to modems. As far as parallel ports go, know the bidirectional parallel port protocols, discussed in this chapter.

Quick Assessment

Identifying common peripheral ports, their cabling, and connectors

1 Serial data is transmitted _____ bit(s) at a time.

2 A serial cable can be up to _____ feet in length.

3 COM1 is commonly assigned to IRQ _____.

4 A _____ signal on pin 4 of a serial connector is used to indicate that the DTE device is ready to communicate.

5 A _____ cable is used to directly connect two computers via their serial ports.

6 Serial devices are controlled by a _____.

7 Parallel cables should not be more than _____ feet in length.

8 The _____ standard covers bidirectional communications through a parallel port.

Trouble-shooting procedures for serial and parallel ports

9 To check for system resource conflicts in the Windows operating system, use the _____.

10 Serial port problems are usually caused by _____ conflicts.

Answers

1 *One.* Check out "Serial Versus Parallel."

2 *50.* Review "Understanding Serial Devices."

3 *4.* See "Setting up a serial port."

4 *DTR* or *Data Terminal Ready.* Look up "DTE to DCE, over."

5 *Null modem.* Take a look at "Cabling the connection."

6 *UART* or *Universal Asynchronous Receiver/Transmitter.* Peek at "Is that UART?"

7 *15.* Review "Looking at Parallel Devices."

8 *IEEE 1284.* See "Keeping up to standard."

9 *Device Manager.* Check out "Troubleshooting a serial port."

10 *System resource.* Mosey over to "Troubleshooting a serial port."

Serial Versus Parallel

Serial and parallel devices, cables, ports, and communications are all based on the same basic premises:

- ✔ Serial data is transmitted one bit at a time.
- ✔ Parallel data is transmitted eight or more bits at a time.

These fundamental differences characterize all comparisons between these two communications modes. To transmit a single ASCII character via a serial port, eight separate one-bit transmissions are needed. On the other hand, a parallel port needs only one 8-bit wide transmission. In some ways, serial communications are somewhat like a single-lane country road, while a parallel transmission is like I-405 with eight lanes. Obviously, parallel communications can handle more data in less time.

Understanding Serial Devices

As I mention in the preceding section, the one or two serial ports that every PC has sends and receives data one bit at a time. However, here are some things you may not know (and even if you do, it's still a good review for the test):

- ✔ Because a serial transmission moves less data than a parallel transmission through the wire at one time, it has more oomph and can travel a longer distance. A serial cable can be up to 50 feet in length (compared to the 15-feet limit of a parallel cable). Beyond this distance, the data begins to lose its oomph and data errors can occur.

- ✔ Most serial devices are external devices that plug onto the PC via a *serial port.* Serial ports are also called *COM ports,* or *RS-232 ports.*

  RS-232 stands for IEEE (Institute of Electrical and Electronic Engineers, Inc.) "reference standard number two hundred and thirty-two," and the term "COM" is used these days to mean serial port.

- ✔ Serial ports are usually added to the PC via an expansion board, although some of the newest computers now have one or two on the motherboard as well. Figure 11-1 illustrates the common serial ports found on a PC.

  If you look at the ports available on the back of the computer, serial ports are easy to recognize because they are always either a 9- or 25-pin male connector. In contrast, a parallel port is always a female connector regardless of how many pins it has. No gender jokes, please!

✔ Serial connectors are called DB-9 and DB-25. The *DB* stands for *data bus,* and the number is the number of pins in the connector. All serial connectors are DB type "D"-shaped connectors, but not all DB connectors are serial.

✔ A serial port is usually a male connector, as shown in Figure 11-1, whereas a parallel port is usually a female connector.

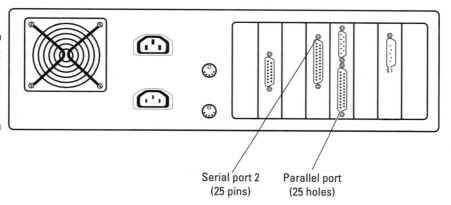

Figure 11-1: DB-9 and DB-25 male serial connectors.

Serial port 2 (25 pins)   Parallel port (25 holes)

✔ PCs only use nine pins in a serial connection, which is why many PCs use the DB-9 connector in place of the DB-25 with its way-too-many and wasted pins. You will find the DB-25 plug on many older PCs, multipurpose adapter cards, and some modems, although it is becoming more and more rare.

✔ Serial ports COM1 and COM2 were included on systems for input/output devices and were assigned IRQ4 and IRQ3, respectively. Some PCs now also support COM3 and COM4, but by default these logical devices are also assigned to IRQ4 and IRQ3, so you may need to switch I/O port and IRQ assignments to accommodate them.

✔ When serial ports are added to the PC via an expansion card (or cards), commonly COM1 uses a DB-9 connector and COM2 uses a DB-25 connector. However, no standard exists for this, so you may need to look at the card to see how the connections are labeled. It should come as no surprise that COM1 is labeled "COM1" and COM2, well you get it.

Setting up a serial port

Every PC technician needs to know and understand how serial devices and ports operate to ensure the proper installation of serial devices. For the A+ exam, you need to be familiar with serial communications terminology, its system resource assignments, and the purpose of a serial port's components.

Table 11-1 lists the system resource assignments for the common serial ports found on most PCs. Be sure you have these assignments engraved into your brain before the test.

Table 11-1	Serial Port System Resource Assignments	
Logical Device	*IRQ*	*I/O Address*
COM1	IRQ 4	3F8h
COM2	IRQ 3	2F8h
COM3	IRQ 4	3E8h
COM4	IRQ 3	2E8h

I don't have any cute little sayings to help you remember these assignments, so you will just have to memorize them. However, the "F8h" part of the I/O address is the same for all the ports, so all you need to do is remember that the odd-numbered ports (COM1 and COM3) have the odd I/O address (3F8h) and the even-numbered ports have the even I/O address (2F8h). In both cases, the IRQ is one more than the first number of the I/O port. It may be easier just to memorize it.

Here are some of the key words in serial-speak that you may find lurking on the exam:

- ✔ **Data bits:** Indicates the number of bits used in the character coding scheme, or data word. Some systems use seven bits and others eight bits, with no other choices available.

- ✔ **Flow control (handshaking):** The embodiment of the protocol used to control the dialog of two serial devices. In general, flow control is used to manage the data flow by sending a character or signal to stop it. Usually the flow control method used also has a means for restarting the data flow. See "DTE to DCE, over" for more details.

- ✔ **Parity:** Actually a group of five choices: even, odd, space, mark, or none. Parity is a way of checking whether the correct number of bits was sent and received. Most modems in use today do not use parity (a parity setting of none). Regardless of the setting, both devices in a serial communications must be set the same.

- ✔ **RTS/CTS (request-to-send/clear-to-send):** Sends signals to specific pins to stop and start the data flow. The CTS signal indicates that a device is ready to accept data, and the RTS signal indicates when a device is ready to send data.

✔ **Stop bits:** Used in certain serial communications to indicate the beginning and end of data words.

✔ **XON/XOFF:** One of the two most common forms of flow control, it sends control characters to stop the flow of data (XOFF) and restart it again (XON). This is the software method of flow control.

DTE to DCE, over

After a serial device such as a modem is connected to the PC, each device is designated as either the Data Terminal Equipment (DTE) or the Data Communications Equipment (DCE). When you connect a modem to a PC, it becomes the DCE and the PC is the DTE. These designations are used to determine which device initiates and controls the conversation between the two devices at various points in their interaction.

Table 11-2 lists the pin assignments of a serial connection.

Don't waste your time memorizing these pinouts. Instead, pay attention to what each pin is assigned to do and the role it would play in passing data back and forth to another device.

Table 11-2	Serial Connection Pin Assignments	
Pin Number	**Designation**	**Activity**
1	Carrier Detect (CD)	Indicates a connection is established.
2	Receive Data (RD)	All incoming data is received on this pin.
3	Transmit Data (TD)	All outgoing data is sent on this pin.
4	Data Terminal Ready (DTR)	The host device (such as the PC) is ready to communicate.
5	Signal Ground	Not used on PC systems.
6	Data Set Ready (DSR)	The connected device (such as the modem) is able to communicate.
7	Request to Send (RTS)	Host device wants to communicate.
8	Clear to Send (CTS)	Connected device is ready to communicate.
9	Ring Indicator (RI)	The telephone is ringing.

The serial connector's pins are used to send signals to create what amounts to a conversation (the *handshaking*) between two serial devices. Picture that each pin is a light that's turned on to indicate the next of a sequence of events. Handshaking accomplishes the hardware flow control (the most common method) between the PC and the modem, as follows:

1. The DTE (Data Terminal Equipment), or PC, turns on the DTR (Data Terminal Equipment), indicating that it's good to go.

2. The DCE (Data Communications Equipment) acknowledges this message by turning on the DSR (Data Set Ready) that says, "Me too."

3. The DTE turns on its RTS (Request to Send) signal to let the DCE know it is ready to receive data.

4. The DCE acknowledges this request with a CTS (Clear To Send) that replies, "Here it comes!"

5. The data flows one bit at a time until one of the devices needs to stop it. This stopping is indicated by either the RTS or CTS being turned off. The flow starts again when the applicable indicator is turned back on.

Review the above steps until you have a good idea of what happens in a serial communications handshake. You're very likely to see a question that asks you about all or part of this sequence of events.

Cabling the connection

The cable used to connect a PC to a modem is called a serial cable, a modem cable, or a straight-through cable. In this cable, all the pins are connected one to one without any twists, crosses, or other fancy arrangements (that is, unless you need to use a 9- to 25-pin converter should the modem cable come with a 25-pin connector and the PC has a 9-pin serial port).

Although few serial port questions are on the A+ exam, there are some. And expect at least one with "null modem cable" as its answer. On occasion, two PCs are connected in a DTE-to-DTE arrangement. When this happens, the cable's pinout is changed to simulate the action of the modem by cross-connecting a number of the pins and creating what is called a null modem, or modem eliminator, cable. Both the modem cable and the null modem cable are generic, and you can purchase them at any electronics store.

Is that UART?

Serial devices are controlled by a *Universal Asynchronous Receiver/Transmitter,* or *UART* for short. This specialized integrated circuit is found either on the device adapter card or on the motherboard (for those that have a serial port mounted on it). The UART chip controls all actions and functions of the serial port, including:

- ✔ Controlling all the connectors' pins and their associated signals
- ✔ Establishing the communication protocol
- ✔ Converting the parallel data bits of the data bus into a serial bit stream for transmission
- ✔ Converting the received serial bit stream into parallel data for transmission over the PC's internal data bus

It is probable that the UART will show up as a close-but-no-cigar answer on one or more questions, so be careful not to confuse it with the port itself. You may be asked something like, "Serial communications are controlled by what device?" And if you're not asked, you should be!

Troubleshooting a serial port

If you're having a serial port problem, it's most likely a system resource conflict. System resource conflicts include problems such as a serial device that fails intermittently or doesn't work at all, another device that stops working when the serial device is installed, or the PC locking up during the boot sequence.

The test requires that you know how to troubleshoot various situations, and you may encounter one on troubleshooting a serial port. Don't worry; there isn't that much to it. Here, let me help you out. To determine the source of the problem, check the following:

- ✔ **Inspect the port for bent pins.** Certain pins absolutely must be straight in order for the device to work properly.
- ✔ **Ensure that the cable is the appropriate cable for the device.** Some serial devices can't use a straight-through or null modem cable.
- ✔ **Check the Windows Device Manager for system resource conflicts.** An IRQ conflict is the most common error in this area. Remember, only one customer to an IRQ at a time.

> ✔ **Be sure that the serial cable is not more than 50 feet long.** Beyond this distance, you lose data integrity, which shows up any number of ways, none of which are good.

Looking at Parallel Devices

For the exam, know how parallel data is transmitted (eight bits at a time), the standard covering parallel port technologies (IEEE 1284 — see the section "Keeping up to standard"), and that parallel ports are used primarily for printers. This section provides you with additional background material.

There really isn't as much to know about parallel ports as there is to know about serial ports. Parallel data moves around much faster than serial data, which is why the internal bus structures of the PC use a parallel format. Parallel ports were originally designed specifically for printers. However, other devices have been adapted to them, including other types of output devices, input devices, and storage devices, all taking advantage of the bidirectional capabilities of IEEE 1284 parallel devices. These include some external CD-ROMs, external tape drives and Zip drives, as well as file transfer software over proprietary cabling.

Oh, and parallel cables shouldn't be more than 15 feet in length.

Keeping up to standard

You're definitely asked about the fact that IEEE 1284 is the standard for parallel ports, bidirectional parallel communications, and perhaps the ECP protocol.

In 1984, parallel port protocols were standardized by the IEEE (Institute of Electrical and Electronics Engineers). The standard, formally titled "IEEE Standard Signaling Method for a Bidirectional Parallel Peripheral Interface for Personal Computers," or IEEE 1284 as it is commonly known, incorporates the two parallel port standards that had been used to that point with a new protocol, creating an all-encompassing port model. The standards included in IEEE 1284 are

> ✔ **Standard Parallel Port (SPP)** allows data to travel one-way only — from the computer to the printer.

✓ **Enhanced Parallel Port (EPP)** allows data to flow in both directions, but only in one way at a time. This lets the printer communicate to the processor or adapter to signal it is out of paper, its cover is open, and so on.

✓ **Enhanced Capabilities Port (ECP)** allows bidirectional simultaneous communications over a special cable, one that is IEEE 1284 compliant. Many bidirectional cables exist, but they may be EPP cables, which do not support ECP communications.

IEEE 1284 established the standard for bidirectional communications on the parallel port, and the ECP protocol allows for full-duplex (simultaneous communications in two directions) parallel communications.

Troubleshooting a parallel port

Trouble with a parallel port is usually in the device attached to it. Because a parallel port is virtually featureless, it either works or it doesn't (and it usually does). Problems are either in the connector (bent pins or blocked holes), the cable (wrong type — SPP, EPP, or ECP), or the device itself.

An outside chance exists that a problem may be a system resource conflict, but only if more than two parallel ports are on the PC. Remember that printers and LPT ports don't use IRQs or DMA channels, but other parallel port devices do. Check for system resource conflicts when troubleshooting nonprinter parallel port problems.

Prep Test

1 A parallel port transmits data

- A ○ One bit at a time
- B ○ Four bits at a time
- C ○ One sector at a time
- D ○ Eight bits at a time

2 A UART chip is used to control

- A ○ The Plug-and-Play BIOS
- B ○ A parallel port
- C ○ A serial port
- D ○ The processor

3 A serial port is almost always

- A ○ A female port
- B ○ A male port
- C ○ A DB-15 connector
- D ○ A 36-pin connector

4 Flow control is used to

- A ○ Restrict data to digital phone lines
- B ○ Control the flow of data by sending a message to start data flow
- C ○ Control the flow of data by sending a message to stop data flow
- D ○ Manage error controls

5 Equipment such as the PC and the printer are designated as

- A ○ DCE devices
- B ○ DTE devices
- C ○ XON devices
- D ○ RTS devices

6 The I/O address of COM1 is

- A ○ 2E8h
- B ○ 3E8h
- C ○ 2F8h
- D ○ 3F8h

7 The two most common connectors used for serial ports are

A ○ Centronics 25- and 36-pin
B ○ DB-9 and DB-15
C ○ DB-9 and DB-25
D ○ Berg and Molex

8 Which of the following should you do when troubleshooting a serial port? (Choose all that apply.)

A ❑ Inspect the port for bent pins.
B ❑ Ensure the cable is the correct type of cable for the device.
C ❑ Check the cable length.
D ❑ Check for system resource conflicts.

9 Which of the following parallel port protocols allows bidirectional simultaneous communications?

A ○ ECP
B ○ SPP
C ○ EPP
D ○ TCP

10 The most common form of software flow control is

A ○ RTS/CTS
B ○ XON/XOFF
C ○ Stop bits
D ○ Handshaking

Answers

1 *D.* A parallel port carries an entire data character using parallel wires to carry each bit. *See "Serial Versus Parallel."*

2 *C.* A UART (Universal Asynchronous Receive/Transmit) chip controls the functions and protocol of a serial port. *Review "Is that UART?"*

3 *B.* Serial ports are usually a male connector, whereas parallel ports are female connectors. *Check out "Understanding Serial Devices."*

4 *C.* While flow control does both, that is, stop and start the data flow, it's primarily a means to stop the flow of data while another action takes place. *Take a look at "Setting up a serial port."*

5 *B.* If the device could have been a terminal on a mainframe, it's Data Terminal Equipment (DTE). If it's used for communications purposes, like a modem, it's Data Communications Equipment (DCE). *Link up with "DTE to DCE, over."*

6 *D.* If you're having trouble remembering the I/O addresses for the IRQs and COM ports, just remember that COM1 comes first and gets the highest address (3F8). Study *"Setting up a serial port."*

7 *C.* These two connectors are very common on the PC, especially for serial ports. *See "Understanding Serial Devices."*

8 *A, B, C, D.* Trick question? Maybe, but you may see questions on the A+ exam like this one. Whenever you see "Choose all that apply" on the A+ exams, be sure that you check every answer that could be a correct answer on its own. *See "Troubleshooting a serial port."*

9 *A.* SPP and EPP are parallel port standards that allow for one- and two-way communications, but both allow communications only one way at a time. TCP is either the stuff in the gasoline or the Internet protocol. *Review "Keeping up to standard."*

10 *B.* RTS/CTS is a hardware flow control method. Handshaking and flow control are synonymous terms, and stop bits are a part of the serial data transmission protocol. *Check out "Setting up a serial port."*

Chapter 12
Printers

Exam Objectives

▶ Identifying printer ports, cabling, and connectors

▶ Explaining printer concepts, operations, and components

▶ Troubleshooting common printer problems

▶ Identifying common printer care procedures

*W*hile society cherishes the idea of a paperless society, it churns out more and more paper with thousands, even millions, of numbers, letters, and symbols to be interpreted as information. The computer was going to create the paperless society and, as near as I can tell, has done just the opposite. If anything, more paper is printed today than ever, and most of the printing is being done by computer printers. Printers come in a variety of models, but they all essentially perform the same task — write information on paper for humans to read.

Little doubt exists that the printer is a very important device to the PC system. In terms of output devices, it ranks right after the monitor in importance. Like the monitor, its importance is what makes its failure all the more disrupting. I can live without my sound card for a while, but when will you have my printer fixed?

In my experience, at least four in ten service or help calls involve a printer in some way. Even if I'm wrong and the number is actually only 20 percent of the calls, of the ten major subsystems of the PC, the printer is still responsible for a disproportionate share of the problems, which is probably why the A+ Core exam has an entire domain and 10 percent of the test devoted just to printers.

Quick Assessment

Identifying printer ports, cabling, and connectors

1   A printer can connect to the PC using either a _____ or _____ connection.

2   The I/O address of _____ is 378-37Fh.

3   Bidirectional parallel interfaces are defined in the _____ standard.

Explaining printer concepts, operations, and components

4   A _____ printer uses an array of printwires to form and print a character.

5   Most laser printers use the _____ process or a derivative of it to print.

6   The _____ is used to uniformly charge the photosensitive drum.

7   The six steps of the laser printer process are _____, _____, _____, _____, _____, and _____.

8   Paper jams in a laser printer most usually occur in the _____ area.

Trouble-shooting common printer problems

9   Laser printer toner consists of _____ -coated iron particles.

10 Never connect a laser printer to a manual _____.

Identifying common printer care procedures

Answers

1   *Parallel* or *serial*. See "Starting at the connection."

2   *LPT1*. Look at "Starting at the connection."

3   *IEEE 1284*. Check out "Keeping up with standards."

4   *Dot matrix*. Review "Dot-matrix printers."

5   *EP (electrophotographic)*. Scan "Laser printers."

6   *Primary or main corona*. Look at "Inside the laser printer."

7   *Cleaning, conditioning, writing, developing, transferring, and fusing*. See "Printing with a laser printer."

8   *Paper pickup or paper feed*. Review "Troubleshooting Common Printer Problems."

9   *Plastic resin*. Review "Inside the laser printer."

10 *Switchbox or A/B switch*. Review Switching around…"

A Printer Is a Printer Is a Printer . . .

The funny thing about printers is that users tend to be rather animated and emotional when they don't work. No matter what type of printer is involved, it usually will, all of a sudden, just stop working. The true definition of a nanosecond is the length of time it takes the user to dial your number after the printer has not immediately spewed forth a document in perfect form. Because of its importance to customers, and the relatively high rate of service call problems relating to printer problems, about 10 percent of the A+ exam covers printers. This means about seven questions of the Core exam and perhaps two or three on the DOS/Windows exam deal with printers, their function, problems, and care. The majority of the questions are about laser printers, but be ready for questions on dot-matrix and ink-jet or bubble-jet printers as well.

Some attributes that all printers share include the following:

- ✔ **They are peripheral devices.** However, attempts have been made to merge the printer into the computer or the monitor (I still shudder over that one).

- ✔ **They are either parallel or serial (or both) devices.** Virtually all printers attach to the computer through a cable and a connector. What more can I say? You don't need fancy, special adapters here — just straightforward, traditional, easy-to-remember-for-the-test connectors.

- ✔ **They have some form of paper transport system to move the paper to and past the printing mechanism.** In every printer, some mechanism is used to push, pull, roll, or slide the paper through the printing process.

- ✔ **They have a printing or marking process.** Somehow characters are formed on the paper. A key or a group of wires strikes an inked ribbon, an ink cartridge sprays heated ink, or a toner cartridge creates an image with an electrical charge.

- ✔ **They have an engine.** Inside the printer resides the intelligence to accept information and commands from the PC and control the process of printing the information as directed.

Starting at the connection

Although some printers can connect through the serial ports (COM1 – COM4), most PC printers connect via the parallel ports (LPT1 – LPT3). LPT ports are designated and numbered according to their I/O addresses by the system BIOS during the boot sequence. Table 12-1 shows the I/O addresses and IRQs typically assigned to the LPT ports.

Memorize the contents of Table 12-1. You definitely see these items on the test.

Table 12-1	LPT Port System Resources	
Parallel Port	*I/O Address*	*IRQ*
LPT1	378-37Fh	7
LPT2	278-27F	5
LPT3	3BC-3BFh	7 or 5

Although Table 12-1 lists an IRQ for each of the parallel ports, most PC printers don't use an IRQ in either DOS or Windows operating systems. However, devices such as external tape or storage drives and the cables associated with file transfer software, such as Laplink and others, that do use interrupts also connect to parallel ports. Two types of connectors are used to connect printers and PCs:

- ✔ **The 25-pin DB (data bus) female connector:** This common connector is used to connect the printer to the PC through a 25-pin male LPT port that's usually mounted on the motherboard or on an adapter card.

- ✔ **The 36-pin Centronics:** This common connector is used at the printer end of the connecting cable.

A parallel cable should never be more than 15 feet in length. See Chapter 11 for more information on parallel and serial ports.

Switching around

You may or may not see a question on switchboxes on the test. You can use a *switchbox,* either manual or automatic, to connect more than one nonlaser printer or any other parallel device or devices to a single parallel port. You can also use them to allow multiple PCs to share a single printer. A dial designates which PC or device is to be connected to the primary device of the switchbox. The devices on the switchbox are called A/B switches because the station designations are generically labeled by alphabetic letters — A, B, C, and so on.

Never connect a laser printer to a manual switchbox. Taking the laser printer on- and offline by changing the active location with the dial creates line noise spikes on the cables connected to the switchbox that can damage the laser printer or the parallel port.

Keeping up with standards

Chapter 11, which covers parallel and serial ports specifically, includes a section on the IEEE 1284 parallel port and protocol standards. If you have not reviewed that chapter or the section entitled "Keeping up with standards," I strongly recommend that you make a point of studying it thoroughly. The IEEE 1284 standard, especially bidirectional communications on a parallel port, is most definitely on the test.

A Plethora of Printers

You can connect many different types of printers to a PC. If you are one of the lucky few who always seem to have the latest and greatest hardware, you probably have a distorted view of the kinds of computers that most users actually have — and it's not the latest and greatest. This view is especially true in printers. Many dot-matrix, inkjet, bubble jet, and even some noisy old daisy-wheel printers are still in use. Not everyone has a laser printer.

Some of the common types of printers are

- **Daisy-wheel:** These printers are still in use but are becoming rare. Daisy-wheel printers are an early type of impact printer that uses a print wheel that works much like the ball on an electric typewriter.

- **Dot-matrix:** These printers create characters by forming a group of hard-wire pins into the pattern of the letter, number, or special character and then striking the entire pin group through a ribbon, forming the character on paper.

- **Inkjet, or bubble jet:** These printers are probably the most popular printer type in use. They are able to produce a better-quality print but without the noise of both the dot-matrix and daisy-wheel printers. In brief, inkjet printers produce an image by heating ink into steam and then "jetting" it onto the paper.

- **Laser:** These printers use a complex printing process to produce very high-quality documents. Laser printers are becoming more common on the desktop, especially with prices continuing to decline.

Daisy-wheel printers

Daisy-wheel printers, because they use a solid form character on a key (or in this case a "petal"), produce what is called letter-quality (LQ) print. Letter-quality is the quality standard achieved by a typewriter. It is the standard by which all impact printers are measured.

You may see a question on the A+ Core exam regarding the daisy-wheel printer, and most likely it will relate to LQ print quality, that the wheel holds the characters to be printed, or the fact that a daisy-wheel printer is very, very noisy.

Dot-matrix printers

You may see a question on the exam relating to how the dot-matrix printer forms its characters, drives its paper, or how its resolution is measured, or all three.

The dot-matrix printer is an impact printer that creates its printed characters using a matrix of very fine printwires to form a pattern of dots. As the number of printwires used to create the character increases, so does its resolution (dots-per-inch) and the quality of the printed image. Each pin, chosen from a matrix of pins, forms a dot on the page, and the pattern of dots creates the printed character. The resulting character is not as good as that created with a daisy-wheel printer, but given the trade-off in noise and speed, you can live with less quality for many documents. The resolution is measured by the number of dots that can be printed in a square inch (dots-per-inch or DPI).

The most common numbers of printwires (pins) in the dot-matrix printer's printhead are 9, 18, and 24. A 24-pin printhead produces *near-letter quality* (NLQ) print. Printers with less than 24 pins are only capable of *draft quality* print, which produces characters with lots of wide-open spaces between the dots.

To produce a character, the print mechanism extends all the printwires needed to create a character. Behind each printwire is a solenoid coil that causes the pin to extend and impact the inked ribbon. A spring then pulls each printwire back into the printhead. Because of the impact used to strike the ink of the ribbon onto the page, dot-matrix printers are commonly used in situations where forms or documents with many carbon copies are created.

The typical dot-matrix printer uses continuous form paper (in contrast to the cut sheet paper used in laser and inkjet printers). Much like a typewriter, dot-matrix printers use a platen, a large rubberized roller under which the paper is fed. The platen provides spring tension to hold the paper in place and move it through the printer. When the platen is rotated by the platen motor, the paper is pushed up and past the printhead.

Dot-matrix printers also support form tractors, or pin-feed tractors, which attach to the platen and are also driven by the platen motor. Form tractors provide a more consistent feed mechanism by using the pin-feed holes along the side of the paper to pull the paper and multiple part forms through the printer.

The speed of a dot-matrix printer is rated in characters-per-second (CPS). Common speed ratings for dot-matrix printers range from 32 to 72 CPS. The actual speed realized from the printer depends largely on its mode of operation. Dot-matrix printers operate in either font (normal text, numbers, and symbols) and dot-addressable (graphics and charts) modes.

The printhead in a dot-matrix printer can get extremely hot and should not be touched while in use. Also, the printhead is never cleaned during preventive maintenance.

Inkjet printers

Don't expect to see many questions on the exam about inkjet printers. However, if you do encounter one, it will very likely deal with the way the inkjet forms its characters.

Inkjet, or bubble jet, printers are probably the most popular printer type in use for two main reasons:

- They are quiet — the inkjet printer is a nonimpact printer, and except for the quiet chattering of its printhead moving back and forth on the page and the sound of the paper feeding through the feed rollers, it is very quiet. Inkjet printers have become very popular in school and college lab settings for this reason.

- Their ink reservoir (which replaces the inked ribbon of earlier printers) is included in a disposable cartridge along with the printing mechanism. This means that each time the ink reservoir is replenished, a new print mechanism is also supplied.

Inkjet printers form characters by squirting ink, using an elaborate ink-stream process with as many as 50 tiny nozzles, to form characters on the paper. The print quality of an inkjet printer is rated in dots-per-inch (dpi). The more dots in the image, the better the image. Inkjets range from 150 dpi to over 1400 dpi on photo-quality printers.

Inkjet printer speeds are rated in pages per minute (PPM). Characters per second (CPS) is not used because the inkjet doesn't form each character separately. Rather, it prints one line at a time across the page. Inkjet printer speeds range from 2 PPM to 9 PPM.

Laser printers

Laser printers are VIT (very important technology) on the A+ exams. To prepare yourself, have a good understanding of laser printer operations in general, and the six steps of the laser printer's printing process specifically.

Laser printers are page printers in that they form and print all the text and graphics for one full sheet or page at a time. Three different printing processes are used in laser printers, each directly attributable to one or more manufacturer(s): EP, HP, and LED. The test covers only EP and HP.

✔ The electrophotographic (EP) process, developed by Xerox and Canon, was the first laser printer technology, and all laser printers use this technology in one form or another. Its characteristics are the use of a laser beam to produce an electrostatic charge and a dry toner to create the "printed" image.

✔ The Hewlett-Packard (HP) process is essentially the same as the EP process, with the exception of some minor operating procedures. It's similar enough to be considered the same process, but different enough to get its own name.

Inside the laser printer

Plan on learning and understanding just about everything there is to know about laser printers for the test. This most definitely includes the following list of major components. You can expect questions on the test that require you to know the overall laser printing process, as well as the role played by key components.

Laser printers use toner to create the image on the printed page. The toner, a dry powder that consists of iron particles coated with a plastic resin, is bonded to the paper during the print process. Toner is supplied to the printer in a removable cartridge that also contains many of the most important parts used in the printing process. Inside the toner cartridge are located the photosensitive drum, a mechanism used to place a charge on the drum, a roller used to develop the final image on the page, and, of course, the toner.

Including the toner cartridge, an additional eight standard assemblies exist in a laser printer. These assemblies are

✔ **The drum:** The drum inside the toner cartridge is photosensitive, which means it reacts to light. The drum holds an electrostatic charge except where it is exposed to light. The laser beam is reflected onto the surface of the drum to create a pattern of charged and not-so-charged spots, representing the image of the page to be printed.

✔ **High-voltage power supply:** The EP process uses very high voltage to charge the drum and transfer and hold the toner on the paper. The high-voltage power supply converts AC current into the higher voltages used by the printer.

- **DC power supply:** Like a computer, most of the electronic components in the laser printer use direct current. For example, logic circuits use +/−5V DC (volts direct current), and the paper transport motors use +24V DC. Also, like the computer's power supply, the laser printer DC power supply also contains the cooling system fan.

- **Paper transport:** Inside the laser printer are four types of rollers that move the paper through the printer. Each rubberized roller or set of rollers is driven by its own motor. The four roller types in the paper transport system are the feed roller or the paper pickup roller, the registration roller, the fuser roller, and the exit roller.

You're asked on the test where most paper jams occur in a laser printer. The answer is the paper transport area.

- **Primary corona:** Also called the *main corona* or *the primary grid,* this device forms an electrical field that uniformly charges the photosensitive drum to −600V as a way to reset it prior to receiving the print image and toner.

- **Transfer corona:** This mechanism moves a page image from the drum to the paper. I cover how this happens a little later, but for now, know that the transfer corona charges the paper and the charge pulls the toner from the drum onto the paper. As the paper exits the transfer corona, a static charge eliminator strip reduces the charge on the paper so that it won't stick to the drum. Not all printers use a transfer corona; some use a transfer roller instead. When working on a printer with a transfer roller, be careful not to touch the roller with your bare hand or arm. The oils from your skin can spot the transfer roller and cause improperly changed paper, which shows up as defects in the printed image.

- **Fusing rollers:** The toner is melted permanently to the page by the fusing rollers that apply pressure and heat, between 165 and 180 degrees Celsius, to it. The fuser — not the use of a laser — is why pages come out of a laser printer hot.

- **Controller:** In effect, this is the motherboard of the laser printer, and it carries many of the same architecture and components of a PC motherboard. It's the controller that communicates with the PC, houses the memory in the printer, and forms the image printed on the page. Memory expansion is possible on virtually all laser printers. Adding memory allows the printer to reproduce larger documents or graphics in higher resolutions or to support additional soft fonts.

A printer that experiences frequent memory overflow errors has a bad memory board, a memory board that was installed incorrectly, or a memory board that needs additional memory. Diagnose this condition in this order.

Printing with a laser printer

Six major steps are involved in printing a page on a laser printer. It's very important that you remember the sequence and activities of each step in the process. A shortcut I've devised to help you remember the sequence is

California Cows Won't Dance The Fandango (CCWDTF)

The first letter in each word represents the steps in the laser printing process: Cleaning, Conditioning, Writing, Developing, Transferring, and Fusing. (You may also see cleaning as the last step in other references, but on the exam, it's listed first.) Also be ready for the test to ask you for the steps backward. Here is what goes on during each step of the EP laser printing process:

1. **Cleaning:** Before a page is started, any remnants of a previous page are cleared away. The drum is swept free of any lingering toner with a rubber blade, and a fluorescent lamp removes any electrical charge remaining on the drum. Any toner removed in this step is not reused but is put into a used-toner compartment on the cartridge.

2. **Conditioning:** The entire drum is uniformly charged to –600V by the primary corona wire (also known as the main corona) located inside the toner cartridge. This charge conditions the drum for the next step.

3. **Writing:** The laser printer controller uses a laser beam and a series of mirrors to create the image of the page on the drum. The laser beam is turned on and off in accordance with the image to be created on the drum. Where the laser's light contacts the photosensitive drum, the charge at that spot is reduced to about –100V. After the image has been transferred to the drum this way, the controller also starts the page sheet through the printer, stopping it at the registration rollers.

4. **Developing:** The developing roller, located inside the toner cartridge, has a magnet inside of it that attracts the iron particles in the toner. As the developing roller rotates by the drum, the toner is attracted to the areas of the drum that have been exposed by the laser, creating the print image on the drum.

5. **Transferring:** The back of the paper sheet, the one that has been waiting patiently at the registration rollers, is given a positive charge that attracts the negatively charged toner from the drum onto the paper as it passes. After this step, the paper has the image of the page on it, but the toner, which is held only by simple magnetism, is not yet bonded to it.

6. **Fusing:** The fusing rollers apply heat and pressure to the toner, melting and pressing it into the paper to create a permanent bond. The fusing rollers are covered with Teflon and treated with a light silicon oil to keep the paper from sticking to them.

Preventive Maintenance and Supplies

Taking proper care of a laser printer can extend its life, especially if the care includes routinely perfomed preventive maintenance. It is important enough that you can expect to see at least one question on the A+ Core exam regarding the cleaning, protection, and preventive maintenance of a laser printer.

Here are a number of common-sense procedures and a few more technical ones that you can use to keep a printer working and reliable:

- Plug the printer into a surge protector or UPS (uninterruptible power supply). For a laser printer, first make sure that the UPS is capable of handling the power demands of the printer at startup; few conventional PC UPS units can.

  Under the heading of you heard it here first, but you will again later: Never plug a laser printer into a conventional PC UPS. Laser printers draw a tremendous amount of power at startup, and few UPS units have enough power to handle the demand.

- Always use the type and weight of paper recommended for the printer to avoid printfeed path jams.

- Clean dot-matrix printers regularly by vacuuming or blowing them out with compressed air.

- Use a wire brush or rubber-conditioning product to clean and maintain the paper transport of an inkjet or laser printer. Never put anything inside a laser printer while it's running to try to clear the paper path, and always wait until the fusing area has cooled down before working in this area of a laser printer. Remember that it generates a great deal of heat melting the toner to the paper and stays hot for some time afterward.

Laser printers have their own special needs when it comes to maintenance, which you should know, test or no test. For the A+ test, you need to know about toner and the cleaning of the primary corona wire. The following list helps you to properly address these special needs.

- The toner in a laser printer is really nasty stuff. If you have ever accidentally dropped a toner cartridge or ignorantly turned one over and shaken it, you know how nasty this stuff can be. Should you ever have a toner spillage accident, or see toner spilled inside the laser printer, don't use your regular vacuum to clean it up. Remember that toner is very fine particles of iron and plastic. The particles are so fine that they seep through the walls of most vacuum bags and get into the motor, where the plastic melts. Special types of vacuum cleaner bags are made for working with toner.

✔ Should you get toner on your skin, never use warm water to clean it off. Warm water may cause the toner to fuse to your skin. It's best to first wipe off as much of the toner with a dry paper towel or soft cloth. Then rinse with cold water, and finish by washing with soap and cold water.

✔ Usually packed with the toner cartridge is a cleaning brush or cotton swab that you can use to clean the transfer corona wire. You can clean the primary corona wire with a cotton swab as well. While cleaning these wires, be very careful not to break them.

✔ During the print process, the laser produces a gas called *ozone*. Most laser printers have an ozone filter that also captures toner and paper dust. Replace or clean this filter in accordance with the manufacturer's instructions in the printer's manual.

✔ Inside the laser printer are two or more mirrors that reflect the laser onto the drum. Using lint-free cloths, periodically clean the laser mirrors — with the power off, of course.

✔ The fuser cleaning pad and the fusing roller can also become dirty and leave unwanted toner blobs on the paper. Check these printer parts regularly and clean them as necessary.

Troubleshooting Common Printer Problems

The A+ exam includes situational questions that require you to respond with the action that should be taken first or next. The troubleshooting sequence for a printer problem is fairly routine for most experienced PC service technicians, and you probably have your own. However, I suggest reviewing the following steps just to refresh your memory for the test.

The first real sign of a printer problem is that paper with printing on it isn't coming out of the printer. When this happens, you can look in four places:

✔ **Printer:** First check to see whether it's powered on, and then check to see whether it's on-line. These suggestions may seem like bonehead stuff, but they are commonly the problem. Make sure that the printer has paper and that the feed tray, roller, or slide is in its proper position for operation. Check for a paper jam; if you find one, clear it, but also notice the point at which the jam occurred and check the rollers and paper feed mechanism carefully. Most paper jams happen right in the paper pickup area, so look there first.

✔ **Cable:** If the printer seems to be generally all right, ensure that the cable is the proper type of cable. Nearly all laser printers and the newest inkjets and dot-matrix printers require an IEEE 1284 cable. If the cable is the right kind, then be sure that it's solidly connected at each end.

> ✔ **Port:** To check the port, use loopback plugs and diagnostic software. Believe it or not, after the printer itself, the port has the next highest failure rate.
>
> ✔ **Software:** In the Windows environment, printers stall for just about any reason. If the printer status shows no problems, and you can't find any other problem, try restarting the system.

Beyond a printer not printing, the most common failure is a bad print image. Regularly cleaning the printer and the printhead as directed by the printer's manuals helps to avoid this problem. It's worth a little bit of time to show customers how to clean these items themselves.

Setting Up a Printer in Windows

You can expect to find a question or two about the procedure used to set up a printer in Windows on the DOS/Windows exam. Familiarize yourself with the process used by actually doing it a few times using different ways to access the Printer group on the Control Panel.

Before you can set a printer in the Windows environment, you must obtain the printer driver for that printer under the specific version of Windows you operate under. If you use Windows 3.*x*, then use a Windows 3.*x* printer driver; for Windows 95, use a printer driver designed for it.

Both Windows 3.*x* and Windows 95 come with a good assortment of printer drivers built in. Some printers still require a separate printer driver and usually include it on a diskette.

Add new printers through the Printers function found on the Control Panel or on the Settings option of the Start Program menu. In either case, the Printers dialog box displays the Add Printer wizard icon (see Figure 12-1). The following lab details the steps you use to add a printer.

Lab 12-1   Adding a New Printer

1. From the Windows desktop, click the Start button to display the Start menu. Access the Settings menu and choose the Printers option.

Or double-click the My Computer icon to display the My Computer folder. Open the Control Panel and choose the Printers icon.

2. With the Printer folder open, choose the Add Printer icon, shown in Figure 12-1, to display the Add Printer dialog box (Windows 3.*x* or Windows 95) or start the Add Printer wizard (Windows 98).

3. If the printer you are adding is not included in the supported printers list, use the diskette or CD-ROM that came with the printer to supply the device driver by clicking the "Have Disk" button when appropriate.

After the printer driver loads, an icon for the new printer displays in the Printers folder.

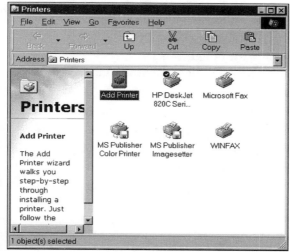

Figure 12-1: Add Printer icon.

Prep Test

1 The paper continuously jams in a laser printer. Where would you look first?

    A ○ Pressure roller area

    B ○ Transfer roller area

    C ○ Fuser roller area

    D ○ Paper pickup area

2 What happens in the conditioning phase of a laser printer?

    A ○ The image is created on the drum.

    B ○ The erasure lamps neutralize the drum.

    C ○ The primary corona applies a uniform charge to the drum.

    D ○ The paper is charged by the transfer corona.

3 The correct order of operations in the laser printing process is

    A ○ Conditioning, cleaning, writing, developing, fusing, transferring

    B ○ Cleaning, conditioning, writing, developing, transferring, fusing

    C ○ Conditioning, cleaning, writing, developing, transferring, fusing

    D ○ Cleaning, conditioning, writing, developing, fusing, transferring

4 On a system on which printing has been working well, the user gets an error message when he tries to print. No changes have been made to the system. After checking whether the printer is powered on, what do you check for next?

    A ○ Is the printer online?

    B ○ Is the printer designated as the default printer?

    C ○ Is the correct printer driver installed?

    D ○ Will the printer print when attached to a different PC?

5 Reducing the negative charge on the areas of the drum that represent the image to be printed is done in which step of the laser printing process?

    A ○ Transferring

    B ○ Conditioning

    C ○ Fusing

    D ○ Writing

6 The toner is deposited onto the drum surface in which step of the printing process?

A ○ Writing
B ○ Conditioning
C ○ Developing
D ○ Transferring

7 Toner is bonded with the paper during which phase of the laser printing process?

A ○ Writing
B ○ Transferring
C ○ Conditioning
D ○ Fusing

8 Which of the following forms the electrical field that charges the drum?

A ○ Transfer corona wire
B ○ Primary corona wire
C ○ Fusing roller
D ○ Cleaning blade

9 A dot-matrix printer with a 24-pin printhead is capable of producing

A ○ Letter-quality print
B ○ Daisy-wheel quality print
C ○ Near-letter quality print
D ○ Graphics only

10 Bidirectional communications on a parallel cable was standardized by

A ○ IEEE 232
B ○ VESA
C ○ Laser printers
D ○ IEEE 1284

Answers

1 *D.* Most paper jams happen right in the paper pickup area when more than one sheet, a crumpled sheet, or a twisted sheet of paper tries to feed into the paper pickup rollers. *See "Troubleshooting Common Printer Problems."*

2 *C.* In this step of the laser printing process, the drum is put into the right condition to receive the print image. *Charge over to "Printing with a laser printer."*

3 *B.* Remember "California Cows Won't Dance The Fandango," and remember that conditioning is longer than cleaning just like California is longer than cows. *See "Printing with a laser printer."*

4 *A.* I know this seems pretty basic, but forgetting the basics gets many PC technicians in trouble. *Check out "Troubleshooting Common Printer Problems."*

5 *D.* This step "writes" the blips on the drum where toner will be placed during the developing step. *Read "Printing with a laser printer."*

6 *C.* I include this question to drive home the comment I make for Prep Test Question 5. Putting toner on the drum "develops" the print image so that it can be transferred to the paper. *Review "Printing with a laser printer."*

7 *D.* Okay, this is the last question of the laser printer's process steps. In the fusing step, the toner is heated to about 350 degrees Fahrenheit and pressed down hard by the fusing rollers. *Take one more look at "Printing with a laser printer."*

8 *B.* To separate the two corona wires in your mind, just remember that the primary corona goes first and charges the drum. The transfer corona is second and charges the paper. *Look at "Inside the laser printer."*

9 *C.* About the best a dot-matrix printer can do with round dots is get the print near the quality of print produced with a solid typeface. *Review "Dot-matrix printers."*

10 *D.* IEEE standard 1284 combines the SPP, EPP, ECL parallel port standards that include bidirectional communications. *See "Keeping up with standards."*

Chapter 13

Communications and Networking Basics

- -

Exam Objectives

▶ Understanding networking concepts

▶ Swapping and configuring network interface cards

▶ Connecting to the network

▶ Networking DOS and Windows

▶ Identifying Internet concepts

▶ Accessing the Internet

- -

*A*lthough data communications has been on the A+ test in the past, networking and the Internet are largely new to the exams. As more and more PCs are connected to local area networks, intranets, wide area networks, and the Internet (especially in office environments), it is important that PC technicians understand the installation of network adapters and the potential impact that repairs to a networked PC can have.

The Internet and World Wide Web, virtually unknown only five years ago, are now the primary reason that some people even have a PC. A growing number of service calls relate to upgrading PCs to access a network or the Internet. For the A+ exam, you need to have an understanding of the basic protocols, terminology, and function of the Internet and how it is accessed.

Although I can't afford a T1 line (a very fast data line), I can still connect to the Internet with a modem. The A+ exam includes questions about modems, but they are considered an FRU (field replaceable unit), along with adapter cards, disk drives, and so on.

You need to know about networks and how they are connected, the Internet and all of its little buddies (the ones that are known only by their initials), and modems. Well, fancy that — I cover all those topics in this chapter!

Quick Assessment

Explaining networking concepts

1 A _____ is used to connect two or more PCs for sharing resources over permanently installed cabling.

2 IEEE _____ is the standard for Ethernet networks.

Swapping and configuring network interface cards

3 Before working on a PC, determine whether it is a _____ PC.

Connecting to the network

4 The two most commonly used connectors for network hardware are the _____ and the _____.

5 The most commonly used cable media is _____.

Networking DOS and Windows

6 _____ is the most common Ethernet network architecture in use.

7 The information needed to check out how Windows 95 has configured a NIC is accessed through the _____.

Identifying Internet concepts

8 _____ is the most widely used network protocol.

Accessing the Internet

9 The software facility used to resolve the domain name to its associated IP address is _____.

Answers

1   *Local area network.* Review "Basic networking terminology you need to know."

2   *802.3.* Check out "Ethernet cabling."

3   *Networked.* Look up "Servicing a Networked PC."

4   *RJ-45 and BNC.* See "Connecting with connectors."

5   *UTP or unshielded twisted pair.* Review "That cable's not my type."

6   *10BaseT.* Check out "Ethernet cabling."

7   *Control Panel and Network icons.* See "Fiddling with network adapters and Windows."

8   *TCP/IP.* Connect to "Moving On to the Internet."

9   *DNS or WINS.* Review "Resolving the domain name."

Networking It Together

About 10 percent of the A+ Core and DOS/Windows specialty exam questions require that you know and understand the following things:

- ✔ Basic networking terms and concepts, including protocols, cabling, and the different ways you can connect a PC to a network
- ✔ How to tell whether a PC is networked
- ✔ The process you use to swap and configure network interface cards (NICs)
- ✔ The possible ramifications of a repair to a networked computer

Networking is one exam domain in which it is very difficult to suggest ways to save preparation time. You can plan on seeing five or six questions on each exam (the Core and the DOS/Windows) relating to networking and the Internet. With such a wide range of topics, predicting just what you may see on the tests is difficult. My best advice is to concentrate on

- ✔ The OSI model (memorize the layers)
- ✔ Networks (topologies and protocols)
- ✔ Network interface cards (NICs), their connectors, and commonly used cable media

That's just about everything.

Basic networking terminology you need to know

A network is two or more computers that have been connected together for the purposes of exchanging data and sharing resources. Networked shared resources range from printers, CD-ROMs, and modems to files and hard disks. Networks can vary in size and scope as well.

Many types of computer networks exist, but you need only be concerned with these:

- ✔ **Peer-to-peer network:** This type of network includes two or more PCs connected to share data files, a printer, or other resources.
- ✔ **Local area network (LAN):** A small business or corporate department may install a LAN interconnecting from two to hundreds of PCs, using permanently installed cabling or perhaps a wireless technology.
- ✔ **Wide area networks (WAN):** A corporation may maintain a WAN using dial-up, leased, or other dedicated communication means.

Also be familiar with the following network terminology and characteristics:

- ✓ **Nodes:** Computers on a network are sometimes called nodes. Computers and devices that allocate resources for a network are called servers.

- ✓ **Topology:** The geometric arrangement of any network is its topology. The most common topologies are the bus, star, and ring topologies.

- ✓ **Protocol:** To operate efficiently, any communications-based system must have established rules to govern its operation. This set of rules is its protocol. Popular protocols for LANs are Ethernet, token ring, and FDDI.

- ✓ **Data packets:** Data, messages, and tokens that are transmitted on any network must conform to the size and format prescribed under the network's protocol. Data packets can also vary between network operating systems (NOS) on the same protocol.

- ✓ **Architecture:** Any network can be classified as either a peer-to-peer or client/server architecture. When all nodes on a network are equal and resources are shared equally, the network is a true peer-to-peer network. When one computer is designated to host programs or files for the rest of the network, it is a server, and the other nodes are clients.

- ✓ **Media:** Nodes on a network are connected by twisted-pair copper wire, coaxial cable, fiber-optic cable, or wireless radio wave connections.

Never tell secrets or trust sales people

All phases of network operations are defined in the layers of the Open Systems Interconnection (OSI) model developed by the International Standards Organization (ISO). The ISO OSI model has seven layers, which you need to remember for the test. Don't memorize what they do, but remember the names of the layers:

- ✓ **The physical layer** is the bottom and most technical layer of the OSI model. This layer defines about what you would expect — the physical components of the network. This includes cables, their media, length, connectors, and so on. The physical layer also defines the characteristics of the electrical signals used to transmit data around the network without assigning any particular meaning to the signals.

- ✓ **The data link layer** assigns meaning to the electrical signals transmitted around a network. This layer determines the size and format of the data sent between the PCs, printers, and other devices (all of which are called nodes) on a network. It also defines the error detection and correction schemes that check to see that the data sent is the data received.

- ✔ **The network layer** provides definitions for the interconnection of two possibly dissimilar networks so that data from one can flow to the other.

- ✔ **The transport layer** breaks data into easily handled message sizes and also provides the identification and addressing that allows a message to find its way from one node to another.

- ✔ **The session layer** carries out the communications between nodes exchanging data. A session must be established before an exchange of data can take place. Don't confuse this layer with a guitar man — he is a *session player*.

- ✔ **The presentation layer** is primarily responsible for the coding and decoding of either compressed or encrypted data sent over the network. Its name comes from its duties that involve the scrambling and unscrambling of data for presentation to the node.

- ✔ **The application layer** provides the linkage for application programs to interact with the network. "Application layer" is a bit of a misnomer. Applications don't interact with this layer. For example, if you want to connect to the network with either Microsoft Word or Netscape Navigator, these applications interact with the network operating system (NOS), such as Windows NT, Novell, and so on, which then interacts with the application layer.

The phrase I use to remember the OSI's seven layers is "Please Do Not Tell Secret Passwords Anytime," which represents <u>P</u>hysical, <u>D</u>ata link, <u>N</u>etwork, <u>T</u>ransport, <u>S</u>ession, <u>P</u>resentation, and <u>A</u>pplication. This little saying can come in handy because you can bet on seeing a question that asks you to identify the seven layers of the ISO OSI model. Some others I've run across that you may use are "People Design Networks To Send Packets Accurately," "Please Do Not Throw Salami Pizza Away," "Please Do Not Trust Sales People Always," or, going backward, "All People Seem To Need Data Processing." You may want to make up your own or create a hybrid.

LAN-ing versus WAN-ing

Personal computers can be connected into networks, at which time they cease to be personal computers and become network nodes or workstations. Getting on a network can be a big deal to a PC. You may think that it's like the PC losing its individual identity and becoming one of a crowd, but actually a networked PC has the best of both worlds. It still has its own identity, but it also has available to it all the resources on the network to offer to its users. That's quite an accomplishment for a PC!

When nodes are directly interconnected within a fairly limited area, they form a local area network (LAN). A LAN can be connected to another LAN to form a bigger LAN. LANs can be interconnected indefinitely, but as long as they are contained within a single physical area, they remain a LAN. Usually a LAN is created using cabling that has been installed in the walls, ceilings, floors — anywhere that it can be pulled through the facility. A little later in this chapter, I explain how LANs can be connected together.

The nodes of a LAN typically fall into one of two groups: clients and servers. A *client* is any node that requests a service from another node on the network. A *server* is the node that receives the request and provides the response. Some clients can also be servers, and servers can be clients as well. However, normally the server is the server, clients are clients, and they are all happy with their lot in life.

When LANs, or nodes for that matter, are connected over longer distances, such as miles, states, or continents, they form a wide area network (WAN). It should be fairly obvious why a WAN is called that. I guess it could be called "directly adapted multiple network nodes," or DAMNN for short, but that just doesn't explain its setup as well. WANs are usually constructed using ISDN, leased line, or other high-speed connections.

A LAN is not the opposite of a WAN, a LAN is not the same as a WAN, and you do not need a LAN to make a WAN. However, WANs are commonly made up of a number of LANs. Got it?

Stars, rings, and pretty nodes all in a row

Creating a LAN is more than just connecting PCs to the network. Beyond the fact that making the connection itself is somewhat involved (more on that later), the network itself must be laid out so that its nodes can be connected easily and the scheme used to facilitate the exchanges between the nodes can work with the physical media's layout. The arrangement used to physically interconnect the nodes and logically serve them is called the LAN's *topology,* or the pattern the LAN resembles if you look at it from high above while squinting your eyes.

The three basic types of network topologies, shown in Figure 13-1, are the star, ring, and bus topologies:

 ✔ **The star topology** is common to ARCNet (Attached Resource Computer Network) networks. Every node in a star network is directly connected to a central server, giving it a starburst look. You have to use a bit of imagination and be willing to visualize all the nodes arranged around the server, instead of the reality that they are all located to one side and resemble one-half of a daisy.

✔ **The ring topology,** which is known more commonly under its commercial name of IBM's Token Ring, creates a network structure in which all the nodes are connected one to another to form a loop that starts and ends at one of the nodes, possibly the server. Like the star, you have to use some imagination to create a ring from the connected nodes.

✔ **The bus topology,** or Ethernet networking, is the most common network topology in use. If the star truly is a star, and the ring is really a ring, then Ethernet networks are installed as a straight line, called a *backbone*. I think it's called a backbone because after you attach all the nodes to the main Ethernet line, it resembles the skeleton of a dead fish — without the head, of course.

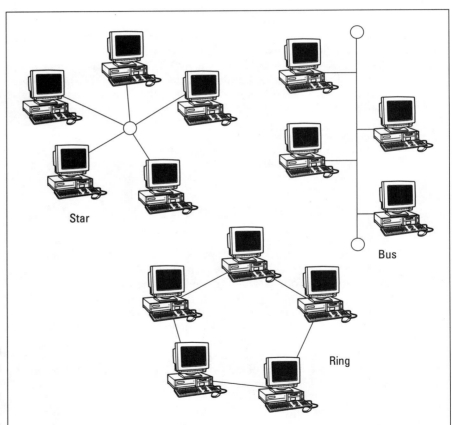

Figure 13-1:
The basic
network
topologies.

Focusing on the Fundamental Features

Networks have essentially five parts: nodes, NICs, cables, connectors, and a network operating system (NOS). For the A+ exam, you are primarily concerned with the NIC and how it is configured and installed into a node (a PC, printer, or other network-capable device). You also need some understanding of the different cable types and how they connect to the NIC. If you know that a network has a NOS, that should cover that part.

A good resource to use for this area is *Networking For Dummies,* 3rd Edition, by Doug Lowe (published by IDG Books Worldwide, Inc.). I recommend Doug's book because it's a good source for networking information and not because I'm trying to suck up.

The network interface card

The network interface card (NIC) is a physical and logical link for a PC to a network. The NIC is installed inside the computer into an unused expansion slot. NICs are available for most of the expansion bus architectures, so getting a card for the slot that's available is easy. If no PCI (peripheral component interconnect) slots are open, use an ISA (industry standard architecture) card or something similar.

When choosing a NIC for a system, try to get one that is Plug-and-Play compatible to make setup easier. Even with Plug-and-Play, a network card can be a pain to set up. Some NICs use DIP switches, some use software, and some use both to create a card's identity and compatibility to the network. The setup needed for the NIC is controlled by two factors: the PC itself and the NOS (network operating system, such as Windows NT, Novell Internetware, and others). If you have the choice, do yourself a big favor and use the same brand and model NIC in every network PC. Mixing NICs on a network can also be a pain, and you know where.

The NIC is a translator that works between the network and the PC. Networks transmit data in a serial data format (one bit at a time), and the data bus of the PC moves data in a parallel format (eight bits at a time). The NIC acts as a go-between to convert the signal from serial to parallel or parallel to serial, depending on its direction. The NIC also formats the data as required by the network architecture.

That cable's not my type

Three basic media are used for network cables: coaxial cable, fiber-optic cable, and cables consisting of twisted pairs of copper wire. In these general categories are more specific cabling types, as illustrated in Figures 13-2, 13-3, and 13-4. You need to know each type of cable and the network architecture it is most commonly used with for the test.

- ✔ **Coaxial cable** (see Figure 13-2). Actually, two types of coaxial cable are used in networks (the type that hooks up your television set is a third type):

  - • **Thick coaxial cable,** which is usually yellow in color and used in what are called *thicknets,* has two conductors. It's made of a solid center wire and a braided metal shield. Foam insulation separates the two, and a sturdy plastic sheathing covers the whole bundle. Thick coax can be used in 500 meter lengths.

  - • **Thin coaxial cable,** used in thinnets, has the same basic construction of thick coax, except it is made of lighter and less expensive materials. This cable is also referred to as RG-58 A/U. The A/U indicates that the core of the wire has a *stranded* core (strands of wire wound together).

- ✔ **Fiber-optic cable** ("fiber" to most network techies), shown in Figure 13-3, has several advantages. It carries a huge amount of data very fast, is small in size, resists corrosion, and is very reliable. On the other hand, it is hard to splice, difficult to install, and it and the devices that connect to it cost more than other types of networking cable.

- ✔ **Twisted pair cable** is available in two types: unshielded and shielded.

  - • **Unshielded twisted pair** (UTP), shown in Figure 13-4, is the most popular type of network cabling in use. UTP has four pairs of wires inside a plastic sheath. Because each of the copper wires (either solid or stranded) is only itself covered with a thin plastic sheath, each pair of wires is twisted a different number of twists per inch to eliminate interference from the other pairs of wire or other electrical devices near the cable.

  - • **Shielded twisted pair** (STP) is common in higher-speed network architectures. STP is very much like UTP with the added bonus of a metallic shield wrapped around the wire bundle to eliminate interference from outside devices, such as electrical motors, fluorescent light fixtures, and so on.

Twisted pair cabling is defined in categories or grades that provide an increasing (as the number gets bigger) amount of protection for outside electrical noise and interference. Networks should be created with cat 3 cable or better, with cat 5 preferred.

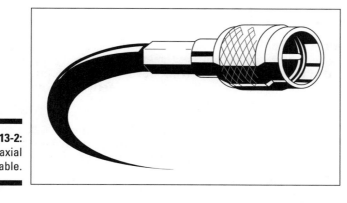

Figure 13-2:
Coaxial
cable.

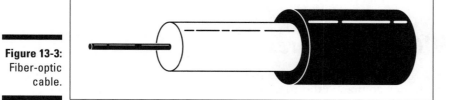

Figure 13-3:
Fiber-optic
cable.

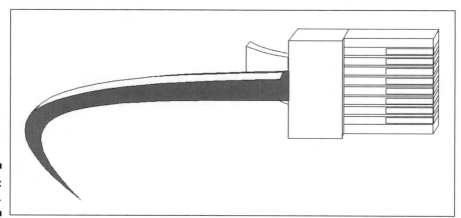

Figure 13-4:
UTP cable.

Connecting with connectors

Different types of connectors are used with different types of cable media. That probably seems like an obvious statement, but the range of connectors is fairly limited in the network world. While several special connectors are used to connect network cables to NICs and other network hardware, the two most commonly used are the following:

- ✔ **The BNC (Bayonet Naur Connector)** is used to connect thicknet network cables to the NIC. *Naur* is the inventor, and *bayonet* is what it's supposed to look like. These connectors are very distinctive-looking.

- ✔ **The RJ-45 connector** looks much like its cousin, the RJ-11 connector, which is used on telephone lines. The difference is that the RJ-45 is physically bigger and connects eight wires, whereas the RJ-11 connects either four or six wires.

NIC architectures

NICs come in different varieties to match the architecture of the network to which they connect: Ethernet, token ring, or FDDI. Here's a description of each:

- ✔ **Ethernet,** or bus topology, uses a full range of network media (using copper or fiber optics) and operates at either 10 Mbps or 100 Mbps. The 100 Mbps Ethernet is called Fast Ethernet. An Ethernet network (local area network) can support about 500 nodes. This is the most commonly installed type of network, probably because it is the cheapest and simplest, the two main characteristics to look for when building a network.

- ✔ **Token ring,** or ring topology, also uses copper and fiber-optic cabling, operates at 4 Mbps to 16 Mbps, and supports about 260 nodes. A token ring network operates very reliably but can be a bear to troubleshoot.

- ✔ **FDDI** (I've heard this pronounced as *fiddy,* but it's usually just spelled out) stands for Fiber Distributed Data Interface. A FDDI NIC contains a laser transceiver that converts its digital data into light to be transmitted on a fiber-optic network or back to a digital signal from incoming light impulses for use by the PC. FDDI is a standard of the American National Standards Institute (ANSI) and the International Standards Organization (ISO) for data networks using ring topology and data speeds of 100 Mbps.

The component on the NIC that handles the data transmission duties is the transceiver. Although it performs different tasks for different network types, its job is to transmit the appropriate data format and signal to the PC and the network. Some NICs have more than one transceiver, common on Ethernet cards, with each attached to a different connector type on the card.

Ethernet Networks

To help you better understand how a node fits into its network, review the three common network architectures. The A+ exam approaches this subject from the perspective of how an individual PC can interrupt the network, if the network goes down.

Ethernet topology

Ethernets are easily the most common network type in use. Although it is generally based on the bus topology, it can also be installed as a star. When installed in a bus design, the nodes are placed on the network backbone with the backbone cable terminated at each end, as illustrated in Figure 13-5.

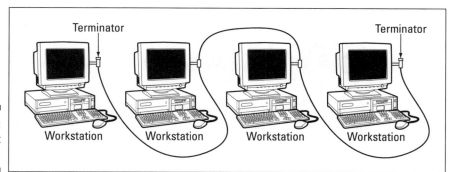

Figure 13-5: An Ethernet bus design.

An Ethernet network can also be clustered around one or more hubs in a star design, as shown in Figure 13-6. A *hub* is a device that connects many devices to a server through a single line. The Ethernet star design is commonly used because it is much easier to lay out, install cable for, and troubleshoot.

Ethernet networks are passive, which means that the nodes (not the network devices such as hubs and routers) do all the work. Messages move around the network from one node to another. Ethernet cables are like

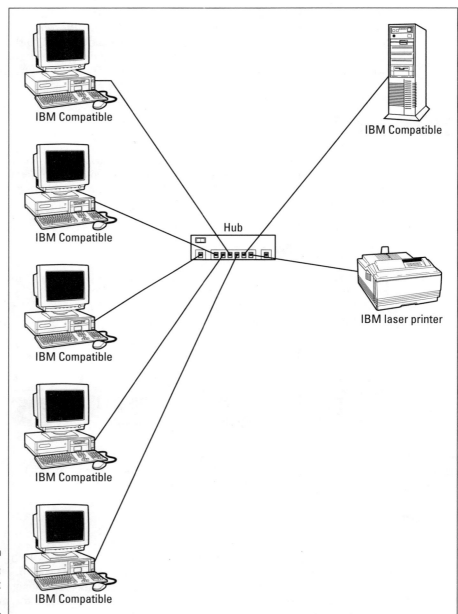

IBM Compatible

IBM Compatible

IBM Compatible

IBM Compatible

IBM Compatible

Hub

IBM Compatible

IBM laser printer

Figure 13-6:
An Ethernet
star design.

pneumatic air tubes that move plastic holders between two points — similar to the drive-up window at the bank and some large warehouse stores. If both ends of the tube were to send holders at the same time, a collision would occur. Then after the line was clear, the senders would try again, allowing one to go first and then sending the other one through.

To avoid this problem with its messages, an Ethernet node checks the line to see whether it is in use before sending a message. If it is busy, the Ethernet waits; otherwise, it sends its message. The protocol used for this purpose by Ethernet devices is *carrier sense multiple access with collision detection,* or CSMA/CD. The name explains what it does: It helps a node sense whether the line is busy, recognizing that multiple devices are accessing the network and looking to avoid message collisions.

Ethernet cabling

The cable types listed earlier in this chapter are given special names in the Ethernet world to describe the cable, its speed, and other characteristics. The IEEE 802.3 standard defines the various versions of Ethernet and its cabling. The cable systems used in Ethernet are the following:

- ✔ **10Base2,** also called thin Ethernet, thinwire, or thinnet, uses light coaxial cable to create a 10 Mbps network with cable segments that cannot be more than 185 meters in length. 10Base2 cables connect with BNC connectors. The NIC uses a T-connector where the cables from two adjacent nodes connect. Ethernet requires that any unused connection must have a 50-ohm terminator.

- ✔ **10Base5,** also called thick Ethernet, thickwire, or thicknet, is the original cabling standard for Ethernet using coaxial cables. The name comes from its 10 Mbps speed and its maximum cable length of 500 meters between nodes. 10Base5 connects with BNC or AUI (attachment unit interface) connectors, which are the big connectors found on many NICs and hubs.

- ✔ **10BaseT,** where the T represents "twisted," uses UTP (unshielded twisted pair) cable to create a 10 Mbps network with cable segments limited to 100 meters. Because it is the least expensive and easiest to work with, 10BaseT Ethernet networks are quite common.

- ✔ **100BaseT** is also called Fast Ethernet and uses STP (shielded twisted pair) cable to create a 100 Mbps network.

- ✔ **10BaseF** uses fiber-optic cable (the "F" in 10BaseF) to create a 10 Mbps network. Fiber-optic-based networks use special connectors, hubs, and NICs to create a network. Fiber-optic cable is commonly used to interconnect between buildings on a network, with copper (UTP/STP) used to connect the nodes to the network. In network tech talk, this arrangement is "fiber to the halls and copper to the walls."

802 point what?

The IEEE (Institute for Electrical and Electronics Engineers), or the "eye triple-e" as some folks call it, has created a group of standards relating to networks that bear the number 802. Within the 802 standard are 12 subcategories that specify the following networking areas:

✔ 802.1   Internetworking

✔ 802.2   Logic Link Control

✔ 802.3   CSMA/CD LAN (Ethernet)

✔ 802.4   Token Bus LAN

✔ 802.5   Token Ring LAN

✔ 802.6   MAN (Metropolitan Area Network)

✔ 802.7   Broadband Technical Advisory Group

✔ 802.8   FiberOptic Technical Advisory Group

✔ 802.9   Integrated Voice/Data Networks

✔ 802.10   Network Security

✔ 802.11   Wireless Networks

✔ 802.12   Demand Priority Access LAN

Meet me at the hub

Ethernet networks using 10/100BaseT involve a clustering device known as a *hub*. The hub serves to consolidate the nodes in a given area and connect to the main system server on one line. The use of a hub allows you to be more flexible about where nodes are physically located, and as long as you have available ports on the hub, a hub makes adding a new node to the network fairly simple. For a network with more than six or so nodes, the network should use a hub and 10BaseT. The fact that a hub and its nodes can be connected into another hub extends the flexibility of the network as far as you want to take it.

Token Ring Networks

The Ethernet is a collaborative development, but Token Ring is an IBM development that is now covered by IEEE 802.5. Its basic premise is that the network's primary cable (backbone) is arranged in a ring (or at least in a loop). The control mechanism used in a ring structure is called *token passing*.

Some time ago, I attended a workshop where the participants formed a circle and passed around a pine branch at the end of the seminar. When each person got the branch, he or she was to share a personal truth about the meeting. When it was my turn, I shared that I now had pine pitch on my hand and hoped it didn't get on my steering wheel. We all have our own levels of truth and sharing.

I'm sharing this story with you now (no tree branch is involved) to illustrate how token passing works. The token, a special packet of data, is passed from PC to PC, node to node, on the network. Any PC that wants to send a message must wait until it has the token, at which time it can send its data. Like the branch in my silly story, the token empowers its holder to use the network.

Nodes connect to the loop through devices called *multistation access units* (MAUs). MAUs are most commonly found on large corporate mainframe sites. Token ring networks are actually configured more like a star with the MAU used as the clustering device. Multiple MAUs are linked together with patch cords to create a logical ring. Because of its physical star configuration, any single station that breaks down has little effect on the ring, as long as the MAU can omit it from the loop.

Token ring networks come in two flavors: 4 Mbps and 16 Mbps.

FDDI Networks

You won't see FDDI on the A+ exam beyond its inclusion as a wrong choice in a multiple choice question. However, just so you know that it's a wrong answer, you may want to review this section.

The FDDI (Fiber Distributed Data Interface) uses fiber-optic cabling to create a network with data transfer speeds of 100 Mbps. A FDDI can support 1,000 nodes and has the flexibility of having workstation nodes as far apart as 2 kilometers. For those of us who are metrically challenged, that's a hair over 1.6 miles.

FDDI technology is sometimes called *a ring of trees* because it creates a ring within a ring logically. The primary ring is the main line of the FDDI network, and the secondary ring serves as either an additional line or a backup to the primary line. Devices can attach to both rings or to just one. A device called a *dual attached concentrator* (DAC) is used to bridge the two rings and attach new devices to the tree. In a way, the DAC is the root of the FDDI tree.

Like a token ring network, the primary control mechanism used by FDDI is token passing. The token passes around on the primary ring unless something happens to it, and the token must be routed onto the secondary ring for all or part of the journey around the ring.

Networking Hardware

For the A+ exam, you need to know the role played by each type of networking hardware. The following list provides information about common devices found in LANs, WANs, and what are now called internetworks that tie together two or more WANs of dissimilar types:

- ✔ **A repeater** amplifies the signals on a cable. Two types of repeaters are used:

  - **An amplifier repeater** picks up the incoming signal and, without making any modifications to it at all, amplifies it and sends it on its way — good, bad, or noisy.

  - **A signal-regenerating repeater** sends out a cleaned-up signal by making a fresh and exact copy of just the good part of the incoming signal and sending out the copy.

- ✔ **A hub** is used as a clustering or connecting point for nodes on an Ethernet network. In many ways, the MAU of the token ring network works much like a hub.

- ✔ **A bridge** is used to interconnect two or more LANs or LAN segments.

- ✔ **A router** (contrary to what my English colleague may say, it is not pronounced "rooter") is an intelligent device that examines the source and destination addresses of network traffic and decides where the message needs to be routed. A router works much like a mail sorter that reads the address on an envelope and then sends it to the appropriate mailbag for delivery. On a network, the address of a message is composed of several segments, each representing the servers, gateways, and routers through which the message must pass to be delivered. The job of the router is to determine the best possible way to send the message to its destination. Not all network protocols support routing — more on that in a moment.

- ✔ **A gateway** connects networks that use different protocols. A gateway is used to interconnect an Ethernet network to a token ring network. In doing this, the gateway must translate and reformat the data packets from the sending protocol to that of the receiving protocol.

Protocols and Other Niceties

In addition to the three network protocols described earlier in this chapter (Ethernet, token ring, and FDDI), other protocols can be used to interconnect PCs to other PCs or to other networks. For the test, you need to know their names, acronyms, and the scope of what they interconnect. The layer that each protocol falls under is really not important, but I include that information to stratify the protocols in the discussion. These protocols are shown in Table 13-1 by ISO OSI layer.

Table 13-1	Protocol Particulars	
Protocol/Layer	**Acronym**	**What It Does**
Point-to-Point Protocol (physical/data link layers)	PPP	Used to connect and manage network communications over a modem
Transmission Control Protocol/Internet Protocol (network/transport layers)	TCP/IP	The backbone protocol of the Internet; very popular for intranets, internal networks using the Internet, and Web work-alikes
Internetwork Packet Exchange/Sequenced Packet Exchange (network/transport layers)	IPX/SPX	The standard protocol of the Novell network operating systems
NetBIOS Extended User Interface (network/transport layers)	NetBEUI (pronounced *Net Booie*)	A Microsoft protocol that is used only by Windows operating systems for LANs with no external connections; does not support routing (addressing through a router to other networks)
File Transfer Protocol (session/presentation layers)	FTP	Used to send and receive files in client/server mode to or from a remote host
Hypertext Transfer Protocol (session/presentation layers)	HTTP	Used to send World Wide Web (WWW) documents, which are usually encoded in HTML (Hypertext Transfer Markup Language), across a network
Network File Services (session/presentation layers)	NFS	Allows the network node to access network drives as if they were local drives, files, and data; also performs the file access and data retrieval tasks requested of the network
Simple Mail Transfer Protocol (session/presentation layers)	SMTP	Used to send electronic mail (e-mail) across a network
Telnet (session/presentation layers)	—	Used to connect to a remote host and emulate a terminal that the remote server recognizes and works with

The last OSI layer is the application layer, on which the clients (such as Web browsers, chat IRCs, e-mail, print services, and network drives) operate. Each of the clients works with the protocols listed in Table 13-1 to connect to the appropriate network resources and carry out its tasks.

Network Operating Systems

Just as the PC needs an operating system to function, the network needs a network operating system (NOS) to coordinate all the sharing, giving, and goodwill going on among its nodes. Probably the two most popular NOSs are Novell's NetWare (or *Intranetware,* as it is now called) and Microsoft's Windows NT Server. Some networks may also use the UNIX operating system or the Linux operating system (UNIX's lighterweight offspring) to manage the network.

For the A+ exam, focus only on the big two NOSs, NetWare and Windows NT.

Dialing up the Windows 95 network

Networking in Windows 95 and Windows NT Workstation is relatively easy. That's good news, because you need to know how to network Windows 95 for the test.

Each of these Windows versions supports TCP/IP, IPX/SPX, and NetBEUI and accesses a network in two ways: direct connection through a NIC installed in the PC and over a modem using what is called *dial-up networking*.

Dial-up networking uses PPP (Point-to-Point Protocol) to send data packets over telephone lines. PPP picks up a packet that has been created by one of the other network protocols and which will be received by a remote PC running that same protocol. PPP is merely the intermediary that carries the data packet over the telephone line. If the packet begins the journey as a TCP/IP packet, it arrives at its destination as a TCP/IP packet.

Dialing up the Windows NT network

Windows NT has built-in services for dial-in remote access — Remote Access Service (RAS). RAS supports a server with one or more modems and increases server security with features such as *call-back security.* Call-back security works like this:

1. A remote user dials in to the NT server from a home or office PC.

2. The RAS server verifies the user's password and login name.

3. The RAS server hangs up on the verified caller. If this seems rude, just wait. There's more.

4. The RAS server calls the remote user back, using a phone number that has been assigned to or designated by the user.

5. The remote end reconnects, and the user is granted access to the network.

Fiddling with network adapters and Windows

When we last checked in on our old buddy NIC, he was just settling in to his new home in a PCI or ISA expansion slot. Having NIC settled in his new home is fine, but that's only half the job of getting the PC connected to the network. On the A+ exam, you can expect a question or two about adding devices to the Windows environment. The device in the question may not be a NIC, but beyond a few specific pieces of data, adding a NIC is much like adding any hardware device. Lab 13-1 lists the steps used to install a NIC in Windows 95 (Windows NT is slightly more helpful and interesting in this process, but the questions on the exam refer to Windows 95).

Lab 13-1	Installing a Network Interface Card in Windows 95

1. **Set the DIP switches and jumpers and then install the NIC in its PC slot.**

   If the NIC is a Plug-and-Play (I hate the PnP abbreviation, so I spell it out) device, you don't have to set its identity and configuration with DIP (dual inline packaging) switches and jumpers. A DIP switch is a block of little rocker or slide switches, and a jumper is a set of pins that can be connected with a cover block to set values on the NIC.

2. **Turn on the PC.**

   Windows 95 detects the new Plug-and-Play device or recognizes the NIC's hardware configuration and configures it to the system.

3. **Check out how Windows 95 has configured the card by using the Control Panel.**

Lab 13-2 lists the steps you use to access the configuration of the NIC card installed in the preceding lab. This is important stuff to know!

Lab 13-2   Accessing Windows 95 Device Configuration

1. **Click the Start button to display the Windows 95 Start menu.**

2. **Choose Settings to display the Settings menu.**

3. **Choose Control Panel — you know what this does.**

4. **Double-click Network to display the Network Devices dialog box.**

5. **Click the Configuration tab, which shows the various networkable devices on the system.**

6. **Find the NIC on the list, highlight it, and click Properties.**

   This step displays the Properties dialog box for that particular device. If the device is not a Plug-and-Play device, the system resources assigned should match those that you physically configured on the card. If it is Plug-and-Play, you can observe the system resources that were assigned to it by Windows 95.

7. **If you want to change the settings (that is, if you truly know what you're doing — otherwise, leave them alone), you can do so and then click OK to save them.**

Living in the Windows Network Neighborhood

Windows 95 allows resources on one PC to be shared across a network with one or more other PCs. This feature allows you to indicate that you want to share your files or printer or both with other PCs and users on the network. This feature is called the Network Neighborhood.

You can share your files and printer simply by indicating to Windows that you think that sharing is a swell idea, and the idea works as long as other users do the same for you. Figure 13-7 shows the networking options used to share files and printers. Unless other users also set their files to be shared, however, file sharing can be a one-sided affair.

Figure 13-7:
Setting
printer and
file sharing
options.

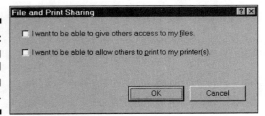

If you click the Network Neighborhood icon and no PCs are shown, check to see that you have enabled printer and file sharing and that other PCs on the network have also set up resources to be shared.

Servicing a Networked PC

One of the primary objectives in the Networking domain of the A+ Core exam is that you can identify when you are servicing a networked PC, which requires some special considerations and actions on your part. Not recognizing that the PC is on a network when servicing it can result in damage to the PC and possibly to the network. The following problems may result from not taking the correct precautionary steps before working on a networked PC:

- ✔ Reduced bandwidth (the data transmission capacity and capability of the network) on the network caused by a faulty NIC signal or improperly set NIC

- ✔ A loss of data caused by an interruption in the network structure

- ✔ A slowdown in the general operation of the network

You can tell whether a PC is networked in a number of ways. Unfortunately, the process is a little more involved than determining the sex of a hamster. First, you pick up the PC and blow gently into the fur around its . . . oops, wrong problem! Some of the ways you can determine whether a PC is networked are listed here:

- ✔ Look at the back of the PC for a network port with a cable attached to it. If you find one, you have a winner — a networked PC.

- ✔ If a network cable is not attached to the back of the PC, it doesn't mean it is not a networked PC; the customer may have already disconnected it. You can ask the customer.

- ✔ If no network cable exists, check to see whether a NIC is installed. No NIC — no network. However, if a NIC is in the PC, you can make other checks to determine whether the PC is networked.

- ✔ If you have access to the hard disk, search it for the tell-tale signs that the PC has been networked: folders or directories with names like NWCLIENT. Or look in AUTOEXEC.BAT or CONFIG.SYS for entries that start networking clients. (This is especially true for Novell software, which places entries in these files.)

- ✔ If you have access to Windows 95, use the Windows Explorer to look for network drives. They usually have drive designators of E:, F:, or higher.

If you determine that the PC is a part of network, follow the steps in Lab 13-3 to perform a repair.

Lab 13-3	Repairing a Networked PC

1. **Check to see whether the PC is logged on to the network.**

   One easy way to check this is to try to open a drive or folder on a network device. If you can open a file, the PC is logged on. If the drive is not available, the PC may be a node, but it is not logged into the network.

2. **If you are working on the hard disk, make a backup of all files.**

   Especially important is backing up any networking information on the hard disk.

3. **Log off the PC as necessary.**

4. **Disconnect the network cable from the NIC card and proceed with the repair of the PC.**

5. **After the repair is complete, reconnect the network cable, verify that the network files are on the disk, and restore them if needed.**

6. **Ask the customer to log on to the network to verify that all is well.**

Moving On to the Internet

Due to the relative overnight success of the Internet and World Wide Web, TCP/IP (the primary protocol of the Internet) is now the most widely implemented network protocol. In addition to its use for the Internet, it is finding success converting local area networks into intranets. An intranet is an internal network that uses the tools and processes of the Internet to access local network resources.

The A+ exam does not expect you to be a cyber-guru, but know the meaning and application of some Internet terminology and features:

- ✔ **TCP/IP (Transmission Control Protocol/Internet Protocol)** is the primary protocol set used to address, transport, and deliver messages on the Internet. The TCP part of the protocol divides an Internet message into data packets for transmission on the network. The IP part of the protocol addresses and sends the packets and then assembles them and provides error-checking at the remote (receiving) end.

- ✔ **An IP** (Internet Protocol — the IP part of TCP/IP) is the numerical routing address assigned to a networked PC and used to route e-mail, Web documents, and FTP files from one PC to another. An example of an IP address is 127.0.0.1, where each of the four segments of the address represents the address of a different subunit of the network.

- ✔ **A domain** is a network server that can be accessed from the Internet to download and upload files. Most domains have a domain name.

- ✔ **A domain name** is used in place of the numerical IP address because IP addresses are difficult to remember. It is much easier to remember www.wholelotofshakinggoingon.com instead of 128.213.254.199, wouldn't you say? Domain names are registered by the InterNIC project to avoid duplicate names. To classify the companies or organizations to which the names are assigned, domain names end with a dot (period) and a three-letter classification abbreviation, like .edu for a school or .com for a business.

- ✔ **Hypertext Markup Language** (HTML) is used to encode documents that contain text and graphics so that a Web browser software program can display the document as the author intended.

- ✔ **Hypertext Transfer Protocol** (HTTP) is the protocol used to transport documents on the Internet and World Wide Web.

- ✔ **A Web browser** is client-end software that uses HTTP to download an HTML document from a remote host site via the Internet and prepares the document for presentation, launches special program coding sequences, or opens interaction with other Web and Internet tools. If the exam mentions specific Web browsers, expect to see either Netscape Navigator or Microsoft Internet Explorer, the big two.

- ✔ **An Internet Service Provider** (ISP) shares its bandwidth with subscribers who contact it via dial-up access. An ISP maintains an Internet presence to facilitate the receipt and delivery of e-mail, the downloading and uploading of data, and any other server-end function you want to use on the Internet. For these services you pay a fee; an ISP is a company that sells you your Internet access.

Addressing a PC

IP addresses are four sets of numbers separated by periods (dots). Because the IP address is 32 bits long, each of the four numbers is 8 bits long, which limits the maximum value of any segment to 255. The highest possible IP address, then, is 255.255.255.255. Because each segment is 8 bits, it is called an *octet,* and the segments are referred to as the first, second, third, and fourth octets. Sounds a little like a singing group — the Octets and their new hit "Home, Home on the Domain."

IP addresses can be assigned as a *static* IP address (a fixed PC location) or as a *dynamically assigned* IP address (changeable).

So what do those abbreviations in Internet addresses mean?

The following table lists the standard five domain name classifications and to whom they are issued:

Domain	Name Ending	Assigned To
.com	Commercial, for-profit companies	For example, www.idgbooks.com
.edu	Education units, including public and private colleges and universities, K-12 systems, and so on	For example, www.wsu.edu
.gov	Governmental agencies	For example, www.whitehouse.gov
.net	Internet providers	For example, www.bmi.net
.org	Not-for-profit organizations, trade associations, and so on	For example, www.comptia.org

Outside the United States, domain names usually end with a country code. Some are easy to figure out, but others are real head-scratchers. For example, the code .uk is easy to figure as the United Kingdom, .de is Germany (Deutchsland), and .ca is Canada. But can you figure out how they get .ch to represent Switzerland, or .eh to mean Western Samoa?

A static IP address is permanently assigned to a node when it is added to the network. Static IP addresses work as long as the network doesn't move, the NIC card is not interchanged with other PCs, or the network is never reconfigured. If a network expects to be reconfigured, however, it should use dynamically assigned IP addresses. Each time the PC is booted, the Dynamic Host Configuration Protocol (DHCP) server assigns it an IP address to use for that session. Both Windows 95 and Windows NT have DHCP clients built in.

Resolving the domain name

Special software is used to convert from the IP address to the domain name and back again. Two primary software services perform this activity:

✔ **Domain Name Service (DNS),** sometimes called Domain Name System, uses a distributed database provided by a top-level domain name server to look up either the domain name (to retrieve its IP address for routing) or the IP address (to get the domain name for display). The IP address assigned to a domain name can change for many reasons. Using DNS to find the IP address from the database allows the entire Internet to adjust and find the new site. The database is maintained by each level of the DNS hierarchy informing those beneath it in the IP structure of new additions or deletions.

✔ **Windows Internet Naming Service (WINS)** also uses a database and is used with Microsoft networks to resolve Windows or Windows NT host names. Its one advantage over DNS is that it records and maintains lookup values for dynamically assigned IP addresses.

Prep Test

1 An FDDI network uses which of the following as its control mechanism?

A ○ CSMA/CD

B ○ CSMA/CA

C ○ 10BaseF

D ○ Token passing

2 The network adapter card component that is responsible for converting the signal between the PC and the network media is the

A ○ Transponder

B ○ Media access control

C ○ NIC processor

D ○ Transceiver

3 From bottom to top, the seven layers of the ISO OSI model are

A ○ Application, Presentation, Session, Transport, Network, Data Link, Physical

B ○ Physical, Data Link, Network, Transport, Session, Presentation, Application

C ○ Application, Presentation, Session, Network, Transport, Data Link, Physical

D ○ Presentation, Application, Session, Network, Transport, Data Link, Physical

4 Which of the following does not use electrical signals to transmit data over the network cable?

A ○ 10BaseF

B ○ 10Base2

C ○ 10Base5

D ○ 100BaseT

5 The _____ is a network device that is used to connect network segments that may use different protocols, such as TCP/IP and IPX/SPX.

A ○ Router

B ○ Gateway

C ○ Bridge

D ○ Repeater

6 Which of the following protocols does NOT support routing?

  A ○ TCP/IP
  B ○ NetBEUI
  C ○ IPX/SPX
  D ○ NetBIOS

7 The most common network protocol in use today is

  A ○ TCP/IP
  B ○ NetBEUI
  C ○ IPX/SPX
  D ○ Ethernet

8 UTP network cable typically has what type of connectors at each end?

  A ○ RJ-45
  B ○ RJ-11
  C ○ AUI
  D ○ BNC

9 The software services that resolves domain names on the Internet, such as www.idgbooks.com, to its IP address is

  A ○ WINS
  B ○ HOSTS
  C ○ DNS
  D ○ DHCP

10 The Windows NT service that allows remote PCs to dial in is

  A ○ PPP
  B ○ IPX/SPX
  C ○ RAS
  D ○ MAU

Answers

1 *D.* FDDI is a fiber-optic ring architecture that has a primary ring and a backup, secondary ring. Token passing is its mechanism for controlling message traffic and collision avoidance. *Review "FDDI Networks."*

2 *D.* The transceiver's name is a combined form of its two actions: transmit and receive. This component performs both of these tasks for the NIC, receiving incoming messages and broadcasting outgoing messages to the network. *Take a look at "NIC architectures."*

3 *B.* You have to be careful on questions about the ISO OSI model's layers and remember that the physical layer is the bottom and the application layer is the top. *Check out "Never tell secrets or trust sales people."*

4 *A.* Trick question, maybe. 10BaseF is a fiber-optic Ethernet implementation, and fiber-optic cable transmits light. *Flash over to "Ethernet cabling."*

5 *C.* Routers are like mail sorters; gateways allow entrance to foreign visitors (from foreign networks); repeaters, well, repeat; and bridges connect LANs and LAN segments, alike or different. *Connect with "Networking Hardware."*

6 *B.* NetBEUI is a Windows protocol that does not support routing. *See "Protocols and Other Niceties."*

7 *A.* The largest network of them all is the Internet, and TCP/IP is its life blood, and it's free, too. *Link up with "Moving On to the Internet."*

8 *A.* Looking like a big telephone connector, the RJ-45 connector is easy to work with and adapts well to use in buildings. *Review "Connecting with connectors."*

9 *C.* Domain Name Service (DNS) is used to translate a domain name to its IP address or back again. *Take a look at "Resolving the domain name."*

10 *C.* Remote Access Service (RAS) supports dial-up access to a Windows NT system. *Connect with "Dialing up the Windows NT network."*

Part IV
Keeping the Computer (And the User) Happy

The 5th Wave   By Rich Tennant

"This part of the interview tells us whether or not you're personally suited to the job of systems technician!"

In this part . . .

Four chapters in this part amount to an overall review of the previous parts. These chapters review the procedures used to take apart the PC, put it back together again, and upgrade key components and the motherboard. These four chapters summarize the technical tasks associated with working as a PC service technician and the safety precautions used to protect both you and the PC in the process.

Two chapters in this part deal with the non-technical or certainly less-technical parts of the job — dealing with the customer directly and preventive maintenance activities that can be used to extend the life of the PC. There is also a chapter on portable systems. Although portable systems is a relatively minor part of the exam, you should review this topic carefully.

Chapter 14
Disassembling the Computer

● ●

Exam Objectives

▶ Identifying electrostatic discharge (ESD) safeguards

▶ Removing field replaceable units (FRUs)

▶ Working safely with high-voltage modules

● ●

*O*ne thing you won't have to worry about being asked on the A+ Core exam is to list the steps used to disassemble (or reassemble) a personal computer. However, you need general background knowledge of the process used to remove (or install) an FRU (field replaceable unit), and the safeguards used to protect FRUs and you from ESD. The best way that I know to help you review the procedure for removing PC FRU modules, such as disk drives, adapter cards, the motherboard, and so on, is to step through the removal of all the PC's modules.

Taking the PC apart isn't difficult, but removing the modules without disrupting everything is what separates the professional PC repair technician from the hobbyist — not that there's anything wrong with hobbyists. The essential skill involved in this process is knowing the difference between an FRU, such as the power supply, and other modules. Beyond your personal safety, you must keep working parts working.

Review this chapter for three things: how the FRU is removed, how the FRU is protected, and the ESD issues involved.

Quick Assessment

Identifying electro-static discharge (ESD) safe-guards

1 A human feels a static charge at about _____ volts.

2 When working on a PC, the power cord should be _____ the wall plug.

3 You should always wear a(n) _____ when working on the PC system unit.

4 You should have _____ and _____ available when working inside the PC so that you can note or diagram the identifying features, orientation, and position of components.

Removing field replace-able units (FRUs)

5 The three standard case types are _____, _____, and _____.

6 You should handle adapter cards and other circuit boards by their _____ to avoid touching the electronic contacts.

7 On newer PCs, the motherboard is secured to the case with _____ and _____.

8 Disk drives are installed into metal enclosures called _____.

Working safely with high-voltage modules

9 The cable that provides power to the front panel of the PC carries _____ power.

10 The power supply should not be opened because it contains _____ that hold high voltage charges.

Answers

1 *3,000.* Charge over to "Getting Ready and Taking Precautions."

2 *Plugged into.* Check out "Avoiding shocking developments."

3 *Antistatic protection device or ESD wrist strap.* Zap over to "Avoiding shocking developments."

4 *Paper and pen.* Review "Checking in: Is the patient ready, nurse?"

5 *Full-size tower, screwless case, and standard desktop.* See "Opening the box."

6 *Edges.* Peruse "Taking out the adapter cards."

7 *Screws and spacers.* Take a look at "Taking out the motherboard."

8 *Bays.* Visit "Undocking the bay."

9 *110V AC.* Charge over to "Grasping the power and removing it."

10 *Capacitors.* Review "Grasping the power and removing it."

Getting Ready and Taking Precautions

You should perform two major activities to prepare for disassembling a PC: ESD preparations and general surgery preparations.

A person can feel a static charge beginning at about 3,000 volts, but electronic circuits can be damaged by a charge of only 30 volts.

Avoiding shocking developments

I can't tell you enough times the importance of protecting the PC and yourself from electrostatic discharge (ESD) and its potential damage and hazards. You can do this in a number of ways:

- The minimum precaution you should take to protect against ESD is to attach an antistatic wrist strap around your wrist with Velcro. The other end of the strap attaches to the PC chassis with an alligator clip. An ESD ground strap contains a resistor that slows down the discharge and protects you. An additional step you can take is to use an antistatic mat under the PC case (in addition to your wrist strap). That way, if you accidentally knock off the clip, you won't pass along a charge to whatever you're holding at the time.

- A supply of antistatic bags is good to have on hand to protect cards and smaller FRUs outside of the case. ESD lurks everywhere. Never let your guard down and always protect your computer parts.

- Leave the power cord plugged into the wall (and the computer, of course). This ensures the best possible electrical ground. (The one exception to this rule is that you want to unplug the power cord before removing the power supply, but I talk about that later in this chapter.)

  One word of caution on where the power cord is plugged at any time — avoid using a power source that carries any electromagnetic interference (EMI) from electrically noisy motors, such as air conditioners, vending machines, pencil sharpeners, or electric lawn mowers, found around the office. EMI can create intermittent problems that are difficult to diagnose.

Checking in: Is the patient ready, nurse?

A year or two ago, I would have told you that you would rarely completely disassemble a PC, especially at a customer's site. However, today customers are trying to maximize the investment in their PC hardware by upgrading their older units. It is not unusual to replace the motherboard, processor, power supply, and adapter cards in upgrading an older PC. This chapter is practical beyond just getting you ready for the A+ exam.

Just to give you a background in the terminology, I use the word *disassemble* (and as many derivatives as I can for variety) to mean the disconnection from cables, extraction of fasteners, and removal of a module to a location outside the case — such as on the workbench or in a box. *FRU* (field replaceable unit) is used on the A+ exam to refer to any component that is replaced as a whole unit and can be installed at a customer site.

If you have a PC available that you can use as a model as you review this chapter, you will remember this information more easily.

Before beginning surgery on your PC, take these actions:

✔ Have your tools standing by and ready for use. If you are lucky enough to have a surgical assistant for this process, all the better, but you're probably on your own. So, to avoid the hassle of clipping and unclipping your wrist strap (and the possibility of forgetting to clip up again) as you run off for a forgotten tool, have your tools ready to go.

✔ Have paper and pen standing by so you can write down or diagram the placement, orientation, and identifying features of the modules, cables, cards, and other vital organs that you remove. Your notes and diagrams will guide you when you are reassembling the PC.

✔ Use whatever means you desire to sort, store, and secure the screws and other fasteners that you remove from the patient. They can easily get lost, scratch the case, or worse — make an awful screeching sound when you drag one trapped under the case across the workbench.

✔ Gather and have available all the support and reference diskettes for the devices installed in the PC. This is even more important if the PC is an IBM Micro-Channel Architecture (PS/2) computer. If you cannot find them, and even if you can, do not disconnect the battery from the motherboard.

When working on the PC, leave it plugged into the wall to provide a solid earth ground.

Taking inventory

You should boot the system and record on paper the system setup configuration data, such as its RAM size and its CMOS setup information. This is a precaution against the unlikely event that you accidentally disconnect or dislodge the CMOS battery, which would have the unfortunate effect of losing the CMOS setup information.

If you are working on a 286 or newer PC, do not disconnect the battery from the motherboard or you will lose the CMOS setup information for sure.

It is a good general practice to keep pen and paper handy when working on any PC to note or diagram any idiosyncrasies of the PC. As horrifying as it may sound, the customer may have worked on the PC or, worse, had his nephew, who's taking a class on Windows, work on it. I hate to scare you like that, but these things happen in life. You never know what you're going to find when you open the box: wires attached together with duct tape, connectors used in odd places, where cables were aligned, and so on. Making a few notes or diagrams as you go can save you many headaches later.

You should also record the model and serial numbers of each major FRU as you go, especially in the shop environment. As the PC is reassembled, verify that the parts that came out are the ones going back in. Replacing a good part with a faulty one inadvertently and introducing new problems to a system would be a "bad thing."

Straight from the "Duh" file comes this reminder: Always close all running programs, shut down the operating system, and turn off the computer before starting to disassemble it. Even though it is still plugged in doesn't mean you can run it while you work.

Removing the Major Components

You need to remember only a few general procedures used to disassemble the PC, and each relates specifically to a major FRU, such as the case, the power supply, adapter cards, RAM, and the motherboard — which just about covers everything.

Opening the box

The logical place to begin the disassembly of the PC is the case of the system unit. To remove the case from any PC, the only tool you should need is a Phillips screwdriver. Newer cases are available that require no tools at all (or so they say).

Unless you are the warranty service provider, be sure that you don't void the warranty on the PC by opening the system unit. Some manufacturers, but not all, put little stickers over the edges where the case parts fit together to warn you that you may be wiping out the warranty by removing the cover.

Be sure that you have on your ESD protection and that you avoid touching any of the internal parts with the cover when removing it.

A variety of system cases types and sizes exist, and each is opened using a slightly different technique:

✔ **Disconnect the cables.** All peripheral device connectors should be removed to get them out of the way. Disconnect the parallel, serial, gameport, video, and other cables connected to the back of the unit. Unplug the mouse and keyboard as well. You may want to use masking or other light tape to label the cables and the plugs to which they were connected.

✔ **Clean the case.** Although not the most technical of steps, this is a practical one. While the case is intact and with peripheral devices removed from its top (desktop models, of course), this is a good time to clean the dust bunnies from the top, back, and sides of the unit. This eliminates the chance that any accumulated gunk will fall inside when you are removing the case's top.

✔ **Remove any protection or appearance bezels.** Some older desktop cases and full-size tower cases have plastic panels mounted on either the back or front for reasons now known only to the case designer. If the PC you are working on has such a panel, it should pull right off. You may need to encourage it with a tweaker to get it started. Check the back of this panel for dust, clean it if needed, and set it aside.

✔ **Remove the case cover.** Manufacturers are getting very clever with cases and how they open and close, but in general, the most common cases are opened in these ways:

 • **Full-size tower case:** The two pieces of this case are a base and a U-shaped cover that fits over the internal components. There are usually three to six Phillips screws located around the edge of the case's back. Pull the case top forward about an inch or so to disengage it from the case bottom and then lift it off.

 • **Standard desktop case:** This is the case type that has been around since the original PC, although it now seems to be fading away. The two pieces of this case fit together in an "L7" fashion, with the front panel attached to the case top, and the back panel attached to the case bottom. The screws are along the edge of the back of the case and are removed with a screwdriver. On older cases, be sure which screws are case screws and which screws hold the power supply. After you remove the screws, push the top forward and either lift it off or continue pushing forward, depending on how it attaches.

 Be very careful not to remove screws that hold internal components (such as the power supply or some connectors) to the inside of the case. Before beginning to remove a screw, always verify to what it is attached.

• **Screwless case:** This type of case, available as either a tower or desktop, can be opened without tools (except for the occasional need to pry a panel loose with a screwdriver). The screwless case comes apart in a number of pieces (front, side, and top panels) that slide-lock into place.

Taking out the adapter cards

After the case cover is off and stored in a safe place, remove the adapter cards next. Generally, you can follow the process in Lab 14-1 for every card.

Lab 14-1	Removing Adapter Cards

1. **Write down or diagram the expansion slot and type (ISA, VL-Bus, PCI, and so on) that the adapter card occupies before you pull it out.**

   This will save you some time when you reassemble the PC. Label any cables attached to the card before you disconnect them.

2. **Record all jumper settings and DIP switch settings before removing the adapter card, if possible.**

   A little dental mirror comes in handy for this step. If you can wait until after you've removed a card and handled it, will you be able to guarantee that you haven't accidentally changed a setting?

3. **Remove the mounting screw that holds the adapter card in place.**

4. **Examine the card for any cables or wires that may be attached to it.**

   In addition to including any you find in your notes and diagrams, it is a good idea to tag any cables or wires with a small piece of tape. Small address labels are good for tagging parts and cables as well.

5. **Grasp the card along its front and back edges and gently rock it front to back until it releases.**

   Avoid touching other circuit boards and the contacts on the bottom of the board with your hand. Handle cards and circuit boards only by their edges or port mountings, and avoid touching the edge connectors.

6. **Lift the card out slowly and look for attached wires or cables that you may have overlooked.**

7. **If you're not going to replace the card, insert a port spacer.**

   A port spacer is a flat metal space holder used to block port openings on the back of the case. The cooling system needs all of these slots filled in order to do its job efficiently.

8. **Store the card in an antistatic bag and do not stack the cards on top of each other.**

If an ESD wrist strap or ankle strap is not available, lean your forearm on one of the metal beams that run across the chassis, and leave your arm in constant contact with the chassis while you lift out the adapter cards.

Undocking the bay

On a case manufactured in the past five or so years, the drive probably is in a metal enclosure designed to hold the various types of drives that conform to a general drive size standard called *half-height*. These enclosures, called bays, allow the device to slip into place either from the front or the back of the bay. Removing a floppy disk, tape, or CD-ROM drive is much easier than installing one. Installing a disk drive can involve mounting problems, cabling considerations, and formatting (see Chapter 15 for more information). However, removing one requires only that you disconnect a few cables, remove a few screws, and slide it out. Okay, it's a little more complicated than that, but not much.

Three things must be considered when removing a disk or tape drive from the PC:

- ✔ It is powered by the power supply through a connector.
- ✔ It is controlled by an adapter board through one or more cables.
- ✔ The drive is attached to the chassis, so it will not move about when in use or when the PC is moved

Each of these considerations is a step in removing the drive from the PC.

Removing the power connections

The power connections for disk and tape drives are fairly easy to find. They are the connectors whose wires extend back to the power supply. You will encounter only two types of connectors: a larger milky-white four-wire connector (usually a Molex connector) and a smaller four-wire connector (a Berg connector) that probably has a clip latch to hold it in place. Here's how to remove them:

- ✔ **Molex connector:** Grasp the connector and gently move it side to side to slip it out of the plug. Don't just yank on it. You can break the connector right off the drive circuit board (and then you have to install a new drive).
- ✔ **Berg connector:** Pry it open gently and slide it apart. Use a tweaker (the small two-ended screwdriver with the pocket clip) or a small screwdriver to lift the latch tab just enough to pull the connectors apart. Again, don't pull on the wires. If needed, use your needle-nose pliers to grasp the plug to pull it out.

You don't need to label drive power connectors, unless you feel compelled to do so. In fact, many come already labeled. There are only two types and each device takes only one type. You can use only the connectors that you have on the power supply, and the plugs are keyed so that you can't install them incorrectly.

Removing adapter cables

Depending on the drive and the form factor of the motherboard, a disk drive is connected to either an adapter card inserted in an expansion slot, or directly to the motherboard. In either case, you will need to remove these cables at this time. Label each cable and its orientation to the power supply (always a good landmark inside the case). Recording the orientation of a disk drive cable means to note on which side the color striped edge is and its orientation to the power supply.

Pull drive adapter cables level and gently. In other words, don't yank them off and pull level and in the direction of the pins.

Detaching a drive from the chassis

The first thing you must do is determine the type of bay the disk drive is installed in. The location and access to drive bays varies with the case, and although two cases may be of the same form factor, the bays may be accessed differently.

Some XT cases are still around that have one full-height bay. Two half-height devices can be stack-mounted in this bay by using a side bracket. This bracket holds one drive above the other with enough space between them for airflow and so that the electronics don't contact each other. When removing a drive (or pair of drives) from an XT case, don't forget the retaining screws in the bottom of the drive bay. XT drives pull out through the front.

AT cases have two (or more) half-height bays that receive drives from the front. A drive is held in place with a pair of small L-shaped retaining brackets that are held in place with a single screw on each side of the drive. To remove the drive, use a screwdriver to extract the retaining brackets and slide the drive forward out of the bay.

Taking out the motherboard

By now, the only item of significance left inside the case should be the motherboard. Depending on the PC's vintage, the remaining steps range from extremely easy to slightly complicated. On any motherboard forms, note or diagram all jumpers, DIP switches, and connectors that require special orientations. The motherboard should be carefully protected in an antistatic bag and placed away from other circuit boards.

If you've managed to get by without your ESD wrist strap to this point, put it on right now! You are now at the point where not wearing it can do some major and expensive damage. Worse yet, the damage may not show up right away; the damage shows up later after the damaged component is stressed further, causing an intermittent or misleading error condition.

PC XT motherboards have one small plastic connector that connects the motherboard to the speaker. Disconnect the speaker connector and remove the two or three screws mounting the motherboard to the chassis, and the motherboard is out.

IBM AT and its clones also have a speaker connector, but they also have a keylock connector. Remove the speaker and keylock connectors slowly because they are adjacent to the memory-size jumper on the AT motherboard. Be careful not to dislodge any jumpers on the board.

AT and related motherboards also have a battery that should be removed with the board and kept connected to the board. Newer AT boards have the battery mounted directly on the motherboard, so just be careful that you don't dislodge it. If this connection is broken, the CMOS chip will lose the system setup configuration information.

Newer AT, Baby AT, and ATX form-factor motherboards are mounted on plastic spacer anchors and held in place with two or three screws attached to the chassis. To remove these motherboards, extract the mounting screws and then slide the motherboard laterally toward the open end of the case to disengage the spacers, and lift the motherboard out of the case by its edges. Leave the spacers in the motherboard.

Pulling out the memory modules

If you also want to remove the memory modules — single inline memory modules (SIMM), dual inline memory modules (DIMM), or dual inline packages (DIP) — be absolutely sure that you are grounded. When working with memory, just touching the case or power supply may not be enough to protect memory modules from possible ESD damage.

Follow the steps in Lab 14-2 to remove memory modules.

Lab 14-2	Taking Out SIMMs and DIMMs

1. **Using your fingers, a slotted screwdriver, or a tweaker, push back the metal tabs holding the chip in the socket.**

   The tabs are located at the end of each memory module socket. With these released, you can then tilt the module.

2. **Gently tilt the first module one way and then the other to release it.**

3. **Tilt each module away from the locking prongs that fit into the holes at each end of the module.**

    Never rock the module side to side or yank it straight up. Record the socket each module comes out of by noting the bank and socket numbers and the chip number. You can use stickers, such as small price stickers, to identify the module.

4. **Place each module in a separate antistatic bag, and store them without stacking them on each other.**

You have your hands full removing a bank of DIP memory chips. Keep these tips in mind:

- Be antistatic. Memory chips are sold in antistatic tubes that you should be able to round up.

- Use a slotted screwdriver, such as the tweaker, to start the process of removing the chip and then gently pry it up and out of the socket with your fingers. You can use an IC puller, but don't blame me for all the bent pins.

- Mark each chip with its bank and socket number and mark the sockets accordingly.

Grasping the power and removing it

These days, the power supply and case are purchased together as a single unit. However, the power supply or the cooling fan in many older AT PCs still in use can wear out and need replacement. Or you may find yourself removing all modules from the case to isolate an intermittent problem source. Unless you have compelling reason to take the power supply out of the case, leave it in.

Treat the power supply as one thing. In other words, don't open it for any reason. Don't even be curious. If any part of the power supply is not working, dispose of it properly and install a new one. Inside the power supply are big nasty capacitors that pack quite a wallop and can hurt you seriously if you touch them — even if you're wearing an ESD strap.

ATX form-factor motherboards have power to them at all times, even when the power supply is turned off. Be sure that you know this for your safety, but forget it when taking the A+ exam: The ATX form-factor is not included — as yet anyway.

Lab 14-3 takes you through the process of removing the power supply.

Lab 14-3   Removing the Power Supply

1. **Turn off the power supply.**

   I'm sure you did this long before getting to this point, but I feel obligated to mention it.

2. **Remove the power cord from the power supply.**

3. **Diagram the orientation or use a grease pencil to mark the edges of the power supply connectors to the PC's front panel, motherboard, and disk drives, and then disconnect them in that order.**

   Use rubber bands to bind the motherboard and disk drive connectors in separate groups.

   The thick black cable that extends to the front panel from the power supply in many PCs carries live 110V AC power straight from the wall socket! If you draw only one diagram of a connector configuration (in this case, where each of the four wires are connected by color), let it be this one. If you connect the wrong wire in the wrong place, it will cause the system to catch fire — but you wouldn't care anymore.

4. **Locate and remove the screws (either Phillips or hex-head) holding the power supply to the back of the case, the side wall, and the chassis.**

5. **Inspect the power supply at this time for faulty, frayed, or broken wires or connectors, and use compressed air to blow out the fan and vents.**

Disassembling the Computer

1 The correct way to remove an adapter card circuit board is to detach any connectors, remove the retaining screw, and then

A ○ Ensure that the power is off

B ○ Grasp the card's front and back edges and rock it gently back and forth

C ○ Grasp the card's top edge and pull straight up

D ○ Grasp the card's front and back edges and rock the board gently from side to side

2 When servicing a PC, to which of the following would you not attach the ESD ground strap?

A ○ To the inside of the case

B ○ To the ground mat

C ○ To the static shielding bag that came with the computer

D ○ To a wall outlet

3 When servicing a computer,

A ○ Be sure that it is not plugged in to the wall socket

B ○ Work only on a clean metallic surface

C ○ Wear rubber gloves to prevent leaving fingerprints on circuit boards

D ○ Leave it plugged in to the wall socket

4 The letters ESD stand for

A ○ Electrostatic discharge

B ○ Extra-sensitive device

C ○ Electric surge detector

D ○ Electrical Statistics For Dummies

5 How much voltage will damage an electrical component with ESD?

A ○ 3,000

B ○ 300

C ○ 30

D ○ 30,000

6 After a circuit board is removed from the system, it should be stored in

A ○ A cool, dry, dark place

B ○ An antistatic bag

C ○ A stack with other circuit boards

D ○ A clean, zippered plastic bag

7 The PC case that is opened without tools is called a

A ○ Snap-tite case

B ○ Screwless case

C ○ Clamshell case

D ○ Mini-tower case

8 The term FRU refers to

A ○ Front or rear unit

B ○ Fully replaceable unit

C ○ A slang term used by PC technicians for modules that can be replaced at the customer site

D ○ Field replaceable unit

9 Disk drives are installed in slide-in compartments called

A ○ Trays

B ○ Bays

C ○ Slips

D ○ Mounts

10 Before you can remove the motherboard, you need to detach which of these connectors at the very last?

A ○ The power supply connector

B ○ The front panel power connector

C ○ The speaker connector

D ○ The keyboard connector

Answers

1 *B.* Answer A is not a bad first step, but that should have been done before you opened the system case. You must avoid stressing the card by bending it side to side or harming the edge connectors by yanking the card straight up. *See "Taking out the adapter cards."*

2 *C.* Unless the static shielding bag is grounded to a solid ground, it won't do you much good. *Charge over to "Avoiding shocking developments."*

3 *D.* This should connect the PC — and you, if you're clipped onto it — to a solid earth ground. *Take a look at "Avoiding shocking developments."*

4 *A.* If you picked anything else, you are remanded to the authority of your local ESD police and shock therapy. *Be absolutely sure that you review "Avoiding shocking developments."*

5 *C.* Just because you can't feel the discharge doesn't mean that it won't damage electronic components. *Zap over to "Getting Ready and Taking Precautions."*

6 *B.* Never stack circuit boards on top of each other even if they are in antistatic bags, and never store a circuit board where it can gather static electricity. *Look at "Taking out the adapter cards."*

7 *B.* This type of case hangs together with panels that interlock and snap into place. *Connect with "Opening the box."*

8 *D.* CompTIA uses this term to refer to all components of the PC that can be replaced at a customer site. *Check out "Checking in: Is the patient ready, nurse?"*

9 *B.* When buying a new case, check out how many bays it includes for disk drives. *Swing over to "Undocking the bay."*

10 *C.* In addition to the speaker, the keylock and battery connectors usually need to be removed before the motherboard can be taken out of the case. *Visit "Taking out the motherboard."*

Chapter 15

Reassembling the Computer

- -

Exam Objectives

▶ Installing field replaceable units (FRUs)

▶ Identifying system modules and their normal operations

- -

*Y*ou can expect to see questions on the exam that require you to know the sequence of steps used in building or rebuilding a PC (however, you won't need to know the minute details). You'll also see questions on how to align and orient cables, connectors, and devices as they are installed in the system.

This chapter focuses on reassembling the PC and completing the process started in Chapter 14 where the PC was dissassembled. If you reassemble a PC that you personally took apart, then you should have little trouble with your extensively abundant and detailed notes and diagrams to guide you. When building a PC from the ground up, then you must verify accuracy and function each step of the way.

The procedures you use to reassemble a PC are essentially the same you use to build one from scratch — with the major exception that you must also deal with the system setup and configuration of the hardware and operating system when building a PC. I give you a very brief overview on the setup and configuration procedure here, but I cover it more extensively in Chapter 4.

When you disassemble a PC, all the work is in front of you. You can see all the modules that you must remove. However, when putting a computer back together, you start with a pile of pieces and work to get them back in working order, with none left over. If the computer isn't assembled (or reassembled) correctly, it will probably have serious problems.

Quick Assessment

Installing FRUs

1 The motherboard is installed on a set of plastic _____.

2 _____ and _____ memory modules are installed in stand-up edge connector sockets.

3 Install the motherboard power connectors with the _____ wires in the center.

Identifying system modules and their normal operations

4 Ribbon cables, used to connect data connections for disk drives, have a color stripe that identifies pin _____ on the cable.

5 When closing up the case, be watchful of _____ and _____, which can be snagged or broken by the case top.

6 The front panel power cable carries _____ to the front panel power switch.

7 If you detached the CMOS battery during disassembly, you must update the _____.

8 Not installing a _____ can result in a boot disk failure.

9 Not installing the _____ can cause the power supply to explode.

10 Controller card failures are likely a cause of the card not being _____.

Answers

1 *Spacers* or *standoffs*. Take a look at "Reinstalling the motherboard."

2 *SIMM; DIMM*. See "Reinstalling memory modules."

3 *Black*. Charge over to "Connecting the power source."

4 *1 (one)*. Become one with "Relating to the Zen of ribbon cable."

5 *Cables, connectors*. Check out "Closing the lid."

6 *110V AC*. Review "Connecting the front panel."

7 *CMOS configuration information*. See "Checking the CMOS and Configuration Data, or Where Did the Battery Go?"

8 *Drive power connector*. Check out "Stating your reinstallment preference: The adapter or the drive first?"

9 *Motherboard power connectors*. Take a look at "Testing the Results."

10 *Seated properly*. Review "Testing the Results."

Putting Everything in Its Place

If you have built or reassembled many PCs, then you probably are reasonably prepared for the A+ exam. As a review, write down the steps you would use along with any safeguards and checks you would use along the way. Then jump to the last section of this chapter — "Testing the Results" — and review it for common device failure modes, several of which will be on the exam in one form or another.

For the A+ exam, make sure you know the general sequence of assembly and the relationship of the major FRUs to one another. You may not see questions that relate directly to how a PC is assembled, but you will see questions that ask which devices are connected with cables, wires, and so on. FRUs are put back into the PC basically in reverse order to the way they came out. Assuming that the power supply wasn't removed from the case, the motherboard (with the memory reinstalled if applicable) goes in first, then the disk drives, the adapter cards, and finally, the case top. If the power supply was removed, it's reinstalled first, with the other components following as stated previously.

Selecting the tools for the job

You need a few more tools to reassemble the PC than you do to disassemble it. You need your ESD (electrostatic discharge) grounding strap; a Phillips, a slotted, and a tweaker (a small pocket-sized screwdriver with slotted and Phillips ends complete with pocket clip); a pair of needle-nosed pliers; and a small flashlight. Mature eyes may also want a small magnifying glass. Probably the most important tool for this job is patience. Take your time. If something isn't right, and no smoke was involved in reaching that decision, take the computer apart and do it again.

Protecting the PC and its FRUs from ESD damage is equally important when putting the system back together. It would be a real shame to damage a component as you are putting it into a PC. Use your grounding straps or take other appropriate precautions.

Remember, you and ESD are together the most threatening element the PC must face in its life. Whatever you can do to reduce this threat gives additional life to the PC. Kind of makes you feel powerful, doesn't it?

The greatest threat to the PC for ESD damage is anyone working on the PC with its case open without proper ESD protection in place.

Putting back the power supply

The power supply is fairly easy to reinstall. Just line up the fan with its hole in the case, and match the power supply to the screw holes and insert the screws. The only safeguard is to make sure that the power supply's cables are not trapped under the case or along its sides.

Install the power supply unplugged to an AC power source. After you install the power supply, plug it in and operate it very briefly to test only the fan. If the fan doesn't operate, check to see whether the power supply's voltage selector is set correctly and that the power cord is seated tightly.

Reinstalling the motherboard

Pay the closest attention to the motherboard and its cables and connections as you reassemble the PC. Putting a floppy disk drive in backward is easily corrected and normally does no harm, but some connectors exist that if put in upside down or simply wrong can harm the devices to which they attach. So take care as you work.

Do not begin the reassembly of the PC without putting your ESD ground strap on and connecting it to the PC case or ground mat.

Lab 15-1 shows you how to reinstall the motherboard.

Lab 15-1	Reinstalling the Motherboard

1. **Orient the motherboard so that its spacers (also called standoffs), shown in Figure 15-1, are aligned with the slots in the bottom of the case.**

2. **Laterally slide the motherboard toward the power supply until the standoffs are firmly snug in their slots.**

3. **Reinsert the mounting screws to anchor the motherboard in place.**

    Be absolutely sure that the motherboard is not in contact with the metal case lining. Contact will definitely give you trouble — if it doesn't short out the motherboard. Look under the motherboard to verify that it is not touching the case anywhere.

4. **To complete this task, reattach the speaker, keylock, and battery connectors.**

    If you were able to leave the battery attached to the motherboard, all the better. Otherwise, you need to set the system's configuration using the CMOS setup utility on the first boot.

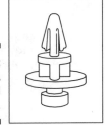

Figure 15-1:
A
motherboard
spacer.

After the motherboard power connectors are installed, you can plug the power cord into the AC wall outlet. It should remain there, providing a solid ground, throughout the rest of the reassembly.

Reinstalling memory modules

Memory modules are installed in a stand-up arrangement in an edge connector socket. Lab 15-2 takes you through reinstallation of either a SIMM (single inline memory module) or a DIMM (dual inline memory module) memory module.

Lab 15-2   Reinstalling a SIMM or DIMM

1. **Insert the module into the socket at about a 45-degree angle.**

2. **Slowly stand up the module, applying even pressure on both side edges, until it snaps into place.**

   If the module will not seat into the socket, it may be backward.

Installing DIP (dual inline package) memory chips takes a lot more patience than is needed with a SIMM or DIMM module and a very steady hand. Where a SIMM or DIMM requires only that you get the module into a slot, DIP memory requires all of its pins to be inserted into separate holes at the same time. If you removed the memory chips during disassembly, you are probably asking yourself why by now. Don't use a chip insertion tool; instead, use tweezers to line the chip over the DIP socket and lightly press one side down. Inspect the other side's pins for alignment, and slowly and gently press it down. When both sides are started (all the chip's pins are in the proper socket holes), use your finger to press it into place.

Connecting the power source

The next step is to connect the power supply plugs to the motherboard. Figure 15-2 illustrates what these connectors look like. These connectors are keyed, which means that they have a built-in feature that prevents them from being installed backward, so you should not be able to plug them on wrong. The only worry you have is getting them reversed. Remember that the black wires of each plug must be aligned together in the middle. These plugs are usually labeled as P8 and P9, but they shouldn't be too hard to find with your labels and the diagram you drew when disassembling the PC.

Figure 15-2:
The motherboard power connectors from the power supply.

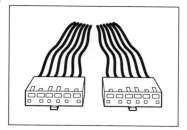

If you forget to connect the motherboard power connectors (P8 and P9), when you turn on the power, the power supply may explode — or at the least make loud ugly noises. So, don't forget to install these plugs.

Connecting the front panel

If the PC has a power cable for the front panel, unplug the PC for the duration of this operation. The front panel cable carries 110V AC power straight from the AC wall socket, and it's not something with which you should take chances. Even if you diagrammed the front panel power switch connector during disassembly, check the power supply's documentation, if available, for the wire color scheme.

The power switch on the front panel closes a circuit that allows the AC power to flow to the power supply. To allow this flow, the power switch has both hot (live) and return (to the power supply) leads. Four wires should be in the front panel power cable:

- **Black and brown:** The hot wires to the front panel
- **Blue and white:** The return wires leading back to the power supply

Whatever you do, don't reverse these wires or use a house-wiring color scheme for what the leads do; you could literally burn up the PC.

After you connect the front panel power, plug the power supply cord back into the wall socket, and then take a deep breath and a break.

Stating your reinstallment preference: The adapter or the drive first?

Some technicians like to install the disk drives before the adapter cards, and others like to do the reverse. Whichever is done first, the same rules apply, just in a different order. Follow your diagram, and reinstall the adapter cards and drives, keeping the cables and cards spaced evenly to allow for good air flow. Place the hard drive as far from the power supply as possible to allow for maximum air circulation inside the cabinet.

For the A+ exam, it doesn't matter which way it's done, but be ready for questions on how cables are connected to adapter cards and the power supply.

A common installation error is forgetting to attach the power cables to disk drives. This error can be a result of the full attention it takes to align the drive in the bay correctly, making sure that round-headed screws are used to anchor the drive in the bay, and that the data connection (the dreaded ribbon cable) is attached correctly. Not attaching the power connector to the drive usually results in a POST (Power On Self Test) boot disk failure.

Relating to the Zen of ribbon cable

In general, ribbon cables connect the same way on either end. However, this versatility can get you into trouble. You must connect the cable so that the wires connect to their counterparts on both connections. To aid you with this connection, the wire representing pin 1 on the cable and connector is usually marked with a red or dark blue stripe along the edge of the cable.

You may have two or more ribbon cables to reinstall. The cable for the floppy disk drive (see Figure 15-3) will be slightly different from the cable for the hard disk or other drives. Be sure you reattach the correct cable to the correct device, although this should not be too much of a problem, because usually they will not attach to the wrong device.

Excuse the veiled sports metaphor here, but an easy way to remember the orientation of a ribbon cable is "Big Red is Number 1." If you forget this phrase, just ask anyone from Nebraska to tell you who's Number 1, and he or she will most likely reply with the Big Red phrase, and you'll be reminded that the red stripe edge of the ribbon cable aligns to pin number 1. See how simply that works? For ribbon cables with a dark blue edge, you'll have to find somebody from Michigan to help you.

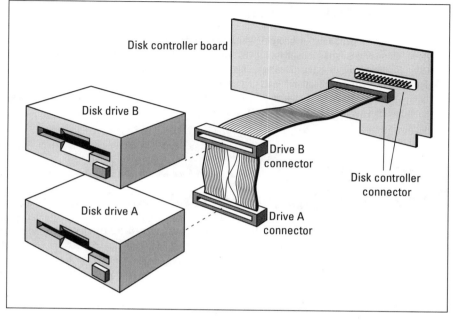

Figure 15-3:
The ribbon cable used for a floppy disk can connect two drives. Note the cable's "twist."

Finding pin 1 on the circuit board is the next step to completing the match. So, how do you tell which end of the connector is pin 1? A small numeral "1" should be printed next to or above the end of the connector that is pin 1. This situation is where a magnifying glass may come in handy, along with the flashlight. If you can't find the printed number, examine the solder pads on the back of the circuit board where the connector is attached. Pin 1 has a square solder pad. These general rules are not universally applied, though, which is why your diagrams are so important.

Watch out for these three common ribbon cable connection errors:

✔ The connector is reversed — sadly, this can do major damage, so chant the mantra "Big Red/Blue is Number One" as you connect ribbon cables.

✔ The connector is attached to only one row — easy to do given the size of the connector and the pins. If caught before the power is turned on, there shouldn't be any damage.

✔ The connector is shifted to the left or right, missing a pair of pins — also easy to do and just as dangerous.

Closing the lid

Reattach the case top. You may want to put the top in place, but leave the screws out until after you've had a chance to test the results. When putting on the case top, watch that you don't snag or trap cables. Cables can become damaged with little nicks or breaks. They may also pull out of connectors, if dragged or dinged by the case top. If the case lid doesn't slide freely into place, investigate why.

Checking the CMOS and Configuration Data, or Where Did the Battery Go?

If you were overly zealous about disassembling every possible FRU in the PC and removed the battery pack or the lithium battery from the motherboard, you are now faced with the challenge of resetting the CMOS setup configuration data. Assuming that the system boots okay, you need to press the appropriate key (depending upon your BIOS version) to open the CMOS setup utility and enter the appropriate data. You did write the CMOS information down, didn't you?

CMOS stands for complementary metal oxide semiconductor, which is a common integrated circuit technology. For more information on CMOS, see Chapter 4.

Okay, so you did remove the CMOS battery. Well, what you need to do is re-enter the CMOS information you captured before you started the disassembly of the PC. The data you need to enter varies slightly with the BIOS version, but generally it includes the following:

- ✔ Floppy disks size and density
- ✔ Hard disk type, and configuration in cylinders, heads, sectors, capacity, and other unique attributes, such as the landing zone (LZone) and others
- ✔ RAM size by type
- ✔ Time and date
- ✔ Parallel port type
- ✔ Serial port type and status
- ✔ Other stuff very specific to your system

If you didn't write down your CMOS settings and then either purposely or inadvertently removed the CMOS battery, you need to do some research to reconstruct the settings accurately. Most newer system CMOSs will detect some of the configuration of the PC, such as RAM size, but you need the manuals for the motherboard and peripherals to get it right.

Testing the Results

The real proof that you reassembled the PC correctly comes when you turn on the power and everything works. However, don't panic if you don't get these results — unless, of course, smoke or flames billows out of the PC.

The following are some common problems associated with PC reassembly:

- ✔ **Motherboard power connectors not installed:** This error is by far the most disastrous and can result in an exploded power supply.

- ✔ **Motherboard solderside contacts touching the case:** On the backside of any circuit board (called its solderside) are the clipped contacts of the electronic components installed on the circuitside of the board. If these contacts touch the metal case lining, some or all of the board may short out.

- ✔ **Reversed data and control cables:** This error can damage a device, but definitely changes how the computer operates, if it operates at all. Align the colored edge to pin 1.

- ✔ **Drive power connectors not installed:** This one isn't so bad; it usually just gets you a boot error beep code or disk boot failure.

- ✔ **Speaker, keylock, and battery connectors not installed:** A very minor problem that comes under the heading of "What a nuisance."

- ✔ **Disk drive, video display, and other peripheral failures:** The adapter card may not be seated properly, may not be anchored with a mounting screw, or may be installed in an incorrect architecture slot.

- ✔ **Floppy drive failure:** The ribbon cable may not be connected properly. The first floppy disk drive (A:) should be connected after the twist, or at the end of the cable.

- ✔ **Keyboard failure:** The keyboard connector may not be installed or not pushed on all the way. Also, if the PC has a PS/2 mouse and its connector is not installed properly, the keyboard may not function.

- ✔ **No lights, no action:** Did you plug it in?

Always be sure that the power supply is switched off before changing any power supply or signal cable connections.

Prep Test

1 What is the likely result of forgetting to attach the power connector to a hard disk during reassembly?

A ○ The power supply will explode.

B ○ A disk boot failure.

C ○ A 601 POST error.

D ○ The hard disk will die an agonizing death.

2 The colored edge of the ribbon cable represents

A ○ Pin 40

B ○ Pin 1

C ○ The Cornhuskers

D ○ The power connector

3 You just installed a hard drive, but it's not working. Why?

A ○ It is connected to the wrong IDE controller.

B ○ The floppy drive is not connected properly.

C ○ The ribbon cable is aligned to pin 1 on the drive.

D ○ The ribbon cable is aligned to pin 40 on the drive.

4 The biggest threat to the PC when being serviced is

A ○ ESD

B ○ Accidental breakage of a component

C ○ Improper tools damaging a component

D ○ Placing components on the wrong type of surface to work

5 When installing SIMMs or DIMMs, you should

A ○ Not ground yourself in case of high voltages.

B ○ Unplug the PC power cable.

C ○ Leave the power cord plugged in.

D ○ Leave the computer power on.

6 The hard disk should be placed as far away as possible from the power supply to provide

A ○ Maximum ESD protection

B ○ Maximum air flow potential

C ○ Minimum EMI interference

D ○ Ample open space for the processor

7 A floppy disk drive failure may be caused by (choose all that apply)

A ❑ The drive power connector may not be installed.

B ❑ The A: drive is not installed after the "twist."

C ❑ Conflicts with the hard disk.

D ❑ No diskette has been inserted.

8 The motherboard is mounted

A ○ On brass standoffs

B ○ On plastic standoffs

C ○ On copper mounting brackets

D ○ Directly on the case's metal lining

9 The front panel power cable from the power supply supplies which of the following to the front panel power switch? (Choose all that apply.)

A ❑ AC power

B ❑ A pair of hot leads

C ❑ A pair of return leads

D ❑ An earth ground

Answers

1 *B.* The BIOS looks to the disk drive to boot from, and not finding the drive, displays a disk boot failure. *Check out "Stating your reinstallment preference: The adapter or the drive first?"*

2 *B.* The colored edge indicates how the cable's connector should be oriented to the adapter or motherboard connector. *Look up "Relating to the Zen of ribbon cable."*

3 *D.* The ribbon cable, which provides the data connection to the drive, must be correctly connected for the device to work properly. *Review "Relating to the Zen of ribbon cable."*

4 *A.* Besides the technician, the biggest threat to the PC when being serviced is electrostatic discharge (ESD). *Take a look at "Selecting the tools for the job."*

5 *C.* This is kind of a trick question, but the PC is left plugged in during all service work (except the power supply, of course). *Jog your memory at "Reinstalling the motherboard."*

6 *B.* There really is no hard-and-fast rule for this, but spacing all the internal components out a bit does help the air flow. *Flow on over to "Stating your reinstallment preference: The adapter or the drive first?"*

7 *A and B.* The floppy disk must be installed in a certain location on the floppy disk cable. *Review "Testing the Results."*

8 *B.* Also called spacers, the motherboard sits up off the case, allowing for air space under the board. *Check out "Reinstalling the motherboard."*

9 *A, B, and C.* This cable must be handled very carefully and installed correctly to avoid its shock hazard and potential damage to the PC. *Look at "Connecting the front panel."*

Chapter 16

Installing New Hardware

• •

Exam Objectives

▶ Configuring IRQs, DMAs, and I/O addresses

▶ Installing and configuring IDE/EIDE and SCSI devices

▶ Installing device drivers

▶ Interfacing with a modem

• •

*I*f the A+ exams reflect the nature of the PC service technician's actual work, then you spend most of your time installing, configuring, and testing new FRUs (field replaceable units), such as adapter cards, hard disks, CD-ROMs, and modems. You also are a walking encyclopedia on IRQs (interrupt requests), DMAs (direct memory access), and I/O (input/output) addresses. The tests include more questions regarding these activities and information than any other area. Therefore, you really need to know this stuff. How well must you know it? Let me explain it this way: About a third of each the Core exam and DOS/Windows exam relates to installing, configuring, and upgrading PC hardware. On the two exams combined (a total of 139 questions) you can expect around 44 questions from this area. I'd say this is something you really need to know.

This isn't the only chapter that you should be reviewing to prepare for this part of the exams. I would also study all of Part II, along with Chapters 17 and 21, to be really prepared.

The A+ Certification exam people claim that no trick questions are on the tests. I guess that all depends on your definition of trick question. Be prepared for questions that are engineered to test that you know why the choices are wrong or right. More than any test you have ever taken, this test is geared to measure your understanding of the relationships of components and their configuration and settings.

In this chapter, I try to summarize all this stuff in one place — a kind of one-stop study center. This chapter would be an excellent one to review just before you go in to take the test.

Quick Assessment

Configuring IRQs, DMAs, and I/O addresses

1 The standard IRQ assignment for COM1 is _____.

2 DMA channel _____ is normally assigned to the floppy disk controller.

3 The standard I/O address assigned to LPT1 is _____.

4 _____ allows a device to pass data and instructions directly to another device.

Installing and configuring IDE/EIDE and SCSI devices

5 Designate the primary hard drive as the _____ and any other hard drives as _____.

6 The colored edge of a hard drive ribbon cable indicates the side that you should connect to _____.

7 An IDE hard drive should _____ be low-level formatted.

8 A SCSI device chain should have _____ installed at each end of the chain.

Installing device drivers

9 A device driver is _____ that communicates directly with a device.

Interfacing with a modem

10 The _____ modem command is used to dial a telephone number using Touch-Tone dialing.

Answers

1 *IRQ 4*. Check out "Assigning System Resources."

2 *2*. Look at "Assigning System Resources."

3 *378h*. Review "Assigning System Resources."

4 *bus mastering*. Take a look at "Assigning System Resources."

5 *master, slave*. See "Designating masters and slaves."

6 *pin 1*. Connect with "Connecting the ribbon cables."

7 *never*. Check out "Configuring the drives."

8 *terminating resistors*. Review "Installing and Configuring SCSI Drives."

9 *software*. See "Installing Device Drivers."

10 *ATDT*. Link up with "ATtempting to Get the ATtention of a Modem."

Assigning System Resources

When you add a new device to the PC, it is assigned system resources through which it will communicate to the CPU and the rest of the system. Make sure that you know the standard assignments as well as what adjustments are possible so that conflicts don't occur between devices trying to use the same resources.

For the A+ exam, you need to have IRQs, DMAs, and I/O addresses down cold. You need to know the cabling and compatibility of hardware devices, especially SCSI and IDE/EIDE.

Sit down, clear your head, and memorize the standard IRQ assignments and their corresponding I/O addresses. Familiarize yourself with the DMA channel assignments, but memorize them only if you have nothing better to do.

Table 16-1 lists the standard IRQ (interrupt request) assignments, their corresponding I/O (input/output) addresses, and the likelihood of a particular IRQ being on the test. I use the following scale to indicate your chances of seeing a specific IRQ on the test:

✔ **No:** Not likely to be on the test.

✔ **Maybe:** It's possible, so prepare for it.

✔ **Yes:** May show up as a wrong answer in a question regarding another IRQ.

✔ **Yes-Yes:** At least one question.

✔ **Yes-Yes-Yes:** Is the focus of more than one question and mentioned in several others.

Table 16-1   Standard IRQ and I/O Address Assignments

IRQ #	Assignment	I/O Addresses	On the Test?
0	System timer	040-043	Maybe
1	Keyboard	060-064	Maybe
2	Link to IRQ9 for IRQs above IRQ7	0A0-0A1	Yes
3	COM2, COM4	2F8-2FF	Yes-Yes
4	COM1, COM3	3F8-3FF	Yes-Yes-Yes
5	LPT2 or sound card	1F0-1F8	Yes
6	Floppy disk	3F0-3F7	Yes
7	LPT1	378-37F	Yes-Yes

IRQ #	Assignment	I/O Addresses	On the Test?
8	System clock	070-07F	Maybe
9	Link to IRQ 2	N/A	Yes
10	Available	N/A	No
11	Laptop PC Cards	N/A	Maybe
12	Bus mouse	238-23B	Yes-Yes
13	Math coprocessor	0F8-0FF	Yes-Yes
14	IDE hard disk	N/A	Maybe
15	Secondary IDE drive	N/A	No

Of all the Yes-Yes-Yes's, the following items deserve one more Yes. They are guaranteed, lead-pipe cinch, for sure, count on it, bet the farm, going to be on the test. That's why I repeat it separately: The IRQ for COM1 and COM3 is IRQ 4. These two serial ports also share I/O address 3F8-3FF.

DMA (direct memory address) channels allow a device to bypass much of the red tape of the motherboard and write or read directly to or from RAM. Not every device gets to be a DMA device, but those that do should not be in conflict. I list the standard DMA assignments in Table 16-2. Chapter 7 covers DMA channels in a bit more detail.

Table 16-2	Standard DMA Channel Assignments	
DMA Channel #	**Standard Assignment**	**On the Test?**
0	Available	No
1	Sound card	No
2	Floppy disk controller	Maybe
3	16-bit sound card (uses two DMA channels)	Maybe
4–7	Available (newer systems only)	Yes

Bus mastering goes one step further than DMA and lets a device bypass not only the CPU, but RAM, too. Bus-mastered devices are intelligent devices that have a microprocessor on board to manage the device, which allows the bus-mastered device to operate concurrent with and independent of the CPU, greatly improving its performance. In fact, bus-mastered devices can pass data and instructions directly to one another without assistance from or disturbing the CPU. Many EISA, MCA, and PCI adapter cards feature bus mastering.

Installing an IDE or EIDE Hard Disk Drive

IDE (Integrated Drive Electronics) allows a system to install up to two disk drives in a series. This interface protocol is also known as ATA (AT Attachment) interface. IDE drives don't require a separate controller card, because this function is integrated electronically on the drive (hence its name). EIDE (Extended IDE) allows up to four disk drives to be installed, two each on two IDE cables. Otherwise, IDE and EIDE are about the same.

Designating masters and slaves

Because the controller functions are integrated into the drive, when more than one drive is installed, you have to designate one as the main dude. Otherwise, the drives would squabble about it and cause chaos. You make this designation through a jumper located on each drive. Set one drive as the master and any others as slaves. If both drives are masters, or if both drives are slaves, neither will work. The exact jumper setting to set a drive to either master or slave varies with the device. Always refer to either a diagram on the top of the disk drive or its documentation to verify the factory setting, which is usually set to master. Exactly how you set the jumper is not important on the A+ exam, only that you know how to.

If you have just installed a second hard drive and the Hard Drive not Present error displays during the POST, you haven't set the master/slave jumpers.

Connecting the ribbon cables

You really must know which end is up on the ribbon cables used to connect hard and floppy disk drives to their adapters. Virtually all ribbon cables have a colored (red or blue) edge that indicates the side with pin 1.

Connecting the ribbon cable in backward, in effect aligning pin 40 to pin 1 of either the drive or the adapter, normally causes the system not to boot and the drive LED on the PC's front panel to light up and stay on. If this happens, you can bet the ribbon cable is flipped.

You can expect to find questions that ask about the number of IDE and EIDE drives that can be installed, the orientation of disk drive ribbon cables, and the need to set the master/slave jumpers when more than one disk drive is installed.

Configuring the drives

IDE/EIDE drives are never low-level formatted, but need to be high-level formatted when first installed in a PC.

Follow the steps in Lab 16-1 to high-level format drives:

Lab 16-1   High-level Formatting an IDE/EIDE Hard Disk

1. Ensure that the drive is properly installed physically and working.

Boot the system from a floppy disk and resolve any POST or boot errors that may occur. If errors occurred in the boot process, reboot after they are resolved.

2. Update the CMOS disk drive types.

Using information from the hard disk itself or from its documentation, enter the appropriate AT drive type in the CMOS setup information.

3. Use the SCANDISK command to check for media errors.

SCANDISK.EXE checks the surface media of the disk for defects and records any bad spots it finds to avoid problems later.

4. Use the FDISK command to create a primary partition and any extended partitions desired.

Remember that Windows 95 requires the primary partition to be at least 32MB. If you are using DOS 3.3 or earlier, the primary partition cannot be more than 32MB. Other partitions can be up to 2GB in size.

5. Use the FORMAT command to high-level format each partition and logical drive.

Each partition will be assigned a logical drive identity. The primary partition is C:, and the other partitions are D:, E:, or other designations depending on drive designations already assigned to other drive types. Each partition (logical drive) must be formatted separately.

The FDISK command creates three primary entities on the hard disk:

✔ **Primary partition:** Used to start the computer from the hard disk and is usually designated as the C: drive.

✔ **Extended partition:** In effect, any of the hard disk not included in the primary partition. You can divide this partition into up to 23 logical drives, which each act as a separate disk with its own drive letter. Extended partitions are occasionally used to install a second operating system.

✔ **Master boot sector:** Also known as the partition table, it contains the master boot program and descriptions of each partition.

Booting multiple operating systems

One of the reasons you would create other logical drives on the hard disk is to install a second operating system, for example, OS/2, UNIX, Linux, or the like. If more than one operating system is installed on the hard disk, you can boot the PC into a different operating system than that on the primary partition.

In order to create the situation where you can choose which operating system you want to boot into, you must edit the MSDOS.SYS file (one of the system files used during the boot process) and add the following command to its [OPTIONS] section:

```
BootMulti=1
```

This option indicates to the boot process that you want to choose the operating system to be started from a menu. Accordingly, a menu listing the boot options displays prior to any operating system being started. You pick the one you want from the menu (which also has the various boot modes of Windows listed), and away you go.

Another way to accomplish the same thing is to press the F8 function key immediately after the POST process stops. It takes good timing to get it, but when you do, it interrupts the normal boot process and displays the boot options menu.

Adding a CD-ROM drive

Installing a CD-ROM drive is pretty easy because its adapter is usually already in the system. CD-ROM drives can share an IDE adapter with a hard disk or be installed into a chain of SCSI devices. Really, the only trick to installing a CD-ROM is getting the sound cable plugged onto the sound card so that you can hear the CD-ROM's audio output on the PC's speakers.

The only things you need to know about installing a CD-ROM drive are in the preceding paragraph. Don't waste a lot of time on laser types or the colors of the standards books (the yellow book is the only one you care about anyway).

Be cautious when working with a CD-ROM drive to avoid possible eye damage by the laser used in the device.

Installing and Configuring SCSI Drives

On the A+ Core exam, you can expect to see questions that include the following facts about SCSI (Small Computer System Interface) devices:

- ✔ SCSI chains can hold up to eight total devices, including the SCSI host adapter.
- ✔ Each SCSI device is assigned an ID number ranging from 0 to 7.
- ✔ The SCSI host adapter is always designated as ID 7.
- ✔ If a SCSI hard disk is to be the boot device, it must be ID 0.
- ✔ The SCSI chain must be terminated with resistors at each end.
- ✔ The CMOS setup for a SCSI hard disk is either just SCSI drive type or drive type 1.
- ✔ SCSI is a very popular choice for external CD-ROM drives.

Three SCSI bus standards exist:

- ✔ **SCSI (SCSI-1):** The original SCSI standard. It uses 50-pin Centronics-style connectors to create an 8-bit data path that supports eight devices on a daisy-chain bus.
- ✔ **SCSI-2:** Adds parity checking and improved methods for installing the terminating resistance. Wide SCSI is a variation of SCSI-2 that uses 68-pin cables, uses a 16- or 32-bit data path, and supports up to 16 devices on its chain.
- ✔ **Ultra SCSI (SCSI-3 or Fast-SCSI):** Transfers data in 20 and 40MB bursts over 8- and 16-bit data paths, respectively. Ultra SCSI is backward-compatible to both SCSI-1 and SCSI-2.

If you install an IDE drive along with SCSI drives, make the IDE drive the boot drive.

Installing Device Drivers

Device drivers are software that communicates directly with the device and acts as a go-between for the operating system and the device itself. Device-driver software is loaded from the CONFIG.SYS file or by Windows 95 and stays in memory as a TSR (Terminate and Stay Resident) program, ready to serve when called.

Installing a device driver in DOS and Windows 3.*x* is a three-step process, as shown in Lab 16-2:

Lab 16-2   Installing a Device Driver in DOS and Windows 3.*x*

1. Copy the device driver software into a hard disk directory.

The device driver's file (usually a .SYS or .EXE) must be present on the boot disk for access by the boot process.

2. Insert the device command into the CONFIG.SYS file.

The following line, used for the mouse driver, is a common device driver entry:

```
DEVICE=C:\MOUSE\MOUSE.SYS
```

3. Reboot the system and test the device under software control. Use the manufacturer's manual to troubleshoot any performance problems.

It is important to see whether the device functions properly when accessed from software because this action exercises the device driver.

In Windows 95, the device driver is normally installed and assigned to a device when Windows 95 installs the device. The device driver then loads each time Windows starts up. Windows 95 comes with an assortment of standard device drivers (especially printers), but most hardware devices also come with their own device drivers on a disk or CD-ROM. In addition, many manufacturers now make available upgraded device drivers that you can retrieve using the Internet and use to replace an existing device driver.

To view or change a device driver for a Windows 95 device, right-click the My Computer icon on the desktop and choose Properties to display the System Properties dialog box. Highlight any device, click the Properties button, and choose the Driver tab to view its driver information. If you want to change the device driver, click the Change Driver button and proceed.

Devices displayed in the Windows 95 Device Manager with a yellow exclamation point symbol are missing a device driver, an IRQ, or another system resource.

ATtempting to Get the ATtention of a Modem

Two types of modems exist: *internal* and *external*. Internal modems are installed in an expansion slot, usually ISA or PCI, and need to be assigned an available IRQ and I/O address. Thankfully, most come with installation software that takes care of most of this for you. You do need to be alert to system resource conflicts, though. External modems attach to an existing COM port; typically, they have little trouble with system resources.

The A+ exam assumes you know how to install a modem and use its manual or software to configure it via its DIP switches and settings. However, the A+ Core exam thinks you should know some of the AT (not to be confused with advanced technology or the early 286 IBM PC of the same name) command set that's used to control a modem when in use. The AT (which is the command for "Please may I have your attention") command set is used to issue dial, hang up, reset, and other instructions to the modem.

Table 16-3 lists some of the most commonly used AT commands. Know them for the test.

Table 16-3 Commonly Used Modem Control (AT) Commands

Command	Meaning
AT	Precedes all modem action commands.
ATDT ppppppp	Dial the ppppppp telephone number using Touch-Tone dialing.
ATDP ppppppp	Dial the ppppppp telephone number using Pulse dialing.
ATA	Answer an incoming call.
ATH0	Hang up immediately.
AT&F	Reset the modem to its factory default settings.
ATZ	Reset the modem to its power-up settings, which may include modifications made by you or the customer.
*70	Cancel call waiting on the line to which the modem is connected.

Many more modem AT commands exist, but for test purposes, focus on those included in Table 16-3.

Prep Test

1 An IDE hard disk drive should be low-level formatted

   A ○ When it's first installed as a new drive

   B ○ After it's partitioned with ScanDisk

   C ○ Before installing a used drive in a new PC

   D ○ Never

2 IRQ is the short form of

   A ○ Internal Resource Quotient

   B ○ Interrupt Request

   C ○ Input/Output Request

   D ○ Internal Request

3 You partition a hard drive using what DOS/Windows command?

   A ○ SCANDISK

   B ○ DEFRAG

   C ○ FDISK

   D ○ SYSEDIT

4 After installing a new hard drive, you turn on the computer. The drive LED on the front of the case comes on immediately when you turn on the power and remains on. The system doesn't boot. What could be the problem? (Choose all that apply.)

   A ❑ The ribbon cable is connected backward to either the drive or the controller.

   B ❑ The hard drive LED wire is reversed on the systemboard.

   C ❑ The master/slave configuration isn't configured correctly.

   D ❑ The adapter card/controller isn't seated properly on the systemboard.

5 A PC has a single IDE and a pair of SCSI hard drives installed. Which should be the boot drive?

   A ○ The IDE drive.

   B ○ The first SCSI drive.

   C ○ The second SCSI drive.

   D ○ Any of the three devices can be assigned as the boot drive.

6 The audio wire that comes out of the CD-ROM should be attached to what device?

A ○ To the case with an alligator clip to provide a ground
B ○ To the audio connectors on the motherboard
C ○ To the sound card
D ○ To the SCSI host adapter

7 After a new hard disk drive is installed and the PC is powered on, you get the message Hard Disk Drive not Present. If all the physical connections are okay, what else may be the problem?

A ○ The hard drive was incorrectly detected during POST.
B ○ There is an IRQ conflict with the drive controller.
C ○ The master/slave configuration is not set up properly.
D ○ The hard drive hasn't been partitioned and formatted.

8 Where are terminating resistors installed on a SCSI chain?

A ○ Only after device ID 7.
B ○ Only before device ID 1.
C ○ At both ends of the SCSI chain.
D ○ The terminating resistors are required only on SCSI-1 chains.

9 The modem command that's used to reset the modem to its factory settings is

A ○ ATZ
B ○ ATDT
C ○ AT&F
D ○ ATH0

10 You may divide an extended partition into

A ○ Two more extended partitions.
B ○ Up to 23 logical drives.
C ○ An unlimited number of secondary partitions.
D ○ You can't further divide an extended partition.

Answers

1 *D.* Never low-level format IDE/EIDE hard drives. They are high-level formatted when first installed in a PC. *See "Configuring the drives."*

2 *B.* IRQs are used by the CPU to communicate and control the PC's devices. *Check out "Assigning System Resources."*

3 *C.* The FDISK command is still the workhorse of disk partitioning. *Take a look at "Configuring the drives."*

4 *A and C.* You should expect a question or two that asks you to identify all the choices that are correct. Both of these conditions can cause the PC not to boot. *Check out "Connecting the ribbon cables" and "Designating masters and slaves."*

5 *A.* The IDE hard drive must be the boot drive in this situation. *Review "Installing and Configuring SCSI Drives."*

6 *C.* In order for the CD-ROM's audio to play out of the PC's speakers, it must be sent through the sound card. *Take a look at "Adding a CD-ROM drive."*

7 *C.* A common reason for a hard drive failure is that its master/slave jumper is not set correctly for the system. *See "Designating masters and slaves."*

8 *C.* The SCSI chain must be terminated at each end of the bus. *Examine "Installing and Configuring SCSI Drives."*

9 *C.* All modem commands begin with AT, and the "&F" command option is used to reset the modem to its factory switch and register settings. Connect with *"ATtempting to Get the ATtention of the Modem."*

10 *B.* The extended partition may be divided into 23 logical drives, each of which may be referenced and accessed by its own drive letter. *Review "Configuring the drives."*

Chapter 17
Upgrading the Motherboard

. . . .

Exam Objectives

▶ Adding and removing motherboard components

▶ Identifying the procedures used to upgrade the BIOS

▶ Using hardware to optimize system performance

▶ Changing the basic parameters of CMOS (Complementary Metal-Oxide Semiconductor)

. . . .

1 recently had to buy a new engine part for the heap of ferrous oxide I laughingly refer to as my car. The price of this part caused me to reflect on whether the car was worthy of it, as opposed to a tow to the car burial grounds. Similarly, while the computing power you get for the price of a PC has steadily increased over the past ten years, the prices of the individual parts, like those for my car, may shock you. However, upgrading an older-model PC is often a better option for a customer than buying a new one.

Upgrading the motherboard is a bit like replacing the crust of a pizza after the pizza has been cooked. All the cheese, sauce, and bits and pieces of pepperoni, olives, and pineapple have to be removed and placed back on the new crust. Of course, the pizza has one advantage over the motherboard — if the toppings aren't in the exact same place, the pizza will still be functional.

The A+ Core exam seeks to verify your knowledge of the processes and components used to upgrade the motherboard and its major FRUs (field replaceable units). Everything inside a PC's case is an FRU except the case itself. For the A+ exam, know what you can upgrade and how you go about it.

Quick Assessment

Adding and removing motherboard components

1 Memory added to a PC must use the same transfer _____ as the existing memory.

2 You can replace older CPUs with a(n) _____ processor.

3 Pentium processors prior to the Pentium II mount in a _____ socket.

4 Removing the battery causes the _____ to lose its data.

Identifying the procedures used to upgrade the BIOS

5 Updating the BIOS under software control is called _____.

6 The BIOS is stored on a _____ chip.

Using hardware to optimize system performance

7 Adding _____ will usually help improve a PC's performance.

8 SRAM is packaged as a _____ module.

Changing the basic parameters of CMOS

9 The key used to access the setup utility displays after the _____ completes.

10 The physical properties of the hard disk are represented by the numerical _____.

Answers

1 *Speed.* Check out "Increasing your memory in three easy lessons."

2 *Overdrive.* Speed over to "Boosting your processor power."

3 *ZIF (Zero Insertion Force).* Review "Updating Pentium processors."

4 *CMOS.* See "Batteries? We Don't Need No Stinking Batteries!"

5 *Flashing.* Take a look at "Replacing the BIOS."

6 *ROM.* Review "Replacing the BIOS."

7 *RAM or memory.* Look up "Increasing your memory in three easy lessons."

8 *COAST* (Cache On A Stick). See "Show me the cache."

9 *POST.* Check out "Updating the CMOS."

10 *Type number.* Review "Updating the CMOS."

Upgrading the Motherboard

For the A+ Core exam, you need to know the major steps to replace the motherboard, add or replace RAM, change the batteries, lube the bit joints, replace the processor, check the cooling oil, and upgrade the BIOS ROM. Okay, you caught me — the bit joints and cooling oil are lifetime systems and don't need to changed, but you must know the sequence of steps used in any of the other upgrade actions, along with the safety and compatibility issues.

The motherboard, CPU, memory modules, SRAM, and virtually everything inside the case, except the case itself, are considered to be field replaceable units (FRUs).

Probably the fastest way to study the processes used to upgrade the motherboard, RAM, and so on, is to do them. Open the case of a PC and run through the steps, described in this chapter and in Chapter 15, you use to add RAM, change the batteries, upgrade the processor, and replace the motherboard. If available, use both a newer Pentium board and an older 286 or 386 board to contrast the particular steps used for each.

Increasing your memory in three easy lessons

The most common upgrade performed on the motherboard is increasing the size of its memory. Adding memory to any PC is the easiest way to enhance its performance and always helps the system run better. Three things exist that you can't have too much of: hard disk space, CPU clock speed, and RAM.

Upgrading memory is a very straightforward task, but you must consider some things beforehand and watch out for them as you go:

  ✔ **Memory type.** Older motherboards (I'm talking ancient here) use *DIP* (dual inline packaging) chips, like the one shown in Figure 17-1. You can easily recognize whether a motherboard uses DIP memory, because it will have row after row of DIP chips on it. More recent motherboards use either *SIMMs* (single inline memory modules), also shown in Figure 17-1, or *DIMMs* (dual inline memory modules). A motherboard with SIMM or DIMM memories has two or more of them standing vertically in their sockets. For the test, know which type of memory is which by sight.

DIMMs and DIPs have very little in common beyond the fact that they are both memory and share the same first and middle names.

Be sure you fully understand the information in the following bullets. You will encounter questions on the test that incorporate this information into situational questions.

- ✓ **Memory speed.** Any new memory added to the system needs to be at the same speed as the existing memory unless all the memory is to be replaced with a faster memory that the motherboard will support. The easiest way to match the memory is to use the last part of the number on the chips. This number usually ends with a dash and a one- or two-digit number. For example, on a 70-nanosecond SIMM, each chip will have a "-70" at the end of the chip number, or on an old 286 PC, the memory may have a "-12" for 120-nanosecond memory.

- ✓ **Memory capacity.** Individual memory chips and modules are available in a number of different capacities, ranging from 32K DIPs to 16MB and higher SIMMs and DIMMs. The number of memory modules needed to provide the memory size desired by the customer depends on how much money they have and the number and type of slots available, in that order. Unfortunately, many combinations add up to what may seem like a simple upgrade. A PC with 16MB may have eight 2MB modules, two 8MB modules, or one 16MB module. If slots are available, you can plug in additional memory of the same type and speed. If all the memory slots are full, you must remove and replace the existing memory.

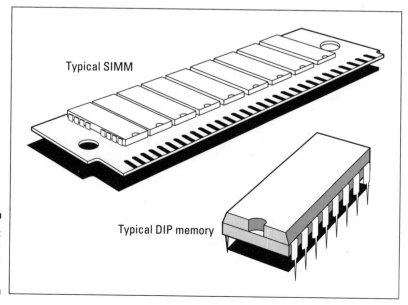

Figure 17-1:
A SIMM and a DIP chip.

Typical SIMM

Typical DIP memory

You must fill DIP memory banks, or SIMM banks, completely before you can begin adding memory to the next bank or banks.

Just because you use the utmost care and a loving touch to add the memory to the motherboard doesn't mean that the computer will trust you and just automatically agree to the memory. Most likely, the PC will give some form of a memory error when it boots. If you have installed the memory correctly, it's fairly certain the PC saw the memory. However, you will need to run the setup utility and update the CMOS (Complementary Metal-Oxide Semiconductor) settings for memory. Don't be surprised if the CMOS memory setting reflects the new memory; if it does, just save it and exit. Review the process you use to set CMOS settings in Chapter 4.

If you have upgraded the memory using DIP memory chips, chances are that in addition to setting the CMOS, you may also need to set a jumper or DIP switch to indicate how much memory is now installed on the motherboard. You must refer to the motherboard's documentation to determine which jumper or switch to change. Extremely old motherboards that do not have CMOS (pre-286) probably are a waste to upgrade in the first place, but most definitely use either jumpers or DIP switches. Chapter 6, although it is about storage devices, includes information on how to set DIP switches and jumpers, which is done the same in all applications.

Show me the cache

Adding additional *cache* memory can help optimize the performance of the CPU and operating system.

Memory caching works in the following way:

1. A cache controller anticipates the data or program module that the CPU (central processing unit) is likely to request next.

2. The data or program code is copied from DRAM (dynamic RAM) and stored in SRAM (static RAM).

3. If the cache controller guesses right, which is about 90 percent of the time, the CPU's next request is satisfied from SRAM at a much faster rate than possible from DRAM.

Prior to the 486 processor, the cache controller was installed on the motherboard on a separate integrated circuit chip. Since the 486, the cache controller is now integrated into the CPU along with an amount of SRAM (static RAM), which is called *internal,* or *level 1* (L1), cache. Systems now boast that they also include additional cache memory. This added cache is called *external,* or *level 2* (L2), cache.

SRAM is usually packaged as a *COAST* (Cache On A Stick) module. A COAST module is installed in a special slot on the motherboard, usually located near the CPU. Like all else, the type of SRAM and the amount a motherboard will support depends on the motherboard. A point of diminishing returns exists to adding cache memory in that no appreciable performance improvement appears for more than 512K of L2 memory cache.

Upgrading the Processor

For the A+ Core exam, understand the processor upgrade options available for pre-Pentium and Pentium motherboards and how to install these options. Also know the evolution of the Pentium processor, which is covered in Chapter 4.

Boosting your processor power

You can do very little to a BP (before Pentium) motherboard to turn it into anything other than a slightly faster version of itself. Putting a Ferrari body on a Pinto creates either a very slow Ferrari or a sleek-looking Pinto. In either case, you've spent money to achieve very little (unless you really like sleek-looking Pintos and slow Ferraris). In that case, processor packages, called *overdrive processors,* can add a little speed to your 386 or 486 PC, which may be all that an installation needs.

Be aware that the upgrade chip must be compatible with the BIOS and processor socket. The documentation with the new chip should list the BIOSes with which it is compatible, or come with a software utility that will accept or reject the system as a home for the new processor. It is probably wiser to make this determination before you actually pay for the processor.

ABSOLUTELY and WITHOUT FAIL take ESD precautions when working inside the case with the memory and the processor. Wear a grounding strap.

After you carefully remove the old processor chip from its mounting (using a chip puller or an old church key, and after breaking three or four fingernails), insert the new chip into the mount. As illustrated in Figure 17-2, you need to pay particular attention to how you place the chip into the socket. Depending on who manufactured the replacement chip, a dot, notch, or blemish of some kind should indicate the pin 1 alignment of the processor to the socket.

Another way to speed up a BP processor is to add a math coprocessor to the motherboard. Some systems, such as the 486DX, already have one built in, but many older processors can benefit from this add-on. The math coprocessor, also known as the *floating point unit (FPU),* allows the CPU to offload arithmetic functions and concentrate on other activities.

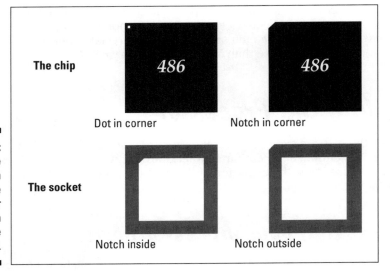

The chip

486 — Dot in corner

486 — Notch in corner

The socket

Notch inside

Notch outside

Figure 17-2: Match the dot or notch of the processor to the notch of the socket.

Updating Pentium processors

You can update most Pentium computers by changing the processor. Pentium processors up through the Pentium Pro mount into a *ZIF* (zero insertion force) socket. To remove and replace the processor, follow the steps listed in Lab 17-1.

Lab 17-1   Replacing the Processor in a ZIF Mounting

1. **Release the handle of the ZIF mount from its little retainer clip.**

   With the handle clipped into place, press down very slightly and pull it away from the little peg that it snaps under to release it.

2. **Lift the handle to release the processor.**

   The old processor chip should pop right out.

3. **Place the replacement processor on the ZIF platform aligned properly.**

4. **Lock the handle by pushing it down and snapping it in place.**

   Before locking down the ZIF handle, check for pins that may be out of the mounting holes along the edges. Do not push on the chip to push it into place. The ZIF socket and handle will pull it into place and lock it down. Zero insertion force means just that — don't push it, don't lean on it.

Not every Pentium, 586, 686, K5, or K6 chip will work on every Pentium-level motherboard. Compatibility issues exist with the data bus, chipset, the socket, and more. An example, but probably not on the exam, is the Pentium II processor, which is in a special package called the Single Edge Contact, which is mounted into an Intel-proprietary socket found only on newer Intel motherboards.

Before using an upgrade processor, check it out. Talk directly to the processor manufacturer's technical support, visit its Web site, or contact the PC manufacturer. The last one can be difficult to do, however, in today's world of clones and custom-built PCs.

Make sure that any Pentium processor has the correct cooling components installed. Some use heat sinks, fans, or both. Some require thermal grease, and some have clips to hold it all into place. The hotter the processor runs, the slower it runs, so be sure it is properly ventilated. If a fan is installed with the processor, be sure to plug it into the power supply. They don't cool so well without power.

You can expect to see some questions on the test that relate to the upgradeability of a Pentium processor. For example, you may see a question that compares the processing speeds and capabilities of the Pentium and the Pentium Pro, including bus speeds and MMX instructions. Table 17-1 lists the Intel processors by their evolution. Yes, there are other manufacturers, but any questions on processor upgrades are about Intel processors only.

Table 17-1	Intel Processors	
Processor	*Processing Speed*	*MMX?*
486DX	25–50MHz	No
486DX2	33–66MHz	No
486DX4	75–100MHz	No
Pentium	60–166MHz	No
Pentium MMX	150–200MHz	Yes
Pentium Pro	150–200MHz	No
Pentium II	233–450MHz	Yes

Replacing the BIOS

Often, all that's needed to make some troublesome problems go away is to upgrade the BIOS (Basic Input Output System). Replacing or upgrading the BIOS ROM chips on a computer can solve many hardware and software incompatibility problems. A customer will be very disappointed to plug in the new toy you sold him or her, only to find that it is DOA (doesn't operate as advertised) because their PC's BIOS doesn't support it.

For the A+ Core exam, know which process is used to update the BIOS in both older and newer computers. What I call an "older PC" has one or more DIP ROM chips that hold the BIOS, and which must be physically replaced. A newer PC uses Flash ROM that is updated with software.

The BIOS ROM chips are usually the ones that have the word "BIOS" printed on top of them, which makes them very easy to recognize. Depending on the system, as many as five ROM chips may hold the BIOS. The motherboard may also have yet another BIOS chip located apart from the others — this one for the keyboard. If more than one BIOS chip exists, you can distinguish by markings that identify each of them as BIOS-1, BIOS-2, and so on. If you decide to be so bold as to replace these chips with an upgraded set (obviously DIP ROM chips), be sure to write down which chip came from each socket and put the corresponding new chip in the same socket.

Upgrading the BIOS by running a software program is called *flashing*. This process is so easy that perhaps customers could even do it themselves — nah! The only real problem with flashing the BIOS ROM can come when the update software is interrupted for any reason, such as a PC crash or power failure. When this interruption happens, no BIOS exists to reboot the system, let alone restart the flashing software. Some motherboard manufacturers now also provide a utility to recover the BIOS should this happen. However, if you do not have this utility, the system is hosed and you must replace the BIOS ROM chip with a good one.

Also, flash ROM viruses now exist that can attack the system through the same door that the flash upgrade software uses. Check the motherboard's manual to see whether it has a jumper that will disable flashing and thus disable the virus. You can always enable flashing again should you ever have the urge to flash the PC.

Updating the BIOS ROM under software control is called *flashing*.

Batteries? We Don't Need No Stinking Batteries!

Unfortunately, the PC's CMOS (Complementary Metal-Oxide Semiconductor), where the setup configuration is stored, does need batteries. With the advent of the BIOS setup utility with the 286 PC, a battery has been a necessity to keep the CMOS powered and holding the system setup configuration information.

In the beginning, AT systems had a special battery that mounted to the case wall with a Velcro strip and plugged on the motherboard through a pigtail. This structure evolved into a small plastic box that held two AA batteries and also hung on the wall of the case by Velcro. Little barrel-shaped batteries soldered, and later clipped, to the motherboard came next, and today, the motherboard has a small clip that holds a lithium battery. The good news is that most CMOS batteries last a long time.

For the A+ Core exam, you need to know two things: that the CMOS is powered by a battery (usually lithium) and that should the battery go dead, be removed, or turned off, the contents of the CMOS will be lost.

Changing the CMOS battery is not necessarily something you do on a regular basis. However, when the system suddenly asks you for the time and date or demands that you reenter the configuration information, it's time to replace it. To change the CMOS battery, follow the steps included in Lab 17-2.

Lab 17-2   Changing the CMOS Battery

1. **Copy down every bit of the setup configuration data stored in the CMOS.**

   When you remove the battery, the CMOS settings revert to their default values. If you have never altered the CMOS, then it's no big deal. However, if you have upgraded the system, added peripherals, memory, and so on, it is a good idea to copy down the current values.

2. **Find the little round red or blue barrel-shaped battery or silver disk located near the BIOS ROM chip held by one or more spring clips.**

   Carefully examine the battery to ensure that it is not attached other than by the clip. On some older systems, it may be wired into the board. If this is the case, check the motherboard's manuals on how to change the battery.

3. **Insert the new battery into the clip or holder.**

   Immediately reboot the system and access the setup utility by pressing the key indicated at the end of the POST process. Enter any values that need to be updated, save the setup, and continue the boot process.

Understand that when you pull out the old battery, the CMOS will be blanked. Unless you have it backed up or written down, the setup information is lost.

Updating the CMOS

For the A+ exam, know the types of information stored in CMOS and how CMOS is accessed.

After you have changed out the motherboard, installed a new CPU, added RAM and cache memory, changed the battery, and saved the customer a bundle by performing computer alchemy, you must enter the new configuration of the PC into the CMOS.

Naturally, the system booted on the first try with no POST errors beeping or displaying, so you are ready to press the secret CMOS access key and enter the mysterious world of the system setup utility. If you don't know the secret key, look in the secret location: on the screen right after the POST completes. It's camouflaged as a boot sequence message, the kind everyone ignores, and looks something like the following:

```
Press <F2> to run SETUP
```

or

```
Press <Del> to enter SETUP or run DIAGS
```

Pressing the secret key mentioned in the secret message opens the CMOS setup utility and a vast assortment of really technical system stuff.

CMOS data is usually organized into basic and advanced information. The basic data includes the following types of entries:

- ✔ **System date and time:** Kept in the CMOS because it always has power and can keep the system up to date. You can change the date and time here, through the DOS DATE and TIME commands, or through the Windows Control Panel.

- ✔ **Type of floppy disk drive or drives on the system:** Usually, four choices are available for each of the two floppy disk drives:

  - 3^1/$_2$-inch, 1.44MB
  - 3^1/$_2$-inch, 720K
  - 5^1/$_4$-inch, 1.2MB
  - 5^1/$_4$-inch, 360K

- ✔ **Drive type of each of the hard disks installed on the system:** The manual that came with your hard disk should indicate the hard disk type. This number ranges from 1 to 48. Each drive type represents a different combination of tracks, heads, sectors, and capacity. Most drives come with installation software that sets this value.

✔ **Amount and type of memory installed on the system:** Even if the BIOS can find and count to the right amount of memory, you may still get an error message that it doesn't agree with the CMOS total, probably because you just added more. The silliest part of this process is that when you look in the CMOS, the correct amount of RAM is probably there already. If so, save it and exit. If not, fix it, save it, and exit.

✔ **Type and number of ports along with their system resource assignments:** Parallel ports are specified as uni- or bidirectional, ECP or EPP. Serial ports are enabled or disabled.

✔ **Disk drive boot sequence:** Indicates the sequence in which the disk drives are to be accessed for a boot sector program. Usually this sequence is set to A: then C:, but it can have other settings.

✔ **Network interface card (NIC):** If installed, its type and resource assignments are configured in CMOS.

✔ **The video adapter card type or architecture:** On some systems, only color or monochrome are saved, but on others, you have a choice of graphics architectures. Remember that changing a video card may also require a change on the motherboard itself through a jumper or DIP switch.

The advanced settings I mention earlier are unique to each motherboard and chipset. These settings can be quite lengthy. Before you changed the motherboard, you wrote down all the CMOS settings, which cannot be entered. You can do some things while you're here to improve the system performance, such as turning on any memory caches or ROM shadows available. Just turn on one new feature at a time. That way, you can back off any that give you a problem.

Prep Test

1 Which of the following are FRUs? (Choose all that apply.)

A ❑ Motherboard

B ❑ Power supply

C ❑ Floppy disk drive

D ❑ Pentium processor

2 ROM usually stores the

A ○ Binary Input Output System

B ○ Basic Input Output System

C ○ System setup utility

D ○ CMOS settings

3 CMOS is the acronym for

A ○ Computer Memory Option Storage

B ○ Common Memory Optional Settings

C ○ Complementary Metal-Oxide Semiconductor

D ○ Computer Metal-Oxide Semiconductor

4 The CPU is packaged in what forms? (Choose all that apply.)

A ❑ SIMM

B ❑ DIP

C ❑ PGA

D ❑ ZIF

5 The chip that you can add to some motherboards to perform math functions is the

A ○ Math simulator

B ○ Arithmetic and logic unit

C ○ Parallel processor

D ○ Math coprocessor

6 Which of the following is not stored in CMOS?

A ○ Floppy disk drive configuration

B ○ Type and amount of memory

C ○ Type and style of mouse unit

D ○ Video adapter type and architecture

7 On a memory chip, the -60 at the end of the chip number refers to

A ○ The number of pins used to install the memory module.

B ○ 60-nanosecond transfer rate.

C ○ 600-nanosecond transfer rate.

D ○ Nothing in particular; it's just part of the numbering scheme.

8 Which of the following processors would be considered to be "faster" than a Pentium? (Choose all that apply.)

A ❑ 486DX4

B ❑ Pentium MMX

C ❑ Pentium Pro

D ❑ Pentium II

9 CMOS is powered by

A ○ A lithium battery.

B ○ A cable from the power supply.

C ○ An AC/DC external power adapter.

D ○ No outside power; none is required.

10 External cache memory is referred to as

A ○ Level 1 cache

B ○ Level 2 cache

C ○ Virtual memory

D ○ RAMDisk

Answers

1 *A, B, C, D*. This is not meant to be a trick question. The A+ exam has many questions like this one, where multiple answers are equally correct. In this case, all of these devices are FRUs. *See "Upgrading the Motherboard."*

2 *B*. The BIOS provides the system with its most fundamental input and output controls. *Take a look at "Replacing the BIOS."*

3 *C*. In actuality, nearly all the integrated circuits in the computer are made using the CMOS technology. However, the term *CMOS* usually refers to the one chip on which system configuration is stored. *Review "Batteries? We Don't Need No Stinking Batteries!"*

4 *B, C*. SIMMs are memory modules, and a ZIF is the socket type that most PGAs are installed into. *Check out "Increasing your memory in three easy lessons" and "Updating Pentium processors."*

5 *D*. Although most newer processors now have this function built in, many early processors did not or had this function disabled for price competition reasons. *See "Boosting your processor power."*

6 *C*. The PC must figure that if you've seen one mouse, you've seen them all, because CMOS ignores the mouse. *Look at "Updating the CMOS."*

7 *B*. Be sure that any new memory added to a system matches the speed of the existing memory. *Flash over to "Increasing your memory in three easy lessons."*

8 *B , C, D*. You will probably see a question or two on the test concerning which processors are better or faster upgrades than other processors. *Check out "Updating Pentium processors."*

9 *A*. But if it is removed, no more memory in the CMOS. *Zap over to "Batteries? We Don't Need No Stinking Batteries!"*

10 *B*. Level 2 memory is effective up to 512K in size. *Review "Show me the cache."*

Chapter 18
Portable Systems

Exam Objectives

▶ Identifying the unique components of portable PC systems

▶ Identifying and installing PCMCIA components

*P*ortable computing has been around for a while now. In the early 1980s, portable systems were nothing like what we have today, but then, what is? The early Compaq, HP, and Osborne portable systems set the stage and established that a market did indeed exist for move-about systems.

The early laptop computers, although smaller than the desktop devices of the time, filled your lap completely and then some. These systems were rarely used on people's laps because most of us don't have arms attached at our hips in order to reach a keyboard on our laps. Portables also were much too big for airline meal trays, a sure killer in the business market. You can still spot anyone who traveled extensively with a laptop computer — one arm is about two inches longer than the other from carrying this "portable" device around.

Today, the notebook computer, so called because it's about the size of a 2-inch binder or notebook, has finally established a size package that the market could truly use just about anywhere. Solitaire anywhere, anytime, anyplace. The latest evolution is the ultimately small palmtop. Technology has finally developed a full-fledged Windows computer that you can literally hold in your hand or fit in your briefcase or even conveniently tuck into your little zippered planner. People no longer need to remember anything at all; they have a computer backed up by a personal appointment system to keep them in the right place at the right time.

Just what the PC service technician's role will be with these devices in the future still remains to be seen, which is probably why the A+ exam has only three or four questions on portable systems. CompTIA recognizes the importance of the portable system and has given it its own domain on the Core exam, but maybe this is to hold a place for future exam versions.

Quick Assessment

Identifying
the unique
components
of portable
PC

1 _____ is the type of portable PC that is the most popular today.

2 A _____ is the power system that allows a notebook computer to be portable.

3 Because of its weight and long life, the _____ type of battery is probably the best choice for a portable PC.

4 Portable PCs use either _____ or _____ memories.

5 Before physically installing a larger internal hard drive on a notebook computer, you can add _____, _____, or _____ using an existing parallel port.

6 The type of LCD display that supports each pixel with its own transistor is called _____.

Identifying
and installing
PCMCIA
components

7 Type I PCMCIA cards are used to add _____ to a notebook computer.

8 A modem is an example of a _____ PC Card.

9 Type III PCMCIA cards can be up to _____ millimeters thick.

10 Changing a PC Card while the system is running is called _____.

Answers

1 *Notebook.* Flip to "Checking Out Portable PC Types."

2 *Battery.* Look at "Examining Portable Power Systems."

3 *Li-Ion.* See "Portable PC battery types."

4 *SIMM or DIMM.* Take a look at "Adding memory."

5 *Zip, Jazz, or tape drive.* Review "Upgrading the hard drive."

6 *Active matrix.* Scan "Comparing active and passive LCD displays."

7 *Flash memory.* See "Focusing on PCMCIA cards."

8 *Type II.* Check into "Focusing on PCMCIA cards."

9 *$10^{1/2}$.* Take one more look at "Focusing on PCMCIA cards."

10 *Hot-swapping.* Look at "Expanding capacity on the fly."

Relating Portable Systems and the A+ Exam

This chapter is the only one in the book that manages to cover every part of an entire A+ Core exam domain (which wasn't all too hard in this case). Because the A+ exams are about what PC service technicians see in the field, and because relatively very few portable computing systems are still in use, there aren't a lot of questions on the exam on this topic — in fact, only three questions.

The inclusion of portable systems on the A+ test recognizes that a growing number of people want to carry a computer everywhere they go. I'm sure people exist who can actually get work done on the airplane and for these folks, a portable PC is the ticket.

Questions on the A+ exam relate mostly to how you add memory and peripheral devices to the portable PC and the best way to dispose of its batteries, which is covered in Chapter 20.

In order to provide you with some background on portable computers, (if you need it), the next few sections cover a little history and terminology. If you want to cut to the chase on portable PCs for the A+ exam, go to the section "Expanding capacity on the fly."

Checking Out Portable PC Types

Many different types and styles of portable systems have been manufactured and sold over the past 18 to 20 years, including the following:

- **Suitcase computers:** I'm not positive that *suitcase* is their actual and official name, but many of the earliest portable systems by Compaq, Osborne, Hewlett-Packard, and others were in cases that clipped, snapped, or locked together like a suitcase. These systems were ingenious in that the keyboard was also the bottom of the case, and that people could actually read 4- and 5-inch monitors.

- **Laptop computers:** This type never did fit on my lap, but then, little does. Most people can balance a flimsy paper plate full of Aunt Esther's lead-weight potato salad easier than actually working with a laptop computer on their lap. However, the clamshell-style cases of these devices, along with some external ports, provided greater capabilities than the suitcase types. However, many still had microdot monitors and displays.

✔ **Notebook computers:** The currently popular type of portable system. What has made notebook computers popular has been that they provide all the capabilities and functionality of desktop PCs. Displays are large, bright, and clear. Notebooks support current processors, large RAM sizes, and high-capacity disk drives. The notebook has raised the portable computer out of its status as the "other computer" to many people's computer of choice.

✔ **Palmtop computers (personal digital assistants):** Currently, these mighty small-fries are very popular among the high-tech business world. They feature support for much of the application and hardware functionality of larger systems, including Windows and smaller versions of word processing, spreadsheets, and other software, and modem and direct cable connections.

Examining Portable Power Systems

Adaptable, lightweight, and portable power sources play a large part in the portability of the portable PC system. Essentially, three general types of power sources for the portable PC exist, each designed to provide it with power either in the office or on the road. The three sources of power for a portable PC are

✔ **AC/DC adapter:** Works very much like the power supply in a desktop computer to convert the wall socket AC power into DC power for the portable PC to use. AC adapters are also used to recharge the portable PC's battery. You are probably very familiar with this type of device because of its use on a wide range of electronic products, including games, calculators, external computer peripherals, and so on.

✔ **Battery:** An integral part of any portable PC because without it, the PC would not be so portable. Instead, users would need very long extension cords and have to depend upon having an AC outlet everywhere they go, which isn't likely. Look for more details on batteries later in this section.

✔ **Docking station:** Provides power and more to the PC. In addition to the power, the docking station enables the PC to connect to full-sized expansion cards and additional ports, and allows the portable PC to connect to and drive the peripherals (monitor, printer, and so on) that are usually found connected to a desktop computer.

Power management systems

Virtually all portable PCs now have some form of a power management system, most commonly a software battery monitor. This system tracks the reserve power of the battery and reports its strength as a percentage. Seventy percent means that you've used only 30 percent of the battery's capacity. Many power management systems also check to see whether the PC is in use and, if not, suspend the PC to conserve the battery's power. Conserving a battery and extending its life is a much better, and less expensive, choice than replacing the battery.

Here are some things that you can do to get the most out of your portable PC's battery:

- Keep in mind that new batteries and those that haven't been in use for a while may require a few discharge and recharge cycles before the battery will take a full charge.

- Portable PC batteries are more effectively recharged if they've been fully discharged. In fact, some power management systems provide a software feature to completely discharge the battery so that it can be recharged.

- Don't constantly recharge the battery by running the portable PC with the AC adapter plugged in. It is actually bad for some portable PC batteries to run while their batteries are being recharged. The conflicting demands of charge and discharge can stress the battery and shorten its life.

- To conserve the battery, turn off a portable PC when it's not in use.

Portable PC battery types

You may see a question on portable PC battery characteristics. In this section, I cover the differences of the battery types used in portable PCs.

Portable PCs use four types of batteries: alkaline, nickel-cadmium (NiCad), NiMH (Nickel-Metal Hydride), and Lithium-Ion (Li-Ion). The characteristics of each follow:

- **Alkaline:** The same batteries you commonly rely on for operation of your calculator, TV remote control, and portable tape player. You use this type of battery in some palmtop computers.

- **NiMH:** Unlike NiCad batteries, these batteries are environmentally friendly because they don't contain heavy metals that can be toxic. They also store up to 50 percent more power than NiCad batteries for the same weight. The disadvantages of NiMH batteries include a shorter life of around 500 charge/discharge cycles, and they cost about 30 percent more.

- ✔ **Li-Ion:** Pronounced "lye-eye-on," lithium is one of the lighter metals and is used to produce a very lightweight, long-life battery. It holds at least twice as much power as a NiCad battery for about half the weight. The downside is its higher cost.

- ✔ **NiCad:** The standard and workhorse of portable PC batteries, it is the heaviest, yet least expensive of the battery types used in notebook computers. You must recharge NiCad batteries every 3 or 4 hours, which can take anywhere from a few hours to as much as 12 hours. NiCad batteries have a charge/recharge life of about 1,000 cycles.

If available for a particular model, Li-Ion is probably the best choice of battery for a portable PC, although it can be more expensive than the other choices.

While sitting around the campfire with other PC service technicians, you may hear horror stories about the *memory effect*. Fear not.

The term *memory effect* refers to the fact that noncomputer NiCad batteries can develop plateaus in their recharge capability when they are repeatedly discharged to the same point and then recharged. However, the memory effect is virtually nonexistent in computer NiCad batteries, especially modern ones.

Working on a Portable PC

If you encounter any questions on working on a portable PC on the A+ exam, you can assume three things:

- ✔ The type of portable PC in question is a notebook computer, unless otherwise stated.

- ✔ The notebook computer has a 486 or newer CPU.

- ✔ The only upgrades that are performed internally are to the RAM and hard drive.

Although portable PCs share the components of and function much like nonportable PCs, their construction is just enough different that it can make upgrading the PC very difficult, if not impossible. The size, and especially the height, of a portable PC dictates that some of the conveniences of the desktop unit must be eliminated. For example, the CPU in a desktop computer is mounted in a ZIF socket that enables easy upgrades. In the portable PC, the CPU is mounted and soldered directly to the motherboard by a process called *surface-mounting,* which practically eliminates the possibility for upgrading it.

Getting to the motherboard

Depending on the manufacturer and model of a portable PC, gaining access to the motherboard likely involves removing the display and/or the keyboard. Some systems, such as the IBM ThinkPad, allow access to interchangeable peripheral devices by raising the hinged keyboard, but getting to the motherboard requires that the keyboard and display come off.

If you really insist on opening a portable PC to get to the motherboard, the first tool you must gather is the computer's documentation. Use this document like a prayer book, referring to it religiously. The next tool you absolutely must have before opening the patient is all the ESD protection you can arrange. Approach your work on a notebook much like a surgeon performing open-heart surgery. In the compact and confined spaces in the portable PC, no room exists for stray dust, hair, or potato chip crumbs.

Modern notebook computers are the products of the type of evil minds that design and engineer automobile engines. The few parts that we can work with are clearly isolated and marked, so that we can still feel involved. The system's documentation is likely to list the few items that you can actually touch.

Adding memory

You can update memory in most notebook computers. Portable PCs use either SIMM (single inline memory module) or DIMM (dual inline memory module) memories, which you install in much the same manner used in larger systems. However, portable systems often prescribe both the total memory that it can support and the increments that you can use to add it. The owner's manual is a good source for determining the right choices.

For example, to upgrade my 486DX notebook's memory from 8MB to 20MB, I had to remove the two 4MB modules and replace them with one 16MB SIMM and one of the 4MB SIMMs I removed, which luckily were at the same speed. In this same scenario, had I wanted to increase to only 16MB, I would have needed two 8MB modules. Therefore, before you rush out and order what you think may work, check the manual.

You can also add memory using a PCMCIA card. (More on that later in "Focusing on PCMCIA cards.")

Upgrading the hard drive

Some notebook models keep their secondary storage units under the keyboard for easy interchange or replacement. In these models, replacing the hard disk drive is a snap. You snap out the old and snap in the new. However, on other models, the hard disk drive is internal, so use other, less arduous ways of increasing storage capacity, if possible. Eliminate the following options before you replace an internal hard disk drive:

✔ You can add removable storage very easily through an existing port. For example, you can add a Zip, Jazz, or tape drive via the parallel port.

✔ You can add a hard disk card via a PCMCIA slot.

✔ If the portable PC supports it, you can interchange the floppy disk or CD-ROM with a second removable hard disk drive.

✔ You can use disk space compression utilities, such as the Microsoft DriveSpace, to increase the effective space of the hard disk.

If none of the above options will suffice, then make sure that you find the right type and size of drive for the specific notebook computer being upgraded. Just about all notebooks take a $2^1/_2$-inch hard disk drive that's either 18 millimeters (mm) tall (if it was made before 1996) or 11mm tall (1996 and later).

Focusing on PCMCIA cards

The Personal Computer Memory Card International Association (PCMCIA) offers a standard for adding additional memory and peripherals to portable computers using credit-card-like cards, also called PC Cards. PC Cards are matched to specifically designated slots on the portable PC, each defined to one of the three particular types and sizes of cards. The three standards revolve around the thickness (and number of connectors) of the card, as follows:

✔ **Type I:** $3^1/_2$ mm thick, these slots have one row of sockets, and are used primarily to add *flash memory,* or SRAM (static RAM). This type of memory is common on PCMCIA cards because it requires less power to maintain it. You can learn more about flash memory in Chapter 5.

✔ **Type II:** $5^1/_2$ mm thick, these slots have two rows of sockets, and used to add modems and NICs to a notebook computer. These cards usually have a pop-out connector for an RJ-11 or RJ-45 connector.

✔ **Type III:** Up to $10^1/_2$ mm thick, these slots have three rows of sockets, and are used to install hard disk drives or support adapters for external CD-ROM, DVD, and tape drives.

Two layers of software exist in the portable PC to detect and support a PC Card when you insert it into the computer:

- ✓ **Socket services:** A layer of BIOS-level software that detects when a card is inserted or removed.

- ✓ **Card services:** Software that manages the assignment and allocation of system resources to the PC Card, such as IRQ and I/O addresses, after the socket services software has detected the card.

You can count on at least one portable PC question on the three types of PC Cards/PCMCIA cards. Just remember, the higher the type number, the thicker the card; a hard disk (Type III) is thicker than a modem (Type II), which is thicker than memory (Type I). Also remember which type of card supports which type of device.

Expanding capacity on the fly

You can change PCMCIA or PC Cards without shutting down the system. This procedure is called *hot-swapping*. You can remove any existing card in the slot and install a new card while the PC is on and the operating system is running.

Expect one of the portable PC questions to be about hot-swapping. The question will more than likely be in the form of "Changing a PC card without powering off the system is called. . . ."

For example, to change from a dial-up modem to a LAN NIC (local area network network interface card):

1. **Remove the connector from the modem.**

2. **Pull out the modem card and store it.**

3. **Push the NIC into the card slot connector.**

4. **Click the LAN cable connector into place.**

Presto Change-o, the notebook is on the network.

Comparing active and passive LCD displays

Liquid crystal diode (LCD) displays have lower power requirements than the CRT-style monitor and can be configured into a flat-panel, which are the reasons these displays are used on notebook computers.

Any exam question on notebook computer displays is likely to ask about these two major types of LCD displays:

- ✔ **Active matrix:** If you have an LCD display on your watch, you have an active matrix display. This type of LCD display has a transistor for each pixel and creates a very crisp image that is easy to read from an angle and has very good resolution. Its downside is that all of those transistors take a lot of power. An active matrix display can clean out a battery in less than two hours.

- ✔ **Passive matrix:** This type of LCD display has two groups of transistors: one along the top edge with one transistor for each vertical column of pixels, and the other along the left side of the display with one transistor for each horizontal row of pixels. Wires form a matrix interconnecting the transistor rows and columns. To darken a particular pixel, power is sent to the transistors on the same row and column as the pixel and down the wires to the intersection point where the pixel sits. This method does use much less power, but it also is much slower and produces a lower-quality image.

You may see a question about the cleaning of an LCD display. LCD displays are covered with a thin sheet of plastic, so avoid any abrasive cleaners and cloths. Use a mild detergent or low sudsing general-purpose cleaner and a lint-free soft cloth.

Prep Test

1 A Type I PC Card is used to

   A ○ Add SRAM to the system

   B ○ Add network capabilities to the system

   C ○ Add a device such as a modem to the system

   D ○ Connect an external device such as a CD-ROM drive

2 A PCMCIA hard drive fits into a

   A ○ Type I slot

   B ○ Type II slot

   C ○ Type III slot

   D ○ Type IV slot

3 Hot-swapping means

   A ○ Installing new devices without the need for a driver

   B ○ Removing and adding internal devices without rebooting

   C ○ Removing and inserting PCMCIA cards while the system is up and running

   D ○ All of the above

4 PCMCIA stands for

   A ○ Personal Computer Memory Card International Association

   B ○ Personal Computer Memory Card Internal Architecture

   C ○ Personal Computer Manufacturers Incorporated of America

   D ○ None of the above

5 After inserting a PC Card into a notebook computer, the system does not recognize the card. What could possibly be the problem?

   A ○ No drivers were installed for the card.

   B ○ The card is inserted in the wrong type slot.

   C ○ The notebook computer does not support PCMCIA.

   D ○ PCMCIA socket or card services has not recognized the card.

6 A modem generally fits in a _____ PCMCIA slot.

   A ○ Type I

   B ○ Type II

   C ○ Type III

   D ○ Type IV

7 What is PC Card socket services?

A ○ Allows PC Cards to emulate ISA devices
B ○ An interrupt level to trap PC Card internal errors
C ○ BIOS-level software that detects the insertion and removal of PC Cards
D ○ A utility that is used to eject PC Cards

8 Passive matrix displays are

A ○ Easier to see at an angle
B ○ Known for their superior image quality
C ○ Able to adjust to quickly changing images
D ○ Cheaper and use less power

9 Which of the following do you use to clean the LCD display? (Choose all that apply.)

A ❑ A mildly abrasive household cleanser
B ❑ Very fine steel wool
C ❑ A mild detergent or general-purpose cleaner
D ❑ A lint-free cloth

10 When working on the internal components of a portable PC, wear

A ○ Eye protection
B ○ Rubber gloves
C ○ No particular special equipment required
D ○ ESD grounding strap

Answers

1 *A.* Type II cards are used to add network adapters and modems and Type III cards are used to plug in external drive adapters. *See "Focusing on PCMCIA cards."*

2 *C.* Type III slots support hard drives. *Review "Focusing on PCMCIA cards."*

3 *C.* Hot-swapping is removing and inserting PC Cards (PCMCIA) without the need to shut down the system. *Take a look at "Expanding capacity on the fly."*

4 *A.* It only seems like a lot of questions are coming from one very short part of the chapter because they are. Expect to see a question on PCMCIA cards. *Visit "Focusing on PCMCIA cards" one more time.*

5 *D.* Unless the Socket services detects the card, Card services will not allocate it system resources. *Look at "Focusing on PCMCIA cards."*

6 *B.* Type I cards are for memory, Type II cards are used for modems, Type III cards are used to add disk drives and NICs, and no Type IV card exists. This is the last question on the PC Card types, I promise. *Review "Focusing on PCMCIA cards."*

7 *C.* Socket services detects when a PC Card is inserted or removed. *Check out "Focusing on PCMCIA cards."*

8 *D.* Passive displays produce a lower-quality display that does not adapt to rapid changes quickly, but it produces a good image and does not use much power. *Look at "Comparing active and passive LCD displays."*

9 *C and D.* Gritty cleansers and steel wool would scratch the clear plastic cover over the LCD display. *Check out "Comparing active and passive LCD displays."*

10 *D.* Above all else, be sure to protect the notebook computer with ESD grounding. Anything else you wear is a matter of personal choice. *See "Getting to the motherboard."*

Chapter 19
Interfacing with the Customer

• •

Exam Objectives

▶ Using effective customer service behaviors
▶ Using good practices for eliciting problem symptoms from customers

• •

*T*he A+ Core exam is somewhat contradictory in the area of customer satisfaction. On one hand, about 10 percent of the test covers it, but your score on that section isn't included in the pass/fail analysis of the exam. I guess this contradiction is CompTIA's way of saying that customer service is a very important area of the test, but because every company may have its own way of doing things, they don't want to penalize anyone who may be confused by what's right and what the company policy may be.

On the A+ test, you can expect to find a few questions that deal with how you should react in a certain situation. If interacting with customers is an area you haven't had much training in — a common problem in technical fields — then read this chapter carefully. You don't find any pictures, graphs, or illustrations, just some information on how to interact with customers in a service call situation.

If you've been in the computer repair field for any length of time, you know what people — I mean customers — can be like. It's a very rare day when a customer calls you up out of the blue just to tell you what a fine job you did on his machine. However, you can count on hearing daily from somebody who's quite upset because her computer isn't doing whatever she thinks it should be doing — and by golly, it worked yesterday!

Good and better ways exist to deal with *customers*. I emphasize the word *customers* because they are very likely the reason you have a job, or a business, or any interest in this test.

Quick Assessment

Using effective customer service behaviors

1 Communications is a continuous _____ loop.

2 Before you can communicate, you must _____.

3 _____ is a way to guide the conversation and keep it on track.

4 Four feedback tools you can apply to let customers know you're listening are _____, _____, _____, and _____.

5 To exceed the customer's expectations is to offer _____ service.

6 Show _____ and _____ for the customer.

Using good practices for eliciting problem symptoms from customers

7 To get customers to provide details on their problem, ask _____ questions.

8 Always express _____ in your ability to solve a customer's problem.

9 When dealing with an angry customer, use _____ to determine the underlying problem.

10 Five personal traits you should demonstrate when visiting a customer's site are _____, _____, _____, _____, and _____.

Answers

1 *Feedback.* See "Communicating."

2 *Listen.* Check out the "Listening to be a better communicator" section.

3 *Effective feedback.* Review "Listening to be a better communicator."

4 *Reflecting, empathetic, querying, and supporting.* Look at "Listening to be a better communicator."

5 *Excellent.* See "Giving excellent service."

6 *Empathy and support.* See "Listening to be a better communicator."

7 *Open-ended.* Take a look at "Providing help over the telephone."

8 *Confidence.* Review "Expressing confidence."

9 *Good listening skills.* See "Dealing with Difficult Situations, or The Customer Who Devoured Cleveland."

10 *Punctuality, professionalism, personal grooming, communications, and accountability.* Review "Going On-Site."

Understanding the Importance of Customer Service

CompTIA members include a number of large companies that do business directly with the public. The funny thing about the public is that if you don't treat them right, they'll find somebody who does. (Unless you're an electric, gas, or telephone utility; then they're stuck with you.) Nobody likes to be mistreated, ignored, irritated, insulted, ripped off, scolded, stood up, or made to feel inferior, and they like it even less when they become your customer.

As a customer, a person has power — the power not to do business with you. If enough people don't do business with you, you don't have any business to do. So as business people, the CompTIA members decided to create some suggested standards of PC service technician behavior when in contact with customers. Of course, you and I don't have a problem in this area, but for all the other PC technical professionals, this standard is an excellent idea. In fact, it's not a bad idea for all occupations.

In this chapter, I focus on the part of the A+ exam that measures how well you can identify excellent customer service behaviors and effective ways for eliciting problem information from a customer. In addition, I cover some personal things you can do to instill confidence in your abilities as a PC service technical professional in your customer.

How much you study for this part of the test is really up to you. Exactly six questions deal with this area on the A+ Core exam. These 6 questions are part of the 69 real questions you are asked, but they do not figure into your pass/failure score. They are scored separately for the record. Some employers, present or future, may ask to see your A+ test results, in which case, they will see how well you did in the customer service and support domain.

Keeping current

Keep your technical skills and knowledge as current as possible by any means available to you. Keeping current is not an easy task, considering the present rate at which technology continues to emerge. A+ certification, and other third-party and industry certifications, such as MCSE, MCP, CCNA, Networking+, and others, is certainly one way to improve your knowledge as well as your marketability. Trade journals, magazines, and surfing the Net can provide you with the latest and greatest trends in technology. Specialized training and certification from hardware manufacturers and software publishers can help you move into new technical areas. Even an occasional class at the local community college can help you explore new areas and refresh old ones.

I don't mean that you should try to know everything; you already know that you can't. However, being current helps you be prepared for new situations or customer questions about new technologies. Saying, "I don't know, but I'll get back to you with an answer" is still perfectly all right. By keeping yourself abreast of current events that impact the computer and its use, you make yourself more likely to know where to look for the answer.

For the A+ Core exam, the primary points in providing good customer service are those skills that provide empathy and support for the customer. Review listening and feedback skills in the next few sections and skim through good telephone (see "Providing help over the telephone") and on-site practices (see "Going On-Site") in this chapter.

Communicating

For far too many people, communicating means talking. What they don't realize is that communication is actually a two-way process. You can talk all you want, but unless someone listens to what you say, no communication takes place. Communication is a continuous feedback loop: I talk to you and you listen; then you respond to me and I listen; I respond to you while you listen, and so on. This process constitutes a conversation. In order for it to work, though, you and I must be equal participants in the dialogue. That doesn't mean that you and I have to speak the same amount of time. It only means that I respect you as an equal with important things to contribute to the communication, and vice versa.

Listening to be a better communicator

Listening is the hard part of communication, which is why it's the most important part. From listening comes understanding. You can't understand what you haven't heard.

One of the most common failures of PC repair technicians (and many other service-related workers) is that they don't listen. I don't mean to say that they don't hear; they hear what the customer says just fine. It's just that they either think they know what the customer is going to say, or they hear with their eyes, by jumping to conclusions about what they see.

When you treat customers with respect and truly listen with interest to what they have to say, two things happen:

- ✔ You find out what needs to be fixed or looked at.
- ✔ The customer will feel comfortable working with you again in the future.

The former is for the present and the latter for the future, but both are good for business.

Ways exist to get the information you need from the customer. Earlier in this chapter, I describe communications as a continuous feedback loop. This loop is what you need to create to get the information you need. How? Let the customer tell you what is wrong while you listen. You may need to guide the conversation and keep it on track, which you can do with effective feedback. *Effective feedback* is your part of the conversation. Take a look at the following conversation snippet:

> The customer says, "This is the most frustrating problem I have ever had."
>
> You say, "I can understand how you might feel that way. When did it first happen?"

In this little dialogue, you let the customer vent some frustration, let him know you're supportive, and guide him to answer an important question. Your comments in the conversation should support, reflect, be empathetic, and continue to query for more information. Using effective feedback provides a mechanism for an effective conversation.

Table 19-1 shows some feedback tools that you can use to let the customer know you're listening.

Table 19-1	Effective Feedback Tools	
Feedback Method	*Conversation Example*	*Effective Because*
Reflecting	Customer: "The diskette drive is not working." You: "Your diskette drive is not working?"	You reflect back what you've just heard as a means of verifying it.
Empathizing	Customer: "This makes me so angry!" You: "I can understand how it would do that."	You're empathetic to the customer's feelings.
Querying	Customer: "I think my RAM is broken." You: "When did you first see the problem?"	Informs customers that you are interested in what they have to say about their problem and that you are listening.
Supporting	Customer: "It has never worked right!" You: "Oh, that's too bad. Let me see whether I can get it working for you."	You show support for the customer's judgment and feelings.

As you can see, only slight differences exist between some of these techniques, and often they are used in combination. As you use these feedback techniques, you soon discover one or two that really work for your personality and speaking style. That's fine — whatever gets the job done!

The answers to customer communication questions on the exam are those in which the service technician shows empathy and support for the customer. Saying things like "I understand," "Oh, that's terrible," "Wow! You've had a rough time of it!", and "I can understand how you'd feel that way" communicate these feelings.

Avoiding jumping to conclusions

Sometimes experienced people deal with customers whom they perceive to be inexperienced or ignorant with the assumption that in no way can the customer provide them with any useful information. You probably know someone just like that or have been treated this way yourself at one time.

It's true that most customers don't have vast experience in diagnosing and troubleshooting computer problems. However, they do know a few things you don't: They know the problem from the perspective of the user. They know why they called you, how the computer is acting, the funny sound it makes, whether smoke came out of the case, and how long it has been doing it (most of the time).

The primary task of any service call is twofold: Establish communication and find out what the problem may be. Without the first, you may never accomplish the second.

Providing help over the telephone

More and more customer service and technical support is provided over the telephone. In this situation, some of the communication techniques I cover earlier also work, but it's more important on the telephone to gain control of the conversation early. You can still be empathetic and supportive of the customer while getting the information you need.

Here are some steps to use at the beginning of the call:

1. **Identify yourself and your company or organization.**

   Use a pleasant and inviting tone of voice and speaking manner.

2. **Ask the caller for his or her name and telephone number and write them down.**

   Use the customer's name throughout the call. Use Mr. or Ms. until you're directed by the customer to use anything else. In addition, in case the connection is broken, you have the customer's phone number and can get back in contact with the customer.

3. **If your company requires a serial number, warranty agreement number, or in the case of a service for fee, perhaps a credit card number, get that information as directed by your company.**

   Do this step in a businesslike, nonapologetic manner.

4. **Using an open-ended question (one that can't be answered yes or no), allow the customer to fully describe the question or problem.**

   Acknowledge the customer's sense of urgency. Record the details and use the effective feedback techniques I outline in Table 19-1.

5. **Before answering the question or addressing the problem, verify your understanding of it by repeating the question or problem back to the customer.**

6. **If you're unable to satisfy the customer in this telephone call, either arrange to call the customer back at a later time or, following the procedures of your employer, make other arrangements accordingly.**

Expressing confidence

One way to put the customer at ease is for you to express confidence in your ability to help the customer solve the problem. This technique holds true whether you're on the telephone or on-site. Expressing confidence doesn't mean that you need to have all the answers. It only means that you're confident that you have the means to solve the problem or answer the questions.

Some ways you can express confidence to your customer are by

- ✔ **Asking questions that are easy to answer in a logical sequence.** You may want to develop a checklist of common service questions and use it in all situations.

- ✔ **Adjusting the technical level of your response to the customer's level of understanding.** "Assume low and adjust up" is a good rule to follow.

- ✔ **Taking your time and not rushing the customer.** When answering or explaining a situation, pause occasionally to let what you've said sink in.

✔ **Knowing ahead of time how to handle a situation for which you need more time or the assistance of another person.** Have a prepared statement ready so that you continue to sound confident. Say something like, "Excuse me, I need to consult with another technician," or "I need to do some research and get back to you with an answer."

✔ **Never be defensive about your answers, your products, or your services.** Be empathetic and supportive to a customer who has had a real or perceived bad experience. Being supportive doesn't mean to run down yourself or your employer, though.

Dealing with Difficult Situations, or The Customer Who Devoured Cleveland

Customers with problems react in many different ways emotionally. It only seems like you get all the truly upset ones. You need to be prepared to handle a difficult situation whether it be over the telephone or face to face. In this section, I describe some situations in which you can expect to find yourself eventually.

The angry customer

Usually an angry customer has either been passed along to you (two or three times maybe), has been hung up on, has been told repeatedly that his problem can't be fixed, or the like. First of all, don't take the customer's anger personally. He isn't angry with you as much as frustrated and tired of getting a runaround. Listen to the problem using good listening skills (see "Listening to be a better communicator") and try to determine what the underlying problem might be. After you establish the problem, treat the call like any other service call.

Mr. or Ms. Know-It-All

Some customers like to play games by withholding information to see how good you really are or to trap you with it later. Or they are overly confident about what they think they know. In either case, remember that they called you for service. Try to use their attitudes and knowledge to your advantage. Ask them for advice, compliment their knowledge, and create a we're-all-in-this-together situation. Use your problem-solving and conversation skills to attempt to work with the customer to solve the problem.

The complainer

Many service managers will tell you that they would rather have complainers for customers than noncomplainers. The reason is that industry statistics show that customers who complain tend to stay customers. Those who don't complain simply move on. If the complaint is legitimate, a sincere apology can help soothe the customer's ill feelings.

The novice

The majority of technical service customers know very little about the computer. This lack of computer knowledge doesn't make them stupid or anything of the kind. Keep in mind that the person you're speaking with may be a medical doctor, lawyer, or plumber — fields you're just as ignorant of. Don't use a lot of computer jargon and never ask the customer to do anything that could possibly damage or impair the computer's operation, or put them at risk of harm. In an on-site situation, ask simple yes-or-no questions to determine the problem symptoms.

The gossip

If, after a problem is solved, some customers don't want to end the telephone call or the on-site conversation, determine whether any other problems need to be solved. If not, summarize what you've accomplished and excuse yourself. You may need to stop using effective feedback and use only yes or no answers. Avoid being rude at all costs.

Going On-Site

Many technicians prefer the anonymity of the telephone and dread going to the customer's site. Others feel the opposite way and would rather work at the customer's site. Regardless, eventually all PC repair technicians find themselves on a service call to a customer site.

Believe it or not, how you act and present yourself is far more important for initial impressions than any of your technical expertise. The keys to making a good first impression include the following:

> ✔ **Punctuality:** If you give an arrival time, be there at that time. If you're unavoidably detained, and very few really good reasons exist for your tardiness, call as soon as you know you won't make it on time, and either reschedule the appointment or give a new time of arrival.

- ✔ **Professionalism:** Respect the customer's place of business. Don't visit with employees outside of determining the problem or fixing it. Don't have your calls forwarded to the customer's business telephone, and don't make lengthy calls on his or her telephone. In this age of cellular telephones everywhere, little need exists for this behavior. Perform the job you're there to do in a professional manner and leave when it's completed.

- ✔ **Personal grooming:** In most cases, you are entering a place of business, so respect that fact by dressing in a way that respects the customer's dress codes. Fortunately, this issue is less of a problem than in the past, with more companies adopting casual dress. Valid safety reasons exist for you not to wear a tie, a scarf, or ruffles, but a blazer or other business attire may be appropriate. Good personal hygiene is a courtesy to your fellow workers and your customers.

- ✔ **Communication:** After you determine the problem, explain in simple terms the nature of the problem and the process and parts to be used to fix it. When you complete the job, brief the customer on the work performed and the parts used.

- ✔ **Accountability:** You're responsible for everything you do. Take responsibility for any mistakes or errors you make. Properly complete all paperwork when you finish the job.

Beyond the paperwork you or your employer requires to document each call, you may want to keep other records on each customer to help you in the future. A well-constructed profile of a customer's computer, indicating the software installed, peripherals, memory size, disk size, operating system, BIOS version, and so on can provide much of the information that the user can't and also help speed up the next service call.

Giving bad service

Like the complainer I talk about earlier in this chapter, customers won't tell you about bad service; they tell other customers. You wouldn't intentionally do a bad job, but it can happen. Remember that you aren't the one making the judgment on the quality of your service — the customer is. Something such as the customer's expectations being unrealistically high, or a policy being unclear as to whether a repair should or shouldn't be performed as warranty work may be the cause for a customer to feel that he or she has received bad service.

The professional thing to do is to correct the situation, or let your employer know about the situation by giving a fair account of what happened. If you think a customer may complain about bad service, let your employer know as soon as possible.

Giving good service

Good service is the goal for many companies. A number of good service standards exist, and many companies follow them closely. The A+ certification testing program is certainly the endorsement of a good service standard. To provide good service:

- ✔ Maintain a positive attitude
- ✔ Focus on solutions, not problems
- ✔ Anticipate other problems that could arise
- ✔ Remember the customer's name
- ✔ Establish credibility with the customer
- ✔ Be punctual
- ✔ Keep promises
- ✔ Show the customers how to help themselves
- ✔ Bring the proper parts and tools to a customer site
- ✔ Be courteous and friendly on the telephone or on-site

And the list goes on. In essence, if you use common sense, treat the customer with respect, and act like you appreciate the customer's business, you'll give good service.

Giving excellent service

Excellent service goes beyond the expectations of the customer. It happens when you help the customer solve problems beyond the scope of a repair or refer them to a competitor because you're not qualified or don't have the equipment to handle a problem. It's a selfless type of service that places the needs of the customer above all else.

Companies that provide excellent service gain great respect and esteem in the marketplace. Although not in the computer business, Nordstrom's department stores, Saturn Corporation (the automobile manufacturer), and Wal-Mart discount stores have all earned a reputation for providing excellent service.

Striving to provide service beyond good is a win-win situation that always reflects well on you and your employer. And that's excellent!

The golden rule of technical support is to provide service and treat others how you would like to be treated.

Prep Test

1 When arriving at a customer site, the service technician should

A ○ Allow the customer to explain his or her problem fully and in their own words using effective listening techniques before beginning to diagnose the problem.

B ○ Look for obvious conditions of failure to reduce the amount of time he has to spend at the customer's site.

C ○ Spend a few minutes chatting with the customer about his qualifications and what the customer thinks the problem may be to establish rapport with the customer, and then excuse himself to begin the actual diagnostic procedure.

D ○ Fix the immediate problem and then begin looking for other problems on the PC to fix to increase the billing amount of the service call.

2 Having a written service quality standard and striving to meet the expectations of the customer is giving

A ○ Average service
B ○ Bad service
C ○ Good service
D ○ Excellent service

3 When Ms. Know-It-All calls:

A ○ Play dumb and let her control the conversation.
B ○ Try to use her attitude and knowledge to help solve the problem.
C ○ Use lots of jargon to deflate her ego.
D ○ Argue with her — that's what she really wants.

4 The golden rule of technical service, which you should follow in order to have satisfied customers, is

A ○ Provide service and treat others how you would like to be treated.
B ○ Provide service and treat others better than you would like to be treated.
C ○ Provide service and always flatter the customer so that they'll think highly of you.
D ○ Provide service and never allow them to know that you don't have all the answers.

5 Which of the following is an example of an empathetic statement?

A ○ "You say that your diskette drive is broken?"

B ○ "I can understand why you might feel that way."

C ○ "That can't possibly really happen."

D ○ "When did you first see this problem?"

6 What are the primary tasks of any service call?

A ○ Repair and paperwork

B ○ Providing customer service and creating follow-up business

C ○ Communication and solving the problem

D ○ Customer relations and profits

7 You are a PC service technician visiting a customer's place of business to fix a problem. Which of the following should you do?

A ○ Let the customer only answer your questions and avoid any lengthy explanations of the problem.

B ○ Perform diagnostics immediately, before speaking with the customer.

C ○ Have the customer attempt to solve the problem on his own while you observe.

D ○ None of the above.

8 How do you deal with a telephone call from a customer who's obviously computer illiterate?

A ○ Avoid computer jargon.

B ○ Ask easy-to-answer, yes-or-no questions.

C ○ Build the customer's confidence by complimenting her when appropriate.

D ○ All of the above.

9 When a very angry customer is routed to you from another technician, you should

A ○ Listen to the problem, using good listening skills, and determine the root of the problem.

B ○ Transfer the call to a supervisor.

C ○ Tell the customer he can't be helped until he calms down.

D ○ Hang up on the customer; nobody should be that rude!

10 Keeping your technical knowledge and skills current helps you to

A ○ Find better-paying jobs

B ○ Ensure you're the most knowledgeable technician in the company

C ○ Get promotions

D ○ Be better prepared for new situations or customer questions

Answers

1 A. Always allow the customer to explain the problem fully before jumping to conclusions about a solution. *See "Avoiding jumping to conclusions."*

2 C. Good service is a high standard that companies strive for. *See "Giving good service."*

3 B. Look at *"Mr. or Ms. Know-It-All."*

4 A. Of course it is. *See "Giving excellent service."*

5 B. Empathetic statements express understanding for the customer's expressed feelings. *Empathetically look at "Listening to be a better communicator."*

6 C. First one, and then the other. *Study "Avoiding jumping to conclusions."*

7 D. Follow good service practices and good listening skills. *Review "Expressing confidence."*

8 D. Try to use the customer's attitude to your advantage and build the customer's confidence by complimenting her when appropriate. *See "The novice."*

9 A. Turn an angry customer into a good customer. *See "The angry customer."*

10 D. Your professional development should be tied directly to performing your job to the best of your ability. *Review "Keeping current."*

Chapter 20

Preventive Maintenance

. . . .

Exam Objectives

▶ Performing preventive maintenance procedures

▶ Using preventive maintenance products appropriately

▶ Complying with environmental guidelines for cleaning products

▶ Detecting and removing viruses

. . . .

An old saying suggests that an ounce of prevention is worth a pound of cure. I'm pretty sure whoever said that wasn't speaking of PCs, but it sure applies to them. Keeping a PC clean, monitoring its parts for wear and tear, and protecting it from the environment and other outside threats are all part of a well-developed preventive maintenance program that can add life span to a PC.

It has always seemed somewhat foolish to me for someone to invest a couple of thousand dollars into a computer system, run it until it dies, and then call the repair technician to perform a Lazarus miracle and raise it from the dead. I'm not talking about the usual, everyday kinds of stuff — you know, the 44-ounce soft drink dumped on the keyboard, the flower vase that spilled water inside the monitor, the metal fingernail file that somehow slipped inside the case, the paper clip stuck in the floppy disk drive slot, or the correction fluid painted on the screen. I'm talking about the truly scary abuse.

I've seen power supplies so choked with dust, smoke residue, and chalk dust that they looked like miniature replicas of Carlsbad Caverns. I've also seen the boot sector virus that has devoured the entire hard disk and half of Cleveland. I won't mention any others for fear that children may read this book. Where's the Computer Protection Services agency when you need it?

The A+ people, CompTIA, recognize the value for preventive maintenance and have included it on the Core exam. Ten percent of this exam covers the Safety and Preventive Maintenance domain, which means that you can expect six or seven questions to challenge your knowledge of how to protect the PC while protecting yourself and the environment. Of these questions, probably two or three deal with preventive maintenance issues or computer viruses, the rest deal with safety issues.

Quick Assessment

Performing
preventive
mainte-
nance
procedures

1 The purpose of a _____ is to prolong the effective life of the computer.

2 _____ is used to blow out the dust and debris found in the keyboard as well as many other FRUs.

3 To clean a mouse ball, use a(n) _____.

4 A(n) _____ is used to clean the floppy disk drive.

Using
preventive
maintenance
products
appropriately

5 Do not use _____ on a mouse ball, because it may shrink or misshape its rubber material.

6 _____ is used to check a hard disk for possible surface errors.

Complying
with
environmen-
tal guide-
lines for
cleaning
products

7 A(n) _____ lists the hazards, proper handling, and storage procedures for a chemical solution.

Detecting
and
removing
viruses

8 A _____ contains a virus program but is not suspected because it imitates a legitimate application.

9 The techniques used by a virus to hide itself from detection are, as a group, called _____.

10 The most common type of antivirus software is the _____.

Answers

1   *Preventive maintenance program*. Review "Applying regular maintenance."

2   *Compressed air*. Scoot over to "The keyboard."

3   *Damp cloth*. See "The mouse."

4   *Floppy drive cleaning kit*. Check out "The floppy disk drive."

5   *Alcohol*. Take a look at "The mouse."

6   *ScanDisk*. Zip over to "The hard disk drive."

7   *MSDS*. Review "Using the right cleaning supplies."

8   *Trojan horse*. See "Horses, worms, and germs."

9   *Cloaking*. Check out "Playing hide and seek with viruses."

10   *Virus scanner*. Take a look at "Combating viruses."

Housekeeping, Safeguarding, and Other Chores

When your computer costs more than your car, as mine does, performing regularly scheduled maintenance, inspections, and cleaning to keep it in good running order is a good idea. Just like a car needs regular oil changes, lubrication, and cleaning, a PC can also benefit from a preventive maintenance program that is regularly applied.

If you're experienced with preventive maintenance programs and how the PC and its components are cleaned and checked for wear and tear, you can skip most of this chapter. However, it may not hurt to quickly review the virus section for terminology.

Applying regular maintenance

The purpose of any preventive maintenance (PM) program is to reduce repairs and extend the effective life of the computer. You can accomplish these goals only if you perform the PM actions on a regular basis. All computer owner's manuals should come with a chart that details what maintenance, adjustments, and cleaning should be performed at specific, periodic intervals. Look in any automobile owner's guide, and you find such a guide tied to the mileage on the car. Each computer should have a similar guide. Table 20-1 is my version of what the guide would include.

Table 20-1	PC Maintenance Schedule Guide	
Frequency	*Module*	*Maintenance Actions*
Daily	System	Run a virus scan of the memory and hard disk
	Hard disk	Create a backup
Monthly	Hard disk	Defrag the drive and recover lost clusters
	Keyboard	Clean the keyboard with compressed air and check for and repair stuck keys
	Mouse	Clean ball and rollers and check for wear
	Monitor	Turn off and clean screen with soft cloth or antistatic wipe
	Printer	Clean with compressed air to remove dust and bits of paper

Frequency	Module	Maintenance Actions
On failure	Floppy disk drive	Clean floppy drive head
Yearly	Case	Clean with compressed air to remove dust and other flotsam and jetsam
	Motherboard	Check chips for chip creep and reseat if needed
	Adapter cards	Clean contacts with contact cleaner and reseat
As required	CMOS	Record and back up CMOS setup configuration
	System	Keep written record of hardware and software configuration of PC system

Table 20-1 doesn't contain everything that could be included, but I think I get most of the biggies. I don't include tasks such as clearing temporary files, checking printer cartridges, and other common-sense preventive measures — such as don't drop, kick, or drop-kick the PC; don't blow cigarette smoke into the floppy disk drive; and don't spill water on the keyboard in the table — but you often see them in PM plans. For the A+ exam, it isn't necessary for you to memorize this or any other preventive maintenance plan, but try to remember the kinds of tasks that should be included in one.

The frequencies used in the table are examples, and depending on the usage of the PCs involved, some tasks may need to be performed more frequently or even less often. Some things, such as daily backups or cleaning a floppy disk's heads only when it fails, are fairly fixed in their schedules in any situation. Whatever the situation, a schedule of maintenance helps achieve the goals of preventive maintenance: saving time and money.

Using the right cleaning supplies

The liquid cleaning compounds used to clean or condition the computer's components, case, and glass surfaces present safety and environmental problems to the user, the technician, and other people. Many of the chemical solvents, cleaners, and their containers may require special handling because they are poisonous or harmful in other ways.

The best tool available for finding out whether a chemical solution poses a threat to you, the user, or the world in general is a Material Safety Data Sheet (MSDS). An MSDS is available for every potentially hazardous chemical product. I use two Web sites to look up any product I'm not completely sure of:

- Northwest Fisheries Science Center — http://research.nwfsc.noaa.gov/msds.html
- Vermont Safety Information on the Internet (SIRI) — http://siri.org/msds/index.html

However, the first place to look for safety information on a product is on its label. Usually, if there is a problem using the product for either you or the PC, it should say so.

The types of cleaning supplies that you are typically concerned about include solutions used to clean the contacts and connections of adapter cards; glass cleaners; and plastic- or metal-case cleaning products.

An MSDS (Material Safety Data Sheet) lists the proper handling and storage procedures for chemical cleaning solutions.

MSDS (Material Safety Data Sheet)

The kinds of information included in an MSDS include the following:

- Section 1. Chemical Product Section
- Section 2. Composition/Information on Ingredients
- Section 3. Hazard Identification
- Section 4. First Aid Measures
- Section 5. Firefighting Measures
- Section 6. Accidental Release Measures
- Section 7. Handling and Storage
- Section 8. Exposure Control/Personal Protection
- Section 9. Physical and Chemical Properties
- Section 10. Stability and Reactivity
- Section 11. Toxicological Information
- Section 12. Ecological Information
- Section 13. Disposal Considerations
- Section 14. Transportation Information
- Section 15. Regulatory Information
- Section 16. Other Information

Performing Preventive Maintenance

The process used to clean and maintain the PC and its components are one of the minor focuses of the A+ exam. Review this section to remind yourself of the general steps and cleaning products used on each FRU (field replaceable unit).

Before you do anything else, you should perform one often-overlooked step — make sure that the PC works! When I was young and foolish and still looking for the bit bucket, I once cleaned a PC until it shined all over, only to find that it didn't have a motherboard. But it sure looked good!

The following sections each concentrate on the preventive maintenance steps of a different FRU. Review this information to get a general understanding of the steps, materials, and products used to clean and protect the PC and its parts. Most of the cleaning questions on the A+ exam deal with the kinds of products (for example, a mild cleaner) and materials (for example, a lint-free cloth) used for cleaning on each device.

The keyboard

Other than the monitor screen, you probably clean the keyboard more often than the rest of the PC. This is because it sits open-faced in the open most of the time, collecting debris, flotsam, jetsam, and all other gunk that floats by or falls in. To clean the keyboard, use the steps shown in Lab 20-1.

Lab 20-1   Preventive Maintenance on the Keyboard

Here are the preventive maintenance steps for the keyboard:

1. **If you really want to get the keyboard clean or want to also do a close visual inspection of it, remove the keyboard cover.**

   Otherwise, you can open a cleaning hole by removing the key caps of the -, +, and Enter keys in the numeric pad at the far-right end of the keyboard.

2. **Using compressed air, blow out the keyboard, sweeping with the air toward the removed key caps.**

   If you removed the cover, you can turn it over, shake it out, and then use the compressed air to clean the internal and cover pieces.

3. **Use nonstatic brushes or probes to loosen any large or stubborn pieces.**

   If the keyboard has had soda pop or the like spilled into it, you may need to wash it. If so, use warm, nonsoapy water to rinse the guck away. You can even run it through a dishwasher with no soap. Just be extra sure that it's completely dry before powering it up.

4. **Replace the key caps or reassemble the keyboard cover.**

5. **To clean the keys and keyboard case, use a soft, lint-free cloth and isopropyl alcohol or a nonsudsing general-purpose cleaner to wipe away any guck, ink, or other indescribable yuckies.**

   The alcohol is good because its evaporation removes any worry about the keyboard being wet. As before, be very sure that the keyboard is dry before sending power to it.

6. **Reboot the system, observing the POST for keyboard errors, and test the keyboard by pressing every key and verifying its action.**

The mouse

Just as it is the mud puddle's fault that the kid is dirty, it is the mousepad's fault that the mouse gets dirty and needs cleaning. Like the keyboard, the mousepad is sitting in the open most of the time getting dusty, wet, slimed, and all else that happens on your desktop. The mouse then rolls over whatever has collected on the mousepad and it gets inside, gumming up the works. To clean the mouse, follow the steps listed in Lab 20-2. To clean the mouse pad, wipe it off occasionally with a damp cloth or get a new one.

Lab 20-2	Preventive Maintenance for the Mouse

Here are the preventive maintenance steps for the mouse:

1. **After making sure that no open applications are on the screen, roll the mouse gently onto its back and, without tickling, remove the ball access slide cover.**

2. **After making sure that your hands are clean, remove and closely examine the ball for pits, cracks, or canyons. Also check to see whether the ball is lopsided or oval-shaped.**

   If the mouse ball has any of these problems, replace it or the entire mouse unit (recommended). Inspect the hole where the ball goes for guck, lint, hair, string, ant colonies, or beaver dams. I'm only kidding about the last two, but you can find some weird stuff inside a mouse.

3. **Inspect the rollers inside the hole where the ball goes for debris or sticky or greasy buildup.**

   To clean the rollers, use a small, flat-blade screwdriver or tweaker (you know, the little pocket screwdriver), the PC technician's friend, to scrape off the guck.

4. **Blow any dust from inside the mouse using compressed air.**

   Don't blow it out with your mouth for two reasons: spit inside the mouse and dust in your eyes.

5. **Use a damp, lint-free cloth to clean the mouse ball. Don't soak it or scrub it, just wipe it clean and let it dry before reinserting it in the hole where the mouse ball goes.**

   Don't use alcohol to clean the mouse ball. Alcohol may shrink the ball or cause it to be lopsided, just like it does to humans.

6. **After placing the mouse ball back into the hole where the mouse ball goes, replace the slide cover and lock it in place.**

   If needed, you can use isopropyl alcohol or a general-purpose cleaner to clean the exterior of the mouse or the mouse pad. Check the mouse pad to see whether it's worn, frayed, torn, or hollow in its center. A beat-up mouse pad can cause lint, bits of rubber, or other guck to go inside the mouse. Mouse pads are cheap, and you can usually garner freebies from stores, manufacturers, or at trade shows (one good reason to go). Your employer may even have some promotional mouse pads for you to give your customers.

7. **Test the mouse, using something other than Solitaire or another game — it just doesn't look right to the customer.**

   Clean the mouse ball with a damp cloth; don't use alcohol on it. Alcohol can dissolve the mouse ball material and cause flat spots and distortion.

The monitor

The glass on the monitor is the part of the PC that should be cleaned the most often, and usually by the customer. Unfortunately, the customer often takes safety chances when he or she does. Lab 20-3 shows the proper cleaning procedure for the monitor.

Lab 20-3   Preventive Maintenance for the Monitor

After making sure that the monitor is working, the preventive maintenance steps for it are as follows:

1. **Turn the monitor off and unplug it.**

   Wait a few minutes before beginning, and do not wear an ESD ground strap.

2. **Using compressed air, clean any dust from the top of the monitor, being careful not to blow it into the open vents.**

   Never open the cover of the monitor! Mean and nasty high voltage lurks inside.

   You can use either isopropyl alcohol or a general-purpose cleaner to clean the outside of the monitor case. The alcohol is probably the better choice, if you can stand the fumes, because it doesn't create a safety hazard if dripped inside the case.

3. **Use an antistatic cleaner to clean the glass of the monitor.**

   Never wash the monitor glass with the power on.

4. **Reconnect the monitor and test the video.**

   If nothing displays, check that the power switch is on, and check the power cord and video connections and the brightness and contrast settings. These connections and settings may have been inadvertently loosened or changed during the cleaning.

The case

Not a lot needs to be done to the case itself to keep it functioning properly. After all, the case doesn't do a heck of a lot — it mostly just gets dusty. However, some preventive maintenance activities exist that you can perform at the system (or case) level to keep the general system functioning well. Lab 20-4 lists these activities.

Lab 20-4   System-level Preventive Maintenance

1. **After powering off the PC and leaving the power cord plugged in, carefully remove the case cover.**

   Before doing anything else, do a visual inspection inside the case to assess any problems that may be written in the dust. Normally, the inside and outside vents may have dust accumulated on them, but if dust is gathering in a place that it shouldn't, the case may have a crack in it, a part may be missing, or some other problem may have developed. Look the case over thoroughly for dust, corrosion, leaking battery acid, dead bugs, moose droppings, and birds' nests. If only lightly dusty, use compressed air to blow it out, using caution not to blow it into your eyes. If you must remove boulders and other chunks, pick them out with tweezers, or if big enough, your fingers.

2. **Check cables and wires for loose connections.**

   Using compressed air, blow out the outside vents of the power supply first, and then its inside vents, the drive bays, adapter cards, and finally the outside vents of the case.

3. **Replace the case cover, taking care not to snag any cables.**

4. **With your bucket of isopropyl alcohol or the general-purpose cleaner, swab down the case, being careful not to slop the mop inside the case.**

5. **Power on the PC and monitor the POST process for errors.**

The floppy disk drive

To perform preventive maintenance on a floppy disk drive or to clean it when it begins to fail, use the steps listed in Lab 20-5.

Lab 20-5   Preventive Maintenance for the Floppy Disk Drive

1. **Verify that the floppy disk drive is working.**

2. **Using a floppy disk drive cleaning kit, clean the read/write heads, following the directions on the kit.**

3. **Test the drive.**

The hard disk drive

The preventive maintenance tasks for the hard disk deal more with optimizing its storage than with physical cleaning tasks. You have no cleaning tasks to perform because the hard disk is a sealed unit. The PM tasks for a hard disk involve the following:

- Backing up the data on the hard disk.

- Running ScanDisk, Norton, or another disk diagnostic software tool to check the surface of the hard disk for errors.

- Running Defrag, Norton Speed, or an equivalent disk optimization program.

Virus Detection and Protection

Viruses are nasty pieces of software that have taken on the characteristics of an infectious disease, spreading germs to infect unsuspecting and unprotected PCs. You can expect a couple of questions on the exam that deal with what a virus is, how it spreads, and how it is detected.

The following characteristics define a computer virus:

- A virus attaches itself to another piece of programming code in memory, on a floppy disk, or on a downloaded file.
- A virus infects a system when the original program executes and also unintentionally runs the virus program code.
- A virus replicates itself and infects other programs, possibly modifying its form and manifesting other behaviors as well.

Horses, worms, and germs

Not all viruses do catastrophic damage to a system. Many viruses are just nuisances or pranks, playing music, simulating system meltdowns, or displaying misinformation during the system boot. Viruses that are malicious can and do cause considerable damage in the form of lost data and altered program code.

Many different types of programs are classified as viruses, including many that aren't actually viruses:

- **Dropper:** The bag man of the virus world. This program installs a virus or Trojan horse on a target system, avoiding detection by most antivirus programs. Droppers are a sophisticated approach to virus infection and are very uncommon.

- **Trojan horse:** Based on Greek mythology. Like the gift horse that hid the attacking army, the viral Trojan horse hides a virus program by imitating or camouflaging itself as a legitimate application. When executed, it springs the virus, often creating other Trojan horses to avoid detection.

- **Worm:** A self-contained program that spreads itself to other systems, usually over a network connection. Worms create many different nasty effects when they run.

- **Virus impostor or gag programs:** Demented jokes created by programmers with not enough to do, obviously. These programs simulate the effects of a virus, scaring users into believing that they have been infected. It's not unusual for users to hear the truth from the jokester, about halfway through the reformatting of their hard disk.

Also keep in mind that some of the nastiest viruses are not viruses at all. Virus hoaxes spread through the rumor mill (especially on the Internet) and tell of untold horrors that will happen at 13 minutes after midnight on the day the creator of a certain candy bar was born, or something like that. Before it gets started, I just made that one up.

Viruses and how they spread

Computer viruses are a form of electronic warfare developed solely to cause human misery. The evil, sick, and quite talented minds that develop computer viruses would like nothing better than to have your boot sectors catch cold or have your disk drives develop dysentery. Five major virus classes exist, each with many subclasses:

- ✔ **Boot sector viruses (system viruses):** These viruses target the boot program on every bootable floppy disk or hard disk. By attaching itself to the boot sector program, the virus is guaranteed to run whenever the computer starts up. Boot sector viruses spread mostly by jumping from disk to disk.

- ✔ **File viruses:** File viruses modify program files, such as .EXE or .COM files. Whenever the infected program executes, the virus also executes and does its nastiness. File viruses spread by infected floppy disks, networks, and the Internet.

- ✔ **Macro viruses:** The newest general class of virus, macro viruses take advantage of the built-in macro programming languages of application programs such as Microsoft Word and Microsoft Excel. Macro languages allow users to create macros, script-like programs that automate formatting, data-entry, or frequently repeated tasks. A macro virus, most commonly found in Microsoft Word documents, can cause as much damage as other viruses and can spread by jumping from an opened document to other documents.

- ✔ **BIOS program viruses:** This type of virus attacks flash BIOS programs by overwriting the system BIOS program and leaving the PC unbootable.

- ✔ **Multipartite viruses:** Especially nasty affairs, multipartite viruses infect both boot sectors and program files.

Because a virus is a program, it can only infect programs. A virus can't hide anywhere that it doesn't blend into the scenery. Viruses that infect graphic files, e-mail, or text files are just myths. It would be like trying to hide a bright red ball among bright white balls. However, viruses can be attached to text files or e-mail and transmitted or copied to a new host system.

Playing hide and seek with viruses

As virus detection software has become more sophisticated, so have the viruses. Most antivirus software works by recognizing a predefined pattern of characters unique to individual viruses, a sort of fingerprint, called its *signature*. As viruses get more devious, they include new ways to elude the virus detectors. These tricks, as a group, are called *cloaking*. Some of the cloaking techniques used are the following:

- ✔ **Polymorphing:** Allows viruses to change their appearance, signature, and size each time they infect a system.

- ✔ **Stealth virus:** Hides its damage in such a way that everything appears normal.

- ✔ **Directory virus:** Hides itself by lying. It changes a directory entry to point to itself instead of the files it is replacing. No actual change is made to the affected files, and they appear normal on directory lists and in Windows Explorer lists, which helps the virus avoid detection.

Combating viruses

Viruses manifest themselves on a PC in a wide variety of ways, including spontaneous system reboots; system crashes; application crashes; sound card or speaker problems; distorted, misshapen, or missing video on the monitor; corrupted or missing data from disk files; disappearing disk partitions; or boot disks that won't boot.

In spite of the efforts of the virus developers, the best defense against virus infection is antivirus software, also called *scanners* or *inoculators*. Don't you just love all this medical talk?

Here are the general types of antivirus software in use today:

- ✔ **Virus scanner software:** This run-on-demand software scans the contents of memory and the disk drive, directories, and files that the user wants to check. This type of software is the most common form of antivirus program.

- ✔ **Memory-resident scanner software:** This kind of scanner stays in memory, automatically checking the environment for viruses.

- ✔ **Behavior-based detectors:** A more sophisticated form of memory-resident scanner, a behavior-based detector looks for suspicious behavior typical to virus programs. Some stereotyping is involved, and some good processes may be interrupted, but being safe is better than being sorry.

  ✓ **Startup scan antivirus software:** This software runs when the PC boots and does a quick scan of boot sectors and essential files to detect boot sector viruses before the PC boots up.

  ✓ **Inoculators:** This antivirus software looks for changes to files and boot sectors and for other evidence left behind by viruses. The inoculator takes a snapshot of clean boot sectors and then periodically compares the snapshots of the clean files to the actual files to check for changes.

Except for inoculators, which look only for the damage caused and not the virus itself, most antivirus software uses a database of virus profiles and signatures for reference. This database should be updated frequently; most antivirus packages include a number of free updates.

Keep in mind that not all detected viruses are viruses. On occasion, what may look like a virus to the virus scanner may be an innocent look-alike program or data file. This detection of the look-alike is called a *false positive*. Before you don your surgical robes and glove up, investigate the virus to find out more about it — how it works and what damage it does. This investigating may save you from removing an important file from a customer's PC because you suspected it to be a virus. Don't get me wrong; most scanner alarms are for viruses, but proceed with caution, especially on a customer's machine.

Prep Test

1 The techniques used by a virus to resist detection are called

A ○ Dodging

B ○ Polymorphing

C ○ Cloaking

D ○ Infecting

2 Information on the hazard of a chemical solution and its safe handling and storage is contained on a(n)

A ○ MSSC

B ○ MSDS

C ○ MSCE

D ○ DSHS

3 To open a hole on the keyboard for dirt and debris to blow out, remove the

A ○ Tab, Caps Lock, Shift, and Control keys from the left end of the keyboard

B ○ Spacebar

C ○ Arrow keys

D ○ Minus, Plus, and Enter keys from the right end of the keyboard

4 The monitor glass should be cleaned

A ○ When the monitor is on

B ○ When the monitor is off

C ○ Anytime using a wet cloth

D ○ Never

5 The major steps for preventive maintenance on a hard disk are

A ○ Defrag, ScanDisk, backup

B ○ Fdisk, Format, ScanDisk

C ○ Backup, ScanDisk, Defrag

D ○ Disassembly, blow dust out, reassembly

6 Which of the following is not actually a virus, although often classified as one?

A ○ Dropper

B ○ Boot sector

C ○ Macro

D ○ Multipartite

7 The process that allows a virus to change its appearance and size each time it infects a system is called

A ○ Macro
B ○ Polymorphing
C ○ Multipartite
D ○ Inoculation

8 A virus threat that exists only in rumor or myth is a

A ○ Hoax
B ○ Stealth
C ○ Multipartite
D ○ Doomsday virus

9 The unique data image that's used by antivirus programs to detect and remove a virus is its

A ○ Profile
B ○ Fingerprint
C ○ Mug shot
D ○ Signature

10 Which of the following is not a type of antivirus software?

A ○ Virus scanner
B ○ Inoculator
C ○ Memory cache scanner
D ○ Behavior-based

Answers

1 *C.* Viruses use a variety of cloaking techniques. *See "Playing hide and seek with viruses."*

2 *B.* Material Safety Data Sheets contain information on all aspects of using, handling, and storing chemical products. *Take a look at "Using the right cleaning supplies."*

3 *D.* These three keys open up a slot on the end of the keyboard through which the chunks can fall out. *Check out "The keyboard."*

4 *B.* The monitor glass carries quite a charge of static electricity, and cleaning it when it is on, especially with a wet solution or cloth, can light up your life. *Look at "The monitor."*

5 *C.* Before you do anything to a hard disk, back it up. Then you can scan it for surface defects and optimize it by defragging it. *Review "The hard disk."*

6 *A.* Besides a dropper, viruses include the Trojan horse, worm, and imposters. *See "Horses, worms, and germs."*

7 *B.* A rather nasty prospect that makes detection of some viruses especially difficult. *Check out "Playing hide and seek with a virus."*

8 *A.* As the story is passed around, the horrors of what the virus can do grows and grows. *Take a look at "Horses, worms, and germs."*

9 *D.* Each virus program has a digital signature that uniquely identifies it. *See "Playing hide and seek with viruses."*

10 *C.* Antivirus software comes in many different types, each suited to the detection and removal of a certain class of viruses. *Review "Combating viruses."*

Part V
The DOS/Windows World

The 5th Wave   By Rich Tennant

What helps the Windows 95 operating system communicate with hardware?

That's easy— a massive, worldwide advertising campaign.

In this part . . .

This part of the book addresses information specifically needed only for the DOS/Windows exam. The A+ exam expects you to be conversant with DOS, Windows 3.*x*, Windows 95, and just a wee bit of Windows NT. You must know how they are installed, configured, and manipulated to perform well on the test. The two chapters in this part focus on different aspects of the information you need to know: installing, configuring and upgrading, and diagnosing and repairing problems with the operating system features.

Chapter 21

Installing, Configuring, and Upgrading

Exam Objectives

▶ Installing and booting DOS, Windows 3.*x*, and Windows 95

▶ Describing OS functions, memory management, structure, and system files

▶ Upgrading the operating system

▶ Accessing network resources

*Y*ou should review some specific things about DOS and the Windows gang before taking the A+ DOS/Microsoft Windows Service Technician Exam. The first four parts of this book focus on the A+ Core Service Technician Exam, and if you are truly ready for it, then you are already halfway home for the A+ DOS/Windows exam as well. Separating PC hardware from PC software is becoming increasingly difficult from a PC repair technician's point of view.

Most of the DOS/Windows exam — nearly 70 percent — measures your knowledge of the material covered in this chapter. Of this percentage, 75 percent of the questions relate to Windows 95, with the rest split fairly evenly between DOS and Windows 3.*x*. These questions test your knowledge of where to find features of the Windows operating system and how and when the features are used.

In many ways, the DOS/Windows exam is much harder than the Core exam. However, if you have installed and used Windows 95 frequently, you probably already know what you need to pass the exam — you just need a refresher course. That's what I give you in this chapter.

Quick Assessment

Describing OS functions, memory management, structure, and system files

1 _____ contains the internal DOS commands.

2 Windows manages its memory in _____.

3 The three core Windows 95 components are _____, _____, and _____.

4 To create a dual-boot situation on a PC, the BootMulti option is set in the _____ file.

5 The _____ records the overall hardware and software configuration and associations of the Windows 95 system.

6 Windows implements _____ by writing memory blocks to a swap file.

7 Before installing Windows 3.*x*, _____ should be used to defragment the hard drive.

8 If the Windows 3.*x* installation hangs up, restart the PC with the _____ command and option.

9 _____ is a file created by Windows 95 that holds a record of the hardware detected during installation.

Upgrading the operating system

10 Microsoft's standard upgrade of Windows 3.*x* to Windows 95 places the Win95 files in the _____ folder.

Accessing network resources

11 Dial-up networking establishes a _____ connection networking over a modem.

Answers

1 *COMMAND.COM*. Review "DOS Basics."

2 *Heaps*. Take a look at "Piling up memory in heaps."

3 *Kernel, user, and GDI*. Review "Windows 95 Basics."

4 *MSDOS.SYS*. Check out "Customizing Windows 95 from inside."

5 *Registry*. Glance over "The Windows 95 registry."

6 *Virtual memory*. Review "Managing virtual memory."

7 *DEFRAG.EXE*. Check over "Installing Windows 3.*x*."

8 *SETUP.EXE /I*. See "Troubleshooting installation problems."

9 *DETLOG.TXT*. Review "Installing Windows 95."

10 *Same*. Check out "Upgrading Windows 3.*x* to Windows 95."

11 *PPP*. Review "Dial-up networking."

DOS Basics

One thing I can say with great confidence is that no questions on the A+ DOS/Windows exam cover installing a DOS operating system. Oh, there are many questions on configuring and using DOS and its commands, but none on installing it. However, you will need to to know about Windows 3.*x* and Windows 95 installations as well as their configuration and use. The A+ exam doesn't cover Windows 98, either.

Before I get too deep into the Windows world, I need to review some DOS facts for the DOS/Windows exam (which means that this information is on the test):

- CONFIG.SYS is not required for DOS to start up.
- COMMAND.COM displays the DOS command prompt.
- EMM386.EXE enables expanded memory and the use of upper memory as system memory.
- ATTRIB changes the file attributes of a DOS file; read, system, hidden, and archive are the DOS file attributes.
- DELTREE deletes a directory and its subdirectories, including all the files contained in the directory and subdirectories.
- Device drivers are loaded as terminate-and-stay resident programs (TSRs) from the CONFIG.SYS file.
- COMMAND.COM contains the internal DOS commands and is required for DOS (as well as Windows 3.*x* and Windows 95) to boot.
- The boot sequence for DOS is IO.SYS, MSDOS.SYS, CONFIG.SYS, COMMAND.COM, and AUTOEXEC.BAT.
- The DOS root directory can hold 512 files.
- DOS memory is divided into *conventional* memory (640K), *expanded* or *upper* memory (384K), and *extended* memory (above 1024K) areas.
- The size of the high memory area is 64K. It is the first 64K of extended memory.
- HIMEM.SYS is the device driver for memory above 640K, which includes expanded (upper memory area) and extended memory areas.
- To load DOS to high memory, use the commands DOS=HIGH and DEVICE=HIMEM.SYS in the CONFIG.SYS file.

Windows 3.x Basics

The name "Windows 3.x" is the all-inclusive name used on the A+ exams for any version of Windows before Windows 95. A+ also seems to support the idea that the Windows software began with Windows 3.0, so you don't need to worry about older versions of the software, such as Windows 2.0 or Windows 286. Windows for Workgroups is mentioned on the test as the work-alike for Windows 95.

The Windows 3.x environment

These Windows 3.x facts may show up on the test:

- Icons are arranged in group files (.GRP) with one group file representing one window.
- The WIN.INI file controls how the desktop looks and how files are associated.
- The file manager in Windows 3.x is called File Manager. Fancy that!
- Device drivers are identified in the SYSTEM.INI file.
- The desktop windows are defined in PROGMAN.INI.
- WIN.INI, SYSTEM.INI, and PROGMAN.INI are text files that you can edit with a text editor.
- Running Windows 3.x on a 286 computer in standard mode requires the file DOSX.EXE.
- Windows 3.x doesn't run unless HIMEM.SYS is loaded.
- As with DOS filenames, Windows 3.x filenames are limited to eight characters plus a three-character extension.

Don't study all the truly user-oriented accessories, games, tools, and applications included in any Windows release. This rule includes anything included in a group window in Windows 3.x or listed on the Start Program menu in Windows 95. Concentrate on the operating system functions (device management, memory management, and so on) of the Windows OS.

Installing Windows 3.x

Installing Windows 3.x isn't done much anymore, but you begin the process by preparing the hard disk and end with a clean boot. If Windows is being installed over DOS, follow these steps included in Lab 21-1.

Lab 21-1   Installing Windows 3.*x* over a DOS Installation

1. **From a DOS prompt, run a DOS CHKDSK /F to recover any lost clusters and then delete the FILEnnnn.CHK files that are created.**

2. **Run a DEFRAG.EXE to defragment the hard disk.**

   One benefit of defragging the hard disk is that you may be able to increase the Windows swap space, which I describe later in this chapter.

3. **If the computer is running DOS 6.0 or a later version, use MemMaker to analyze and optimize UMB (upper memory blocks) utilization.**

   MemMaker edits the CONFIG.SYS and AUTOEXEC.BAT files to load device drivers and other TSRs to UMB, which frees conventional memory.

4. **Verify that CONFIG.SYS and AUTOEXEC.BAT are correct before proceeding.**

   Windows makes modifications to these files as well, so remove any unnecessary or conflicting commands.

5. **Run the SETUP.EXE command from the first Windows 3.*x* disk.**

   The setup routine offers two installation choices:

   - Express setup makes many of the system configuration choices for you. Unless you change the target drive or directory, the system is installed into C:\WINDOWS.

   - Custom setup allows you to customize which features and tools are installed. You can also change the target directory or drive. This version of the setup also gives you control over printer driver installation.

In either Windows 3.*x* Express or Custom setup procedures, you're asked whether you want to change the target drive or directory. If you want to do so, change the drive by typing the new drive letter. To change the directory, use the browse button.

Troubleshooting installation problems

Several common problems may occur during a Windows 3.*x* installation. If you encounter a problem, refer to the following list of problems and remedies:

- ✔ **Setup continually asks for the same disk.** Check to be sure that the metal slide on the disk is not stuck, and verify that the correct disk is in use. Otherwise, the disk may be faulty. Try the disk a few more times, and if it still doesn't work, get a new disk.

✔ **The printer attached to the PC is not listed as a supported model.** Check the printer's documentation to see whether work-alikes can be substituted to complete the installation. Then contact the printer manufacturer for a Windows driver.

✔ **Setup gives you the message "Not enough disk space."** If you run out of disk space during the installation, abort it and use the Custom setup to pare down the options being installed and disk space required. If you have already done that and are still getting this message, you need to get a bigger hard drive (or possibly use a disk compression utility). Microsoft recommends that around 14.5MB of hard disk space be available to install Windows 3.*x*.

✔ **Setup hangs up.** When this happens, the problem is probably in the hardware detection phase of the installation. The best way around this problem is to reboot the computer and restart the installation with SETUP /I. The /I option bypasses the hardware detection phases and allows the installation to complete. (This question is probably on the test.)

Managing virtual memory

Although Windows 3.*x* is an operating environment that runs on top of DOS, it does have some memory management tricks of its own. The primary trick is virtual memory.

Main memory can be temporarily freed up by transferring the contents of some memory segments onto the hard disk into a *swap file*. Windows 3.*x* implements swap files in three ways:

✔ **By creating temporary files:** Windows applications can extend their temporary storage requirements outside of memory by creating temporary files.

✔ **By creating application swap files:** Windows can table the activities of an application and write its program code and data to special swap files in the temporary file area. When the application resumes, these files are restored to memory.

✔ **By creating virtual memory:** In 386 enhanced mode, Windows 3.*x* can create additional virtual memory by writing memory blocks to either a temporary virtual swap file (WIN386.SWP) or a permanent archive (swap) space (386SPART.PAR).

Piling up memory in heaps

Windows manages its memory in allocated memory segments called *heaps*. Windows creates five basic heaps that are allocated to applications and utilities as needed. The amount of memory assigned to a heap is limited by DOS memory management, which is why on a PC with 128MB of RAM, you can still get "out of memory" error messages from Windows. The error message is most likely referring to a situation in which one of the heaps, probably the system or GDI heap, has run dry. This happens when applications fail to release their memory allocations back to the heap when they terminate — and a situation called a *memory leak*.

The five heaps in Windows are as follows:

- ✔ **The system heap** includes the memory assigned to applications and system utilities. Virtual memory is included in this heap.

- ✔ **The GDI heap** is the memory used to display the GUI *(Graphical User Interface)* and its elements, including icons, fonts, and the mouse pointer. GDI stands for *graphic display interface.*

- ✔ **The user heap** holds the information on elements with which the user is interacting. These elements include open and minimized windows, dialog boxes, printer events, and the desktop layout.

- ✔ **The menu heap** holds all desktop and application menus and any associated data.

- ✔ **The text heap** holds all text elements of the Windows desktop and user interfaces, including Windows help functions.

Windows 95 Basics

A good way to study Windows 95 basics is to practice navigating around the various Properties functions in Windows 95, including right-clicking on the desktop, on the My Computer icon, from the Settings menu, and from the Control Panel. Look at the Device Manager, Printers, and Networks functions. The exam has questions about how to access these options.

Windows 95, as an operating system, is very much like Windows for Workgroups (Windows 3.11). However, know some of the important differences between Windows 3.*x* and Windows 95:

- ✔ Windows 95 supports the 16-bit code of the DOS/Windows 3.*x* environment as well as 32-bit programming.

✔ Windows 95 supports Plug-and-Play devices. Windows 95 refers to all non-Plug-and-Play cards as *legacy* cards.

✔ Windows 95 has three core components that share the processing load:

   • **Kernel** (KERNEL.DLL) contains the essential operating system functions, including memory, file, and I/O management, and application support.

   • **User** (USER32.DLL/USER.EXE) controls all elements of user interface including the mouse, keyboard, I/O ports, and the desktop layout.

   • **GDI** (GDI32.DLL/GDI.EXE) creates the graphical user interface and controls printing. This component is on the test.

✔ Windows 95 implements the concept of the virtual machine, which allows it to run applications from other operating systems (mainly DOS) in a nearly native environment.

Installing Windows 95

Windows 3.*x* releases were usually installed from diskettes, but Windows 95 is released on CD-ROM. The Windows 95 CD-ROM usually starts by itself when you close the CD-ROM tray, but if it doesn't, you can start the installation with the SETUP.EXE command. If you allow the CD-ROM to autoplay (that is start by itself), *Install Win 95* is one of the choices on its menu. Otherwise, you can access the CD-ROM's contents (and the SETUP.EXE file) with either the Windows Explorer or the My Computer icon.

Windows 95 begins the installation in real mode but soon switches to its normal run state in protected mode. The installation process is rather uneventful outwardly, compared to the activity of the Windows 3.*x* installation, but Setup is busy recording information into a series of log files. One of these files, DETLOG.TXT, records the hardware detected during installation. Another log file, DETCRASH.LOG, records the devices that failed to respond during the detection phase, and yet another file is a record of the activities of the setup process — SETUPLOG.TXT.

If Setup hangs up or if the system crashes during the installation, turn off the power to the system and then turn it back on. Restart the installation as before. During the boot procedure, Setup looks at the DETCRASH.LOG and the SETUPLOG.TXT files to determine what was already installed and what was attempting to install when the system failed. Setup skips the step that it determines caused the crash and continues with the installation. The log files help keep the system from making the same mistake twice. You need to complete the installation later, after you diagnose the problem hardware, correct it, and use the Control Panel to install it.

Windows 95 has had a midversion update called "OSR2" (Operations Service Release 2), which many are now unofficially calling "Windows 95b." This update of Windows 95 fixed many operational problems and added FAT32, an improved file management technique. OSR2 is not a new release of Windows 95 but instead an upgrade and bug fix. For the A+ exam, remember OSR2 and FAT32 together. FAT32 is discussed later in this chapter.

Customizing Windows 95 from inside

Just as you can add shortcuts to the Desktop and install applications to the Windows 95 Start⇨Programs menu to customize the Windows 95 interface, you can also change how Windows 95 allows another operating system to boot, eliminate the splash screen, the Windows logo pages, and other of its displays, and a few other system-level attributes and characteristics, if you want. You make these changes by editing the MSDOS.SYS file.

You don't need to worry about most of the MSDOS.SYS options listed here beyond reviewing the types of options that you can set, but be sure that you remember the BootMulti option and what it does.

If a computer has more than one operating system loaded and you want to select which system should boot, you add the following command to the [OPTIONS] area of the MSDOS.SYS file:

```
BootMulti=1
```

Set BootMulti to 0 (zero) to indicate that only Windows 95 should boot. You may set these other options in MSDOS.SYS as well:

- ✔ Setting **BootKeys** to 0 disables the function keys during the boot cycle.
- ✔ Setting **Logo** to 0 leaves the screen in text mode and doesn't display the Windows logo.
- ✔ Setting **DoubleBuffer** to 1 enables double buffering for a SCSI drive.
- ✔ Setting **BootFailSafe** to 1 includes Safe mode in the Startup menu that displays automatically after a crash or abnormal shutdown or when F8 is pressed immediately after Windows 95 starts.
- ✔ Setting **LoadTop** to 1 loads COMMAND.COM in the top of conventional memory.

If you edit the MSDOS.SYS file, make sure that the file remains greater than 1,024 characters in length when you are finished.

The Windows 95 registry

Windows 3.*x* is a virtual forest of .INI files that contain the configuration and execution instructions for Windows and its installed applications, but Windows 95 has consolidated much of this information into a feature called the *registry*. Windows 3.*x* had a perfunctory registry that was contained in a file called REG.DAT, which contained some limited information on the system, but it was nothing like the registry used by Windows 95. The Windows 95 registry is a special database that contains a complete profile of the system configuration and program settings, eliminating the need for many .INI files.

The registry records the overall hardware and software configuration and associations of the Windows 95 system. You can expect to see at least three or four test questions about the Windows 95 registry. Know these facts about the registry:

- The two registry files are USER.DAT and SYSTEM.DAT.
- The file extension for backups of these files is .DA0.
- The registry is organized in a tree hierarchy around six major keys. (See Table 21-1 for the names and contents of these keys.) Each key is a major branch of the registry database and holds information relating to the subject of the branch.

The registry is made up of six major keys or branches, each of which has a number of subkeys structured in a tree hierarchy. Within each key is a number of values, each of which has corresponding value data. The six major keys of the Windows 95 registry are listed in Table 21-1.

Table 21-1	The Major Keys of the Windows 95 Registry
Key Name	**Contents**
HKEY_CLASSES_ROOT	File associations and OLE data.
HKEY_USERS	User preferences, including desktop setup and network connections.
HKEY_CURRENT_USER	On a PC with only a single user, this key is a duplicate of the HKEY_USERS key. However, on a PC with multiple logins, it contains the preferences of the currently logged-in user.
HKEY_LOCAL_MACHINE	The hardware and software installed on the system.
HKEY_CURRENT_CONFIG	In addition to duplicating the HKEY_LOCAL_MACHINE key when running, this key also contains any configuration changes made in the current session and information on the printers and fonts installed.
HKEY_DYN_DATA	Records system performance information and keeps information on Plug-and-Play devices.

For the test, you need to know that the registry is organized into keys and the contents of each key so that you can recall this information upon seeing the key name. The A+ exam asks you to match the key to the type of information that it contains.

The registry's backup files

The registry is kept in two files, SYSTEM.DAT and USER.DAT. Each time the system boots, backup copies (with a .DA0 extension) are made of these files. If Windows 95 starts and can't find one of the registry files, Windows 95 uses the backup copy. If both files are missing, Windows starts in Safe mode and displays the Registry Problem dialog box, from which you can indicate that you want to restore both files from their backups and then restart the system.

Editing the registry, if you dare

You use the REGEDIT.EXE program to edit registry files. Make changes to the registry only with extreme caution and care. Be sure that you back up both the SYSTEM.DAT and the USER.DAT files before making any changes to the registry. You may want to back up these files before you install new Windows software to the system as well, because each installation modifies the registry. Figure 21-1 is a screen capture of this program displaying the contents of a registry.

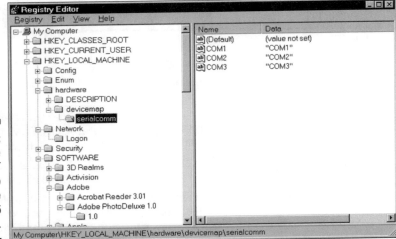

Figure 21-1:
Use the
REGEDIT
program to
edit the
Windows 95
registry.

Windows 95 memory management

Study these facts about Windows 95 memory management:

- ✔ Windows 95 starts in real mode so that it loads any legacy and 16-bit drivers and then switches to protected mode for 32-bit operations. The 32-bit drivers are called *virtual device drivers* and usually have a .VXD or .386 extension.

- ✔ If all device drivers are 32-bit, Windows 95 doesn't need CONFIG.SYS.

- ✔ Virtual memory management is automated under Windows 95. Unlike Windows 3.*x*, you don't set the size and type of swap files; Windows 95 does it all automatically.

- ✔ Windows 95 doesn't use SMARTDRV.EXE or SHARE.EXE, which free up conventional and upper memory space. Instead, the features provided by those files are built into Windows 95 directly.

File Management in the Windows World

Different versions of Windows manage files stored on secondary storage in different ways. The differences revolve around the various FAT (File Allocation Table) strategies and the number of characters allowed in a filename.

FAT, VFAT, and FAT32

Although their names make them sound like three dietary evils, FAT, VFAT, and FAT32 are file organization techniques used in Windows 3.*x* and Windows 95. Windows 3.*x* uses the 16-bit FAT (File Allocation Table) to index the contents of hard disk clusters and the files that they contain. Each FAT entry contains the information about each hard disk cluster and the file or data stored in that cluster.

Windows 95 supports VFAT (Virtual, not Very, FAT), which is a 32-bit FAT that also provides the LFN (long file names) feature. Windows 95 (after OSR2 is applied) also supports an updated file allocation table scheme that can be used in place of VFAT called FAT32, but don't worry about that being on the test.

File management with Windows 3.x

File Manager is the tool used to manage secondary storage devices in Windows 3.x. File Manager presents the contents of the floppy disk, hard disk, CD-ROM, and other drives as a tree structure. Windows 3.x refers to the file grouping divisions on a disk as *directories*. Remember that memory and file management in Windows 3.x uses DOS facilities, because Windows 3.x is not technically an operating system, but rather an operating environment.

If you've never seen File Manager in Windows 3.x, it looks very much like the Windows Explorer of Windows 95, with some subtle functional differences, such as how files are manipulated from one directory to another. The one functional difference that you may be asked about on the DOS/Windows exam is how file attributes are changed in the File Manager.

Lab 21-2 details the process used for changing file attributes in the Windows 3.x File Manager:

Lab 21-2	Changing File Attributes in Windows 3.x

1. **Select the file by clicking on the filename in the right-hand window.**

2. **Choose Properties from the File menu.**

   The Properties dialog box for the highlighted file opens.

3. **Change the attributes of the highlighted file by clicking the check boxes provided in the Properties dialog box.**

Compressing (not depressing) data

A system running DOS or Windows 3.x is not likely to have a 10GB hard drive. In fact, it is very likely to have only 200MB or less. To overcome the demand for hard disk space by Windows applications without having to purchase a bigger hard disk, disk compression utilities sprang forth.

Disk compression stores the data on a hard disk in one very large compressed file, creating a logical drive, a disk subdivision created and maintained by software. The data is stored using a mathematically encoded algorithm to reduce its storage requirements. The data is then managed (coded and decoded) into and out of the big compressed file. Available storage space is reported in terms of effective capacity, creating the illusion that the hard disk is bigger than it really is. It's not bigger — it just stores more compressed data. A 200MB drive can effectively store 300 to 350MB of data.

Disk compression techniques in Windows 95 are only slightly improved from those used in DOS and Windows 3.*x*. Under Windows 95, a logical "host" drive is created to hold the compressed volume file (CVF). The CVF is very much like the *really big and complicated file* used in the earlier versions. The program released with Windows 95 to create and manage compressed hard disk files is the DriveSpace utility. Once you use DriveSpace, it becomes a part of the environment and translates data in and out of the CVF.

The good news about compressing data files is that the hard drive holds more files than it can when the files are uncompressed. The bad news is that the hard drive holds more files than it can when the files are uncompressed. Yes, disk compression is both a good thing and a bad thing. If you ever want to uncompress your data files for some reason, you must delete enough of the files (hopefully backed up somewhere) to make the compressed file fit on the hard drive uncompressed.

Another potential problem with disk compression is that the data is in one really big and complicated file. Any corruption to the file loses all the data, which is why files that must be available to the operating system, such as swap files, are placed on an uncompressed drive outside of the compressed drive by Windows 95.

Managing the hard drive with Explorer

Windows 3.*x* uses File Manager as the primary tool for managing the contents of secondary storage devices; Windows 95 uses Windows Explorer in a similar manner. You can access Explorer from either the Start menu or by right-clicking the My Computer icon and choosing Explorer. You use Explorer to create, modify, move, and find files and folders. A Windows 95 folder is what Windows 3.*x* and DOS call a directory. Windows 95 allows folders and files to be moved using drag-and-drop, as well as the usual method of cutting and pasting or copying and pasting.

For some reason, the A+ exam emphasizes how file management tools are used to change file attributes. I don't know about you, but this isn't something I do often. However, it may be on the test, so Lab 21-3 details the steps you take to change a file's attributes:

Lab 21-3   Changing File Attributes in Windows 95

1. **Right-click the filename to display the shortcut menu and choose Properties.**

2. **Click the General tab on the dialog box that appears.**

3. **Change the file attributes and then click OK.**

   If you can complete this lab, you understand the basic navigation of Explorer.

Upgrading Windows 3.x to Windows 95

For a standard Microsoft upgrade from Windows 3.x to Windows 95, Windows 95 files are loaded into the same folder, usually C:\WINDOWS, and upgrade the Windows 3.x runtime files to Windows 95 runtime files. To create a dual-boot system with both versions of Windows, Windows 95 is installed into a separate directory. You can expect to see questions on the test about both installing Windows 95 over Windows 3.x and creating a system with both versions.

Installing Windows 95 over the top of a Windows 3.x installation is considered the standard Microsoft upgrade procedure. However, should you want to be able to start either version, to continue to run older versions of application software for instance, you only have to change the target drive or folder for Windows 95 during its installation.

For a system that has both Windows 95 and Windows 3.x on it, Windows 95 must be the normal boot version. Windows 3.x would then be started when the system was MS-DOS mode.

Installing Hardware in Windows 95

In the hazy, lazy days of Windows 3.x and DOS, installing hardware was a simple matter of plugging in the hardware and editing the CONFIG.SYS file to load the hardware's device driver. Installing hardware may not have been *that* simple, but that's a fairly close description of the process.

Windows 95 is more discriminating than its predecessors. It classifies hardware devices into four groups:

- **Plug-and-Play (PnP):** Windows 95 is a Plug-and-Play operating system. It configures a Plug-and-Play device even if the PC's BIOS is not Plug-and-Play compliant.

- **32-bit supported devices:** Windows 95 carries a number of 32-bit device drivers for peripheral devices that it directly supports. These drivers are included on its CD-ROM and are loaded automatically when the devices are detected.

- **Unsupported 32-bit devices:** These devices may be compatible with a user's computer, but Windows 95 does not include drivers for them. The manufacturer usually supplies compatible drivers on a floppy disk.

- **Legacy cards:** These 16-bit or 8-bit adapter and interface cards may cause system resource conflicts. They are usually configured through DIP switches and jumpers.

If Windows 95 recognizes the device as a supported device, hardware installation proceeds with virtually no input needed from you. If a device is not Plug-and-Play compliant, but is still a supported device, Windows 95 suggests system resource assignments and just needs confirmation from you to complete the installation. Windows 95 usually needs intervention only for legacy cards, unsupported devices for which a device driver, typically supplied by the manufacturer, is needed.

Networking in Windows 95

A PC service technician must be familiar enough with networked PCs to be able to tell whether a PC is networked before working on it and must be able to test newly installed networking hardware as well. In Chapter 13, I cover the details of networking PCs, but some specific issues regarding networking with Windows and DOS are covered on the DOS/Windows exam. You can expect questions about how you determine whether a DOS/Windows 3.*x* PC is networked, as well as questions about dial-up networking and direct cable connections.

You can usually tell whether a DOS computer is networked by looking in its root directory. A tell-tale sign is a directory named C:\NWCLIENT or something like that. Also, in the CONFIG.SYS or AUTOEXEC.BAT file, you see network configuration statements and client programs being launched from directories with the tell-tale names.

Dial-up networking

Any Windows 95 system that uses a modem to connect to a network — whether it is a LAN, WAN, or the Internet — uses dial-up networking (DUN) to make the connection. DUN creates a point-to-point protocol (PPP) connection between two computers over a telephone line. In effect, PPP causes the modem act like a network interface card. PPP is the telephone line protocol that transports the actual network protocol over the telephone lines to carry out the network interaction by the connected PCs.

Dial-up networking automatically installs the Dial-Up Adapter (no abbreviation for this one) and the Client for Microsoft Networks (this one either). These tools carry out the network dialogue by configuring the outgoing data packets to fit the protocol of the remote network (whether it is NetBEUI, IPX/SPX, or TCP/IP) and translate the incoming data packets from the network protocol for local use. The remote network in this case is the network you have connected to using DUN. In order to communicate with it or any of its workstations, servers, or features, you must speak its language (protocol). DUN, Dial-Up-Adapter, and the Client for Microsoft Networks are the tools used to translate your messages into the proper format and form understood by the remote network, and vice versa.

Direct cable connection

To create a peer-to-peer network environment, Windows 95 computers can be directly connected for communications using either a null modem serial cable or a parallel cable connected to the standard ports on PCs. One of the primary purposes of any network is sharing resources, and the only reason for peer-to-peer networking to exist is resource sharing. However, for this pinnacle of cooperation and trust to succeed, the directly connected computers must open up to each other.

Peer-to-peer networking works only between Windows 95 PCs that have the file-and-print sharing component installed. After file-and-print sharing is activated, you use Windows Explorer to designate which drives and folders are shared.

Prep Test

1 What is the order of the DOS boot sequence?

A ○ IO.SYS, MSDOS.SYS, COMMAND.COM, CONFIG.SYS, AUTOEXEC.BAT
B ○ MSDOS.SYS, IO.SYS, COMMAND.COM, CONFIG.SYS, AUTOEXEC.BAT
C ○ COMMAND.COM, IO.SYS, MSDOS.SYS, CONFIG.SYS, AUTOEXEC.BAT
D ○ IO.SYS, MSDOS.SYS, CONFIG.SYS, COMMAND.COM, AUTOEXEC.BAT

2 Each entry in the FAT uses one

A ○ Cluster
B ○ Sector
C ○ Cylinder
D ○ Volume

3 What software device driver is required to run Windows 3.*x*?

A ○ EMM386.EXE
B ○ HIMEM.SYS
C ○ PROGMAN.INI
D ○ LOADHIGH

4 Windows organizes its memory into

A ○ Keys
B ○ Conventional, Upper, Extended
C ○ Heaps
D ○ Clusters

5 The Windows 95 registry is organized into

A ○ Trees
B ○ Hives
C ○ Registrations
D ○ Keys

6 The core components of Windows 95 are

A ○ Explorer, Control Panel, Settings
B ○ Kernel, User, GDI
C ○ Plug-and-Play, Dial-Up Networking, Desktop
D ○ Menu, Desktop, Explorer

7 When Windows is installed on a system using file compression, where should the swap file be located?

A ○ In the compressed drive's root directory
B ○ Wherever Windows places the file automatically
C ○ In the Windows directory
C ○ On the uncompressed drive

8 If Windows 3.*x* Setup halts during installation, what action should you take?

A ○ Restart the PC, run A:\SETUP.EXE, and choose Recovery Mode when prompted.
B ○ Contact your dealer or Microsoft for replacement diskettes.
C ○ Restart the PC and run A:\SETUP.EXE again. The halt was probably a fluke.
D ○ Restart the PC and run A:\SETUP.EXE /I.

9 Which two files hold the Windows 95 registry?

A ○ SYSTEM.INI and WIN.INI
B ○ SYSTEM.REG and USER.REG
C ○ SYSTEM.DAT and USER.DAT
D ○ REG.DAT and SETUP.REG

10 The programs used by Windows 3.*x* and Windows 95 to manage hard drive files and directories, respectively, are

A ○ PROGMAN.INI and WIN.INI
B ○ File Manager and Windows Explorer
C ○ Program Manager and Desktop
D ○ .SWP files and .PAR files

Answers

1 *D.* Remember that CONFIG.SYS, if present, is used before COMMAND.COM. *Review "DOS Basics."*

2 *A.* Sectors make up clusters, and cylinders and volumes are the stuff of UNIX and mainframes. *Review "FAT, VFAT, FAT32."*

3 *B.* Windows 3.*x* doesn't run without HIMEM.SYS loaded. *Review "The Windows 3.x environment."*

4 *C.* Both Windows 3.*x* and Windows 95 organize memory into heaps that are allocated to support specific functions of the core components. *Review "Piling up memory in heaps."*

5 *D.* The registry is made up of a series of major keys, each of which has an associated tree hierarchy related to it. *Review "The Windows 95 registry."*

6 *B.* The Kernel contains the essential operating system functions; User controls the user interface; and GDI creates the GUI and controls printing. *Review "Windows 95 Basics."*

7 *D.* Any files that must be available to the operating system or to start the system should be stored outside the compressed master file. *Review "Compressing (not depressing) data."*

8 *D.* The /I option bypasses the hardware detection phase of the setup to complete the installation and allows you to add your devices manually. *Review "Troubleshooting installation problems."*

9 *C. Review "The registry's backup files."*

10 *B.* The File Manager in Windows 3.*x* and Windows Explorer in Windows 95 are used to manage hard drive files, folders, and directories. *Review "Managing the hard drive with Explorer."*

Chapter 22
Diagnosing and Repairing Problems

● ●

Exam Objectives

▶ Recognizing and correcting common boot sequence errors and messages
▶ Correcting Windows printing problems
▶ Diagnosing and troubleshooting DOS and Windows problems
▶ Running DOS applications in Windows
▶ Creating an emergency boot disk

● ●

A significant part of working with DOS and Windows as a PC service technician involves resolving issues between the PC and its operating system. About 20 percent of the questions on the A+ DOS/Windows exam relates to how you deal with DOS and Windows problems, or at least the ones that can be duplicated.

If you have worked with Windows for any length of time, you know very well that it can have its days. Some days, it's weird, and other days, it's not normal. When dealing with customers, it's important that you're able to quickly and authoritatively respond to a problem with something other than a look of surprise and the claim that, "It's never done that before." Many operating system problems are rooted in the same causes, and how you deal with these causes is what A+ has deemed important.

The degree of difficulty of the DOS/Windows exam is a bit up and down. Parts of the test are simple, basic things that just about anyone can figure out just from using either operating system. Other parts of the test include very detailed, sophisticated errors, the kind not necessarily encountered by everyone with only six months on the job. However, in this chapter I include information to cover most of the questions you should encounter on this exam.

Quick Assessment

Recognizing and correcting common boot sequence errors and messages

1 The sequence in which the system files load and execute in a DOS boot is _____, _____, _____, _____, and _____.

2 The "Incorrect DOS Version" error message indicates an incompatibility between a DOS command and _____.

3 Windows 3.x doesn't run without _____ loaded.

4 Division by zero or memory addresses outside of an allotted area can cause a _____.

Correcting Windows printing problems

5 A printer that was working before has stopped working. After checking the power and making sure that the printer is turned on, you should next check to see whether it's _____.

Diagnosing and trouble-shooting DOS and Windows problems

6 The utility you use to detect and repair bad clusters on the hard drive is _____.

7 The _____ is a feature of Windows 95 Help to guide you through the resolution of hardware conflicts.

Running DOS applications in Windows

8 The Properties dialog box of a DOS program displays the contents of its _____.

Creating an emergency boot disk

9 The /s option of the FORMAT command is the same as using the _____ command to copy system files to a disk.

Answers

1 *IO.SYS, MSDOS.SYS, CONFIG.SYS, COMMAND.COM,* and *AUTOEXEC.BAT.* Review "The DOS boot sequence."

2 *COMMAND.COM.* Review "Friendly old DOS error messages."

3 *HIMEM.SYS.* Review "Wonderful Windows 3.*x* error messages."

4 *General Protection Fault.* Review "Dealing with Printers and Printer Problems in Windows."

5 *Online.* Review "Dealing with Printers and Printer Problems in Windows."

6 *SCANDISK.* Review "Diagnosing and Troubleshooting Problems Using DOS and Windows Utilities."

7 *Conflict Troubleshooter.* Review "Diagnosing and Troubleshooting Problems Using DOS and Windows Utilities."

8 *PIF (program information file).* Review "Running a DOS Program in Windows 95."

9 *SYS.* Review "Creating an Emergency Boot Disk."

Recognizing and Correcting Common Boot Sequence Errors and Messages

The focus of boot sequence error messages, at least those that deal with the operating system, is quite different between DOS and Windows. Errors issued from the DOS world are in many ways more friendly than those of the "user-friendly" Windows world. DOS messages are straightforward and deal with problems or exceptions in its startup files. DOS seems perfectly happy to let the POST (Power On Self-Test) deal with any environmental problems the PC may have. Windows, especially Windows 95, deals with its entire operating environment well beyond the POST.

Much of the Diagnosing and Troubleshooting domain of the DOS/Windows exam consists of knowing the sequence of events that occur in the boot sequences of DOS, Windows 3.*x,* and Windows 95, and recognizing error messages and their associated corrective actions. Memorize the boot sequences and familiarize yourself with the error messages in each environment.

The DOS boot sequence

Virtually every PC goes through about the same sequence of events when starting up, regardless of the operating system it uses. This process is called the boot sequence. The name boot comes from "bootstrap," as in "pulling yourself up by your own bootstraps." Memorize the DOS boot sequence for both the Core and DOS/Windows exams because it is still a favorite test topic. Remember the exact sequence of the actions, especially software tasks.

After the POST processing validates the system, the operating system loads, as in the following steps:

1. The CMOS indicates the sequence in which the disk drives (A:, C:, and so on) are scanned for a boot record.

2. If the boot device is the C: drive, the Master Boot Record (MBR) loads, and its program locates the boot partition.

3. If the boot disk is the A: drive or if the C: drive boot is continuing, the DOS Boot Record (DBR) loads, and control passes to it.

4. The DBR loads the IO.SYS and MSDOS.SYS files (which is most of DOS) and passes control to them.

5. IO.SYS loads CONFIG.SYS (required by DOS systems), which sets the environment and loads the device drivers.

6. The COMMAND.COM command interpreter then loads, and control passes to it. COMMAND.COM loads and executes the AUTOEXEC.BAT and then displays the user interface (the command prompt).

The DOS boot sequence is IO.SYS, MSDOS.SYS, CONFIG.SYS, COMMAND.COM, and AUTOEXEC.BAT.

A question you may see on the test asks when the DOS boot sequence ends. I bet that many people miss this one. The DOS boot sequence ends when the AUTOEXEC.BAT finishes and displays the command prompt or a shell menu.

Friendly old DOS error messages

An error message from the DOS boot sequence provides immediate feedback on any error you have made either by omission or commission. You have left something out or put in an error, ever so slight, but enough that DOS doesn't work. Table 22-1 lists some common DOS boot sequence error messages and what you can do to correct them. Expect to see one or two questions about these errors on the test.

Table 22-1	DOS Boot Sequence Error Messages	
Error Message	*Condition*	*Corrective Action*
Missing operating system	The MBR can't find a bootable partition. Either the disk hasn't been formatted and had the system copied to it, or a virus is squatting all over your partition table.	Either format the disk with the FORMAT C: command using the /s option, or use an antivirus program to scan and clean the disk.
Non-system disk or disk error, replace and press any key	Usually means that you forgot to remove your data disk when you booted the PC, and it is now trying to use the disk as a boot disk.	Pop the disk out of the drive and press any key to continue the boot sequence. You see this error on Windows machines, too.

(continued)

Table 22-1 *(continued)*

Error Message	Condition	Corrective Action
Incorrect DOS version	The COMMAND.COM in the root directory and an internal command, issued in either of the CONFIG.SYS or AUTOEXEC.BAT files or at the command prompt, are not of the same DOS version.	You need to either track down the correct COMMAND.COM or use the SETVER command to trick DOS into believing that it's running the correct version. You can use SETVER to set the current version to an older version. This problem is common with CD-ROM drivers.
Error in CONFIG.SYS line XX	Something is amiss in the CONFIG.SYS.	Use EDIT to open and examine the suspect line and make the appropriate adjustments. If a line number isn't displayed with the Error in CONFIG.SYS message, you can use the F8 key to slow the boot to the pace of one instruction at a time.
Bad or missing DRIVER.DRV	If CONFIG.SYS can't load a device driver, it issues this message, replacing the word DRIVER with the name of the missing driver. CONFIG.SYS loads device drivers last, so chances are that the system will still start, but without the driverless device.	Locate the driver and correct the entry in CONFIG.SYS.
Bad or missing COMMAND.COM	Somehow or another the COMMAND.COM file is no longer in the root directory.	If you have not squirreled one away in the DOS directory, you may need to reinstall DOS. However, more than likely, you have a copy of it on either a backup or floppy boot disk. Copy COMMAND.COM to the root directory and reboot.

The only error messages you can expect from the AUTOEXEC.BAT file processing are the "Illegal or unknown command, file, or directory" messages. The easiest way to isolate these errors is to use the F8 key to step through the commands one at a time.

Following the PATH

This place is as good as any to talk about the PATH= statement that should be present in the AUTOEXEC.BAT file. The PATH statement establishes the directory sequence and priority as to where the operating system is to look for command-line files it is given to run. For example, the following statement in the AUTOEXEC.BAT file means that DOS commands and WIN.COM can execute from any directory on the disk.

```
PATH=C:\DOS;C:\WINDOWS
```

Any other directories added to the PATH statement extend this capability to their commands. A common problem, and one you are likely to be asked about on the test, is that although a directory is included in the PATH statement, if the PATH statement is included in the AUTOEXEC.BAT file after the WIN.COM execute statement, the PATH statement doesn't take effect prior to the start of Windows. Therefore, it is not available in a DOS window opened by Windows.

The Windows boot sequence

Because Windows 3.*x* isn't an actual operating system, but rather an operating environment, it actually uses the DOS boot sequence and then adds a few more steps. Typically, WIN.COM executes from the AUTOEXEC.BAT file.

Windows 3.*x* uses several configuration (called *initialization* or *.INI*) files to define the graphical user interface (GUI) and its input and output devices. These files contain such things as the size of the screen, the display font, the colors of the desktop, and the speed settings for the mouse. These files include the following:

- ✔ **CONTROL.INI:** Defines the user desktop, including colors, wallpaper, background, and any screen saver options in use
- ✔ **MOUSE.INI:** Defines operational settings for the mouse
- ✔ **PROGMAN.INI:** Defines the group windows and the icons included in each
- ✔ **SYSTEM.INI:** Defines hardware settings, defaults, and the Windows multitasking parameters
- ✔ **WIN.INI:** Defines the working relationships of Windows 3.*x*, including printers, fonts, file associations, and applications

Wonderful Windows 3.x error messages

Table 22-2 lists some common boot sequence error messages you may see from Windows 3.x (in addition to those listed in Table 22-1).

Table 22-2	Windows 3.x Boot Sequence Error Messages	
Error Message	*Condition*	*Corrective Action*
HIMEM.SYS not loaded	HIMEM.SYS is the device driver for extended memory and the high memory area (HMA). Windows 3.x doesn't run unless it's loaded.	Add a DEVICE=C:\WINDOWS\HIMEM.SYS line in the CONFIG.SYS.
Unable to initialize display adapter	Windows 3.x is having trouble getting the video adapter card to respond or play fair. Possibly, Windows doesn't have an embedded driver for the adapter or the display itself.	You can usually solve this problem immediately by changing the device to a VGA type and then either loading the manufacturer's driver or diagnosing a problem with the video card itself if the VGA doesn't work. If you have a disk from the manufacturer for the device driver, click on the Have Disk button when asked for the disk.
Swapfile corrupt	Somehow, the virtual memory swap file has been corrupted.	Use the Control Panel's 386 Enhanced mode virtual memory function to reestablish either a permanent or temporary swap file.
A device referenced in WIN.INI could not be found (The actual message for this error condition varies, but this is the gist of it.)		Edit the WIN.INI file and verify its contents. Focus on any device drivers launched from within this file.

The Windows 95 boot sequence

The Windows 95 boot sequence is just a little different from that of DOS and Windows 3.x. Its steps follow:

1. After the BIOS performs the POST, and if the PC has a Plug-and-Play BIOS, Plug-and-Play devices are configured.

2. The partition table is accessed, and the boot record activates IO.SYS.

3. The Windows 95 boot sequence performs partially in real mode and then switches to protected mode. Beginning at this point, the boot sequence performs in real mode.

4. The MSDOS.SYS is checked for any Windows 95 boot parameters (such as BootMulti or BootMenu).

5. If all is normal, the message "Starting Windows 95" displays, and the sequence pauses for two seconds to wait for a function key.

6. If file compression is in use, DRVSPACE.BIN loads.

7. The registry (SYSTEM.DAT) is checked, and if it's valid, it loads.

8. Windows 95 performs hardware detection and identifies any new hardware.

9. If the CONFIG.SYS and AUTOEXEC.BAT files exist, IO.SYS processes their commands.

10. The boot sequence switches to protected mode.

11. WIN.COM executes.

12. The VMM32.VXD file and all virtual device drivers included in the Windows 95 registry or the SYSTEM.INI file load.

13. Windows 95 core components — Kernel, GDI, and User — load, along with the Explorer and network support.

14. Any applications in the startup (RunOnce) section of the registry start.

15. The boot sequence ends.

The actual pathname in the registry is

```
Hkey_Local_Machine\Software\Microsoft\Windows\CurrentVersion\RunOnce\
```

If the Windows 95 boot sequence experiences any problems, restart it and immediately press the F8 key after the message "Starting Windows 95" appears. This action displays the BootMenu, which includes the option to boot the system in Safe mode. Safe mode boots Windows 95 without its startup files, which results in only the essential device drivers being loaded. If the computer can successfully boot in Safe mode, you know that the problem is in a device or its driver.

Another BootMenu option that can help isolate a boot problem is the selection for Step by Step Confirmation. This choice allows the system to boot by displaying system file entries one at a time for you to include or exclude from the boot process. Answering "No" to every option is the same as booting in Safe mode, and Windows 95 reverts to that mode automatically.

If Windows 95 won't boot in Safe mode, the system may have any of the following problems:

- The CMOS settings are incorrect.
- A hardware conflict exists, such as advanced BIOS settings, IRQ conflicts, duplicated COM ports, or defective memory modules.
- The MSDOS.SYS file contains an erroneous setting.
- Set the video drivers to either VGA.DRV or VGA.VXD, both of which you can find on the Windows 95 CD-ROM.

You may also want to examine the contents of the BOOTLOG.TXT file located in the root directory. This file contains a log file of the results of device driver activation. The last line should list the driver attempting to load when the error occurred.

Really nice and friendly Windows 95 error messages

Because DOS has taken all the really neat bad error messages, Windows 3.*x* and Windows 95 have had to resort to messages that actually make sense on occasion. Table 22-3 lists some of the very best errors that Windows 95 has to offer.

Table 22-3	Windows 95 Boot Sequence Error Messages	
Error Message	**Condition**	**Corrective Action**
No error message	The boot sequence stops at a point after the POST and before Windows 95 starts. Quite likely, the problem is a boot virus or some equally scary problem with the MBR.	Run FDISK with a /MBR option to rebuild the MBR. You may want to scan the disk with an antivirus program first.
GPF in USER.EXE	The User core component has run out of file space.	Add the line FILES=100 to the CONFIG.SYS file.
0E or 0D exception errors	0E errors refer to bad memory, and 0D errors are video problems.	If this problem persists on a reboot, examine the CMOS for exceptions and verify the device drivers in use. Try switching to VGA video mode.

Error Message	Condition	Corrective Action
Out of Memory	This error is usually caused by the GDI and System heaps filling up and by memory leaks — programs that end without releasing their memory allocations.	Reboot the system and reduce the activity on the system.
Windows error accessing system registry	The system registry may be corrupted.	Reboot to the Safe mode command prompt only and reset the restricting file attributes on the SYSTEM.DAT file (ATTRIB -s -h -r SYSTEM.DAT) and then rename SYSTEM.DAT to something like BADSYSTEM.BAD.

Dealing with Printers and Printer Problems in Windows

Printing from Windows is perhaps one of its more reliable activities, but when printing doesn't work, most customers are at a loss for what to do, especially if the PC is networked. Table 22-4 lists some of the more common problems that customers may encounter, and the ones you are likely to encounter yourself on the A+ exam.

Table 22-4	Common Windows 95 Printer Problems
Problem	**Corrective Action**
The printer won't print.	Is it plugged in? Is it turned on? Is it online? Is the cable attached? Is the correct printer driver installed? Is paper loaded? Users can do something, even without knowing they have done it, to change the existing physical or logical environment.
The document was generated (user saw the little animated graphic showing it being generated), but nothing is coming out.	See preceding entry. Also, make sure that the print spool isn't paused. To release it, click the printer icon shown on the right corner of the Taskbar, highlight the print job, select Document from the menu bar, and click off the Pause Printing selection.

(continued)

Table 22-4 *(continued)*

Problem	Corrective Action
The printer won't go online, and the LCD display continues to show "Warming Up."	The printer and its driver are set for bidirectional parallel port printing, but somehow a unidirectional cable is installed. (You can expect a question about this one on the test.)
The printing is garbled and page advances are crazy.	Most likely, either an incorrect or incompatible driver is assigned to the printer. The easiest way to fix this problem is to delete the printer from the Settings Printers folder and reinstall it with the correct driver. You may need to download the driver from the manufacturer's technical support Web site.
The print job is generated and is sent to the printer, but nothing happens.	The printer settings, in the Printer properties, is set to print to the wrong port (LPT1 or LPT2). This and many other unexplained printer problems may also have nothing to do with the printer, its driver, or the cable. Rather, the CMOS settings for the printer port (LPT1) are not set correctly, or the setup in the Windows Device Manager is not set to the appropriate protocol (ECP, EPP, or Standard). Read the manufacturer's manual and adjust the port to the proper setting using the Control Panel System Device Manager choices.

Several Windows and non-Windows system problems are sometimes harder to explain because they occur intermittently or because nobody, including Microsoft, has come up with a reasonable enough explanation for them. Here are the best explanations I can muster for the ones likely to be on the test:

✔ **General Protection Fault (GPF):** A wide range of reasons exists why a Windows application can get a GPF, including division by zero, corrupted memory addressing, and more. The best remedy for an application that repeatedly dies with GPFs is to uninstall the application, reboot the system to rebuild the registry, and reinstall the application.

✔ **System lock up:** The list of reasons why this problem occurs in any system (DOS or Windows) is myriad. Essentially, all you can do is reboot the system. Occasionally, a lockup is accompanied by the blue screen of death, but sometimes it happens out of the clear blue sky (no relation). If a particular application or device consistently locks up the system, you may need to isolate it for diagnosing the problem.

✔ **System busy:** This message usually accompanies the blue screen of death. It suggests that you can wait for the system to become available or reboot. Depending on your patience, you can wait a while before you reboot. As I mention previously, if this problem consistently happens in the same application or device, you should pursue diagnosing it.

✔ **Application will not start or load:** Enough system resources may not be available to start the job, or the application's .EXE file may be corrupted. If the application should be able to load but won't, then uninstall, reboot, and reinstall it. You may also need to add more memory or hard disk space. One other reason for this problem may be that it's a DOS application that may not be able to run in a Windows DOS window. Try running it after rebooting into MS-DOS mode.

✔ **Cannot log on to network:** Let me count the ways: The network configuration has been changed or corrupted, the cable is missing from the NIC, the network itself is down, the user has been removed from the network users list, and so on. On the Windows 95 system, check out the Network settings on the Control Panel and, if all is well there, check the network end before opening the hardware to check it.

Diagnosing and Troubleshooting Problems Using DOS and Windows Utilities

You need to be familiar with when, why, and how the most common DOS and Windows diagnostic utilities and their options are used to troubleshoot and diagnose system problems. Table 22-5 lists the most commonly used DOS/Windows utilities.

Table 22-5	DOS/Windows Diagnostic Utilities	
Utility Name	**Purpose**	**Options**
ATTRIB	A DOS command that you use to change the attributes of a file on a disk. The attributes of a file include read only, system, hidden, and archive.	You enter the options r (read), s (system), h (hidden), and a (archive) with either a plus or a minus to add or remove an attribute. For example, $+r$ designates a file as read-only.

(continued)

Table 22-5 *(continued)*

Utility Name	Purpose	Options
CHKDSK	A DOS and Windows utility that you use to locate lost clusters, which are clusters that the FAT can't determine where they belong.	Using the /F option saves these clusters in files placed in the root directory with names like FILE0000.CHK. The idea for the .CHK files is that you can recover them. Don't waste your time trying and just delete them.
DEFRAG	A DOS and Windows utility that you use to reorganize the hard drive content so that clusters are placed in adjacent sectors, which speeds up hard disk operations.	
EDIT	A DOS command that you use to edit text files, including .BAT, .DAT, and .TXT files.	
FDISK	A DOS and Windows utility that you use to partition a hard drive prior to formatting and copying the system files to it.	An option you may find on the test is the /MBR option, used to rebuild the master boot record.
MEM	A DOS utility that displays the current status and assignment of memory.	The /Classify option shows the configuration of the memory on a PC.
MSD	A DOS utility that you use to view system resource assignments, memory, ROM, UARTs, and other internal hardware, such as IRQs, DMA channels, and I/O port addresses.	
SCANDISK	Used by both Windows and DOS to detect and repair bad clusters on the hard disk. SCANDISK attempts to move data from bad clusters to good ones.	
SYSEDIT	A Windows utility that you can use to view and modify the CONFIG.SYS, AUTOEXEC.BAT, and .INI files.	

Here are some Windows 95 tools you may be asked about on the test:

✔ **Device Manager:** You use this tabbed dialog box to view and manipulate the status of system devices, their drivers, system resources, and compatibility.

✔ **Conflict Troubleshooter:** A feature within Windows 95 Help that you can access through the Index under "conflict, hardware." This tool steps you through the resolution of a hardware system resource conflict.

✔ **Control Panel:** This window contains icons for many of the system features and configuration setting utilities, including the mouse, networks, modems, printers, and more.

✔ **SYSEDIT:** This utility is still available and allows you to view the CONFIG.SYS, AUTOEXEC.BAT (if any), and the WIN.INI files all at once.

✔ **REGEDIT:** You can use this Windows 95 utility to edit the registry files, if you dare.

Running a DOS Program in Windows 95

DOS programs need to have a DOS-like environment created before they can run in the Windows 95 world. The steps listed in Lab 22-1 are an example of what's required to create such an environment:

Lab 22-1	Running a DOS Program in Windows 95

1. **Using the Windows Explorer, choose the DOS program you want to execute.**

2. **Right-click the filename and click Properties.**

   The Properties Dialog Box that appears displays the details of the PIF (program information file) for the application.

3. **Click the Memory tab to display the settings for how much conventional, expanded, and extended memory needs to be made available to it when it runs.**

   Setting this option to Auto allows most DOS programs to run just fine in the default environment. DOS programs that have problems sometimes suffer from too much memory (especially conventional memory) being assigned to them. In this case, you can limit the amount of memory assigned to a program.

4. **Other settings, including the screen size (window size), whether Windows 95 is to be displayed for the window, and whether to enable or disable dynamic memory allocation, are set on the other tabs of the DOS program's Properties box.**

Some DOS programs won't run in a Windows 95 window, and when they try, they get errors such as illegal operation messages. The first-aid remedy for this type of error is to check the Protected box on the Memory tab of the Properties dialog box and then begin fiddling with the program's memory requirements. If the program's manual, which I'm sure you have readily available, doesn't list the program's memory requirements by type, you're left experimenting or running it in MS-DOS mode. You switch to MS-DOS mode through the Start menu's Shut Down option.

When the DOS program finishes, you have to reboot the system to return to Windows 95. Needless to say, this option should be the last resort for running a DOS program. It would be far better to spend the bucks for a newer, more compatible version, if you can.

The bad news is that if the program crashes, it crashes everything. Windows 95 is actually still running, but it's in MS-DOS mode. Therefore, if the application quits, so does Windows 95.

If a DOS program persists in failing, you can change a number of settings on the program's Properties dialog box. Try changing only one setting at a time, so that you don't overshoot the mark and need to undo something. These settings may be mentioned in a question concerning what you must change to allow a DOS program to run in the Windows 95 environment:

✔ Disable the Allow Screen Saver option on the Misc tab.

✔ Disable the Dynamic Memory Allocation setting on the Screen tab.

✔ Disable the Fast ROM Emulation setting on the Screen tab.

✔ Change the Idle Sensitivity toward Low.

✔ Select the Full-Screen option on the Screen tab.

Dealing with Viruses

Viruses are nasty pieces of software that have taken on the characteristics of infectious diseases, spreading germs and infecting unsuspecting and unprotected PCs. You can expect a couple of questions on the exam that deal with what a virus is, how it spreads, and how to detect it. The A+ exam reflects that the industry believes viruses to be a serious problem, and you should expect to see two or three questions relating to viruses on the test.

What you are expected to know is what the different types of viruses are, where they come from, and how to get rid of them on the Microsoft DOS/Windows exam. Review Chapter 20 for the details you will need on viruses.

Creating an Emergency Boot Disk

The exam definitely contains at least one question on how to create a floppy boot disk for use in an emergency.

In DOS, enter the command

```
C:\> FORMAT A: /S
```

The /s option acts the same as the SYS command to copy the system files to the disk.

In Windows 95, follow the steps in Lab 22-2.

Lab 22-2   Creating a Boot Disk in Windows 95

1. **Open the Control Panel and click Add/Remove Programs.**
2. **Choose the Startup Disk tab.**
3. **Click Create Disk.**
4. **Follow the bouncing ball prompts.**

Prep Test

1 What action can you take to get around the "Incorrect DOS version" error message?

A ○ Reboot.

B ○ Use SETVER to report a different version of DOS.

C ○ User SETVER to upgrade the application to the new DOS version.

D ○ Reinstall the correct version of DOS.

2 What is the order of the DOS boot sequence?

A ○ IO.SYS, MSDOS.SYS, COMMAND.COM, CONFIG.SYS, AUTOEXEC.BAT

B ○ MSDOS.SYS, IO.SYS, COMMAND.COM, CONFIG.SYS, AUTOEXEC.BAT

C ○ COMMAND.COM, IO.SYS, MSDOS.SYS, CONFIG.SYS, AUTOEXEC.BAT

D ○ IO.SYS, MSDOS.SYS, CONFIG.SYS, COMMAND.COM, AUTOEXEC.BAT

3 Which two of the Windows 95 heaps can fill up and cause "Out of Memory" errors?

A ○ System and GDI

B ○ System and User

C ○ GDI and User

D ○ System and Menu

4 Which Windows 95 applet do you use to create an emergency boot disk?

A ○ Add/Remove programs

B ○ System properties

C ○ Windows Explorer

D ○ Settings

5 The IO.SYS and MSDOS.SYS files load by which DOS boot sequence element?

A ○ CMOS

B ○ COMMAND.COM

C ○ DOS Boot Record (DBR)

D ○ Master Boot Record (MBR)

6 The four configuration files of Windows 3.x are

A ○ IO.SYS, MSDOS.SYS, COMMAND.COM, AUTOEXEC.BAT

B ○ MOUSE.INI, WIN.BAT, WIN.INI., SYSTEM.INI

C ○ Swapfile, User, GDI, Menu

D ○ CONTROL.INI, MOUSE.INI, PROGMAN.INI, SYSTEM.INI, WIN.INI

7 In a Windows 95 boot sequence, what loads immediately after WIN.COM executes?

A ○ SYSTEM.DAT

B ○ VMM32.VXD and the virtual device drivers

C ○ DRVSPACE.BIN

D ○ Kernel, GDI, and User core components

8 The respective exception error codes for memory and video problems in Windows 95 are

A ○ 0E and 0D.

B ○ 0F and 387h.

C ○ GPF and I/O.

D ○ Windows 95 has no exception error codes for memory and video.

9 The Windows 95 boot mode that loads only the essential hardware drivers is

A ○ Normal.

B ○ Safe mode.

C ○ Short mode.

D ○ No Load mode.

Answers

1 *B.* You use the SETVER command to make DOS appear to be an older version for older applications. *Check out "Friendly old DOS error messages."*

2 *D.* You really need to know this one for the test. *Take a look at "The DOS boot sequence."*

3 *A.* These two heaps handle the user interface and the applications started by the user. Should they run out of memory, they are unable to effectively operate the desktop environment. *Look over "Really nice and friendly Windows 95 error messages."*

4 *A.* In Windows 3.*x*, you use the File Manager, and in DOS, you use the FOR-MAT command. *See "Creating an Emergency Boot Disk."*

5 *C.* The MBR loads the DBR, which loads the IO.SYS and MSDOS.SYS. *Look up "The DOS boot sequence."*

6 *D.* The initialization files contain the system information used to create the desktop. *Check out "Following the PATH."*

7 *B.* The 32-bit VXD drivers are loaded by WIN.COM. *Review "The Windows 95 boot sequence."*

8 *A.* You have probably seen this error accompanied by the red X of death or the blue screen of death, a new wrestling tag team. *Take a look at "Really nice and friendly Windows 95 error messages."*

9 *B.* Safe mode provides you with an opportunity to identify which hardware device may be causing a problem. *See "The Windows 95 boot sequence."*

Part VI
The Parts of Ten

The 5th Wave   By Rich Tennant

SHERLOCK HOLMES TAKES THE A+ CERTIFICATION EXAM.

In this part . . .

After you have scheduled yourself to take the test, you can begin preparing for the test in earnest. This part includes some great places to get study guides, test demonstrations, and other information to help you prepare. Also included in this part is a list of things you should think about or do before, during, and after the test.

Chapter 23

Ten Ways to Prepare for Your Test Day

. . . .

In This Chapter

▶ Get there early

▶ Review your lists

▶ Do the tutorial

▶ Take your time

. . . .

Get to the Test on Time

When you schedule your exams, you are at the mercy of the testing center in your area as to the time you can take the test. You must schedule around its hours of operation. I took my test at a community college library's media and testing center that was open pretty much all day and into the evening, as well as Saturdays. The choice of time and day is up to you, within the limits of the testing center.

Make sure that you get to the testing center at least one-half hour before your test time, or even earlier if you want to do some last-minute studying. The last thing you want or need is to be rushing to make the test time (that you set yourself, remember) and be agitated when you begin the test. Get there early, find a quiet place, relax, have a cup of coffee, tea, Postum, or whatever helps you relax, and go over the *A+ Certification For Dummies* Cheat Sheet and your notes.

Review Your Notes One Last Time

In the time right before you check in, review the things guaranteed to be on the test: IRQs and I/O addresses, DOS memory allocation, laser printer operations, the OSI model, and the items included as Instant Answers throughout this book. What these items have in common is that they each involve a list or sequence of things. Right before the test you should review your cheat phrases (salami pizza, California cows, and so on) and other reminders. You may not benefit by cramming conceptual topics, but a last-minute cram with lists can help you focus on the test.

Check In on Time

A few minutes before your scheduled test time, check in with the test administrator. Be sure that you have the two pieces of identification you were asked to bring. Because only one needs to be a picture ID, your driver's license, passport, or work badge (if it also has your signature on it) should work. You will also need a second identification that has your full name on it. A credit card should do fine. You can't carry your notes or books with you into the test area, so surrender them all willingly. Don't play tug of war with your notes; keep yourself relaxed and focused on the test. Remember that this test is something you wanted to do and that it is a good thing.

Do a Brain Dump, But Do It on the Plastic

You're not allowed to bring, nor will you be supplied with, scratch paper. Instead, you will be given sheets of plastic or a dry-erase board and a dry-erase pen. These items are for you to use for notes during the test. You must leave them behind after the test. You can have as many of these as you would like, so take a couple.

After you're situated at your station and have been given your basic instructions, unload your lists. Write down as much of the lists and sequences, and special relationships, such as I/O addresses and IRQs, you can remember. You can then refer to your notes during the exam without getting flustered about whether you're remembering something correctly.

If you're taking both exams on the same day, concentrate on only the test at hand. You should have scheduled at least a one-hour break between the two tests to give yourself time to come down from the adrenaline rush of passing the first test and getting a quick review before the second. You can take the tests in any order you please. Also, if you pass your first exam, don't get overly confident about the second.

Whether it is better to schedule the two tests on different days is really up to you. Some would advise you that it is better to schedule them a week apart so you can focus your study on each test. Because so much overlaps in the material tested, however, taking them together is not too difficult. Scheduling also depends on how far you must travel to take the test. For example, I had to drive 3.5 hours to get to the testing center, which highly motivated me to take the tests together.

Do the Tutorial!

At the beginning of the test session, you will be offered a tutorial on the test from the Sylvan Prometrics testing system. Don't be a twit and think that if you've seen one online test, you've seen them all. Take the time to casually move through the tutorial. Your time doesn't begin until you start the test, so don't start the test until after you've reviewed the tutorial. The tutorial contains examples of each type of question included on the test. It also shows you how to display and hide illustrations and figures used with a question. Use the tutorial as a way to relax and get ready for the exam.

Ready, Steady, Go

When you're ready to begin, take a deep breath, clear your head, and start the exam. If you're taking both exams on the same day, you have 75 minutes to answer the 70 questions on the Core exam and then another 75 minutes for the 74 questions on the DOS/Windows exam.

If you're taking the Core exam, remember that seven of the questions don't count against your pass/fail score. Six of the questions relate to customer interaction and are scored only for information purposes, and one is merely to ask your permission to use your name in connection with the fact that you've passed and been certified. You have all 75 minutes to deal with only 64 questions, so don't rush. Take your time, but check the time remaining (it displays in the upper-right corner of the display) occasionally.

If you're taking the DOS/Windows exam, you have 75 minutes for its 70 questions. This time frame still leaves more than a minute per question. Even if you're not a particularly fast test-taker, you should have plenty of time as long as you stay on task.

Mark Questions You Want to Think About

The Sylvan Prometric test software allows you to mark a question with a checkbox so you can review it again later. You should also make a note on your plastic as to why you have marked this question, such as the following:

33. Is it A or D? First impression is D.

41. B or D?

61. Isn't this asked a different way earlier in the test?

Avoid the temptation to mark every question. You don't need to mark a question to review it later.

Answer Every Question

Some people recommend that you read through an entire test before you begin answering its questions. Don't waste your time reading the entire exam before starting. Instead, answer all the questions you're sure of and mark the ones you're not. If you're in the least hesitant on a question, choose your best choice, and then mark it. At least this way, you can't forget to answer it at all. Don't leave any questions unanswered. When in doubt, make as educated of a guess as you can, but give an answer. Blank is wrong!

Watch Out for Questions with Multiple Right Answers

If you go through the tutorial, you will learn that a question with a single right answer uses a radio button for its answer, and questions with multiple correct answers use checkboxes. Be on the lookout for this subtle difference and when confronted with checkboxes, check all the answers that are correct. If you get only one of two or more answers, the question is as wrong as if you entered no answers at all. Not many of these questions are on the exam, but be alert to them.

No Hootin' and Hollerin' Please

The good, and sometimes bad, part of taking a Sylvan Prometric interactive online test is that you get your results immediately. As soon as you finish the test, you know not only whether you passed or failed, but also how well you did in each domain. Of course, if you pass, you don't much care right away which areas you could improve. However, if you fail, this information can be helpful for next time.

It is considered bad manners to celebrate boisterously at your terminal when you pass. However, when that happens, take along my congratulations and those of the entire ...*For Dummies* team for a job well done.

Chapter 24

Ten Really Great Web Sites for Study Aids

In This Chapter

▶ A+ exam study materials on the Web

▶ Other resources you can use to prepare for the A+ exams

*V*ariety is one of the keys to preparing for the A+ exams. By using a number of different study tools and aids, you can see many ways of asking the same question. This helps prepare you for whatever format the A+ tests use.

A number of sites on the Web simulate the test content and format fairly accurately. Some are free; some slightly more. The free ones are certainly worth their cost; the others — *caveat emptor.* You will need to balance how much you want to spend on study aids to prepare yourself for a $200 test. Of course, if you don't pass, the cost of the test begins to multiply. Be cautious when buying study aids, and look for the bargains that are out there.

Be especially alert for study aids that are still for the old tests. One surefire way to tell whether the study aid is old is that it contains Macintosh materials. Another tip-off is that Windows 95 is not mentioned at all.

The Web sites and other resources listed in this chapter are sites I believe you will find helpful without having to spend a fortune. Please understand that all of these sites did exist at the time this book was written. If any of these sites have disappeared, you can always search for others. Remember that searching for "A+" will get you nowhere, so search for "Aplus" or "certification."

CompTIA.org

This should be your first stop when preparing for the A+ exams. This site is the proverbial "horse's mouth" for the A+ tests. While it may not be the best-looking, organized, or fastest site on the Web, it does have the answers to just about any question you would have about taking the test.

```
http://www.comptia.org/Ct_aplus/
```

The CompTIA site displays a series of commercial training company banner ads if you are looking for preparation courses, materials, or practice tests.

AFSMI.org

The Association For Services Management International (AFSMI) markets the A+ exam internationally (outside of the U.S.). It has created a Web site that provides a lot of background information on CompTIA, Sylvan Prometrics, and the exams. This site has perhaps 20 pages of A+ information, and although much of it duplicates the CompTIA site, it is certainly more readable.

```
http://www.afsmi.org/aplus/
```

A few sample questions are included in what CompTIA calls the exam blueprint, which lists the test objectives and domains. They also have a page listing some additional sources of study materials and courses.

Visit this site as early in your preparation process as possible, and then again right before the test to revisit the test-taking tips and scheduling information.

Selftest.co.uk

This British site offers probably the best freebie test demo on the Web. In fact, its practice test, of all the practice tests available on the Web, is probably the one most like the real thing.

```
http://www.selftest.co.uk/download.htm
```

You can download a sample A+ test demo and a few other certification tests as well. The idea is that if you like the practice tests, you can buy the full-blown test simulators. If you can afford it, it may not be such a bad idea.

AplusExam.com

Other than having a very pretentious name, this site offers a very good CD-ROM-based product. The product, called Aplus Certify, contains four sample tests for each of the A+ exams, as well as a cram guide for each exam. You can find a sample exam on the Web site that demonstrates the content on the CD.

```
http://www.aplusexam.com/
```

If you can overlook the hokey multimedia gimmicks and occasional misspelled word on the CD, the content is actually very accurate to what you can expect to find on the A+ exams.

QuickCert.com

The URL listed for this site opens a registration form for a demo version of the QuickCert practice test.

```
http://www.quick-cert.com/demo.html
```

Please be patient when downloading the demo; it took me three tries to get the whole file, but remember that it is free and really worth the effort. The format of the demo test is very much like that of SelfTest and Marcraft but contains MCSE test information. If you are interested in this product for A+, you have to buy it.

Marcraft International (MIC-INC.com)

Of the free downloadable practice tests, this one is probably the most challenging. The questions are written in such a way that you must think about both why an answer is correct as well as why the other answers may be wrong. The Marcraft full-blown practice test study aid is reasonably priced, and if you haven't already shot your bankroll on other study tools, it's worth buying.

```
http://www.mic-inc.com/Aplus
```

By all means, try out each of the demos available before buying one. You may actually find one for free that does the job for you. If you plan to use only interactive practice tests (not the best idea in my opinion), then the Marcraft product is not a bad choice.

LeLogic.com

This company sells a six-month access to a set of online tests for a fairly reasonable fee. The site also includes a 15-question, timed sample test. However, this test is of more value to see how the LeLogic system works than to prepare you for the A+ exams.

```
http://www.lelogic.com/index.html
```

However, if the sample test is indicative of the tests available (written by "actual college instructors"), this could be the best bargain of the study aids you can buy. One warning, though: LeLogic's tools work only with Netscape Navigator. In fact, the site warns that it will not work with Internet Explorer at all.

DaliDesign.com

Dali Design (as in Hello, Dali) has created a product it calls PREP! for A+ that is an excellent study and test prep aid. The sample test includes 54 questions that can be downloaded in both a Windows 95 or Windows 3.x version.

```
http://www.dalidesign.com/prepap/apdef.html
```

The full PREP! for A+ contains 540 questions that Dali Design has taken from "actual A+ Certification test experiences" so that all the test topics are included. If you like the sample test, the price on the full test engine is very reasonable.

PCGuide.com

The PC Guide is not an A+ site specifically, but it is without a doubt the most comprehensive site on PC hardware on the Web. Even if you don't use this site to round out your studies for the A+ Core exam, you should probably bookmark it for later reference.

```
http://www.pcguide.com/
```

The honorable thing to do would be to purchase the site's content in CD-ROM form to encourage the author of this site's content to continue maintaining this excellent Web site.

Amazon.com

What, you ask, is a book company doing in the list of A+ sites? Well, whether you use Amazon.com (my favorite), Barnes and Noble, Borders, or another online bookstore, these sites can provide you with a list of the very latest A+ exam guides, cram books, and question banks available in print. The test simulators are good, especially if you buy some of the complete test banks, but a study guide in print form is a good way to study when you are away from the PC, like on an airplane.

```
http://www.amazon.com
```

Visit this site and search for Aplus.

CramSession.com

Of the exam-related sites, this one has the best organization and information. It is perfect for that last-minute cram before the test.

```
http://www.cramsession.com/aplus/
```

As you get closer to the exam day, use this site to finely hone your memory banks for the test. It can also be used as you first get started to outline the areas you need to study.

Other Resources You Should Consider

Perhaps the best of the resources are my favorite books from my favorite publisher, not to mention my favorite authors:

Upgrading & Fixing PCs For Dummies, 4th Edition, by Andy Rathbone

Windows 95 For Dummies, 2nd Edition, by Andy Rathbone

Networking For Dummies, 2nd Edition, by Ned Lowe

DOS For Dummies, Windows 95 Edition, by Dan Gookin

In spite of the fact that this is a shameless plug, these books are an entertaining and informative way to brush up on your PC repair, Windows, and networking knowledge. You need to have some fun while studying, and at least this way you'll have an excuse for that smile on your face.

Part VII
Appendixes

The 5th Wave   By Rich Tennant

"I can never remember — are the bubble lights VESA or PCI?"

In this part . . .

This part contains sample questions from each domain of the two A+ exams to help you prepare for the test. Understand that on the actual test, some domains have more questions than are included here, and others have fewer questions. Use these questions as indicators of the types of questions you can expect to see on the test. If you do fairly well on these questions, then you are probably reaching your peak.

Included with this book is a CD-ROM that contains many tools to help you prepare for the test, including a test engine that generates practice tests for you in a variety of combinations. Check out Appendix B for more about the CD.

Appendix A
Sample Test

H ere are some sample questions from each of the domains included on the two A+ examinations. This appendix is not meant to represent an entire test. These questions are intended to give you an idea of the type of questions and the subject matter to expect. Practice with these questions, and if you do well, you are probably just about ready to take the tests.

Core Examination

Installation, Configuration, and Upgrading

The following questions are samples of what you may find on the A+ Core exam within each of the exam domains.

1 Which of the following connectors are used with a mouse? (Choose all that apply.)

A ❏ mini-DIN-6

B ❏ PS/2

C ❏ DIN-5

D ❏ DB-9

2 COM1 is commonly assigned the same IRQ as which other serial port?

A ○ COM2

B ○ COM3

C ○ COM4

D ○ LPT1

3 An ESD wristband should not be worn when working on which of the following?

A ○ Motherboard

B ○ Memory modules

C ○ Disk drives

D ○ Monitor

4 Which of the following is not an FRU?

A ○ Motherboard

B ○ Case

C ○ Hard disk drive

D ○ Memory module

5 When servicing a PC, where would you attach the ground strap to prevent ESD? (Check all that apply.)

A ❏ To the inside of the case

B ❏ To the static shielding bag that came with the computer

C ❏ To the ground mat

D ❏ To the PC's power supply

6 What type of cabling is used by an internal SCSI device?

A ○ Centronics-50 cable
B ○ 50-pin ribbon cable
C ○ 15-pin ribbon cable
D ○ 34-pin ribbon cable

7 Processor chips mount to the motherboard in which of the following forms? (Check all that apply.)

A ❏ PGA
B ❏ ZIF
C ❏ SIMM
D ❏ DIP

8 What is the I/O address for the first parallel port?

A ○ 3F8h
B ○ 378h
C ○ 2F8h
D ○ 278h

9 What is the colored edge on a disk drive ribbon cable aligned to?

A ○ Pin 1
B ○ Pin 2
C ○ Pin 40
D ○ Either pin 1 or pin 40

10 In which of the following is the system setup configuration information stored?

A ○ BIOS ROM
B ○ CMOS
C ○ chipset
D ○ SRAM

11 What is electrical resistance is measured in?

A ○ Amps
B ○ Ohms
C ○ Volts
D ○ Watts

12 The microcomputer operates on _____ current electricity.

A ○ Alternating
B ○ Direct
C ○ Switchable
D ○ Directional

Diagnosing and Troubleshooting

13 After powering up a PC, you almost immediately hear a series of beeps, and there is a 300-series error code on the display. What is likely the problem?

A ○ Motherboard failure
B ○ Serial port problem
C ○ Keyboard problem
D ○ Hard disk drive failure

14 After you have installed a new hard drive in a PC, if the display remains dark and the computer does not boot when restarted, what should you check?

A ○ The configuration of the hard disk
B ○ The alignment of the ribbon cable
C ○ The CMOS settings
D ○ The hard disk's power connection

15 The term POST refers to what?

A ○ Power Off Safety Testing
B ○ Pulsating Oscillator Stress Testing
C ○ Power On Self Test
D ○ Power On Stress Test

16 Which of the following protect against voltage spikes? (Check all that apply.)

A ❑ Surge suppressor
B ❑ Battery backup UPS
C ❑ Line conditioner
D ❑ A grounded wall outlet

17 What would you do to reset CMOS to its default settings, including passwords?

A ○ Press the Del key during POST processing
B ○ Use the CMOS battery jumper
C ○ Replace the ROM BIOS chip
D ○ Remove the CMOS battery

18 How can you determine the amount of physical memory on a PC?

A ○ Enter the CMOS and look at the memory amount entered there.
B ○ Hold down the Esc key during the boot process.
C ○ Read the display during the POST processing at system startup.
D ○ All PCs are limited to 1MB of memory.

Safety and Preventive Maintenance

19 How should you dispose of used laser printer toner cartridges?

    A ○ Place them in a plastic bag and throw them in the trash.
    B ○ They should be refilled by the user.
    C ○ Send them to the manufacturer or a recycler.
    D ○ No special handling is required.

20 What is the software utility used to group data in contiguous clusters?

    A ○ DEFRAG.EXE
    B ○ SCANDISK.EXE
    C ○ EMM386.EXE
    D ○ CHKDISK.EXE

21 A monitor is considered an environmental hazard because it contains

    A ○ lead
    B ○ phosphor
    C ○ mercury
    D ○ plastic

22 Published information on the handling, use, and storage of hazardous chemicals is MSDS. What does MSDS stand for?

    A ○ Material Safety and Disposal Specification
    B ○ Material Storage and Disposal Specification
    C ○ Material Safety Data Sheet
    D ○ Material Storage Data Specification

Motherboard/Processors/Memory

23 Which of the following are motherboard form factors? (Choose all that apply.)

    A ❑ Baby AT
    B ❑ ATX
    C ❑ AT
    D ❑ XT

24 Which of these processors does not incorporate a math coprocessor?

    A ○ Pentium
    B ○ 486DX
    C ○ 486SX
    D ○ Pentium Pro

25 MMX refers to

A ○ Memory module extensions
B ○ Multimedia extensions
C ○ Multimedia cross-references
D ○ A model name with no specific meaning

26 What is the width of the Pentium processor's address and data bus, respectively?

A ○ 16- and 32-bits
B ○ 32- and 32-bits
C ○ 32- and 64-bits
D ○ 64- and 64-bits

Printers

27 What is the sequence of steps used in the laser printing process?

A ○ Charging, cleaning, writing, developing, transferring, fusing
B ○ Charging, fusing, writing, developing, transferring, cleaning
C ○ Cleaning, charging, writing, developing, transferring, fusing
D ○ Cleaning, charging, fusing, developing, transferring, writing

28 A parallel printer cable should not exceed

A ○ 5 feet
B ○ 10 feet
C ○ 15 feet
D ○ 25 feet

29 What is the standard that covers bidirectional parallel printing?

A ○ IEEE 1284
B ○ IEEE 1394
C ○ RS-232-C
D ○ TCP/IP

30 In which phase of the laser printing process is the drum electrostatically erased before it receives a new image?

A ○ Charging
B ○ Cleaning
C ○ Writing
D ○ Transferring

31 Parallel printer cables that feature a bar connector are

A ○ DB-25 Male

B ○ DB-9 Female

C ○ 36-pin Centronics Male

D ○ 36-pin Centronics Female

Portable Systems

32 Which of the following statements are true concerning a Type III PCMCIA (PC Card) slot?

A ❑ 5.5 millimeters thick

B ❑ Used to install disk drives and external drive adapters

C ❑ Type III cards are thicker than Type II cards

D ❑ Type III cards can be hot swapped

33 PCMCIA is an acronym for

A ○ Personal Computer Manufacturers Council and Industry Association

B ○ Portable Computer Manufacturers Council International Association

C ○ Personal Computer Memory Card Interface Adapter

D ○ Portable Computer Memory Card International Association

Basic Networking

34 What is the most common network protocol in use?

A ○ NetBEUI

B ○ IPX/SPX

C ○ AppleTalk

D ○ TCP/IP

35 An RJ-45 connector is used with which cable type?

A ○ Telephone line

B ○ UTP

C ○ Coaxial

D ○ Fiber optic

36 The hardware that must be added to a PC to connect it to a network is a(n)

A ○ NIC

B ○ BNC

C ○ UTP

D ○ FDDI

37 When installing a network using 10BaseT, what devices must be terminated?

A ○ Each end of the bus

B ○ Each hub

C ○ Each router

D ○ Nothing needs to be terminated

Customer Satisfaction

38 When you first arrive at a customer's site, what should you do first?

A ○ Immediately perform diagnostics on the PC to determine the real problem.

B ○ Check in with your employer to find out when you are due at the following customer's location.

C ○ Ask the customer to explain in his own words what the problem is and listen actively and use effective feedback techniques.

D ○ Let the customer give you his version of the problem solely for the sake of customer relations, acting as if you are listening, and then perform diagnostics to determine the problem.

39 What do you believe is the most effective way to deal with an angry customer?

A ○ Resolve her problem as quickly as possible.

B ○ Ignore her and repair the problem.

C ○ Notify your boss about this difficult customer.

D ○ Tell her you will return to work on her PC when she can be more professional.

40 The customer has explained the problem as thoroughly and completely as he can. What is your next action?

A ○ Begin work on the PC.

B ○ Try to establish rapport with the customer by asking about his family or hobbies.

C ○ Summarize what you understood the customer to say and offer one or more possible solutions to the customer.

D ○ Avoid telling the customer how wrong he is, but ask him about a different problem and solution.

Microsoft DOS/Windows Exam

Function, Structure, Operation, and File Management

1 Which of the following files are required for operating system startup?

A ❑ CONFIG.SYS
B ❑ IO.SYS
C ❑ AUTOEXEC.BAT
D ❑ MSDOS.SYS

2 Which file displays the DOS prompt?

A ○ IO.SYS
B ○ AUTOEXEC.BAT
C ○ COMMAND.COM
D ○ MSDOS.SYS

3 What is the file management utility in Windows 3.*x*?

A ○ Windows Explorer
B ○ Control Panel
C ○ Program Manager
D ○ File Manager

4 The DOS root directory can hold how many files?

A ○ 256
B ○ 512
C ○ 1024
D ○ There is no limit on the number of files that can be stored in the DOS root directory.

5 DOS filenames are limited to a length of

A ○ 256 characters
B ○ 8 characters plus a 3 character file extension
C ○ 8 characters total
D ○ 254 characters plus an unlimited file extension

6 What does the ATTRIB +r *.* command do?

A ○ Forces all files in a directory to a read-only attribute
B ○ Removes the read-only attribute from all files in a directory
C ○ Adds the letter "r" to the end of all filenames in a directory
D ○ Forces all files on the disk to be read-only

7 Device drivers are loaded from which file?

A ○ AUTOEXEC.BAT
B ○ WIN.INI
C ○ SYSTEM. INI
D ○ CONFIG.SYS

8 Which utility can be used to edit system files in Windows?

A ○ EDIT
B ○ SYSEDIT
C ○ WordPad
D ○ NotePad

9 Which DOS command is used to remove a directory, its subdirectories, and all of their contents?

A ○ XCOPY
B ○ RMDIR
C ○ DELTREE
D ○ DEL

10 DOS and Windows store all directory entries in the

A ○ Directory file
B ○ Master boot record
C ○ FAT
D ○ Root directory table

11 The _____ command is used to copy all of the files and subdirectories from one directory to another.

A ○ COPY
B ○ XCOPY
C ○ COPY /A
D ○ XCOPY /S

12 In order for Windows 3.x to load, which file must have already been loaded?

A ○ EMM386.EXE
B ○ HIMEM.SYS
C ○ WIN.INI
D ○ SYSTEM.INI

Memory Management

13 What software enables expanded memory and the use of upper memory as system memory?

A ○ HIMEM.SYS
B ○ EMM386.EXE
C ○ EMM386.SYS
D ○ LOADHIGH.SYS

14 Which of the following files is the extended memory manager?

A ○ HIMEM.SYS
B ○ EMM386.EXE
C ○ LOADHIGH.SYS
D ○ HIMEM.EXE

15 What are the four sections of DOS/Windows memory?

A ○ Conventional, expanded, extended, reserved
B ○ Conventional, extended, high memory area, expanded
C ○ Conventional, expanded, high memory area, extended
D ○ Reserved, conventional, upper memory area, extended

Installation, Configuration, and Upgrading

16 Which utility is used in Windows 95 to partition a hard disk drive?

A ○ WINDISK
B ○ DRVSPACE
C ○ MSD
D ○ FDISK

17 What is the maximum size of a disk partition in Windows 3.*x*?

A ○ 500MB
B ○ 1GB
C ○ 2GB
D ○ 4GB

18 Which Windows 95 command is used to edit the Registry?

A ○ SYSEDIT
B ○ REGEDIT
C ○ REGCLEAN
D ○ REGSVR

19 What Windows 95 startup mode allows you to correct any hardware or configuration problems that occurred during startup?

A ○ Normal mode
B ○ MS-DOS mode
C ○ Debug mode
D ○ Safe mode

20 Which command must be placed into the AUTOEXEC.BAT file to start Windows 3.*x* from DOS?

A ○ WIN.INI
B ○ WINDOWS.EXE
C ○ WIN.COM
D ○ PROGMAN.EXE

21 Which files make up the Windows 95 Registry?

A ○ SYSTEM.DAT and USER.DAT
B ○ USER.SYS and SYSTEM.SYS
C ○ REG.DAT and SYSTEM.SYS
D ○ GDI.EXE and GDI.SYS

22 What is the default boot device priorities on a PC?

A ○ A:, C:, B:, D:
B ○ C:, A:, D:, B:
C ○ C:, A:
D ○ A:, C:

23 If the Windows 3.*x* installation fails, which command can be used to restart the installation?

A ○ SETUP /I
B ○ SETUP /R
C ○ RESTART /I
D ○ SETUP /X

24 To access the properties function of the Windows 95 Desktop, you should

A ○ Double-click the My Computer icon.
B ○ Right-click the Desktop and choose Properties.
C ○ Access Settings from the Start Menu.
D ○ Right-click the My Computer icon.

25 To access the Boot Menu on a Windows 95 PC, after the Starting Windows message appears, press

A ○ F5

B ○ F6

C ○ F8

D ○ F10

26 What is the order of the DOS boot sequence?

A ○ IO.SYS, MSDOS.SYS, COMMAND.COM, CONFIG.SYS, AUTOEXEC.BAT

B ○ MSDOS.SYS, IO.SYS, COMMAND.COM, CONFIG.SYS, AUTOEXEC.BAT

C ○ COMMAND.COM, IO.SYS, MSDOS.SYS, CONFIG.SYS, AUTOEXEC.BAT

D ○ IO.SYS, MSDOS.SYS, CONFIG.SYS, COMMAND.COM, AUTOEXEC.BAT

Diagnosing and Troubleshooting

27 What action can you take to get around the "Incorrect DOS version" error message?

A ○ Reboot.

B ○ Use SETVER to report a different version of DOS.

C ○ User SETVER to upgrade the application to the new DOS version.

D ○ Reinstall the correct version of DOS.

28 Which type of virus masquerades itself as a legitimate program?

A ○ The stealth virus

B ○ The Trojan horse

C ○ A dropper

D ○ A worm

29 Which two of the Windows 95 heaps can fill up and cause "Out of Memory" errors?

A ○ System and GDI

B ○ System and User

C ○ GDI and User

D ○ System and Menu

30 The four configuration files of Windows 3.*x* are

A ○ IO.SYS, MSDOS.SYS, COMMAND.COM, AUTOEXEC.BAT

B ○ MOUSE.INI, WIN.BAT, WIN.INI., SYSTEM.INI

C ○ Swapfile, User, GDI, Menu

D ○ CONTROL.INI, MOUSE.INI, PROGMAN.INI, SYSTEM.INI

31 In a Windows 95 boot sequence, what loads immediately after WIN.COM executes?

A ○ SYSTEM.DAT

B ○ VMM32.VXD and the virtual device drivers

C ○ DRVSPACE.BIN

D ○ Kernel, GDI, and User core components

32 The respective exception error codes for memory and video problems in Windows 95 are

A ○ 0E and 0D

B ○ 0F and 387h

C ○ GPF and I/O

D ○ Windows 95 has no exception error codes for memory and video.

33 What is the Windows 95 boot mode that loads only the essential hardware drivers?

A ○ Normal

B ○ Safe mode

C ○ Short mode

D ○ No Load mode

34 Division by zero or memory addresses outside of an allotted area can cause a

A ○ Parity error

B ○ Exception error

C ○ System halt

D ○ General protection fault

35 A printer that was working before has stopped working. After checking the power and making sure the printer is turned on, you should next check to see

A ○ Whether the printer drivers are functioning

B ○ Whether the printer is online

C ○ Whether there is paper in the printer

D ○ Whether there is toner in the printer

36 The /s option of the FORMAT command is the same as using the _____ command to copy system files to a disk.

A ○ SYS

B ○ XCOPY

C ○ SYSEDIT

D ○ FDISK

Networks

37 What are the common LAN network topologies? (Choose all that apply.)

    A ❑ NetBEUI

    B ❑ Ethernet

    C ❑ Ring

    D ❑ Star

    E ❑ TCP/IP

38 Which of the following is not a commonly used Internet protocol?

    A ○ FTP

    B ○ HTTP

    C ○ TCP/IP

    D ○ IPX

39 The layers of the OSI model (top to bottom) are

    A ○ Network, Physical, Transport, Data Link, Session, Presentation, Application

    B ○ Physical, Data Link, Network, Transport, Session, Presentation, Application

    C ○ Application, Data Link, Network, Physical, Presentation, Transport, Session

    D ○ Physical, Data Link, Network, Transport, Session, Application, Presentation

40 What service is used to resolve Internet domain names into IP addresses?

    A ○ NetBIOS

    B ○ WINS

    C ○ DNS

    D ○ HTTP

Core Examination Answers

1 *A, B and C.* The mini-DIN 6-pin and the PS/2 connectors are essentially the same and are common to bus mouse and motherboard connectors. The DB-9 connector is used for serial mouse units. There is no such thing as a DB-5 connector. *See Chapter 11.*

2 *B.* COM1 and COM3 share IRQ4. *See Chapter 7.*

3 *D.* The monitor contains a large capacitor. Should it discharge through you, it may kill you. *Review Chapter 10.*

4 *B.* The case is not considered a field replaceable unit. *See Chapter 4.*

5 *A and C.* The PC should be plugged into a wall socket providing you with a solid ground. *Review Chapter 14.*

6 *B.* The key to this answer is internal. Some external SCSI devices use Centronics cables. *See Chapter 6.*

7 *A and D.* Since the 286 processor, the pin-grid array has been very popular, and before that the dual inline packaging mode was used. *See Chapter 4.*

8 *B.* The I/O address assigned LPT1 is 378 hexadecimal. *See Chapter 10.*

9 *A.* Remember "Big Red is Number One." *See Chapter 6.*

10 *B.* The CMOS holds the configuration information used by the BIOS to boot the system. *See Chapter 4.*

11 *B.* Know what each of the electrical measurements measure. Ohms measures resistance or continuity. *See Chapter 2.*

12 *B.* The external AC power is converted into DC power inside the PC. *See Chapter 8.*

13 *C.* The 3xx series of POST error messages are keyboard errors. *See Chapter 9.*

14 *B.* Any time the PC does not boot from a newly installed disk drive, check the data cable. *Review Chapter 6.*

15 *C.* Power On Self Test is a system integrity check run by the BIOS. *See Chapter 4.*

16 *A, B, and C.* The wall outlet, while it provides a ground, is the villain you're protecting the system from. *See Chapter 8.*

17 *B and D.* Either of these methods will reset the CMOS to its default settings. *See Chapter 4.*

18 *C.* The POST process displays the amount of physical memory detected on the PC. *See Chapter 4.*

19 *C.* They should be recycled to the manufacturer or a recyler. *See Chapter 12.*

20 *A.* DEFRAG relocates data more efficiently on the disk. *See Chapter 6.*

21 *A.* A monitor contains leaded glass, which poses a health and environmental problem. *See Chapter 10.*

22 *C.* Material Safety Data Sheets contain instructions for handling, storing, and using chemical products. *See Chapter 20.*

23 *A, B, and C.* The XT is long gone. The AT set the standard, and Baby and ATX are newer versions. *Review Chapter 4.*

24 *C.* The 486SX was made market-ready by having its math coprocessor disabled. *Review Chapter 4.*

25 *B.* MMX added 57 instructions to the Pentium chip. *See Chapter 4.*

26 *C.* The address bus is 32 bits and the data bus is 64 bits. *See Chapter 4.*

27 *C.* California Cows Won't Dance The Fandango. *Review Chapter 12.*

28 *B.* Some say 15 feet, but stick with 10 feet for the test. *See Chapter 12.*

29 *A.* IEEE 1284 sets the standard for all parallel protocols. *See Chapter 12.*

30 *B.* Be sure you know what each of the laser phases do. *Review Chapter 12.*

31 *C.* The 36-pin bar. *See Chapter 12.*

32 *B, C, D.* Type III cards are 10.5 millimeters thick. *See Chapter 5.*

33 *C.* PCMCIA cards are not called PC Cards. *See Chapter 18.*

34 *D.* The popularity of the Internet has made TCP/IP the most popular protocol. *Review Chapter 13.*

35 *B.* RJ-45 connectors are most commonly used with unshielded twisted pair copper wire. *See Chapter 13.*

36 *A.* A network interface card is used to connect a PC to a network. *See Chapter 13.*

37 *D.* Okay, so it was a trick question. 10BaseT doesn't require termination. *See Chapter 13.*

38 *C.* Let the customer explain the problem to you while you pay attention. *See Chapter 19.*

39 *A.* The best way is to do a good job and do it quickly. *See Chapter 19.*

40 *C.* Be polite, attentive, and understanding. *See Chapter 19.*

Microsoft DOS/Windows Exam Answers

1 *B and D.* The others are needed to start the PC environment but not the operating system. *See Chapter 21.*

2 *C.* COMMAND.COM is the command line interpreter for DOS. *Review Chapter 21.*

3 *D.* This one is almost too easy, but it's on the test, so take heed. *Review Chapter 21.*

4 *B.* You can count on this question being on the test. *Review Chapter 21.*

5 *B.* Eight characters are allowed for the filename, plus the "dot" and the three character file extension. *See Chapter 21.*

6 *A.* ATTRIB assigns or removes attributes using the plus and minus signs. *Review Chapter 21.*

7 *D.* In the DOS/Windows 3.x world, loading device drivers is the primary function of CONFIG.SYS. *Review Chapter 21.*

8 *B.* Windows 3.x files WIN.INI and SYSTEM.INI appear in the SYSEDIT window for editing. *Review Chapter 21.*

9 *C.* DELTREE deletes an entire directory structure. *Review Chapter 21.*

10 *C.* The File Allocation Table contains a record of how the disk clusters are used. *Review Chapter 21.*

11 *D.* The /S option indicates structures (subdirectories) are to be copied. *Review Chapter 21.*

12 *B.* Windows needs HIMEM to be running so it can load. *Review Chapter 21.*

13 *B.* EMM386.SYS is the memory manager for expanded memory. *See Chapter 5.*

14 *A.* HIMEM.SYS is the device driver for extended memory. *See Chapter 5.*

15 *C.* Conventional, expanded (reserved), high memory, and extended. *See Chapter 5.*

16 *D.* Windows 95 did not create a new graphical interfaced partition tool. *See Chapter 16.*

17 *C.* Although Windows 95b eliminated this limitation. *Review Chapter 16.*

18 *B.* REGEDIT is kind of obvious, but it's the one. *See Chapter 22.*

19 *D.* Safe mode loads only the essential device drivers. *See Chapter 22.*

20 *C.* Windows is just another program to DOS. *Review Chapter 21.*

21 *A.* The SYSTEM.DAT AND USER.DAT files are the registry. *Review Chapter 21.*

22 *C.* First the disk driver with the Master Boot Record, usually C:, and then the A: until it finds the boot program. *Review Chapter 6.*

23 *A.* The /I option tells SETUP to ignore hardware detection. *Review Chapter 22.*

24 *B.* There are other ways, but this is the fastest and most straightforward. *Review Chapter 22.*

25 *C.* Pressing F8 immediately after the Starting Windows message appears in the boot sequence. *See Chapter 22.*

26 *D.* Remember that CONFIG.SYS, if present, is used before COMMAND.COM. *Review Chapter 21.*

27 *B.* SETVER lets DOS be whatever version an application needs it to be. *See Chapter 22.*

28 *B.* Like its mythological namesake, it appears to be something else and then strikes. *Review Chapter 20.*

29 *A.* These two heaps handle the user interface and the applications started by the user. Should they run out of memory, they are unable to effectively operate the desktop environment. *See Chapter 22.*

30 *D.* The initialization files contain the system information used to create the desktop. *See Chapter 22.*

31 *B.* The 32-bit VXD drivers are loaded by WIN.COM. *Review Chapter 22.*

32 *A.* You have probably seen this error accompanied by the red X of death or the blue screen of death, a new wrestling tag team. *Review Chapter 22.*

33 *B.* Safe mode loads only what Windows 95 needs to run, eliminating all of the unsafe user stuff. *See Chapter 22.*

34 *D.* GPFs are never fun. They also occur for memory parity errors. *Review Chapter 22.*

35 *B.* This is a very common cause of nonworking printers. *See Chapter 12.*

36 *A.* SYS is how system files can get on a drive without impacting existing files. *See Chapter 22.*

37 *B, C and D.* The rest are network protocols and not topologies. *Review Chapter 13.*

38 *D.* IPX is a Local Area Network protocol and not an Internet protocol. *Review Chapter 13.*

39 *B.* Please Do Not Tell Secret Passwords Anytime. *Review Chapter 13.*

40 *C.* Domain Name Server converts domain names into IP addresses. *Review Chapter 13.*

Appendix B
About the CD

● ●

On the CD-ROM

▶ The QuickLearn game — a fun way to study for the test

▶ Practice and Self-Assessment tests to make sure you're ready for the real thing

▶ Practice test demos, including Dali Design's PREP!, BeachFrontQuizzer Software, CICPreP!, and a demo from MicroTech USA, exclusive to *A+ Certification For Dummies*

● ●

System Requirements

Make sure that your computer meets the minimum system requirements shown in the following list. If your computer doesn't meet most of these requirements, you may have problems using the contents of the CD.

✔ A PC with a 486 or faster processor.

✔ Microsoft Windows 95 or later.

✔ At least 16MB of total RAM installed on your computer.

✔ At least 32MB of available hard drive space to install all the software on this CD. (You need less space if you don't install every program.)

✔ A CD-ROM drive — double-speed (2x) or faster.

✔ A sound card for PCs.

✔ A monitor capable of displaying at least 256 colors or grayscale.

✔ A modem with a speed of at least 14,400 bps.

Note: To play the QuickLearn game, you must have a Windows 95 or Windows 98 computer — the game will not run on Windows NT. You must also have Microsoft DirectX 5.0 or a later version installed. If you do not have DirectX, you can download it at www.microsoft.com/directx/ resources/dx5end.htm.

Using the CD with Microsoft Windows

To install the items from the CD to your hard drive, follow these steps:

1. **Insert the CD into your computer's CD-ROM drive.**

2. **Click Start⇨Run.**

3. **In the dialog box that appears, type** D:\SETUP.EXE.

   Replace *D* with the proper drive letter if your CD-ROM drive uses a different letter.

4. **Click OK.**

   A License Agreement window appears.

5. **Read through the license agreement, and then click the Accept button if you want to use the CD. After you click Accept, you are never bothered by the License Agreement window again.**

   The CD interface Welcome screen appears. The interface is a little program that shows you what's on the CD and coordinates installing the programs and running the demos. The interface basically enables you to click a button or two to make things happen.

6. **Click anywhere on the Welcome screen to enter the interface.**

   The next screen lists categories for the software on the CD.

7. **To view the items within a category, just click the category's name.**

   A list of programs in the category appears.

8. **For more information about a program, click the program's name.**

   Be sure to read the information that appears. Sometimes a program has its own system requirements or requires you to do a few tricks on your computer before you can install or run the program, and this screen tells you what you may need to do, if necessary.

9. **If you don't want to install the program, click the Go Back button to return to the previous screen.**

   You can always return to the previous screen by clicking the Go Back button. This feature enables you to browse the different categories and products and decide what you want to install.

10. **To install a program, click the appropriate Install button.**

    The CD interface drops to the background while the CD installs the program you chose.

11. **To install other items, repeat Steps 7 through 10.**

12. **When you finish installing programs, click the Quit button to close the interface.**

You can eject the CD now. Carefully place it back in the plastic jacket of the book for safekeeping.

To run some of the programs on the *A+ Certification For Dummies* CD, you need to leave the CD in the CD-ROM drive.

What You'll Find on the CD

The following is a summary of the software included on this CD.

Dummies test prep tools

This CD contains questions related to A+ Certification. The questions are similar to those you can expect to find on the exams. I've also included some questions on A+ topics that may or not be on the current tests or even covered in the book, but they are things that you should know to perform your job.

QuickLearn Game

The QuickLearn Game is the *...For Dummies* way of making studying for the Certification exam fun. Well, okay, less painful. OutPost is a DirectX, high-resolution, fast-paced arcade game.

Answer questions to defuse dimensional disrupters and save the universe from a rift in space-time. (The questions come from the same set of questions that the Self-Assessment and Practice Test use, but isn't this way more fun?) Missing a few questions on the real exam almost never results in a rip in the fabric of the universe, so just think how easy it will be when you get there!

Practice Test

The Practice Test is designed to help you get comfortable with the A+ testing situation and pinpoint your strengths and weaknesses on the topic. You can accept the default setting of 60 questions in 60 minutes, or you can customize the settings. You can pick the number of questions and the amount of time, and you can even decide which objectives you want to focus on.

After you answer the questions, the Practice Test gives you plenty of feedback. You can find out which questions you got right or wrong and get statistics on how you did, broken down by objective. Then you can review all the questions — the ones you missed, the ones you marked, or a combination of the ones you marked and the ones you missed.

Self-Assessment Test

The Self-Assessment Test is designed to simulate the actual A+ testing situation. You must answer 60 questions in 60 minutes. After you answer all the questions, you find out your score and whether you pass or fail — but that's all the feedback you get. If you can pass the Self-Assessment Test fairly easily, you're probably ready to tackle the real thing.

Links Page

I've also created a Links Page, a handy starting place for accessing the huge amounts of information about the A+ tests on the Internet. You can find the page, `Links.htm`, at the root of the CD.

Commercial demos

A+ Test Demo, from MicroTech USA

The MicroTech demo test was especially and exclusively developed for *A+ Certification For Dummies*. For more information on MicroTech, check out its Web site at `www.microtech.com`.

CICPreP!, from Prep Technologies, Inc.

CICPreP! features A+ sample questions and a testlike environment. It's a great resource for everyone seeking A+ certification, because it covers the new requirements. For more information on Prep Technologies and the full version of this product, visit `www.mcpprep.com`.

BeachFrontQuizzer

BeachFrontQuizzer is one of the favorites among A+ Core Service Technicians and A+ DOS/Windows exam crammers. More information is available at `www.bfq.com/apluscert.html`.

CET's A+ Test Prep!, from Certify, Inc.

Windows-based, interactive certification assessment software with many special features. For more information, visit `www.apluscertification.com/aplus.htm`.

PREP! For A+ 2.0, from Dali Design

The sample features over 50 questions to get you started. To find out more about the full practice test, visit http://dalidesign.com/prepap/apad.html.

Self Test A+ Certification Software, from SelfTest

This exam series covers all objectives set by CompTIA, so that you can be confident about the actual exam. To find out more about Self Test, visit www.selftest.co.uk/aplus_practice_tests.htm.

Super Software's A+ Certify Exam

This demo is another good resource for test questions and sample exams. Check out its Web site at www.aplusexam.com.

If You've Got Problems (Of the CD Kind)

I tried my best to compile programs that work on most computers with the minimum system requirements. Alas, your computer may be somewhat different, and some programs may not work properly for some reason.

The two most likely culprits are that you don't have enough memory (RAM) for the programs you want to use, or that you have other programs running that are affecting installation or running of a program. If you get error messages such as Not enough memory or Setup cannot continue, try one or more of the following procedures and then try using the software again:

✔ **Turn off any antivirus software monitor that you may have running on your computer.** Installers sometimes mimic virus activity and may make your computer incorrectly believe that it is being infected by a virus.

✔ **Close all running programs.** The more programs you're running, the less memory is available to other programs. Installers also typically update files and programs; if you keep other programs running, installation may not work properly.

✔ **In Windows, close the CD interface and run demos or installations directly from Windows Explorer.** The interface itself can tie up system memory or even conflict with certain kinds of interactive demos. Use Windows Explorer to browse the files on the CD and launch installers or demos.

✔ **Add more RAM to your computer.** This is, admittedly, a drastic and somewhat expensive step. However, if you have a Windows 95 PC, adding more memory can really help the speed of your computer and enable more programs to run at the same time.

If you still have trouble installing the items from the CD, please call the IDG Books Worldwide Customer Service phone number: 800-762-2974 (outside the U.S.: 317-596-5430).

Index

• *M* •

• *X* •

• *Z* •

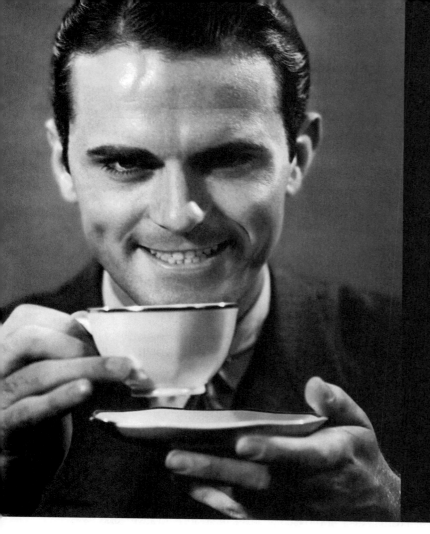

"Upset? Why should I be upset? So I couldn't reschedule my exam this weekend and still had to show up at precisely 8:00 Monday morning. And so what if it took till 10:39 before it was finally ready for me to take it. Does that bother me? Nooooooooooo. I'm just going to sit right here and drink my nice lovely cup of tea!"

Hint: Now is not a good time to tell him he should have tested at a VUE Authorized Testing Center.

With VUE's real-time web-interface you can register or reschedule your exam 24 hours / 7days a week, not just when someone happens to be answering the phone. Also, all VUE Testing Centers are tied into our powerful registration system, so you can register and pay at the site, and be taking your exam minutes later. And if you want to take another crack at an exam that you just 'sub-optimized', a VUE testing center should have your exam ready in less than five minutes.

Also, VUE is the only testing network that live-links your records directly with Microsoft and Novell's certification databases; you can test at any VUE Testing Center with the assurance and confidence that your results will get where they need to go.

To register for a Microsoft exam call toll free 888-837-8616 (USA & CAN), to register on the Web or to obtain a complete list of world-wide toll free phone numbers go to www.vue.com/ms

When it really matters, test with VUE.

Microsoft Certified
Professional
Exam Provider

VUE®

VIRTUAL UNIVERSITY ENTERPRISES

a division of NCS®

For more information, go to
w w w . v u e . c o m

©1998 NCS, Inc. All rights reserved.

IDG Books Worldwide, Inc., End-User License Agreement

5. **Limited Warranty.**

   (a) IDGB warrants that the Software and Software Media are free from defects in materials and workmanship under normal use for a period of sixty (60) days from the date of purchase of this Book. If IDGB receives notification within the warranty period of defects in materials or workmanship, IDGB will replace the defective Software Media.

   (b) IDGB AND THE AUTHOR OF THE BOOK DISCLAIM ALL OTHER WARRANTIES, EXPRESS OR IMPLIED, INCLUDING WITHOUT LIMITATION IMPLIED WARRANTIES OF MER-CHANTABILITY AND FITNESS FOR A PARTICULAR PURPOSE, WITH RESPECT TO THE SOFTWARE, THE PROGRAMS, THE SOURCE CODE CONTAINED THEREIN, AND/OR THE TECHNIQUES DESCRIBED IN THIS BOOK. IDGB DOES NOT WARRANT THAT THE FUNCTIONS CONTAINED IN THE SOFTWARE WILL MEET YOUR REQUIREMENTS OR THAT THE OPERATION OF THE SOFTWARE WILL BE ERROR FREE.

   (c) This limited warranty gives you specific legal rights, and you may have other rights that vary from jurisdiction to jurisdiction.

6. **Remedies.**

   (a) IDGB's entire liability and your exclusive remedy for defects in materials and workmanship shall be limited to replacement of the Software Media, which may be returned to IDGB with a copy of your receipt at the following address: Software Media Fulfillment Department, Attn.: *A+ Certification For Dummies,* IDG Books Worldwide, Inc., 7260 Shadeland Station, Ste. 100, Indianapolis, IN 46256, or call 800-762-2974. Please allow three to four weeks for delivery. This Limited Warranty is void if failure of the Software Media has resulted from accident, abuse, or misapplication. Any replacement Software Media will be warranted for the remainder of the original warranty period or thirty (30) days, whichever is longer.

   (b) In no event shall IDGB or the author be liable for any damages whatsoever (including without limitation damages for loss of business profits, business interruption, loss of business information, or any other pecuniary loss) arising from the use of or inability to use the Book or the Software, even if IDGB has been advised of the possibility of such damages.

   (c) Because some jurisdictions do not allow the exclusion or limitation of liability for consequential or incidental damages, the above limitation or exclusion may not apply to you.

7. **U.S. Government Restricted Rights.** Use, duplication, or disclosure of the Software by the U.S. Government is subject to restrictions stated in paragraph (c)(1)(ii) of the Rights in Technical Data and Computer Software clause of DFARS 252.227-7013, and in subparagraphs (a) through (d) of the Commercial Computer–Restricted Rights clause at FAR 52.227-19, and in similar clauses in the NASA FAR supplement, when applicable.

8. **General.** This Agreement constitutes the entire understanding of the parties and revokes and supersedes all prior agreements, oral or written, between them and may not be modified or amended except in a writing signed by both parties hereto that specifically refers to this Agreement. This Agreement shall take precedence over any other documents that may be in conflict herewith. If any one or more provisions contained in this Agreement are held by any court or tribunal to be invalid, illegal, or otherwise unenforceable, each and every other provision shall remain in full force and effect.

Installation Instructions

To install the items from the CD to your hard drive with Microsoft Windows, follow these steps:

1. **Insert the CD into your computer's CD-ROM drive.**

2. **Click Start⇨Run.**

3. **In the dialog box that appears, type** D:\SETUP.EXE.

   Replace *D* with the proper drive letter if your CD-ROM drive uses a different letter.

4. **Click OK.**

   A License Agreement window appears.

5. **Read through the license agreement, and then click the Accept button if you want to use the CD. After you click Accept, you'll never be bothered by the License Agreement window again.**

   The CD interface Welcome screen appears.

6. **Click anywhere on the Welcome screen to enter the interface.**

   The next screen lists categories for the software on the CD.

7. **To view the items within a category, just click the category's name.**

   A list of programs in the category appears.

8. **For more information about a program, click the program's name.**

   Be sure to read the information that appears. Sometimes a program has its own system requirements or requires you to do a few tricks on your computer before you can install or run the program, and this screen tells you what you may need to do, if necessary.

9. **If you don't want to install the program, click the Go Back button to return to the previous screen.**

   You can always return to the previous screen by clicking the Go Back button. This feature enables you to browse the different categories and products and decide what you want to install.

10. **To install a program, click the appropriate Install button.**

    The CD interface drops to the background while the CD installs the program you chose.

11. **To install other items, repeat Steps 7 through 10.**

12. **When you finish installing programs, click the Quit button to close the interface.**

    You can eject the CD now. Carefully place it back in the plastic jacket of the book for safekeeping.

IDG BOOKS WORLDWIDE BOOK REGISTRATION

We want to hear from you!

Visit **http://my2cents.dummies.com** to register this book and tell us how you liked it!

- ✔ Get entered in our monthly prize giveaway.
- ✔ Give us feedback about this book — tell us what you like best, what you like least, or maybe what you'd like to ask the author and us to change!
- ✔ Let us know any other ...*For Dummies*® topics that interest you.

Your feedback helps us determine what books to publish, tells us what coverage to add as we revise our books, and lets us know whether we're meeting your needs as a ...*For Dummies* reader. You're our most valuable resource, and what you have to say is important to us!

Not on the Web yet? It's easy to get started with *Dummies 101*®: *The Internet For Windows*® *98* or *The Internet For Dummies*, 5th Edition, at local retailers everywhere.

Or let us know what you think by sending us a letter at the following address:

...*For Dummies* Book Registration
Dummies Press
7260 Shadeland Station, Suite 100
Indianapolis, IN 46256-3945
Fax 317-596-5498

™

...FOR DUMMIES

**BESTSELLING
BOOK SERIES**